Engraved by A.H. Ritchie.

John Urquhart

MEMOIRS,

INCLUDING

LETTERS, AND SELECT REMAINS,

OF

JOHN URQUHART,

LATE OF THE

UNIVERSITY OF ST. ANDREW'S.

BY WILLIAM ORME.

WITH A PREFATORY NOTICE AND RECOMMENDATION,

BY ALEXANDER DUFF, D.D., LL.D.

"Multis ille bonis flebilis occidit."—*Horat Carm.*

—— What though short thy date?
Virtue, not rolling suns, the mind matures;—
The man of wisdom is the man of years."—YOUNG.

STEREOTYPED BY J. FAGAN.

CONTENTS.

CHAPTER III.

CHAPTER IV.

CHAPTER V

PREFATORY NOTICE

AND

RECOMMENDATION.

BY THE REV. DR. DUFF.

Having been personally acquainted with the subject of the following memoir, I was requested, during my recent visit to the United States, by my revered friend James Lenox, Esq., of New York, to look over the last English edition, and mark what alterations might advantageously be made in a projected American edition of the work.

This revision, hitherto delayed from unavoidable causes which it is needless to recount, has now been accomplished. As the general result, it may be stated that several minor mistakes, into which the Biographer had inadvertently fallen, have been corrected; that various passages of inferior importance, or of merely local or ephemeral interest, have been omitted; that the essays of a purely literary or philosophical character have been extruded from the body of the work and thrown into an Appendix; and finally, that the whole has been broken up into the more convenient division of chapters.

With many it may be a matter of doubt, whether the essays ought not to be excluded altogether. But, on mature consideration, it has been thought that the same reasons which weighed with the Biographer in originally introducing them, may well be regarded as still sufficiently valid in warranting the continued retention of them. They are not numerous; they do not occupy any considerable or disproportionate space; and they may serve to show the students of mere secular philosophy, how, between true science and true religion, there is not only no real discrepancy, but a beauteous and mutually enhancing harmony; and how, with the utmost ease, precision, and intelligence, a Christian young man, whose whole soul was inflamed with the spirit of missions, could, in the ordinary course of his academic career, and at the call of duty, turn aside and successfully grapple with some of the most abstruse and perplexing questions in ethics and political economy. Considered as the college exercises of a youth of little more than sixteen, they cannot but be pronounced as no ordinary productions. Their simplicity, as Mr. Orme has truly remarked, constitutes their charm; the *lucidus ordo* is most delightfully exemplified in every one of them; his thoughts constantly flow in a train peculiarly clear, always natural and unaffected; and the easy diction in which he expressed himself was the perfect picture of his mind.

The grand object, however, of the memoir is, to exhibit the rise, progress, and formation of the religious character of the individual whose short life is illustrated. Amid the many clustering excellencies that adorned that character, by far the most prominent and striking was the evangelistic spirit and self-devotion by which it was so peculiarly distinguished. It was this which chiefly conferred on it at once its lustre and its *uniqueness*. The Church of Christ in all lands can happily point to not a few young men of sincere and shining piety; but, unhappily, to very few, who, at the age of young Urquhart, have been privileged to obtain and cherish so marvellously clear and intelligent an apprehension of the duty of exemplifying that piety by a solemn act of personal dedication to the God-like enterprise of the world's evangelization.

It is under this more distinctive aspect of it, that I would earnestly crave the special attention of Christian young men in general, and more particularly of Christian students and candidates for the ministry, to the life of John Urquhart.

In his case, we find the true *rationale* of personal dedication to the cause of missions, unfolded with singular point and clearness. In early youth it was his inestimable privilege to enjoy the benefit of religious training, under the instruction and example of pious parents. Being naturally of a mild, gentle, amiable, guileless, Nathanael-like disposition, such example and instruction could not fail to have their due effect, in not only restraining him from the commission of gross outward sin, and saving him from the contagious influences of evil companionship, but also in superinducing a habit of internal conformity to the practices of Christian devotion and worship. Still, until he had passed his fourteenth year, there is no evidence whatever of his having undergone the great change of the *new birth* in the soul. On this subject, his own statement to his pastor, Mr. Orme, is perfectly explicit. Writing, in April, 1824, he says, "My first impressions of danger, as a sinner, were caused by a sermon you preached, on a Lord's day evening, about a year and a half ago. At the time, I was very much affected; it was then, I think, that I first really prayed. I retired to my apartment, and with many tears confessed my guilt before God."

This first partial awakening occurred towards the close of the autumn of 1822. Soon afterwards he went, for the first time, to the College of St. Andrew's. There his first religious impressions became somewhat blunted, though not effaced. On his return home in the summer of 1823, he tells us that he began to feel less pleasure in the exercises of prayer, and praise, and reading of the Scriptures; yea, that these employments became a weariness to him, and were at last almost totally neglected. "My soul," he adds, "reverted to its original bent, and the follies of this world wholly engrossed my attention, and had I been left in that state, I must have inevitably perished."

But the Lord, who is rich in mercy, and who delighteth not in the death of the wicked, had better things in store for him. Through the powerful operation of the Holy Spirit, a process of illumination and conviction was commenced and carried on in his soul, until at last it issued in manifest conversion to God. Returning to St. Andrew's, for the second time, towards the close of the autumn of 1823, he was enabled, before the end of that session, thus to write: "God, in his infinite mercy, has again been pleased to call my attention to the things of eternity. For some months back, I have been led to see the utter worthlessness of earthly things; to see that happiness is not to be found in any earthly object. And I think I have been led to seek it where alone it is to be found — in Jesus crucified for me. I have felt great pleasure in communion with God; and I have felt some love, though faint, to the Saviour and to his cause. I have had a long struggle with the world. I have counted the cost, and I have at last resolved that I will serve the Lord."

Under these re-awakened and more vital impressions, and as a scripturally ordained means of heightening and permanizing them, he at once resolved openly to profess his faith in Jesus, by formally entering the communion and fellowship of a Christian church. Relative to this decisive step, his biographer with equal truth and emphasis remarks, that his reasons for taking it, "were those by which he appeared to have been invariably influenced in his religious course. He first sought to ascertain what was the will of God; and on arriving at a satisfactory conclusion on this point, he was then prepared to encounter all difficulties which stand in the way of full compliance with it. He delayed not, but hastened to keep the commandment."

On being received as a member of the Church of Christ, he not only felt keenly alive to the seriousness and solemnity of the step he had taken, but entertained the most humbling sense of his own weakness and unworthiness, — coupled, however, with a well-grounded reliance on the all-sufficiency of his covenant God: "I see," he remarks, "many temptations in my way, and I feel that I am not able in myself to withstand them. May God perfect his strength in my weakness, and may he enable me henceforth to live, *not to myself*, but to *Him* who died for me, and who rose again; *to offer my body a living sacrifice, and to devote all the faculties of my mind to his service.*"

These were no mere words of course, expressive of aspirations that were to perish with the utterance. No; they were the spontaneous effusion of an intensely conscientious and ingenuous mind. From the day that he united himself, as a member, to the body or visible Church of Christ, by a deliberate act of public communion, it was clear to all around, that he regarded himself, in strictest literality, as "no longer his own," but as one "bought with a price;" and therefore bound to serve his divine Lord and Redeemer, with "soul, body, and spirit, which were his." Suddenly startled out of the dreamy indifference and illusory visions of old nature — arrested in his downward career towards the fiery lake — snatched as a brand from the burning — and overwhelmed under a vividly realizing sense of so great a deliverance, he might well have given expression to the actual inner workings and new spiritual instincts of his soul in words like these: "Lord, what wilt thou have me to do? How can I most effectually testify my adoring gratitude and love? Here am I a sinful, guilty rebel, ransomed by thy blood from the power of sin, and death, and hell, and the grave; do with me what thou wilt, for I am thy servant, under obligation the most absolute to be and to do whatsoever thou wilt."

Assuredly, in his case, there was no first consulting with mere flesh and blood! No tacit reserve in favour of mere natural tastes or antecedent predilections! No partial or half deference to the whims or humours, the likings or prejudices of friends! No plausible transference, through a voluntary humility, of individual personal responsibility to the arbitrary decision of others! No secret clinging or cleaving to any favourite or previously cherished scheme or department of labour! No timorous respect to the ordinary routine or stereotyped conventionalities of ecclesiastical usage! No! "Here I am, Lord, whenever, wherever, in what way soever *thou* wilt have me to serve thee — only do thou show me, that I may promptly obey,"— seems but the faithful and compendious embodiment of the real feelings and convictions of his heart.

It was, then, when in this Isaiah-like, Paul-like mood and frame of mind, the true spring and source of noblest self-renunciation and most heroic self-sacrifice, that the Lord was pleased powerfully to impress his mind with a desire to devote himself to the Christian ministry, in direct connection with the reat work of heathen evangelization, as the sphere in which, if rightly improved, most glory might accrue to God, and most good to the souls of men. Thus it was, that in his case, the evangelistic spirit, which ultimately led to so solemn an act of personal consecration, was coeval with the dawn and manifestation of the new birth in his soul. Planted there, as in a soil prepared by the Holy Spirit, and watered by the dews of the heavenly grace, the tender germ gradually sprung up into stature and strength, keeping pace with the growth of the new man, until, at last, it bore the ripened fruit of an unconquerable resolve.

It is true that with the subject of missions, in its general aspects, he had long been well acquainted. It was one in which his pious parents and pastor were deeply interested. It was, therefore, linked with many of his earliest and most familiar home associations. But it was not until he himself was sought out, effectually called, and quickened, as one of the lost, that he began to feel the influence of a Saviour's example and command constraining him to consider, whether it might not be his own duty, in imitation of his divine Lord and Master, to go forth in person, into "the waste howling wilderness" of sin and death, to seek and to save the lost! The discovery of his own ruined condition by nature, opened up to his unsealed vision a new and appalling prospect of the whole world lying in wickedness, and exposed to endless miseries here and hereafter. The felt realization of the joy and blessedness of pardon and sanctifying grace to his own soul, from the Fount itself of redeeming love, inspired him with new and unwonted motions of sympathy and compassion towards the perishing, as well as new and unwonted desires to be honoured as the herald to them of the glad tidings of a great salvation. An overpowering sense of grateful loyalty to Him to whom he owed his own everlasting life, inspired him with an uncontrollable longing to do what in him lay, to advance that glorious cause of the world's evangelization, in the consummation of which alone He shall see of the travail of his soul and be satisfied. Thus it was that, in him, the first stirring of the missionary spirit was not the impulse of a mere ordinary philanthropy — not the fitful gleam of a doating imagination — not the fond vision of chivalrous romance — not the sudden movement of excited feeling — not the wild project of adventurous enterprise — not the momentary flash and sparkle of an ebullient enthusiasm. Oh, no! It was the welling forth of a divine sentiment of pity and compassion, gratitude and love, from the profoundest depths of a renovated spirit — it was the lighting up of a radiant and enduring principle of life and energy in a soul, now struggling in the new pathway of holy duty, to disengage itself wholly from the smoke and tarnish of a turbid earthly atmosphere.

Still, he was very young and inexperienced, not having yet completed his sixteenth year. On this account, with a judgment pre-eminently sound, he resolved, in the first instance, to keep his newly awakened thoughts and desires to himself, spreading them out before God only, and seeking for further light from the illumination of the Holy Spirit, in the reading of Scripture, meditation, and prayer. A better evidence of perfect calmness and sobriety, coupled with earnest determination, could scarcely be afforded, than was indicated by this course of action. "If," wrote he, even at a later period, "if my wish to preach the gospel of Christ among the heathen, have

2

in it aught of the romance of a boyish imagination, a few years' thought and experience will extinguish its ardour; but if the Lord has appointed me to declare his name among the Gentiles, and that wish has been implanted in my breast by the Spirit of God, delays and disappointments will but foster its growth, and make it yet more vigorous." How sagaciously he had thus judged, the result abundantly proved.

After the lapse of a considerable period, devoted to *private* readings, meditation, and prayer, he resolved in his intense anxiety to learn his Lord's will in the matter, to seek for light from every available extraneous source, steadfastly watching the leadings of Providence with a filial eye. Conscious of his own liability to err, and with a diffidence and modesty peculiar to the sincere inquirer after truth and the path of duty, he was led, among other means of enlightenment, to ask counsel from friends to whose candour and practical wisdom he might look with some degree of confidence; not that such counsel might form a decisive or determining element in the case, but simply furnish materials for the confirmation or correction of his own immatured judgment. It was to his pastor, Mr. Orme, that in his letter of February 18th, 1825, he very naturally and properly first unbosomed his mind on the subject, stating that he had long considered the object of the missionary enterprise, as "one of the most important, perhaps, the most important, which can engage the mind of a Christian;" that, "for some time he had even seriously thought of devoting his own life to the cause of missions;" that he was "aware of the difficulties to be encountered, and of the danger of rashly forming a resolution of such importance;" that "even the desire he had thus expressed was the fruit of much meditation and prayer;" and that he had "communicated it to Mr. Orme in order to have the benefit of his advice."

But while he thus sought the counsel of experienced friends, it was from the Bible that he drew his chief inspiration and guidance;

praying at the same time, for the illumining influences of the Holy Spirit. The substance of his cogitations and conclusions in this direction he himself supplies. In a letter to a friend, July 8th, 1825, he remarks as follows:—

"In connection with this matter, I have been led to consider more attentively those passages of Scripture which refer to missionary exertions, and the result has been a deeper impression than ever of the duty of engaging in this work. It is very true that much has to be done at home; that there are many here, as my friend Craik writes, who 'can only be considered in the light of more criminal heathens.' But this is a wilful ignorance; they are not 'perishing from lack of knowledge.' And this argument, if carried to its full extent, would stifle missionary exertions to the very end of the world. What would have been the consequence had the apostles resolved not to leave Jerusalem till every one of their brethren according to the flesh was truly converted? The Gentiles would not have received the glad tidings of salvation to the present hour. This was not the commandment the apostles received, however; and accordingly they acted in a very different manner. They were to preach the gospel to all nations, *beginning* at Jerusalem. The nation of the Jews had a claim upon the first preachers of Christianity which our countrymen have not upon us. They were not only their 'brethren according to the flesh,' but they were also God's chosen nation; and as such it was right that they should enjoy a pre-eminence over all others, in first receiving the proclamation of pardon. But how did their brethren, the apostles, act even to this favoured nation? They made a full declaration of salvation through Christ; they made a free tender of the mercy of Jehovah; but by almost all this mercy was slighted and rejected. By thus sinning against greater light, these individuals became *more criminal* even than the heathen. Did the apostles, therefore, think that they should not go forth to the heathen till all these rejecters of the truth were convinced of the error of their ways? No; that very rejection of the gospel by their countrymen was a signal for their departure. 'Seeing ye *reject*,' &c., 'behold, we turn to the Gentiles.' Had the gospel been proclaimed in like manner to *all* other nations, the apostles would have felt it their duty to have laboured assiduously among their brethren at home. But, while there remained a single nation on the face of the earth that had not received the knowledge of salvation, they felt that the parting commandment of their Master was not yet fully obeyed; and while they lived, they made it their business more and more fully to execute that command. But their missionary spirit died with them; and at the present hour that commandment remains still unobeyed. Is it difficult, in this case, to see the path of duty? Besides, I cannot see that by preaching at home we hasten the coming glory of the Church. God has promised that all shall *know* him. He has not promised that all shall *serve* him. On the contrary, he has said that he will gather his people out of every nation, kindred, and tongue, and people; which evidently implies that *all* shall *not* be his people. Far be it from me to depreciate the work of the ministry at home. It is a most important work. But still, while there are any sitting in darkness and the shadow of death, it must yield in importance to the missionary field. Besides, who can tell what an effect our neglect of God's commandment to preach to *all* nations may have in causing him to withhold his Spirit from the exertions of Christians at home?"

In a subsequent letter he supplements this clear, simple, resistless scriptural statement, by the following very impressive view:—

"I still am inclined to think that the publication of the gospel as a message of mercy to sinners is the grand object for which the Christian ministry was instituted; at least it is one of the greatest objects. I do think that even the edification of the body of Christ yields to it in point of importance. We believe that if a sinner once embraces the gospel he cannot finally fall away; and even if his progress in the divine life should be slow, we know that in a very few years at the farthest, a full display of the glories of the divine character must burst upon him. Now, whether is it a more important work to rescue a sinner from hell and place him in this condition of safety, or to antedate, in a very slight degree, the happiness of a future state in one who has believed? For, all our advances in the knowledge of divine truth here must be held insignificant, when compared with the immense addition to our knowledge and our happiness, which we shall receive at that time when the dim conceptions of faith shall be exchanged for the bright realities of actual vision. I beg that you would not understand me as estimating lightly the work of grace in the hearts of believers. It is only when contrasted with the work of regeneration that I would ever think of it as of secondary importance. But I am not sure that the work of grace would go on more slowly in the hearts of believers, from the attention of the pastors being more called to the work of evangelizing the heathen. I do think in the present day we are apt to trust too much to public ordinances, and I would almost like to see Christians more thrown upon the resources of private devotion, and more direct communion with God. Our knowledge of divine things, to be sure, is small; but, O that our piety were but equal to our knowledge!"

As a further means of furnishing himself with sufficient data to ensure an intelligent and solidly based resolution, he sought and obtained, in the autumn of 1825, a personal interview with Mr. Townley, formerly a missionary in Bengal, and Dr. Morrison, the celebrated Chinese missionary, then resident in London. To them he openly expressed the wish he had for some time fostered, to devote himself, if the Lord willed, to missionary labours. As China, on account of its magnitude and their comparative neglect by the Christian world, presented the strongest claims to his mind, he looked forward to it as his probable future mission-field. He, accordingly, attended Dr. Morrison's instructions in Chinese, that he might gain as much insight into "the mode of studying the language as might enable him, should he wish to pursue it, to do so alone." And his biographer testifies that the papers he left behind sufficiently evinced how ardently and successfully he entered into the study of that difficult language.

Returning with his friend Mr. Adam, who had devoted himself to the missionary cause, about the end of October, to St. Andrew's, they both resolved to apply themselves afresh to their general studies, and to a thorough examination of everything relating to missions. For this purpose, they searched the sacred Scriptures, and summed up their inquiries under the heads of *precepts*, *prophecies*, *examples*, and *promises*. In order to render the investigation the more complete, they also resolved, at the same time, to collect from other sources, all the accessible information on the interesting subject. In this way they carefully perused Brown's History of Missions, Horne's, Ward's, Milne's, and Judson's Letters; the lives of Martyn, Brainard, and Chamberlain; Ward's History of the Hindus, &c., praying more earnestly than ever for wisdom and direction from above.

It is surely not possible to imagine anything more enlightened or judicious than the preparatory course of inquiry thus systematically pursued. No rashness, flightiness, impulsiveness, flashy enthusiasm, or ephemeral excitement here! On the contrary, all is characterized by a singular calmness and sobriety of spirit, comprehensiveness of aim, and persevering steadfastness of purpose, the clear indications of a simple, earnest, honest, conscientious desire to ascertain the divinely prescribed path of duty.

And what was the result? A growing conviction of the paramount claims of the heathen field, and of the duty of personal engagement in the missionary cause. Accordingly, as he had been led to give the first intimation of his long cherished *desire* on the subject to his friend Mr. Orme, so, on the 10th of March, 1826, he deemed it proper to convey to him the first announcement of his *final decision*. In that admirable communication, he tells how Mr. Adam and himself had made the subject of missions a matter of daily consideration throughout the session, reading nearly all the principal works relating to it; how he had thus obtained much sounder views of the matter than before; how the brilliant colouring of romance, if it previously existed in any degree, had faded from the picture, only leaving its outlines more strongly and broadly marked than before; how he was distressed by the prospect of those temptations before which so many of the missionary agents had fallen, and yet, how he felt encouraged to trust in God who could enable him to stand in the midst of all temptations; how he saw more clearly than ever that unwavering faith in God's promises and closeness of communion with him, were among the many requisites in the character of the missionary; how, the further he proceeded in his inquiries, he was impressed more deeply than ever with the duty of engaging in this department of the ministerial work; and how, as the result of the whole, "*after deliberately viewing all sides of the question, and candidly comparing the claims of our home population and the heathen world, and earnestly seeking for direction from Him who has promised to be the guide of his people even unto death, he had come to the final resolution of devoting himself to the service of God among the heathen.*"

His first *public* announcement of this final resolution was made, about the same time, towards the close of his concluding address to the members of the St. Andrew's University Missionary Society. It was in these terms: "The matter" (of personal engagement) "some time ago presented itself very forcibly to my own mind, and I felt that it at least demanded my serious consideration. As I have proceeded with my inquiries on the subject, the difficulties seemed to have gathered thicker on the prospect, but the convictions of duty have grown stronger too. The arguments for personal engagement seem to me to have acquired the strength of a demonstration. I have, therefore, resolved, with the help of God, to devote my life to the cause; and I have only solemnly to charge every one of you who are looking forward to the ministry of Christ, to take this matter into most serious consideration."

The writer of these remarks happened to be present when these sentences were uttered, and he can testify to the deep and solemn impression which they produced. It was not that they displayed aught of the artistic in style, the fascinating in rhetoric, or the brilliant in oratory. Ah, no. In themselves, the words were abundantly simple, artless, and unendowed. But there was, notwithstanding, a spell-like charm in them which at once reached the heart and caused it to vibrate to the innermost core. The address was on the subject of "personal engagement in the work of missions." The preacher commenced with a somewhat abrupt and hurried intimation which instantaneously aroused and arrested general attention. As he advanced, step by step, every statement seemed so clear and strong in common sense — every illustration, so apt and telling — every address to the head and heart, so backed and fenced round and round by scriptural authority — and all, so firmly clenched by that consummating announcement, which proved beyond the possibility of cavil or debate, that the earnest advocate was no mere special pleader who strove to influence others by appeals which had failed in practically convincing himself — that the cumulative argument seemed to bear down on the sincere and candid mind with a force all but resistless. And then, there was something so touching, so melting even, in that youthful expression of countenance, when lighted up with the kindliness of an unearthly sanctity — something so piercingly persuasive in those suffused eyes, when glowing with the fire of wistful longing and fervent entreaty — something so soul-thrilling in that naturally sweet, soft, mellow, silvery voice, when quivering with the pathos of out-gushing emotion from a surcharged heart, — that the combined effect of the whole might well be said to have been overwhelming. For a moment, it appeared as if all present were ready to rise up and march forth as a united phalanx into the battle-field; and few there were who did not then at least resolve to submit the subject to an examination with which it had never been honoured before; while of some, it can be added that they did not pause till they found themselves across oceans and continents, in front of the bristling hosts and frowning citadels of heathenism.

When his long and sore soul-travail had thus fairly brought his final resolution to the birth, one would have thought that it would have been joyously hailed, with general acclaim, by the friends of Jesus. But, no. Already, while merely prosecuting his earnest researches on the subject, he had met with not a little discouragement on the part of those from whom he had good reason to anticipate a different reception. And now, the formal announcement of his final decision seemed only to be the signal for an onset of more positive and determined opposition. But, it was not to be expected that a resolution which had been the deliberate result of so much patient, pains-taking conscientious inquiry — accompanied with so much fervent prayer and devout waiting upon God — could be easily shaken. It was not like Jonah's gourd, the growth of a day, destined to wither, before the first attack of an insect foe, in the morning of a summer's day. It rather resembled the monarch oak, which, slow in growth, gradually attains to a robustness of strength, that enables it not only to defy, but acquire increased tenacity of root and texture from every assailing tempest. The result abundantly proved that every antagonistic argument and appeal only recoiled on their authors, with a quicker and yet more vehement rebound, — thus furnishing fresh and incontestable evidence of the massive solidity — the adamantine firmness of the basis on which the resolution had been founded.

It is, therefore, with feelings of deepest pain, on account of his friendly but misjudging opponents, and intensest admiration of the heavenly-minded youth — in whom sage-like wisdom seemed so rarely blended with childlike simplicity, and the tenderest sensibilities intertwined with the stern, heroic, martyr-like spirit — that we find so many entries like the following, in his subsequent journals and letters: "He" (a venerated professor whom he greatly esteemed and loved) "tries to persuade me to stay in this country, but I do not think his arguments powerful." "I have been in Glasgow twice. I met Mr. Erskine there as well as Mr. Ewing," (colleague of Dr. Wardlaw in the Theological Seminary), &c. "All are against my being a missionary; but I have heard no arguments against it that seem to me at all conclusive." "Have you been thinking more of missions? I find every body dissuades and discourages me, urging the great wants of our own country. I think I feel the claims of our own land as strongly as some who urge them against my plans. But still this does not prevent me from feeling the immense argumentative force of the simple fact, that nothing has yet been done for heathen nations, proportioned to their vast extent; and nothing to fulfil the wide command of our Lord." "I have been partly terrified out of the idea of attempting publication, from the decided opposition *our* sentiments on this subject have met with, when I have laid them before those whom I have, from infancy, looked up to as men mighty in the Scriptures. Do not mistake me: my own convictions are by no means weakened. Every prayer deepens their impression. And at times of closer communion with God, a brighter light seems to be shed on the path before me. My own conscience must be my guide." "On the subject of missions every prayer strengthens my purpose. I am aware of the glare of romance, which fancy may throw round the idea of Christian expeditions to foreign lands; but I have tried to make due allowance for this; I have prayed that a youthful imagination might not lead me astray. The result is, I am every day more and more convinced that my convictions on this matter are founded in Scripture." "On consulting my friends" (parents and others, when on a visit to Perth) "I was astonished to find them even more opposed than before. There seemed to be even some disappointment that I had not by this time, abandoned the idea of being a missionary altogether. Had the impulse on my mind been a mere boyish fancy, in all probability this would have been the case, exposed as I have been to influences altogether unfavourable. But I trust there is no enthusiasm in supposing that the impression has been made by the Spirit of God, when time, and meditation, and prayer make it deeper and deeper. Still, my relations are quite against my views."

In connection with this determined and continued opposition which he had to encounter, to the very last, from Professors, ministers, relatives and acquaintances, Mr. Orme endeavours to present a plea, partly apologetic, and partly explanatory.

One of the dissuasive arguments frequently adduced — rather a favourite one with fond parents and doating friends — was, the alleged weakness and delicacy of his constitution. But apart from the grand fact, that all are in the hands of a gracious and sovereign God, who can preserve the weak, though exposed to the greatest peril, and strike down the strong, though placed in circumstances the most advantageous, Urquhart was persuaded of the soundness of the opinion of the physician whom he had consulted, coinciding as it did with that of the most experienced on the subject: "That no physician could predict how any particular constitution would suit a hot climate; and that, in general, persons of a *thin, spare habit,*" (like his own), "were more likely to stand than those who were *stouter.*"

Another of the redoubtable and stereotyped arguments with which he was constantly plied — the favourite one with Theological Professors and home pastors, who yet, at times, can eloquently declaim on the awful spiritual necessities of the heathen, and the glory and grandeur of the missionary enterprise — was, the urgent claims of home; implying, that he possessed some special fitness, from the peculiarity of his tastes and talents, for home work. Now, the real fact was, as stated repeatedly by himself, that he was led, in the very consideration of the missionary question, to regard more attentively the state of his own country as to religious knowledge. And no one can carefully and candidly read the many communications in which the subject is discussed by him, without perceiving how thoroughly he had examined, and how intelligently he had appreciated the claims of home; yea, how diligently he had laboured, as time and opportunity were afforded, in supplying the wants of home, by teaching Sabbath-schools, collecting young men around him, holding prayer meetings with the poor, visiting from house to house, distributing tracts; and yet, how vastly, in the case of one like himself, who simply strove to learn *where* the Lord's cause had *most need* of his *personal* services, the claims of the heathen were felt to preponderate.

But a truce to all such objections! From whatever quarter they proceed, they are of "the earth, earthy." Professors of religion, indolently and sinfully suffer themselves, for the most part, to be so entrenched in antecedent prejudices, preferences, and predilections, that their minds can very seldom indeed fairly look the subject in the face. Nay, more! The real truth is, that the teeming brood of ordinary objections will be found to spring from a deeper source than any that appears on the surface, or any that is usually avowed. The saddening and discreditable fact ought not to be glozed over or disguised, from the cowardly fear of offending man — however lofty in talent, station, or influence; or however endeared by ties of earthly relationship — that there is, in the minds even of most of the friends and supporters of missions, a thoroughly inadequate apprehension of two most vital gospel requirements: — First, a thoroughly inadequate apprehension of the *real nature* and *extent* of the *self-sacrifice,* which the gospel *demands* of *all* true believers; though such self-sacrifice be not a super-eminent grace, expected to belong only to a chosen few of transcendent piety, but one of the primary constituent elements of the Christian character — the destitution of which would argue not so much weakness of faith, as the non-existence of genuine faith altogether: — and secondly, as thoroughly inadequate an apprehension of the *real nature* and *magnitude* of the missionary enterprise, and of the *peculiar claims* of heathen nations, viewed in the light of *Scripture prophecy* and *divine commands,* as compared with those which, for ages, have enjoyed the blessed dispensation of the gospel. Hence it is, that, too often, even pious professors and ministers would begrudge young men, that are rarely gifted by nature and grace, to the heathen world; as if the conduct of a great war in the territory of a powerful foe demanded less talent, genius, or energy, than the commandership of a peaceful garrison in one's native land; or, as if the procedure which God himself exemplified in separating Paul and Barnabas, the mightiest of apostles and apostolic men, from the great and flourishing Church of Antioch, to become his ambassadors to the realms of heathenism, constituted no precedent, and challenged no imitation! And hence, also, it is, that, too often, even godly parents would begrudge a beloved son to the glorious work of proclaiming the unsearchable riches of Christ among the Gentiles; as if he were *their own,* and not *His,* whose claims, as Creator, Preserver, and Redeemer, are altogether paramount; or, as if the divine declaration, "that God *so* loved the world that he gave his only begotten Son, that whosoever believeth on him should not perish, but have everlasting life," constituted no example, and imposed no practical obligation!

How far the painful and harassing course of dissuasion and resistance, so obstinately and unyieldingly persisted in by parents, acquaintances, and friends, may have acted on Urquhart's keenly sensitive nature, so as injuriously to affect his bodily health and help to precipitate a fatal issue, it were vain for us now to surmise. On this extremely delicate point, every reader of the narrative must be left to judge for himself. One thing is certain, that, up to the very last, his own mind remained firm and unshaken as the iron rocks amid the ceaseless buffetings of old ocean. The *last* entry in his journal, referring to the commencement of the attack which soon terminated his earthly career, very touchingly shows, as his biographer has well remarked, how the ruling passion — his devoted attachment to *personal* service in the missionary cause — appeared strong in death. After recording the doctor's professional verdict, he remarks: "This has distressed me a good deal, *as it may unfit me for the East; which I have long contemplated as the scene of my labours.* But the Lord knows what is best."

Verily, the good and the gracious Lord did know what was best; and He now began visibly to take the whole matter into his own hands. He who knows the heart, well knew how sincerely and devoutly it was in the heart of the youthful Urquhart personally to labour in the distant fields of heathen evangelism. And, doubtless, the approving sentence, that it was good to have cherished such a purpose in his heart, has been duly registered in the book of the Divine remembrance. But, as endless obstacles were interposed in his way, by parents and friends on earth, the Lord was pleased, in his sovereignty, to decide the question, by taking him to himself! They would not consent to his serving his divine Master in foreign climes below; and so, *he* transferred him to a nobler service in the climes above! They would not consent to his leaving home and fatherland, on an embassy of mercy to perishing millions; and so, in loving-kindness to him and in rebuke to them, the Lord ordained that what they would not willingly suffer him to attempt by his life, *he* would honour and enable him to accomplish more effectually by his early death! It is known that, already, the perusal of this memoir has been sanctified as the means of quickening the desire of some, and confirming the timid resolve of others, to go forth as the heralds of salvation to the unevangelized tribes of earth. These, then, may truly be regarded as his substitutes and representatives in the heathen world, which he had so longed to visit and help to save. And souls rescued by their instrumentality from the bondage of sin and Satan, may yet hail him in the realms of everlasting day, as, in an important sense, their honoured spiritual progenitor.

Recommending, therefore, this volume, with all earnestness, to the members, and especially the juvenile members, of the evangelic churches of America, my fervent prayer is, that the lessons which it is so well fitted to teach, may not be lost on old or young, — that the perusal of it may, under God, be blessed to the stimulating of their souls to holier and more self-denying endeavours for the advancement of Christ's cause and kingdom in the world — that the mantle of the saintly, devoted, and now glorified Urquhart may fall on not a few youthful, ardent disciples, who, imbued with a double portion of his spirit, may be privileged to rear the standard of the cross over many a hitherto unconquered province of Satan's empire.

ALEXANDER DUFF.

MARCH, 1855.

PREFACE TO THE FIRST EDITION.

BY THE REV. WM. ORME.

I HAD scarcely received the intimation, alike unexpected and distressing, of the death of my beloved young friend, when I was importunately solicited to give some account of him to the world. The reasons for making this application to me, will be sufficiently apparent to the reader of the volume, so that no explanation on that point is required in this place. Prompted at once by my love for the individual, and by a sense of duty to God, whose grace and goodness were eminently illustrated, I assented to the request, before I knew what it would involve. I had then no correct idea of the nature of the materials which existed, and supposed that a very small number of pages might include all that I could furnish of sufficient interest. No sooner, however, was my purpose made known, than, besides the papers left by himself, which were more numerous and valuable than I had supposed, his friends and fellow-students poured in upon me such a number of letters and communications, that I have found great difficulty in keeping my selection even within the bounds to which the work has finally extended.

The individuals who have thus supplied some of the most valuable parts of the volume, and have contended who should bear the most decided testimony to the character and talents of him whom "they admired when living, and adored when lost," though occasionally mentioned, in connection with the correspondence, will, I am sure, experience some gratification, in having their names more distinctly connected with this memorial of their departed friend. It is due from me to say, that without their aid, I must have failed in doing justice to his character and history. It is due from the readers of this volume, if they shall experience any gratification from those letters, which, I consider, to be no less beautiful as compositions, than they are admirable in sentiment. And it is especially due to that sacred and Christian friendship, which subsisted between them and him who has gone to receive an early, but a full reward. I earnestly pray, that the band of youthful spirits, united at St. Andrew's, may, "when the dispersed of Israel are gathered into one," be again united, to rejoice together in the fruits of their sacred association.

The following are entitled to an honourable place in this statement: —Mr. John Adam of Homerton, between whom and the deceased there was a solemn agreement to labour together among the heathen, should Providence permit. Mr. Alexander Duff, still, I believe, a student, the earliest friend of John, at the University. Mr. William Alexander, his latest companion while there, and who is still prosecuting his studies with a view to the Christian ministry. Mr. Henry Craik, now at Exeter, between whom and John, a most powerful attachment appears to have subsisted, which rendered his death almost overwhelming. Mr. William Tait, son of the Rev. William Tait, of the College Church, Edinburgh. Mr. William Scott Moncrieff, of Edinburgh; Mr. Herbert Smith, of Egham, Surrey; Mr. James Lewis, Mr. Alexander Reid, and Mr. Robert Trail.

To other individuals, besides these, I have also been indebted for some valuable contributions; but whose names, I could not, with propriety, mention. They will accept of my affectionate acknowledgments for the readiness with which they allowed me the use of the letters which I have published.

Besides those testimonies, which I have used throughout the work, both to support my own opinion of the talents and character of the deceased, and to illustrate the points of view in which they were contemplated by others, there is one, which is entitled to a distinguished place in this memorial. Knowing that John had been a favourite pupil of Dr. Chalmers; and that, between the Doctor and him, a very intimate friendship had obtained, before I did anything myself, I wrote to Dr. Chalmers to inquire if he could undertake the office of biographer, and offering him, in that case, all the information and documents I possessed. In answer to this, I received the following letter, which confers a high value on the work that contains it, and shows the estimate which was formed of this admirable youth, by one of the most eminent men of the age.

"St. Andrew's, *Feb. 12th*, 1827.

"*My Dear Sir*—I received your letter some days ago, but have been prevented, by various engagements, from replying to it so soon as I could have wished.

"I had been previously applied to, from another quarter, for a Memoir of John Urquhart; and felt myself obliged to decline, in consequence of other engagements. I have less difficulty in pleading the same apology to you; for your superior opportunities, and earlier acquaintance with him, point you out as the person on whom the task is most properly devolved.

"He is altogether worthy of the biographical notice which you purpose. My first knowledge of him, was as a student, in which capacity, he far outpeered all his fellows; and in a class of uncommon force, and brilliancy of talent, shone forth as a star of the first magnitude.

"I do not recollect the subjects of his various essays; but the very first which he read in the hearing of myself, and of his fellow-students, placed him at the head of the class in point of estimation: a station, which he supported throughout, and which was fully authenticated at the last, by the highest prize being assigned to him for those anonymous compositions, which are submitted to my own judgment, and among which, I decide the relative, and respective merits, without any knowledge of their authors.

"For several months, I only recognised him as a person of fine taste, and lofty intellect; which, teeming forth, as they did from one who had not yet terminated his boyhood, gave the indication, and the promise, of something quite superlative in future life. It was not till after I had, for a time, admired his capacities for science, that I knew him as the object of a far higher admiration, for his deep and devoted sacredness.

"It was in the second session of my acquaintance with him, that I devolved upon him the care of a Sabbath-school, which I had formed. In the conduct of this little seminary, he displayed a tact, and a talent, which were quite admirable, and I felt myself far outrun by him, in the power of kind and impressive communication; and in that faculty, by which he commanded the interest of the pupils, and could gain, at all times, the entire sympathy of their understanding. Indeed, all his endowments, whether of the head or of the heart, were in the best possible keeping. For example, he was alike literary and mathematical, and combined the utmost beauty of composition, with the rigour and precision of the exact sciences. But his crowning excellence was his piety; that virtue, which matured him so early for heaven, and bore him in triumph from that earth on which he hath so briefly sojourned. This religious spirit gave a certain ethereal hue to all his college exhibitions. He had the amplitude of genius, but none of its irregularities. There was no shooting forth of mind in one direction, so as to give a prominency to certain acquisitions, by which to overshadow, or to leave behind, the other acquisitions, of his educational course. He was neither a mere geometer, nor a mere linguist, nor a mere metaphysician; he was all put together; alike distinguished by the fulness, and the harmony of his powers.

"I leave to you, sir, the narrative of his higher characteristics. I have spoken, and fully spoken, of the attainments of his philosophy; to you it belongs, to speak of the sublimer attainments of his faith.

"Had I needed aught to reconcile me to the transition which I have made, from the state of a pastor to that of a professor, it would just be the successive presentation, year after year, of such students as John Urquhart; nor, in giving up the direct work of a Christian minister, can I regret the station to which Providence has translated me, at one of the fountain heads of the Christian ministry in our land.

"Yours, very truly,

"THOMAS CHALMERS."

MEMOIR

OF

JOHN URQUHART.

CHAPTER I.

Introductory observations — John's birth, and early education — John sent to the Grammar School of Perth — Mr. Duff's account of him while there.

BIOGRAPHY is not dependent for its usefulness on the length of an individual's life, or on the station which he occupies in society. Were this the case, the longest livers, or the most dignified personages would constitute the chief subjects of this species of writing. But so far is this from being the fact, that the great body of those who live to advanced years, and occupy the high places of the earth, pass out of it with little more than an antediluvian notice, — "They lived, begat sons and daughters, and died."

Such a record is all that the vast majority of these persons deserve. They live for time, and they live for themselves. In their characters none of the elements of an enlarged and immortal benevolence exist. To the present state of being, all their views and wishes are limited, and with the objects which minister to their own gratification, they are almost entirely engrossed. When they have finished their day, therefore, they have obtained, such as it is, their reward. As while they lived, the world was nothing to them, except as it conferred enjoyment; so when they die, they are nothing to the world, which in their death has sustained no loss. The blanks which such deaths occasion are quickly filled up. The candidates for the pleasures and honours of the earth are innumerable: and they are generally too busy in attending to themselves, to think much of their predecessors, or to derive either warning or improvement from their fate.

It is admitted that the lives of such persons will frequently supply a large portion of what is called incident, which is too generally regarded as the principal charm of biography. In proportion to the number of extraordinary events, unlooked-for occurrences, and strange combinations, is supposed to be the value of the memoirs or the life; while all the while the events illustrate no principle, develop no specific class of causes, and furnish little or no instruction to the reader. They appear as if they were stuck upon the subject, instead of growing out of his character, and might, for anything we can see, as well belong to a hundred other persons, as to the hero of the story.

The life of the most interesting person whom this world has produced, whose actions were entirely directed to the affairs of the world, and whose training had little bearing on the enjoyment and occupations of a better state, must be of less importance than the life of the least individual in the kingdom of heaven. In the former case, the results, as far as the person himself is concerned, terminate with time; in the latter, they embrace eternity. Here the germs of an immortal existence are planted; here the roots are struck, of that tree of life which is destined to fill the celestial paradise with its sweetest and most fragrant fruits;

here the first elements of the heavenly sciences are learned; and here commence those dispositions and habits which shall grow to perfection in the courts of the Lord.

The writer of the following pages has no romantic tale to tell; but he regards it as one of some interest, or he would not tell it. It will be found to contain nothing of the poetry or fiction of religion, which are so eagerly sought by the sickly sentimentalists of the age. It records none of those splendid acts of religious heroism, the external glory of which the men of the world are sometimes disposed to admire, while they hate the principles which produce them. His aim is to present a faithful, though he is conscious it is only an imperfect, portrait, of one dear to himself by many recollections; whose mind was cast in one of nature's finest moulds, and highly polished, not by art and man's device only, but by the Spirit of the living God; whose character rose to maturity more rapidly than that of any individual he ever knew, and who lived as much in a short time, as most who have been honoured to adorn the doctrine of the Redeemer. Should the simple story of his short pilgrimage enforce on the minds of his youthful associates, the importance of cultivating his virtues and following his example; and lead others to examine the nature of that religion which was the object of such devotion to a mind of no ordinary vigour and acuteness, great will be the reward. In that case, it may at last appear that John Urquhart lived not in vain; and that the time spent in recording his history has not been unprofitably employed.

The subject of these memoirs was born in the town of Perth, on the seventh of June, 1808. As his parents are both alive, it would be indecorous to say much more than that, professing the faith of our Lord Jesus Christ, they felt the importance of devoting their offspring to him, and of bringing them up in the nurture and admonition of the Lord. To his mother in particular he was indebted for his earliest ideas and impressions; and of her tenderness and attention to him, he retained, as will afterwards appear from his letters, the liveliest and most grateful recollections.

From the extraordinary quickness and precocity which distinguished him, more than usual encouragement must have been presented to instil into his mind the elements of knowledge and religion; and I have reason to believe that advantage was duly taken of his docile and inquisitive disposition, to direct his attention to the most interesting of all subjects. It is not often that we can trace the impressions of childhood in the future habits and character of the man. They are made during a period in which the mind is inattentive to its own operations, and unconscious of the nature of the process which it is undergoing. The effects remain after the cause which produced them is forgotten. The writing upon the heart often becomes legible, only when the hand which traced it is mouldering in the dust; and the prayers which have been frequently breathed over the cradle of infancy, sometimes do not appear to have been heard, till after prayer has been exchanged for praise. These considerations, as well as the appropriate promises of the word of God, ought to induce Christian parents to commence their work of instruction with the first dawn of intelligence, and not to be dispirited because they do not soon reap a visible harvest of success. To this, as to other departments of service, the language of inspiration is applicable: "In the morning, sow thy seed, and in the evening, withhold not thy hand: for thou knowest not whether shall prosper, either this or that, or whether they both shall be alike good."

At five years of age he went to school, and, from having a remarkably sweet and melodious voice, soon became an object of interest as one of the finest readers among his juvenile associates. Shortly after, also, he was sent to a Sabbath evening-school, there to receive instruction of a more strictly religious nature than can be communicated in the seminaries of every day instruction. At this school he remained, I believe, with occasional interruptions, till a short time before he went to the University.

My young friend was indebted to Sabbath-school instruction, in a degree which cannot be fully ascertained or known in this world. There his mind was richly stored with divine truth, the full benefit of which did not appear at the time, but afterwards, in the rapidity with which he grew in knowledge after he felt the full power of the gospel. There those principles were implanted and strengthened, which tended to preserve him when he was exposed, an unguarded boy, to the imminent temptations of a University. There those moral feelings were first touched, which, in due time, arrived at that degree of sensitiveness, as to be incapable of bearing what was evil, and of relishing, in the most exquisite manner, all that was lovely, and pure, and excellent.

From the English school, he passed, in his ninth year, into the Grammar school, then conducted by a respectable scholar, Mr. Dick, under whose care, and that of his successor, Mr. Moncur, he remained four years. I have little to remark during this period of his life; but that he made distinguished progress in acquaintance with the classics is evident from the prizes which he obtained, and from the appearance, which he made when he first entered St. Andrew's, of which notice will afterwards be taken.

I am not aware of all the prizes which he gained during the time of his attending the Grammar school; but, in 1820, he obtained the second prize at the fourth class; and in the following year, the last of his attendance, the second prize at the first class.

When it is remembered, that he was only thirteen years of age when he left school, it will not appear surprising, notwithstanding his future eminence, that I have nothing of sufficient importance to mention during this period of his life. He was remarkably lively and good tempered, when a boy; and enjoyed, I believe, the general good-will and affection of his school-fellows. As he acquired everything with great facility, study was in general no labour to him. But during the last part of his attendance on Mr. Moncur's classes, he was very diligent; as he frequently rose at four or five o'clock in the morning, to prepare the lesson for the day. I forget how many books of Virgil he professed, besides other things, at the last examination; but I know the number was considerable. Though the ardour, or rather enthusiasm, of Mr. Moncur, in inspiring his pupils with the loftiest ambition of classical eminence, was extraordinary, and the effects of it, on the students, wonderful, John acquitted himself so well, that he carried off the second prize. The best account I can give of his progress, and of the esteem in which he was held by those who knew him, at this time, has been furnished me by his intimate friend, Mr. Alexander Duff, who was his associate in study for several years, in Perth, and during all the time he spent at St. Andrew's. It confirms my own statement, which was written previously to receiving it. He writes me as follows: —

"I first became acquainted with John Urquhart in the year 1820, at the Grammar school of Perth. Early in the year 1821, I entered into habits of the most intimate friendship with him, and scarcely a day passed without our being in each other's company for several hours, till the vacation of the school in the end of July. We generally prepared our lessons together; and thus, I had full opportunity of marking the dawn of that intellectual superiority which he afterwards exhibited. With almost intuitive perception could he discern the truth of many a proposition, which, to an ordinary mind, is the result of painful and laborious investigation. And finely could he discriminate between the truth and falsehood of many a statement which was embellished with all the alluring drapery of a poet's fancy. With singular acuteness could he estimate the real weight and value of an argument: and with an ease and readiness, far beyond ordinary, could he unravel the intricacies and discover the true meaning of a difficult and disputed passage in the classics. The *ingenuity* of some of his conjectures regarding the import of a sentence, and the derivation of certain words, was, I distinctly remember, highly applauded by his teacher. With a mind thus richly endowed by nature, he prosecuted his classical studies with the greatest fervour and perseverance; and though *far* inferior to the majority of his class-fellows in years, he uniformly appeared among the *foremost* in the race of distinction. During the summer of 1821, he was singularly active. For the most part, he rose every morning between three and four o'clock, and directly issued forth to enjoy its sweets. And should you, at any time, during the course of the morning, cast your eyes along that beautiful extensive green, the North Inch of Perth, you could not fail to observe, in the distance, this interesting youth moving along the surface like a shadow wholly unbound to it; sometimes in the attitude of deepest meditation, and sometimes perusing the strains of the Mantuan bard, which afforded him peculiar pleasure. Some of the fruits of these early perambulations, when most of his school-mates were enjoying the slumbers of repose, appeared in his having committed *entirely* to memory, four of the largest books of the Æneid. He was highly esteemed by all who attended the school. For, while his superior intellectual attainments commanded their admiration, that amiable simplicity and guileless innocence, which formed such predominating features in his character, necessarily commanded their love. You never heard him utter a harsh or unbecoming expression; you never saw him break forth into violent passion; you never had to reprove him for associating with bad companions, nor for engaging in improper amusements. In every innocent pastime for promoting the health, in every playful expedient for whetting the mental powers, none more active than he: but in all the little brawls and turmoils that usually agitate youthful associations, there was one whom you might safely reckon upon not having any share. And yet, with all his talents, and amiableness, and simplicity, I cannot venture positively to affirm, that there appeared, at that time, anything like a decided appearance of vital Christianity in the heart. One thing I can affirm, that, in our daily and long-continued conversations, religious topics did not form a considerable, or rather, any part of them. The love of what was good, and abhorrence of what was evil, had been so habitually inculcated from childhood, that the cherishing of these feelings might seem to have acquired the strength of a constitutional tendency; and the abandonment of them would have been like the violent breaking up of an established habit; still at this very time, the hand of God might have been silently, though efficaciously working. It is not for us to decide on those secret things that belong to the Lord. But, at whatever period the life of faith truly commenced, I believe it to be the fact, that his progress in it was so gradual and imperceptible as to elude observation."

Being still too young to be trusted alone at a University, and at a distance from his father's house, it became a question, how to dispose of his time for at least a year longer. After consulting with other friends and myself, his father determined on sending him to the Perth Academy for one session. Here, under the instruction of Mr. Adam Anderson,* a gentleman well known for his high scientific attainments, and Mr. Forbes,† now the successor of the Rev. Dr. Gordon, in Hope Park Chapel, Edinburgh, he prosecuted those studies in the mathematics, in natural philosophy, chemistry, and other branches which have been long and successfully taught at that respectable seminary. He received, at the end of the session, the first prize

* Late Professor of Natural Philosophy, in the University of St. Andrew's.

† Now Rev. Dr. Forbes, one of the ministers of the Free Church, Glasgow.

in the second class; and another prize for the best constructed maps.

This last circumstance induces me to mention that there was great neatness in everything which was done by my young friend. He possessed the love of order and elegance in a very remarkable degree. It appeared in the arrangement of his little library, in the keeping of all his things, in attention to his person; and, in short, in all that was capable of evincing the possession of a mind perspicacious, well balanced, and sensitively alive to everything ridiculous or offensive.

Hitherto no serious impressions on his mind had become apparent. That he was not altogether without them, appears from references made to this period of his history at a future time. His constant association with religious people, the preaching of the gospel which he regularly attended, in connection with his peculiarly impressible mind, must have subjected him to occasional convictions, which, though not permanent, prepared him in a measure for the deep impressions which were afterwards made upon him. The death of Mr. Moncur, the master of the Grammar school, under exceedingly painful circumstances, appears also to have deeply affected him. But the time had not yet come, when the full view of his own character, and of the grace and power of the gospel, were to be experienced.

Few persons have been placed in the same circumstances with young Urquhart, without feeling certain religious emotions; though, alas, in a vast majority, those feelings are subsequently entirely erased, or only remain in a very faint and inefficient remembrance. Association with the world; the pursuits of business or pleasure; or, what the

Scriptures admirably denominate, "The lust of the flesh, the lust of the eye, and the pride of life," cause many a fair "blossom to go up as dust," and destroy hopes of the most flattering nature. But when it pleases God to cause these early convictions to take root, and ripen, the future life of the individual is often remarkably blessed. His earliest and best years are devoted to the enjoyment and service of Christ; if cut off soon, it must be matter of rejoicing that his youth was given to God; if spared long, he has the delightful privilege of obtaining a full reward.

CHAPTER II.

Difficulties in determining his profession — He is sent to the University of St. Andrew's — Letter to his father, giving an account of his gaining the first bursary — Letter to his mother — His success at the end of the first session — Mr. Duff's observations on his conduct at this time — Return to St. Andrew's — Letter, giving an account of his early impressions, and change of mind — Remarks on this subject — His views of Christian fellowship — Success at the end of his second session.

THE period had now come when it was necessary to determine the future career of this interesting boy. Various objects presented themselves to the minds of his anxious parents. They thought of the professions of the law, and of medicine, and perhaps of another profession also, though they feared to avow it, especially to himself. It is not improbable that his own mind was directed to the ministry; but as he had given no decided indications of piety, neither his father nor myself encouraged him to think of it. Convinced of the deep injury done to religion, by the education of men for the ministry, who afford no evidence that they themselves know the truth as it is in Jesus, I consider the encouragement of such persons, the greatest wrong which can be done to their own souls, and to the Church of Christ. In some instances, it is true, the salvation of the gospel is afterwards received by them; in numerous instances it is altogether and finally rejected, although the most solemn obligations are submitted to, to preach it; and in many cases there is reason to fear, a cold orthodoxy is all that is ever attained. Under the influence of these causes, Christianity has sustained more injury than from all other things. The ruin of any church may be dated from the time that it commences the training of men avowedly for the ministry, from their infancy.

This is a different matter from a Christian parent, devoting, in his own mind, to the work of God, a promising youth, provided he shall become a partaker of divine grace. In that case, it will be his duty to give him such an education as his circumstances admit, and which may eventually further the object of his wishes. Such were the views with which I tendered my advice to the elder Mr. Urquhart, respecting the education and prospects of his son. I was powerfully convinced, that, should it please God to call him to the knowledge of himself, he had all the elements of an accomplished and attractive preacher. He had a fine voice, a pleasing address and appearance, besides being remarkably fond of knowledge, and diligent in its pursuit. To himself I said nothing; but I pointed out these things to his father, and convinced him of the importance of giving his son such an education, as might suit any of the professions in which the knowledge of literature is required. To everything except study, he always manifested great reluctance or aversion; so that the path of duty to send him to St. Andrew's became at length clear.

The high satisfaction which this afforded to John was very evident. The buoyancy and vivacity of youth, no doubt, appeared, in the prospect of going to a new scene, especially as that scene was a University. But he was to be placed among those to whom he was almost an entire stranger, to be separated from his own family, which he had never before left, except for a few days together, and to be made, in a great measure, his own master. These considerations could not fail to make on his delicate mind, some painful impression.

His parents, too, could not but feel the risk to which they were exposed, though he had hitherto conducted himself with much propriety and success. He possessed a large portion of good sense for his years. He was exceedingly steady and persevering in all his habits; and was ardently set on rising to eminence in some honourable department of life. But he was yet a boy; having only completed his fourteenth year. To many temptations he was now to be exposed, from which he had before been exempted, or the influence of which had been in a degree counteracted. Dangers of a very formidable kind frequently assail an inexperienced youth, not only from the associates of his academical pursuits, but from some of those pursuits themselves. But the election had been made; it was therefore necessary to commit him to the care and blessing of God.

I feel pleasure in remembering, that, with his father, I accompanied him to St. Andrew's, and thus far assisted in introducing him to that scene of usefulness, and perhaps, in the best sense, I might say, of glory, in which he was destined to act a conspicuous and an important part. Lodgings of the humble kind, which are generally occupied by the young men who attended that University, whose circumstances and prospects are not of a superior description, were provided for him. The respective professors on whose lectures he was to attend, were spoken to, and he was commended especially to the watchful care of my respected friend, the Rev. William Lothian, minister of the Independent congregation, whose ministerial labours he was to enjoy, on the Lord's day. Of that gentleman's kind and affectionate attentions, John ever spoke with great warmth; and to him he was indebted for much useful instruction, in private as well as in public.

Here I cannot allow the opportunity to pass without bearing my public and decided testimony to the liberal principles on which the Universities of my native country are conducted. At these important establishments, no distinction of party is acknowledged. They are open to men of all professions. No subscription is required at entrance or in any stage of future progress. Their highest honours are attainable by the Dissenter as well as by the Churchman; and, in the distribution of their rewards, I am not aware that any difference is made in consequence of the candidate not being of the established faith. At St. Andrew's all the students are required to attend public worship on the Lord's day, at the College church; but a young man has only to signify that he is a Dissenter, and that he means to attend regularly at the dissenting chapel or meeting-house, and his attendance with his fellow-students is at once dispensed with. It is due to both parties that I should state, that John Urquhart entered the College of St. Andrew's as the son of dissenting parents;* while there, he regularly attended a dissenting meeting, and became a regular member of a Dissenting Church; he left it with a mind unaffected on the subject of dissent; and throughout his course of study, he received from all the professors, the most marked and affectionate treatment. Of their kind and honourable conduct, he always spoke with the warmest respect and gratitude.

Of this impartiality he had soon a very substantial proof.

* Of the Congregational body.

Contrary to the wishes of his father, he was determined to offer himself as a candidate for one of the exhibitions, or bursaries, as they are termed, in Scotland; most of which have been left for the encouragement of young men at the commencement of their college career, with a view to help them to defray the expenses of it. Though the sum is usually small, it has often proved highly beneficial; not merely in aiding those whose resources are rather limited, but in exciting and stimulating the successful candidate to further exertion. The effect produced in this way on the mind of my young friend, I have no doubt, was both considerable and beneficial. But, as happily his own account of his trial and his success remains, I shall allow him to tell the story of his first adventure himself. In a letter to his father, dated St. Andrew's, 7th of November, 1822, he writes as follows:—

"My Dear Father—The bursaries are at last decided. Tuesday was the day appointed for the competition; we met accordingly, at ten o'clock in the morning, and got a passage to translate from Latin into English, which we gave in at two o'clock. We were then allowed an hour for dinner, and assembled again at three, when we had another version to turn from English into Latin, which we finished about six o'clock. We were then, without getting out, locked up in a room to wait till we were called in our turn to be examined upon an extempore sentence. I was not called upon till near eleven, when I was dismissed for that night. The professors met yesterday to determine the bursaries, from the exercises that had been performed the day before. There were no less than *thirty-three* competitors, and as I knew many of them to be very good scholars, from their answers in the public classes, I had given up all hopes of getting one. You may then judge of my very agreeable disappointment, on going last night to know the determination, to hear that I had gained the *first* bursary. I could not believe it till we, who had got bursaries were called in, and informed of it by the Principal.

"I began my letter with the decision of the bursaries, and have dwelt on them so long, because I thought it would be the most agreeable intelligence I could communicate. The whole four bursaries are equal in regard to value, being each *eight pounds* a session, for four years, if the person continues at the College for that time. It has certainly greatly relieved my mind, as my expenses here will now be comparatively easy. I was very dull, of course, for the first two or three days I was here, but since Alexander Duff came, I have been happy enough with my situation. I feel every comfort that I could have at home, excepting the presence of my friends. Mr. Lothian has been unremitting in his kindness to me ever since I came."

This letter shows satisfactorily the attainments he must have made, when at the early age of fourteen, he could gain the first bursary among thirty-three competitors, the great body of whom must have been much further advanced in life than himself. It affords evidence, also, of that spirit of exertion and independence which distinguished him to the last. It was his desire to be as little burdensome to his parents as possible; and everything which enabled him to diminish that burden, he grasped at with avidity. His wants were very easily supplied; and could I, with propriety, communicate the details and evidence

5

of his economy, which are now before me, I am sure they would excite no ordinary degree of surprise. Possessed, even at this early period, of a generous and self-denying spirit, he nobly sacrificed everything which it was possible for him to give up, so that the expense of his education might affect as little as possible the other branches of the family.

The time of a young man attending the classes of a University must be so fully occupied, that it would be foolish to expect that much of it should be spent in letter writing. Besides, many letters may be written which contain nothing that would be proper to meet the public eye.

The following extract from a letter to his mother, discovers his affection for her, gives some account of his employments, and shows how busily and constantly he was engaged.

"St. Andrew's, December 12, 1822.

"My Dear Mother — I confess that I ought to have written to you before now; I shall make no excuse for not doing so; but shall only say, that it by no means proceeded from forgetfulness or neglect of you. If there is any one of you that I remember more than another, you are that one; and, indeed, I must be kept in constant remembrance of you, by the comforts you are sending me every opportunity. The flannels, &c., which you sent last, were very acceptable; the mittens you sent me were also very seasonable; but I hope you were not, in any way, depriving yourself of them for my sake; for, if I thought so, I could have no pleasure in wearing them.

"I was happy to hear by my father's last letter, that you were keeping free of your complaint. I hope you are still so; and David* also. I always feel a kind of uneasiness in being absent from you all; but to hear that you are all well removes the greater part of it. For my part, I am keeping my health better here than ever I did before. I have not had the slightest head-ache. This, I am convinced, proceeds in a great measure from regularity. Every hour is employed much in the same manner every day. My meals are also strictly measured in the same quantity. I rise every day at seven o'clock, (with candle-light of course,) go to the Greek class at eight, and remain there till nine; take my breakfast and go to the library between nine and ten; go to the mathematics from ten to eleven; the Greek again from eleven to twelve; take a walk between twelve and one; go to Latin from one to two; dine between two and three; study till four; take a walk between four and five; and am in the house the rest of the night: you have thus a history of the time I have spent since I came here.

"This has been a very dry letter, but you may expect a better next.

"And believe me to be,
"Your very affectionate and obedient son."

By the same conveyance, he wrote his eldest brother a playful letter, enclosing a plan of St. Andrew's, sketched with his pen, with very considerable accuracy and neatness.

He paid a visit of a few days to Perth, during the Christmas vacation of College, and returned to prosecute his studies with increasing ardour and diligence. When the end of the session arrived, he bore off the silver medal, which is the highest prize of the junior Greek class, which

* His eldest brother.

he attended. He also received "Xenophon de Cyri Expeditione," as a prize in the junior Latin class. In the senior mathematical class, taught by Professor Duncan, he obtained "Simpson's Conic Sections," as one of the prizes; but which in order, I have not ascertained. This success could not fail to be flattering to a young and ardent mind; yet I do not recollect that he seemed much elated by it on his return. He seldom spoke of himself; and though to me he was accustomed to speak freely, he rarely adverted to his exertions, and scarcely at all to the honours which he had obtained.

I have reason to believe, indeed, that the good work was slowly and imperceptibly going on in his soul. I know that he was then in the habit of reading the Scriptures regularly every day, and that he and his companion frequently joined together in prayer. His uniform correctness of conduct and regularity in attending the means of grace on Sabbath, encouraged the hope that a decided profession of religion would be made at no distant period. In such a case as his, no very marked or visible transition could take place. His mind, familiar from infancy with divine truth, had not to acquire a theoretical knowledge of it. Not the intellectual perception of the gospel, but the moral taste for its beauty and adaptation, was the thing required. The former is a mere human attainment, the latter is the doing of the Lord. Man may cultivate and enlarge the understanding; but God only can touch and renovate the heart. Our expectations in regard to this were not disappointed.

The following extract of a letter from his companion Mr. Duff, confirms these observations, and shows what a change must afterwards have taken place.

"During the session of College at St. Andrew's, in 1822–3, he and I lodged together in the same room. He was still the same John Urquhart, though more ripened in intellect, and, if possible, more amiable in deportment. He attended the junior Greek and Latin classes, and the second mathematical class. He gained the first prize in the Greek, a prize in each of the competitions in the Latin, and a prize in the Mathematics; all this he accomplished with little labour or exertion. He spent much time in reading books from the public library: of what description these generally were, I do not now remember; but one he read and re-read with peculiar satisfaction, 'The Memoirs and Writings of Henry Kirke White.' He took great delight in walking along the sea-shore, and exploring the rocks which so abound in the neighbourhood of the town. Throughout the whole session we regularly engaged in the worship of God morning and evening; but I fear there was much coldness, and much formality in almost every exercise. With neither of us I fear, was religion then made *the great object.* There was little appearance of the savour and unction of divine, little appearance of real joy and delight in communion with God, little in short, to manifest the earnest longing, the devout aspiration, the holy zeal of him whose piety is deeply rooted in the heart, and tinctures more or less with its own sacredness, every thought and feeling, every word and action. The Bible was read, but I fear that the spiritual meaning of the Bible was not understood, and the subduing power of its doctrines not felt. Prayers were regularly offered; but I fear that the real *spirit* of prayer was wanting — the fervent outpouring of the heart to God. The wonders of redeeming love formed but a small share of our discourse:

our own individual interest in the great salvation, formed not a prominent subject of eager inquiry and anxious examination. In this manner passed the session of 1822–3, without any remarkable incident."

He passed the following summer at home with his friends, without any circumstance occurring worthy of notice; and in the beginning of November, 1823, returned to St. Andrew's to attend his second College course. Scarcely any of his correspondence during this session remains. He appears to have been very busily engaged in his various studies; and yet it was towards the close of this period, that he was led to make that decided profession of religion, which he was enabled to maintain to the last. I cannot express the gratification I felt on receiving the following letter from him; and which, notwithstanding its peculiar references to myself, I hope I shall be forgiven for presenting entire. I had not previously heard of his taking the step to which it refers.

"St. Andrew's, April 13, 1824.

"My Dear Sir — It is with feelings of a very peculiar nature, that I sit down at present to write to you. Since I saw you last I have been admitted a member of a Christian Church. I determined to write to you at present for several reasons. I have long considered you as one of my best friends, and as a sincere servant and follower of Jesus Christ; and your preaching was the first instrument in the hand of God, of leading me to think seriously of an eternal world. To you, therefore, I have determined to reveal every feeling, and to open the recesses of my heart.

"My first impressions of danger, as a sinner, were caused by a sermon you preached on a Lord's day evening, about a year and a half ago. At the time, I was very much affected; it was then I think, that I first really prayed. I retired to my apartment, and with many tears confessed my guilt before God. These impressions were followed by some remarkable events in the providence of God, which struck me very forcibly. About that time, I had a proof of the inability of earthly wisdom and learning to confer true happiness, by the melancholy death of Mr. Moncur. On leaving my father's house to come here, shortly after, I felt myself in a peculiar manner dependent on Jehovah. I was removed from the care of my earthly father, and from the intercourse of my earthly friends; and I felt great pleasure in committing myself to him who is the father of the fatherless, and a friend to those that have none. My companion used to join me morning and evening in the reading of the Scriptures, and prayer. In these, and in attending on the more public exercises of God's worship, I had some enjoyment, and from them, I think, I derived some advantage. On my return home, however, last summer, I began to feel less pleasure in these employments; they began to be a weariness to me, and were at last almost totally neglected. My soul reverted to its original bent, and the follies of this world wholly engrossed my attention. Had I been left in that state, I must have inevitably perished. But God is rich in mercy; he delighteth not in the death of the wicked. In his infinite mercy, he has again been pleased to call my attention to the things of eternity. For some months back, I have been led to see the utter worthlessness of earthly things; to see that happiness is not to be found in any earthly object; that

"'Learning, pleasure, wealth, and fame,
All cry out, It is not here,'

And I think I have been led to seek it where alone it is to be found, in 'Jesus crucified for me.' I have felt great pleasure in communion with God; and I have felt some love, though faint, to the Saviour, and to his cause. I have had a long struggle with the world; I have counted the cost, and I have at last resolved that I will serve the Lord. I have long been kept back from openly professing my faith in Jesus from an apprehension lest my future conduct might bring disgrace on the religion of the Saviour. But I have begun to think that this proceeds, in a great measure, from self-confidence, and from not trusting implicitly to the promises of God. He that hath brought me thus far, will not now forsake me; he that hath begun a good work will perfect it until the end.

"On Thursday s'ennight, after imploring the Divine direction, I felt it my duty to apply for admission to a Christian Church; since then, I have conversed with two of the members; and, being proposed last Lord's day, I was received into their number. I have thus, my dear sir, as far as I can, related to you without reserve, my various feelings, and my state of mind since I first was impressed with a sense of the importance of religion. I have yet many doubts whether I have been really renewed by the grace of God. Of this my future life must be the test. I see many temptations in my way, and I feel that I am not able in myself to withstand them. May God perfect his strength in my weakness, and may he enable me to live henceforth, not to myself, but to him who died for me, and who rose again; to offer my body a living sacrifice, and to devote all the faculties of my mind to his service. And now, my dear sir, pray for me, that he who is able to stablish me according to the preaching of Christ Jesus, may keep me from falling, and make me in the end more than a conqueror. At present, farewell; I hope to see you soon. Give compliments to Mrs. Orme, to my parents, and all friends."

"P. S. You may, perhaps, think I have been rash in joining myself to the church here, when I have a prospect of returning to you in so short a time. I can only say that I felt it my duty to apply immediately, that I have before experienced the danger of procrastination, and that I consider it much the same whether I be in the first instance to be connected with the church here, or with that in Perth, and that our friends here were all of the same opinion. In connecting myself with that body of Christians, to which you and my parents belong, I think I have not been influenced by the prejudices of education, but a sense of duty, and the writings of the apostles themselves."

This letter bears all the marks of the most ingenuous and candid disclosures of the leadings of Providence, and the workings of his own mind. It shows the gradual and pleasing manner in which he had been led to receive and obey the truth; and that although he had been much engaged in literary and scientific pursuits, and ardently attached to them, the powerful operations of the divine Spirit had carried forward the process of illumination and conviction, till it at last issued in his decided conversion to God. His reasons for taking the step which he had adopted, were those by which he appears to have been invariably influenced in his religious course. He first sought to ascertain what was the will of God; and on arriving at a satisfactory conclusion on this point, he was then prepared to encounter all difficulties which stood in the way of full compliance with it. He delayed not, but hastened to keep the commandment.

How much it is to be regretted that prudential considerations, or sinful timidity, induce many individuals, long after they have received the truth, to keep at a distance from the fellowship and ordinances of the Church of Christ. Instead of looking at the command of God, and considering the shortness and uncertainty of human life, they allow year after year to pass away in inquiring and doubting; or resolving and calculating, instead of deciding and acting. The consequences are a deprivation of personal comfort, to a great extent; the formation of habits most unfavourable to the decision of religious character, and injuries of various kinds being done to the souls of others.

It is as clear as possible, that at the beginning, no sooner did men believe the gospel, than they associated together for the observance of all the institutions appointed by Christ in his Church. There was then no neutral ground on which they could stand, between the world and the Church of God. No man is recognized in the New Testament as a Christian, who is not a member of a Christian society. Yet not a few can reconcile themselves to remain in the perfectly anomalous situation of doing all that Christianity seems to require, but making that profession of it which lies at the foundation of everything else.

I am aware that human barriers have sometimes been presented, by which some have been improperly kept at a distance from the fellowship of the gospel, who ought to have been welcomed into it. But I fear, in the majority of instances, the evil is to be traced to erroneous ideas of the gospel, inadequate impressions of divine authority, and to a want of that firm and decided principle, which, wherever it exists, will conquer trivial and even considerable difficulties. Providence is frequently pleaded as an excuse, while its arrangements are only putting our sincerity and principles to the test. As he who observeth the clouds will not sow, so he that will not go forward in doing the will of God till all difficulties are removed out of the way, will always find something to hinder him.

The plea set up by many, that they are afraid they may be left to bring disgrace on religion, is admirably adverted to by my young friend. A more superficial thinker would have ascribed this feeling to humility and self-distrust; he, with nicer discrimination, ascribes it to self-confidence. Provided our obedience were in any instance the result of our own strength, we might be justified in exercising delay on this principle. But as from first to last we are called to depend on the strength of another, the case is very different. He who enables us to believe, and flee from the wrath to come, will assuredly preserve us from dishonouring him, if our confidence is properly reposed. Many refuse to believe in Christ, on the plea that their sins are too great for them to hope that they may be forgiven. This they call humility; while in fact it is the deceitful operation of pride. It is obvious that if they thought they were better, they would not feel the same difficulty; because they could then come to Christ with greater confidence of acceptance. Many think they are not good enough to observe the Lord's Supper; as if the observance of it ought to be suspended on their goodness or merit. It is intended exclusively for Christians; but under that denomination, it includes all of every grade in the profession, who really know and love the Lord. It is designed, not for the perfect, but as the means of promoting perfection in those who are aiming to attain it. It is intended, not for the full, but for the empty soul; and will always prove useful in invigorating the life of godliness.

The following extract of a letter written long after, to the Rev. W. Lothian, pastor of the church which he joined, both illustrates his grateful feelings, and his strong attachment to the church under his care.

"I am chargeable with many faults, and carelessness is not among the least of them. I will not offer any apology, or pretend to make an excuse for not writing sooner, for my own conscience condemns me. But be assured it has not proceeded from a want of Christian love, or a forgetfulness of the many spiritual blessings I have enjoyed under your ministry, and in communion with the church under your care, or the many acts of kindness shown me by many of its members. No! I will never forget St. Andrew's; and the place where first I professed myself a follower of the Lord, and the little body of Christians who first gave me the right hand of fellowship, will be remembered with lively gratitude and delight, when the associations of literary and social intercourse shall have been effaced, by the impression of other scenes, and different pursuits. How different is our friendship from that of the world! Distance of time and place cannot weaken it, since neither can remove us from Christ. So long as we love him who begat, so long shall we love those who are begotten of him; and coldness of love to our Christian brethren can only be produced by lukewarmness in our love to God. Forgive my wandering; I sometimes forget that I am writing a letter."

"The account which he gave," says Mr. Lothian, "of his religious views and experience, on being received into church, was very satisfactory, and discovered great knowledge of the Scriptures in one so young. He particularly mentioned the advantage he had derived from parental instruction, and from hearing the gospel faithfully preached. I thought it my duty to remind him, that by casting in his lot with us, he would be deprived of that patronage which might otherwise have held out to him prospects of temporal advancement. He, however, said, that he had examined the subject for himself, and could not conscientiously unite himself to any other body of Christians."

The propriety of Mr. Lothian's caution will appear when we reflect on the tender years of young Urquhart, on his highly promising talents, on the temptations incident to a college life, and on the little inducement which he could have, under such circumstances, to connect himself with a small, and in the city of St. Andrew's, a despised independent church. Difficult as the circumstances were, he maintained his consistency and integrity of character to the last. And such was the power of principle, and his attachment to the body to which he belonged, that when on his leaving St.

Andrew's, a very desirable situation was put in his power, he would not accept of it, till the parties were informed that he was a Dissenter, and that the full liberty to act according to his own principles was the *sine qua non* of his acceptance. I mention these things chiefly as evidences of his sincerity, decision, and steadiness.

Important as these matters were, it must not be supposed that he was so absorbed by them as to neglect his professional studies. The best evidence of the contrary is furnished by the fact, that at the end of the session, which took place after he joined the church at St. Andrew's, he obtained again some of the best prizes. A second time he received the silver medal, as the best scholar in the senior Greek class; and also the second prize, "Xenophon de Cyri Institutione," in the same class. In the third mathematical class, he also obtained one of the best prizes. His distinguished attainments as a Greek scholar, were thus noticed by Professor Alexander: "He prosecuted his studies with unremitting assiduity; evinced talents and attainments in Greek literature of the first order; and in each session carried off, as he well merited, the highest prize of distinguished scholarship."

On his return home, I had the opportunity of conversing fully with him on the nature of his religious views, the great change which had taken place in him, and the object which he was now led to pursue. I found his mind, as I expected, devoted to the Christian ministry; and it now became my pleasing duty to encourage his resolution, and direct his reading with a view to that object. Possessing, as he evidently did, the leading qualifications to form a popular preacher, I hailed the day when it might be my privilege to introduce him in some form to the elevated and responsible employment of the ministry. I forget whether he then said much, or anything to me respecting the object to which he finally directed all his attention, the work of a Christian missionary. I entertain little doubt, however, that he then thought of it; but as my views of his talents led me to think of the home, rather than of the foreign service, I must have chiefly directed his mind towards the former.

While he was at home during this vacation, he wrote an essay on the Nature and Design of the Mission of the Saviour on Earth, intended, I believe, for some magazine, which promised a prize for the best essay on the subject. I remember that he showed it me; but I am unable to say whether he sent it. His accurate knowledge of the gospel, and the ease with which he could express himself respecting its nature and design are here strikingly illustrated. I believe it is the first piece of extended composition which he wrote, and cannot therefore be so perfect as some of his subsequent pieces. But the language requires as little apology as the sentiment. The former is as simple as the latter is dignified.*

This paper contains a very excellent view of all the leading truths of the gospel. They are every one of them stated fairly, and are all blended together in admirable harmony. No undue importance or prominence is given to any one topic, while the practical design of the whole is constantly kept in view. It discovers a discrimination and justness of conception, as well as an extent of acquaintance with divine truth, very rarely to be found in a youth of sixteen.

Even at this early period, and while so little accustomed

* See Appendix A.

to composition, he was above the ambition of fine writing. Here is no attempt at it; and yet the language is admirable for its appropriateness and simplicity. His mind was evidently filled with the importance of the subject; and from the abundance of his heart his mouth spake. His only object was to express himself clearly and forcibly; and in this he completely succeeded.

My personal intercourse with him was shortly after this time brought nearly to a close. In consequence of removing to London, our subsequent connection was maintained chiefly by letters. He employed himself, of his own accord, after my removal, for several weeks, in making out a catalogue of my library; classifying the books, as well as numbering them and registering their titles. It is now in my possession, and evinces, at once, his correctness and diligence, and his love for the proprietor, as it must have cost him considerable labour. That labour, however, I am sure he never thought of; it gratified, in a small degree, his love of books, as he amused himself by looking at many of them as he passed them through his hands; and it afforded him the far higher gratification of doing an unsolicited service to a friend whom he loved. I now deeply, but unavailingly, regret, that my opportunities of personal usefulness to him, were not, on my part, sufficiently cultivated. I too often neglected the present, by anticipating the future; and thus allowed many occasions to pass away, which might have been employed in promoting his advancement in knowledge and piety. Still, I trust, that intercourse was not altogether without profit. He is gone before, to the region where are no defects. May it be my privilege to follow, and to meet him there at last!

CHAPTER III.

Introduction to Dr. Chalmers — Attends the Moral Philosophy class — First appearance at this class — Letter to his father, on the formation of the University Missionary Society — On the same, and other topics — Mr. Duff's account of the progress of his religious views — Letter to his parents, on the death of a younger brother — Letter to Mr. Orme, partly on the same subject — Letter to his mother — Letter to his brother — Letter to his sister — Letter to an afflicted friend — Letter to the same — His diligence at Dr. Chalmers' class — Letter to a young friend — Letter to his father — Success during the third session at College — View of John's talents and character at this time, by a fellow-student.

Two events of considerable importance belong to his return to St. Andrew's, for the third session, in November, 1824 — his introduction to Dr. Chalmers, and attendance on the Moral Philosophy class, taught by him; and the formation of a Missionary Society among the students of the University. Of the Doctor, young Urquhart had long been a passionate admirer; and, to be one of his pupils, was the object of his most ardent desire. He was too modest to anticipate the enjoyment of Dr. Chalmers' personal friendship, in the high degree in which he afterwards enjoyed it; but which it is evident was most gratifying to both parties.

Moral Philosophy, as it has been usually taught at the Scottish Universities, is one of the most dangerous and ensnaring studies in which a young man can engage. Instead of being, as the designation of the science imports, the philosophy of morals, it is commonly treated as the philosophy of mind, and is chiefly directed to the varied and perplexing phenomena of mental perception and operation. Instead of connecting ethics with the revealed will of Gòd, it has too often been employed to gender scepticism, and foster the pride of intellect. Hume and Malebranche, Berkeley and Reid, are more frequently appealed to than the writers of the Bible; and many a young man who went with his principles tolerably correct, if not altogether established, has left the class a sceptic, or a confirmed unbeliever. The occupation of this chair by such a man as Dr. Chalmers is of incalculable importance. It secures against the danger of those speculations which—

"Lead to bewilder, and dazzle to blind,"

and provides that morals shall not become the enemy, but the handmaid of religion.

With missionary objects, young Urquhart's early associations had made him familiar; and his mind having become deeply impressed with the importance of eternal things, he was exceedingly desirous of interesting others in the noble object of missionary exertion.

Of his first appearance in the Moral Philosophy class, and, also of the exertion which he made to accomplish the other object, I have been furnished with a short account, by his bosom friend, and contemplated associate in foreign labours, Mr. John Adam. The following extract from a letter to me relates to both:—

"My first acquaintance with John Urquhart, commenced at St. Andrew's, in the winter of 1824. I had gone chiefly for the sake of Dr. Chalmers' Lectures to that University; and, besides my brother, was totally unacquainted with any of the students. The first subject given out as an essay to the class, was on the divisions of philosophy. The Doctor had introduced us to his department of the academical course, by some general observations on this topic. He wished us each to give an abstract in our own terms, before entering on the main business of our investigating moral philosophy. Not as yet familiar with any of my fellows, I was particularly struck when one of the youngest in the class, with simple dignity, (though, as he told me afterwards, with great perturbation of mind,) read an essay, which, for purity of style, for beauty of imagery, and a masterly delineation of thought, exceeded everything we had then heard. Nor could I but rejoice, when at the conclusion, a universal burst of admiration (which was evidently participated in by the Professor), proceeded from all present. I need only say, that his character, thus established, was maintained during the whole course. The decision of the prize, both by Dr. Chalmers and his fellow-students, awarded him the first honour they had it in their power to bestow.

"Soon after his first appearance in the class, I was happily introduced to him, at the house of one of Mr. Lothian's deacons, a Mr. Smith, when he mentioned a plan he was then meditating: viz., to attempt the formation of a Missionary Society, such as they had at Glasgow, which should not be confined to the Hall of Theology. This project was carried into effect a few days after; and a number of names having been collected from the Philosophy College, a junction was formed with a small society that had already existed amongst the students of divinity.

"During the term of this session, my friendship for John was cemented; and by studying together, by walks, and frequent intercourse, we became so attached, that, not to have seen one another for a few hours, was an extraordinary occurrence."

In a letter to his father, of the date of November the 3d, he communicates some particulars on the same subjects.

"My Dear Father — I arrived safe here the same day I left you, and am again very comfortably settled in my old lodgings.

"We have been attempting to form a Missionary Society in our College, to co-operate with one which the divinity students formed last year. We do not expect very large contributions, and the assistance which we can render to the cause may be, comparatively, but trifling: but the great object we have in view is to obtain and circulate missionary intelligence among the students; a thing which, we trust, with the blessing of God, may prove useful to themselves; and, though not directly aiding the cause, may, in the end, prove highly beneficial to it. For this purpose, we propose holding monthly meetings for the purpose of reading reports, and conducting the other business of the society. We wish also, if possible, to collect a small library of books connected with the subject; and what I have chiefly in view in writing to you about it is, that you may send any reports, or sermons, or other works, connected with missions, which you can obtain. You may mention the thing to any of our friends who you think could favour us with any of such publications, which will be very thankfully received. The formation of such society in such circumstances is, I think, peculiarly interesting; and may, if properly conducted, be productive of the most interesting results; and I am sure the friends of the Saviour will be happy to assist us in our operations. In asking for subscriptions, we have hitherto met with no refusals; and, though we have not yet got many, I have no doubt but it will succeed."

The following, written a little after this, notices the state of St. Andrew's, and some other things relating to the formation of the University Missionary Society:—

"St. Andrew's, December 15, 1824.

"My Dear Father—As I do not intend coming home at Christmas; and, as it will be some time before I need to send my box, I sit down to write you a few lines at present. I received yours along with a parcel containing a new watch, about a fortnight ago; for which I feel very grateful. I am as comfortably situated this year as I could wish. I have been introduced to some very excellent companions at Dr. Chalmers' class. The Doctor has brought a good number of students from other Universities, many of them of very polished manners, and, I think, not a few of very decided piety.

"The Doctor has thus not only increased the number of the students, (which, this year, amounts to about two hundred and fifty;) but those who have come for his sake, being mostly of evangelical principles, he has thus, though indirectly, wrought a great change on the religious aspect of our University. It is to this chiefly, that I would attribute the success with which my efforts have been crowned, in attempting to form a missionary society in our College. We have got about forty subscribers, and have already had two meetings, which we purpose to continue monthly. There have also been formed a number of Sabbath-schools, one of which is taught by Dr. Chalmers himself, and the rest by students. And, besides this, several meetings are held, by select parties of students, for social worship. Such a change, I did not certainly expect to see in my day. And this has not all gone on without opposition. Not only were we refused a room in the College for our missionary meetings, but the minds of the people of the town are so influenced that, even yet, we are not quite sure of a place to meet in regularly.

"On the whole, our College seems, at present, to present an aspect something similar to that of the University of Oxford, in the days of Hervey and Wesley. Among the rest of my class-fellows, there is a young man who seems to be very zealous in the cause of truth. He goes out to the country and preaches every Sabbath afternoon, at a place called Dunino; a place very much neglected; and on Sabbath evenings, he has a meeting of fishermen, to whom he preaches.

"With all this to render me happy, the remark of the shepherd of Salisbury Plain is still applicable to me: that 'Every man has his black ewe;' I have not been able to get any teaching," &c.

These letters show how much his mind was now occupied with promoting the spirit of missionary enterprise among his fellow-students. Instead of wondering that he should have met, at first, with some opposition to his plans, when we consider the materials of which colleges consist, it is rather surprising, he should have been so successful. The state of religious zeal in the University of St. Andrew's, had, for many years, approached nearer to the freezing than to the boiling point. The first attempt, therefore, to rouse and kindle the flame, could not fail to produce a certain degree of commotion. This, however, our young friend, and his associates met in a Christian manner, and overcame by their prudence and good sense. Dr. Chalmers was early engaged in its support; and others of the Professors also came afterwards to encourage it. His friend, Mr. Duff, gives the following account of the progress of John's religious views and feelings at this time, and of his exertions in forming the Missionary Society among the students:—

"At the beginning of the session of 1824–5, the traces of a gathering and growing piety were very observable. 'Out of the fulness of the heart the mouth speaketh;' and, accordingly, religious subjects became with him, the great, the constant, the delightful theme of conversation. Christianity was not now with him, a mere round of observances—a matter of cold and heartless formality. It engrossed all his thoughts, it gave a direction to all his actions; and his chief concern was how to promote the cause of his Redeemer. One evening, early in the session, a few of his companions met in his room. The main topic of conversation was the blindness of the understanding, and the hardness of the heart, with its entire alienation from God. This led to a discussion upon the influences of the Spirit in removing the various obstacles that oppose the reception of the truth as it is in Jesus. On this subject Mr. Urquhart's thoughts were striking, and his views luminous. Our attention was then directed to the resistance made to the offers of the gospel by the men of the world, and the want of universality in its propagation. The efforts of enlightened Christians in publishing the glad tidings of salvation, and the operations of missionary societies, were then largely spoken of. The vast, the paramount importance of this object as involving the interests of time and eternity, was acknowledged by all. The question was suggested, Is it not possible to form a Missionary Society among the students? By some the idea was reckoned chimerical, from the coldness and apathy well known to prevail among the members of the University. By others, among whom was Mr. Urquhart, it was strenuously urged, that a vigorous effort should, at least, be made for the purpose of forming an association for the promotion of so good a cause. I cannot now state the precise amount of influence which Mr. Urquhart's arguments had on those present; only he was most urgent and impressive in maintaining the propriety of the scheme, and its probability of success. Paper was accordingly produced, and the prevailing sentiments stated: the object being to procure a sufficient number of subscribers friendly to the missionary cause, to justify the formaton of a society. A small association of divinity students had met on the preceding year, in a private room, with the intention of reviewing and supporting missions. It was suggested, therefore, that a union might be formed between the divinity and philosophy students, (in the event of the latter coming forward,) so as to form an active and efficient body of members. The whole scheme, so ably advocated by Mr. Urquhart, succeeded far beyond the most sanguine expectations. And thus originated the St. Andrew's University Missionary Society, which now ranks among its friends and supporters more than one-third of all attending the University."

As this society occupied so much of his thoughts, and was, in fact, productive of some very important results to himself and others; and, as the mode of conducting its affairs was formed very much after the model of the St. Andrew's Missionary Society, of which Dr. Chalmers was the President, I am glad that I can give some account of the latter from his pen. It was furnished to "The St. Andrew's University Magazine," a small monthly work, published by those of the young men attending the theological and philosophy classes; and to which Urquhart was an occasional contributor. Though written the following year, it may be read appropriately in connection with the present period of my young friend's life.*

The interesting views and reasonings of this well-written paper are deserving of attention from the friends of missions. It shows how much may be made of this subject by men of a discursive and philosopic turn of mind; and were missionary meetings occasionally conducted in the manner pursued by Dr. Chalmers, they would prove more interesting and instructive than they often do. Considering the period during which exertion has been made to propagate Christianity among the heathen, and the number of persons who are employed in the work, both at home and abroad, it is surprising that some work, on what might be called the philosophy of missions, has not yet appeared. The only things, approaching to this character, are the

* See Appendix B.

"Hints on Missions," by Mr. Douglas, of Cavers; and the work on "The Advancement of Society," by the same highly gifted individual. But the former of these productions too accurately corresponds with its title, to answer the purpose to which I refer; and in the other, the subject is only noticed as one among many. From these works, however, the germ of a highly valuable essay on the subject of Christian Missions to the heathen might be obtained.

What we want is not an increase of reports of yearly proceedings, and arguments derived from the Scriptures, to persuade us that it is our duty to engage in this good work; but a condensed view of the knowledge and experience which have been acquired during the last thirty or forty years. What appear to be the best fields of labour? —what the most successful mode of cultivating them?—what the kind of agency which has been most efficient, and least productive of disappointment?—what the best method of training at home, for the labours and self-denial to be encountered abroad?—whether are detached and separate missions, or groups of missions and depôts of missionaries, the most desirable? These, and many other questions, require a mature and deliberate answer. The materials for such an answer exist. And can none of the officers whose time is wholly devoted to the management of our Missionary Societies furnish such a digest? Are they so entirely occupied with the details of business, as to have no time or inclination left for looking at general principles? Were more attention paid to the ascertaining of such principles, and more vigour and consistency manifested in prosecuting them, there might be less of glare and noise; but, assuredly, there would be a prodigious saving of labour, property, and life; and, in the end, a greater degree of satisfaction and real success.

"The first requisite in benevolent operations," says Mr. Douglas, "as in all other undertakings, is system; a fixedness of design, and a steady adaptation of the means to the end. Opposite to that of system, is the pursuing of what are called openings, or the being caught with every change of circumstances and drawn by every chance of success into new paths of pursuit, having no connection with each other, and leading to remote terminations. Every step gained in a system, strengthens; every step gained without it weakens. The first object acquired leads to the possession of the second, and that to the attainment of the third, if all the objects to be attained are originally chosen with reference to the accomplishment of a plan. Every new object, where there is no system, divides the already scattered forces; and success, if pursued, might dissipate them entirely, and leave but the vain pleasure of having a number of defenceless stations, each calling for assistance, and all calling in vain, while the society only retained the empty boast of an extended line of operations, and of being equally helpless and inefficient in every quarter of the globe. On a system, each part strengthens the other, the line of communication is held up entire; as each point is gained, the whole advances; they are all in movement towards the same position, and they rest upon the same centre of support."

I cannot pursue the subject further, but the existing circumstances of our missionary institutions call loudly for the consideration of these judicious remarks. I return to the narrative.

Not satisfied with his exertions in establishing and aiding a missionary society, and thus contributing to diffuse the gospel abroad, John felt it his duty to do all the good in his power to those among whom he lived. This led him at the commencement of this session to engage in teaching a Sabbath-school, in a village a few miles distance from St. Andrew's. To this place he was in the habit of going regularly every Lord's day evening, and occasionally, also, on other days, when he could find time, for the purpose of conversing with the parents; thus endeavouring to interest them in the spiritual welfare of their children, and in their regular attendance at the school.

These engagements have often been productive of the most beneficial effects on young men intended for the ministry, as well as on the minds of the rising generation. They stimulate to the examination of the Scriptures, accustom the teacher to an easy and familiar method of speaking and address; and increase his acquaintance with the peculiarities of human character. The difficulties he experiences in conducting such seminaries, and accomplishing his wishes, will be found to arise from many of the same causes which operate on the "children of a larger growth," whom he may afterwards be called to instruct. And the mode of meeting these difficulties by a combination of faithfulness and affection, of perseverance and prayer, will habituate him to the exercise of principles and dispositions of the last importance, in discharging the duties of the Christian ministry.

To this kind of service my young friend was much attached, as well from choice as from principle and a sense of duty. He was sensible of the benefit which he derived from it himself; and, therefore, wherever he was, though but for a short time, he endeavoured to collect a few young persons around him. From the great amiability of his disposition, he never failed to bring them together, and to attach them to him; and, from his happy method of engaging their attention, he was always rewarded, in seeing their love to the exercise, as well as their personal attachment to himself. On his return home, at the end of the session, he succeeded in establishing a meeting of a few young men, of his own age, in his father's house, once a week, for conversing about the Scriptures, and for prayer; the benefit of which some of them, I hope may yet enjoy. While there, also, during the summer vacation, he taught a Sabbath-school in the neighbourhood of Perth; thus evincing his sincerity and diligence in the improvement of every opportunity of usefulness which he could command.

Having noticed his feelings and views in regard to personal religion, and to the work of the gospel abroad, and his exertions to promote its interests at home, it will now be proper to advert to his progress in his literary pursuits, especially in that class in which he made so distinguished a figure. A certain description of persons, who are not altogether opposed to religion, but who feel exceedingly cool in regard to its claims, both upon themselves and others, are much disposed to allege, that if the attention of a young person is much occupied with religious subjects, other things which he ought to pursue, must be neglected. It is admitted that there is some difficulty in perfectly adjusting the relative and proportionate claims of religious and other pursuits, especially during the more active period of human life. Wisdom is necessary to direct in this, and in many other matters, which cannot be determined by the language of the Scriptures. To which preference is due, no doubt can be entertained. "Seek ye first the kingdom of God and his righteousness," is a plain injunction applicable to all circumstances, and at all periods of our existence. True wisdom consists in obeying that injunction, which will never fail to secure the fulfilment of the promise, "and all these things shall be added unto you." Should there be in any instance an excess in devoting what may be considered too large a portion of attention to religion, surely it is a very pardonable offence. If it be an error, it is an error on the safe side. Allowances are made for individuals following the bent of a powerful genius, when that genius is directed towards some earthly object; but, unhappily, if the bent of the mind is toward religion, the feeling which is manifested is very different. What is an amiable and praiseworthy enthusiasm in the one case, is denounced as miserable and misguided fanaticism in the other. The conduct which raises an artist or a poet to the summit of earthly glory, places a Whitefield and a Martyn in the pillory of the world's scorn.

It is no common thing to find a mind so nicely poised and balanced, as to be capable of giving every subject of examination its proper degree of attention, and every object of pursuit its just measure of importance. It will too generally happen that when one thing, whether of a secular or spiritual nature, obtains firm possession of the mind, other things will, to a certain extent, be dislodged. There is usually, to employ the expressive phraseology of Dr. Chalmers, "a shooting forth of the mind in one direction;" and when this happens, other things must be obscured and left behind. If, according to Spurzheim, the faculty of common sense consists in the harmonious arrangement and operation of all the other senses, it is very evident that the faculty is by no means so *common* as the phrase imports.

As it regards religion, however, I am inclined to think, this is one of the libels which its enemies are ever disposed to propagate against it. They maintain in the face of all evidence, that the men who are clamorous on the subject of the spiritual wants of others, are usually defective in their generosity to supply their temporal necessities. In vain we appeal to our Howards and Wilberforces, and thousands besides, in refutation of the calumny. It will be reiterated till the world is regenerated.

I apprehend that it will often be found that our religious men are among the most ardent and devoted students. Few men have distinguished themselves more when at College, than Martyn, and Kirke White; and I am happy that I can add the name of Urquhart to the list of persons, who, under the noblest considerations, devoted their fine talents and unconquerable ardour to the pursuits of literature and science, that they might lay their crowns as scholars at the foot of the cross.

I hesitated for some time whether I should give a few of his essays in the Moral Philosophy class; fearing they might not do full justice to his merits, and that to some readers they might not be sufficiently interesting. But, knowing the opinion of these essays, entertained by such a man as Dr. Chalmers, and observing the beautiful simplicity of language and felicity of illustration which they discover; by which the most abstruse subjects are rendered not only intelligible, but attractive, I have resolved to present them. The reader will thus see that he who was so much at home in religion, was not a stranger in the walks of philosophy.*

While engaged in these interesting exercises of his academical course, and in the prosecution of his plans of usefulness, he was called to sustain a painful trial, in the death of his youngest brother. Nothing of this kind had before occurred in the family, within his knowledge. He was suddenly summoned to Perth; and after spending a few days by the dying bed of his brother, and endeavouring to interest his mind in religion, he returned to St. Andrew's, as the nature of the complaint left it very uncertain how long his brother might continue. On being informed of his death he wrote to his father and mother, as follows:—

"St. Andrew's, January 17, 1825.

"My Dear Parents—It is a remark which I have somewhere heard, that God tries to bring us to himself by mercies; but if this has not the effect, he makes use of trials. Like the affectionate father of rebellious and disobedient children, he tries to win us by love; and it is only our obstinate perseverance in our own ways which forces him to use the rod. It is true, that our very afflictions are signs of God's love towards us; for, 'whom he loveth he chasteneth.' But it is equally true, that they are signs of his displeasure. We, as a family, have long been favoured with every blessing; and it becomes us to ask, if we have been as grateful and as obedient as became the children of so many mercies. A serious review of the past, will make us wonder that our Father has been so long-suffering; that he has withheld his chastening hand

* See Appendix C.

so long. It becomes us, then, to repent of our unthankful and repining disposition, and to humble ourselves under the mighty hand of God.

"It is a joyful thing, that, in the time of affliction, God does not hide his face from us, nor remove us far from him. But it is the very end of all our trials to bring us to himself by drying up our channels of happiness, to lead us to the spring from whence those channels were supplied; by breaking the cisterns which we have hewed out for ourselves, to lead us to the fountain of living waters.

"I think I may say, 'it has been good for me to be afflicted;' it has driven me to the Bible, and to a throne of grace, as the only consolations; and never did the truths of the gospel appear more precious. My Christian friends here have been very attentive to me, and seem to have sympathized with me in earnest.

"This is certainly a warning to each of us, to be also ready — a solemn exhortation to be active in the cause of Christ; and whatever our hand finds to do, to do it with all our might; knowing that there is no knowledge nor device in the grave whither we are fast hastening.

"I am anxious to know what impression this solemn event has made on the minds of my yet remaining brother and sister. Death can sometimes affect the soul which has been unmoved by the most solemn admonitions, and the most impressive eloquence. I am very sorry that it is out of my power at present to write to them.

"The ways of God are very mysterious. Had I been here during the Christmas holidays, I could, in all probability, have got a situation, which would have enabled me to support myself, and even, in a year or two, to have given you some assistance. It was a situation as tutor in a very pious family in England. I had been recommended as a fit person for the place, but as it had to be occupied immediately, it was given to another, who is there by this time. From all the accounts I got of it, it seemed a place where I could have been very happy; and I could not help feeling disappointed. But it is a happiness to think that it is a gracious Father that overrules all things; and that he does all things well.

"P. S. Give me a more full account of the latter part of my poor brother's illness."

Shortly after this, he wrote me a long letter, partly on the same subject, and partly giving me an account of various affairs then transacting in St. Andrew's, which he knew would interest me.

"St. Andrew's, February 18, 1825.

"My Dear Sir — I am really quite ashamed that I have not sent you a letter long before now. I intended writing by Dr. R———, when I sent up the catalogue of your library; but it occurred to me that at such an early period of your new settlement, when you must have been so much occupied with the bustle and the confusion attending such an event, it would have been altogether out of place for *me* to trouble you with a letter. It is now a month or two since my father informed me in one of his letters, that he had heard from you, and that you had kindly expressed a wish that I would write to you from St. Andrew's. I really have no proper excuse for delaying so long; suffice it to say, that this is not the first time I have sat down to address you; and that I might fill my sheet to no purpose, in telling how often I have taken up the pen, and what circumstances have hitherto prevented me from finishing my letter. You have, in all probability, heard before now, that death has at last entered our family, and has snatched away the youngest and healthiest of us all. Poor Henry had thought himself dying from the first day he took to his bed, and had expressed a great desire that I should be sent for. My father accordingly sent for me; and on my arrival at home, I found my brother in a state of very great agony, and quite unable to converse with me. I was anxious to speak to him about that world whither he was evidently fast hastening; but so excruciating was his pain, that he could not listen. I can remember, when I asked him, after he had been violently crying out from the pain in his head, what was the cause of all his suffering, how expressively he answered, that it was sin. And at another time, on asking him if he was afraid to die; he told me, No. But these short answers were all I could obtain from him; the painful nature of his distress did not permit longer conversation. After staying at home about a week, I found that I was waiting for a change which might yet be far distant; and that I was losing my own time without being able to render any service to my brother. I therefore resolved to return; but I think I shall never forget the bitterness of that parting. I felt far more then, than when I heard afterwards, that my brother was gone. Henry begged of me not to go away, and my mother with tears entreated me to remain; but I thought it my duty to leave them; and in the issue, it has proved much better that I did so; for my brother lingered for weeks after. I cannot say whether I was more depressed or relieved by the letter which brought the tidings of his death. I rejoice to think that his body was freed from very exquisite suffering; but with regard to his soul all was uncertain. I would indulge the hope, that his suffering may have been rendered the means of bringing him to trust in that Saviour about whom he had so often heard. But it rests with God. To us there has been given no certain assurance of his happiness. I hope I have myself been enabled to see in this dispensation, the hand of an all-wise Father; and that it has not been without a beneficial influence on my own soul. Separated from my earthly relations, and deprived of the comfort which their sympathy might have inspired, I was forced to seek consolation from that Friend who never leaves his people. Never did I feel so much the need of the consolations of the gospel; and never did its declarations appear more cheering and consolatory. I could feel not only submissive, but thankful. I could say with Conder, when in a similar situation:—

> 'Oh, to be brought to Jesus' feet,
> Though sorrows fix me there,
> Is still a privilege.'

But I have to regret that the impression has been of such short continuance, and that my heart seems ready to go back again to the vanities of the world. I can easily perceive that if the gospel have not an abiding influence on the conduct, the mere sentimental tenderness, and deadness to the things of earth, which are produced by the death of a friend, may, and will soon be forgotten. I know you will forgive me for dwelling so long on this painful theme. You will remember that the wound is yet green; and you know from experience how the mind, in such circumstances, loves to brood over the cause of its sorrow.

"I must proceed to give you some information about St. Andrew's. I might tell you of the prosperity of the College; the increase in the number of the students, &c.; but as these things cannot much interest you, I shall just shortly advert to some religious institutions which have been formed among us, and to the spiritual state in general of our town and University. Dr. Chalmers has effected a good deal by his own example and his own exertions; but he has even been more useful in drawing to this place a number of pious young men of various denominations, who have been the instruments of bringing about a great change in the externals, at least, of our University. We cannot indeed say, that any great moral renovation has been effected; but the machinery, at least, has been erected, which, with the blessing of God, may be the means of effecting it. We have now Sabbath-schools taught by members of the University; and meetings for prayer among the students; and, what is more astonishing still, a University Missionary Society, consisting of about sixty members, who meet once a month for the purpose of promoting the objects of the society. In connection with this last institution, we have formed a small library of missionary books, which have mostly been sent us in presents; and from the circulation of which, I anticipate great good. This is an institution in which I take particular interest, as I have long considered the object which it has in view one of the most important, perhaps, the most important, which can engage the mind of a Christian. And for some time I have even seriously thought of devoting my own life to the cause of missions. I had long wished to find a companion who could enter into my own views on this subject; and such an one I think I have fallen in with this session. His name is Mr. Adam; he had been boarded for some time with Mr. Malan, of Geneva, and he seems to have imbibed much of the spirit of that excellent man. We have sometimes talked over the subject of missions together, and I hope we may be yet honoured to preach the gospel to the heathen. I am aware of the difficulties to be encountered; and of the danger of rashly forming a resolution of such importance; but even the desire I have expressed to you, is the fruit of much meditation and prayer. And I have communicated it to you, in order to have the benefit of your advice. I shall always look to you as one of the best friends I have on earth, and I trust my father in Christ Jesus. I wish you would send me word about the institution at Gosport. I have heard there is a great deficiency in the number of students. I entreat that you will pray for my direction in this matter of so great importance with regard to my spiritual happiness.

"I may mention, by the way, that we have a Mr. H——— here, a Baptist minister, from London; of whom, perhaps, you may have heard. He has come to attend Dr. Chalmers, and has been very useful here. He and my friend, Mr. Adam, have established several preaching stations in the country round, where the people seem eager to hear the gospel.

"I am sorry that I am so soon obliged to conclude; for I have not told you the half of what I have to communicate. When I heard from home, my friends were well; and the church had given Mr. Jack a unanimous call.

"Perhaps I have been too free in still retaining the

Hebrew books you were pleased to lend me. I am devoting all my spare time to the reading of the Psalms.

"I shall be very much gratified by a letter. Perhaps you may be interested to hear that I preached, for the first time, on Saturday last, to a few of my fellow-students, who have formed themselves into a society for extempore preaching. We meet in the Divinity-Hall. Farewell."

The reader, I am sure, will join me in admiring the beautiful combination of Christian principle and brotherly affection contained in these letters. There is no affectation of feeling; but the utterance of it in the simplest and most impressive language. He dwells on the slight indications of religious feeling which his brother could give, with evident delight; and fondly cherished hope as far as the circumstances admitted. The account of the progress of religion and of the juvenile association, is also very interesting. It shows how completely his heart was now engaged; and, from this time, I considered him devoted to the work of God among the heathen, should Providence be pleased to spare his life. I accordingly wrote to him to encourage and cherish, rather than to stimulate him, which, I perceived, he did not require. The sermon to which he refers, as his first essay in this kind of composition, remains among his papers; and would do credit, in point of sentiment and expression, to a minister of some years standing.

Having been the principal means of establishing the University Missionary Society, he appears to have taken a very active part in its management. And as an evidence how much it engaged his mind, and how fully he thought on all the bearings and aspects of the great work,

I must introduce an essay which he read at one of its meetings, held on the 12th of February; a few days before the writing of the preceding letter.*

He was too busy about this period to spend much time in correspondence; but a few of his letters, though short, I must introduce. They will show the strength and delicacy of his natural feelings, and how tenderly he was alive to all the charities of human life. A sentence is sometimes more indicative of feeling and sentiment than a volume.

"St. Andrew's, February, 1825.

"My Dear Mother — If ever in my life I felt quite oppressed and burdened with kindness, it was on the receipt of your very kind communication after my brother's death; and I am quite ashamed that I have not long before now found means to express my gratitude. My friends seem to have vied with each other, who should be kindest, and who should pay me most attention; and had I not been quite overburdened with business, you should have had a letter long before now. At the time you sent, I had a very severe cold, which seemed to show some disposition to settle in my breast; but I am now tolerably well again. Nothing, however, could prevent my good landlady, on the recommendation of Mr. Smith, who called on me, from ordering flannels for me, which of course has greatly assisted in emptying my slender purse. I have just received my father's letter of the 4th, and am exceedingly happy to hear that the church have all come to one mind concerning Mr. Jack. The choosing of a minister is in general one of the most trying times to our churches;

* See Appendix D.

and I think we have much reason to bless God that roots of bitterness have not been permitted to spring up and trouble us. Things are going on pretty well among us. The people round about seem to be hungering and thirsting after righteousness. Mr. Adam preached in the country on Friday, at a new station, where the people themselves had requested that some one should come. There is a great want of labourers — they have pressed Mr. R——— into the service, but still there is employment which is more than enough for them."

"St. Andrew's, February 22, 1825.

"My Dear Brother — I have sometimes blamed, or rather pitied you, (for it is not a legitimate subject of blame,) for a want of feeling; and I am quite sorry I have ever done so; for the deep pathos that runs through some of your letters, which are, notwithstanding, expressed in all the unaffected and unstudied simplicity of nature, convinces me that I have been very far mistaken. I recollect of being very much struck by your truly pathetical, yet artless account of the death of T. Greig, which was contained in a letter you sent me about a year ago; and I have been still more affected by your very touching allusion, in your last, to the death of our brother. I would indulge the hope that this event may have proved a blessing to us as a family. In all the communications I have received from home, there has, I think, been displayed a spirit of greater tenderness than usual. With your own short letter I have been particularly pleased. You could not have given me a more satisfactory proof that this dispensation has been in some degree blessed to you than the feeling of self condemnation which your letter breathes."

"My Dear Sister — I have the expectation of seeing you so soon, that it may be thought almost unnecessary for me now to write to you: but I cannot think of letting the session pass without sending you a letter. I was gratified to hear from Mr. Muir that you had written a letter for me. I am quite sorry you did not send it, for I am sure that those very things which seemed blemishes to you would have enhanced its value to me. It is an easy and unstudied effusion of sentiment which constitutes the great charm of epistolary correspondence. I wish you would always write to me the simple dictates of your own heart without any external interference whatever, and with the fullest confidence, that, what you write will never meet any eye but my own. I hope to see you now in a few weeks, and to be able to devote a good part of my time in the summer months to your education. I hope you have been going on with your French. I should have written you a much longer letter had it not been that I expect so soon to see you personally."

In these letters the feelings of nature are expressed in a very interesting manner. The letter to his brother contains some very delicate touches, and manifests much tact and discrimination, as well as great ingenuousness and deep concern for the salvation of his soul. May his prayers and expostulations not be in vain!

The two following, though the last is without date, appear to have been written during this session.

"St. Andrew's, March 13, 1825.

"My Dear Friend — This is Sabbath evening, and it is now pretty late, yet I cannot think of letting my father go without writing by him. I have had but little experience in the feelings of the afflicted, but yet I can remember how the receipt of a letter from a friend, or any such little incident, would sometimes mitigate, in a degree, the pains of disease, by chequering the dull and tedious hours of confinement. And, if in this way I can have any hope of ministering to your comfort, it were surely most ungrateful of me to let slip, through negligence, a single opportunity of doing so. My father tells me that you are still very poorly; but you know, from experience, far better than I can tell you, that every affliction works for the good of them that love God. You must have a satisfaction in feeling that every trial through which God has carried you, has been an additional proof of his love to you, and of your interest in a Saviour! A satisfaction which that individual, whose religion (like mine) has been all in the sunshine of prosperity, cannot enjoy. I have not yet proceeded far on the voyage of life, and hitherto all has been smooth and prosperous; but I sometimes look forward with dread foreboding to the many tempests which I may have to encounter on life's rough sea, and to the many waves of trouble and distress which roll between me and that peaceful shore, where 'billows never beat, nor tempests roar.' And at such times I could envy the case of that bark, which, like yours, has long been tossed by many a tempest, but which has weathered them all, and is just about to drop anchor in the peaceful haven. But I feel that this is a sinful feeling, and proceeds from weakness of faith. It is doubting his word, who has said, 'when thou walkest through the fire it shall not burn thee; and through the waters, they shall not overflow thee.' I am sorry that I am obliged here to conclude abruptly, as my time is gone. May the Lord support you in all your trials!"

"MY VERY DEAR FRIEND—I cannot think of leaving you, as we parted last night, without some expression of what I feel at your *often repeated* kindness which has entailed upon me a debt of gratitude which I can never discharge. All that I am, and all that I have, are devoted, I trust, to the service of God; and the only way that I can ever repay the kindness of Christian friends is by redoubling my ardour in the great cause for which we all live, and for which we all die. If this shall be the effect of your generosity, it will produce to you a double reward, and to me a double benefit. You will not only enjoy the thought that you have gained the lasting gratitude and good wishes of a fellow-pilgrim in this world, but when this world, and all the things that are therein, shall be burnt up, you will be rewarded a thousand-fold as having contributed, in some degree, through that unworthy individual, to promote the interests of a cause, the noblest that ever occupied the thoughts of men or of angels; I had almost said, of God himself.

"And if your kindness prove to me, as I trust it will, a stimulus to greater exertion in the cause to which I am devoted, that will be an infinitely greater benefit than all the advantages it may directly confer. Thus may the Lord make your kindness a double blessing both to the giver and to the receiver. And to his name be all the thanks and all the glory."

The two preceding letters would do credit to any pen as specimens of natural and unaffected epistolary correspondence; while the sentiments they contain, and the spirit which they breathe, would not be unworthy of the most mature Christian. The fears respecting the future, which he so beautifully expresses, were never realized. His tender bark was indeed ill fitted to encounter the storms and perils of this world; and therefore infinite goodness brought it speedily to "the land of glory and repose."

Dr. Chalmers' class seems to have occupied the principal share in his attention during this winter; and in moral philosophy and political economy, he appears to have made great proficiency. Besides his notes of the Professor's lectures, and the papers which he wrote on the various subjects which were assigned, or voluntarily undertaken, he composed a synopsis, or analysis of Smith's Wealth of Nations, the favourite class-book of Dr. Chalmers, and which has contributed more to produce correct views of society, and of the science which is now so popular, than any production of the age. My young friend read this work evidently with great care; and though he must have generally admired it, and agreed in its statements and reasonings, he did not blindly adopt them. His essay on the Distinction between Productive and Unproductive Labour, will evince that he could think for himself, and discover even in the able work of that most profound thinker, positions that are not altogether tenable.*

Every one must admire the acuteness and talent displayed in this essay. More than common discernment was necessary to catch the author of the Wealth of Nations tripping; but still greater talent was required to detect the fallacy and expose the mistaken reasonings by which the theory was supported. A discovery, when made, often

* See Appendix E.

appears very simple and easy; but the mind which makes that discovery, and the process which leads to it, belong not to the common order, and may be far removed from vulgar apprehension.

Among his papers, which were written about this time, are several fragments, on subjects of great importance; and while I feel deep regret that they are imperfect, I cannot throw aside even the fragments of such a mind. The first is on Written Language, in which his object appears to have been to prove that it is of divine origin. This is a view of the subject not peculiar indeed to him, but still not usually adopted by philosophers and philologists; though I confess it has long appeared to me the only tenable hypothesis. The employment of hieroglyphics, and the use of them to record facts of a certain kind, are easily accounted for; but the discovery of alphabetic writing is a very different matter. The extraordinary simplicity of alphabetic characters, and their still more extraordinary power, render it improbable that they should be the discovery of chance, or the invention of a barbarous people: while the impossibility of arriving at any great degree of civilization or scientific advancement without them, supposes that the discovery must have preceded. If reason and language are the gifts of God, it is not going too far to say, that both are imperfect and very limited in their operation without the use of a written language. In order to preserve and authenticate a divine revelation, a fixed medium of that revelation seems absolutely necessary; and, perhaps, it would not be difficult to suggest reasons amounting to high probability, that when the law was given to Moses, the first knowledge of alphabetic writing, and the first specimen of it were then communicated. But this is not the place to pursue such an inquiry.*

Among his other pursuits during this busy session, he wrote several discourses on passages of Scripture. Some of them were read to Mr. Lothian, others of them to a small number of his fellow-students; but none of them, I believe, was used in any other way. They are all illustrative of the soundness and clearness of his mind; the accuracy and extent of his knowledge of the Scriptures; the philosophical turn of his thinking; and his prevailing disposition to connect all his pursuits with the missionary enterprise, in which even then, he ardently wished to engage. I am very much deceived if the discourse, which I give as a specimen, will not be considered an extraordinary effort of so young a mind.†

I do not know whether the writer of this admirable discourse ever saw the "Hints on Missions," by Mr. Douglas; but there is a passage in that little work so applicable to the subject of this discourse, and so important in itself, that I shall here take the liberty to introduce it: —

"While belief is connected with truth, we shall never want converts; and while the belief of truth impels to the communication of truth, we shall never want preachers.

"'I believed, and therefore have I spoken.' Here is a measure derived from heaven to judge of the sincerity of belief. The laws of the human mind are not circumscribed within degrees and parallels. He who has no desire to proclaim the gospel abroad, has none to proclaim it at home, and has no belief in it himself; whatever profes-

* See Appendix F. † See Appendix G.

sions he may make, are hollow and hypocritical. Bodies of Christians who make no efforts to christianize others, are Christians but in name; and the ages in which no attempts are made to send the glad tidings to heathen countries, are the dark ages of Christianity, however they may suppose themselves enlightened and guided by philosophy and moderation.

"The ages of Christian purity have ever been the ages of Christian exertion. At the commencement of Christianity, he who believed in the gospel, became also a preacher of the gospel. 'We believe, and therefore we speak.' The effort was correspondent to the belief, and the success to the effort. Christians grew and multiplied, and their very multiplication insured a fresh renewal of their increase. The primitive prolific blessing was upon them, and one became a thousand." *

If the subject of these memoirs borrowed the hint from the above passage, of which I have no evidence, it is very clear that he has duly improved upon it. His discourse exists but in the first rough draft, and appears therefore under every disadvantage. I have not altered one sentence, and scarcely corrected even a word; yet with all these drawbacks, it affords evidence that it is the production of a master-mind. The argument is exceedingly ingenious, and is sustained with a degree of ability and felicity of illustration, which reflects the highest credit on the powers of the author. The simplicity of his own views of religion, and the deep earnestness with which he pleads for the full practical influence of Christianity are truly delightful. How happy would it be for the individuals themselves, for the church, and the world, did all who enter on the office of the ministry feel the force of the high and hallowed views which are here stated.

The references to natural religion, as it is called, contained in this discourse, induced me to introduce an essay on that subject, which he wrote as a class exercise at the close of this session. The subject is one on which a great deal of ignorance has been discovered, and a vast portion of error propagated. The religion of nature will, I fear, go a very little way to inform the understanding, still less to regulate the affections, and no way at all to satisfy God, or pacify the conscience of a sinner. Whether unassisted reason is capable of accomplishing all that my young friend, with many others, contends for, is not perfectly clear; but no one can doubt the admirable and beautiful manner in which he conducts his own argument, and the justice which he does to the claims of the revelation of God.*

From his correspondence I select the following letter to a young friend, who was then about to sustain a severe loss in his mother, a most amiable and eminently devoted Christian. It is marked with much tenderness and faithfulness.

"St. Andrew's, March 12, 1825.

"On looking over your last letter, the most important, indeed the only intelligence it conveys, is an answer (which I regret is such a painful one) to my inquiries about your mother's health. From what my father tells me, I fear the worst, and I cannot help dreading you may have lost her ere now. At all events, from the nature and virulence of her disease, your hopes cannot be very

* See Appendix H.

sanguine. I am writing to one who has either just lost, or who is every day expecting to lose, the dearest of all earthly relatives; and in either case, I should feel I was doing violence to all the finer feelings of our common nature, did I indulge in a strain of writing that was light or frivolous. There is something in the near view of death, either prospectively or retrospectively, which solemnizes the gayest heart, and disposes the most thoughtless to serious reflection. There is something in that tender sorrow which attends the death of one that is dear to us, which, for a time, subdues the pride of the haughtiest, and turns the eye of the most worldly, for a time, to heaven. If ever that spiritual blindness is removed, which hides from our view all that is beyond the grave, it is, when by the death of a near friend, we are led, as it were, to the very outskirts of this world, and can thus take a nearer view of that world which lies beyond it. You will excuse me, then, if, in such circumstances, I call to your remembrance, and press upon your attention, those sacred precepts which your mother has often taught you, and of which she herself has been a living exemplification. I know the dislike of the young mind to religion; I have felt it, but it is a dislike which should be fought against. I know the alluring prospects of happiness which this world holds out; but short, as has been my experience, I have found that they are deceitful. I know the difficulty that there is in standing out against the laugh and sneer of young and gay and light-hearted companions; but, I can assure you, that you will be enabled to bear it, and even to rejoice under it. All that I wish you to do is, to *consider* the things of spirituality: if you but do this, your belief will follow; and your joy, in believing, as a natural consequence. Perhaps your mother is yet lingering in this world; if so, it is my prayer, that she may yet be restored to you. But perhaps, even now, you are mourning her loss; if so, it is my prayer, that your affliction may send you to seek for consolation in the exercises of devotion. If this be the result of your trial, it will prove to you a real blessing, and you will find you have exchanged an earthly parent for an heavenly one."

It was towards the close of the session, he wrote for the prize at the Moral Philosophy class, proposed by Dr. Chalmers. It appears, that, till near the end of the term, he had no intention of becoming a competitor, and that it was not till within four or five days of the period fixed for the giving in of the essays, that he set himself in good earnest to the task. To this, and several other subjects of importance he refers, in the following letter to his father:—

"St. Andrew's, April 18, 1825.

"My Dear Father—I am happy to be able to inform you, that I did *not* speak at the meeting at Cupar, nor ever had the slightest intention of doing so. I have been intreated by some of our friends, and have been reproved for want of zeal by others, because I did not come forward and preach in the country, but I have withstood both intreaties and reproofs. Mr. Reid has been pressed into the service, and even Mr. ——, at the risk of being called to an account by the Presbytery, preached one Sabbath at Denino. I acknowledge that I have much higher ideas of preaching than are generally entertained among our brethren; and I do sincerely think, that it has been one of the greatest evils (perhaps, for a time, a necessary one,) in our system, to bring forward people to preach who were not rightly qualified for this most important of all engagements. I think, from what you say in yours, you do not seem to have a right idea of the prize essay which I said I was writing. Most perfectly do I agree with you, that I stand no chance of gaining it; but, at the same time, I should have thought it a breach of duty, and was afraid it might offend Dr. Chalmers, did I not give it in. They were entirely motives of this nature, which induced me, after I had burned an essay I had written, in order to compete for the prize, to write another when the time was almost run out. I am sure you will not think me capable of so much presumption, as to expect that a production, which cost me only five days' labour, at spare hours, should come into competition with those which have cost my competitors the continued application of four months.

"I feel sincerely grateful for your letter. It is exactly what I need at present. I feel the praise which is of men, to be one of the severest trials I can meet with, and to be more especially the besetting temptation of an academic career."

The modesty which formed a marked feature of his character, is strongly indicated in this letter. Though he had been frequently urged to preach, and to speak at some public meetings, he had decidedly refused to do so. He considered himself much too young to appear in public; and in his ideas of preaching, I most fully concur. Those who did not know him, might suppose there was something of affectation in his intimations of having no expectation of the prize. But his friends at College, as well as myself, are persuaded that this was really the state of his mind, notwithstanding the effort which he made.

"He was distinguished," says Mr. Duff, "for a remarkable diffidence in his own abilities, uncommon though they were. An instance of this occurred during his second session. The subject of a prize essay was proposed by the Professor of Logic. Mr. Urquhart began to write the essay, and brought it nearly to a close; when, upon reading it, he was so dissatisfied with its merits, that he threw it into the fire. He was, however, encouraged to renew the attempt, and prosecuted the subject with vigour. He submitted the performance to a fellow-student, whose tried abilities rendered him capable of estimating the talent with which it was executed. He was much struck with the superior excellence of the essay, and strongly advised Mr. Urquhart to give it to the Professor. Notwithstanding this encouragement, having once more read the essay himself, he was so much displeased with its execution, that he burnt it without any hesitation."

The highest prize was assigned him for the essay composed under the circumstances adverted to in the letter to his father. The opinion of Dr. Chalmers is evident, from his having awarded it, and from the sentence which he has written upon the last page of the essay itself. In this opinion, not only did the class in general concur, but even those individuals from whom he had carried off the boon.*

Besides gaining the first prize at the Moral Philosophy class, on the subject prescribed by the Professor; he gained also the first prize for the best essay read in the class. He had also distinguished himself in the private Greek class; and, indeed, in all the departments to which he directed his attention. "In estimating his success," says a fellow-student, "it must be remembered, that there

* See Appendix I.

never was at St. Andrew's a more brilliant assemblage of talent and of genius, attracted from all parts of the kingdom, by the fame of Dr. Chalmers, than there was during the session of 1824–25." In this opinion, it will be seen from Dr. Chalmers's letter, how fully he concurs.

Perhaps I cannot do better than introduce, at the conclusion of the course of Moral Philosophy, the account of him, with which I have been favoured by another of his fellow-students, and a competitor along with him for the prize. It contains some traits of character worthy of being preserved, and besides showing the estimate which was formed of him by others, is highly creditable to the talents, and still more the generous feelings of a fellow-candidate. It is not necessary that I should subscribe to every sentiment which it expresses; but the description is, on the whole, correct and faithful: —

"The seeds of talent, wherever they were sown, could not fail to spring up under the fostering eloquence of Dr. Chalmers. His enthusiasm, intense, and almost approaching to juvenile extravagance, communicated its ardour to every mind that could appreciate his bold and original speculations in moral and political philosophy, or could be animated by the eloquence with which they were illustrated and enforced. Mr. Urquhart caught, in common with his fellow-students, the contagion of the example, which emanated from the chair. The activity of his mind was awakened, and the veneration which he entertained for the character, and admiration of the genius of his professor, were the strongest motives to exert his own. I remember well the impression which his first essay made upon his class-fellows, and the flattering, though merited approbation it received from his professor. He began in a low, timid, faltering voice, shrinking from the silent and fixed attention of a public display, till by degrees his voice assumed a firmer tone, and when he closed it was not without animation and feeling. As his unpretending manners, and his previous public examinations, had given but little promise of his talents, the triumph was the more complete, as it was unexpected. Not to feel vain or proud of the distinction which literary eminence confers, is a modesty of nature but rarely found, even among those who have been longest accustomed to the homage of the public. To a young man, though the sphere in which his merits are displayed is narrower, yet the novelty of the feeling, combined with the gentler sensibility of his mind, renders the impression irresistible. It is, perhaps, the proudest moment of his life, when he is first commended for his literary acquirements, his taste, or his promise of future talent. That Mr. Urquhart was insensible to this praise, would be saying too much. Such an indifference would have proved rather a want of feeling, than an absence of vanity. But whatever secret pleasure he may have felt, it was betrayed by no assumed airs of consequence or pride. Those who were attracted by his talents were not repelled by his vanity. He levied no contribution of admiration from his friends, as a tax to his merit; and as no one could be less disposed to gratify others at the expense of truth, so none was ever less solicitous of flattery. In his intercourse with his fellow-students, there was a total absence of all ostentation or pretension. No one was forced in his presence upon the disagreeable conviction of his own inferiority, so that without any of the arts of pleasing, or those popular qualities that attract general favour, he had made many friends, but no enemies. Few fancied they saw in him a rival to their own ambitious hopes; and when he crossed the path, and gained the hill in advance, it was with so noiseless a step, and with so little show of a triumph, that he either escaped the vigilance of his competitors, or they pardoned his success for the manner in which it was obtained. What they might imagine themselves entitled to, for their superior talents, they willingly resigned to his virtue. Indeed, a little observation of the world shows, and the remark is applicable to every period of life, that men are more easy under a defeat than a triumph, and that the prosperous might enjoy their success without envy, if they had the prudence to conceal it. Not that by this reflection we mean to resolve Mr. Urquhart's modesty into a refinement of selfishness. His conduct was equally remote from that haughtiness, which is one of the forms of pride; and from that affectation of humility, which is often the same passion under a new disguise. Nature in him had not learned to conceal her feelings, and still less to assume those which did not belong to her. Reserved without pride, and grave beyond his years, without any mixture of severity, he avoided the promiscuous society of his class-mates, not from any feeling of superiority, but partly from the timidity of his disposition, and from a want of sympathy in their ordinary sports and conversation.

"'Concourse and noise, and toil, he ever fled.'

"This disposition was as beautifully illustrated as the action was characteristic of his modesty, in his conduct on that day in which the prizes were distributed, at the close of the session, and of which he was to bear away some of the most distinguished and honourable. While the more ambitious and showy youths, had selected a distant station in the hall, that they might advance to the spot where the prizes were distributed, through a line of admiring spectators, Mr. Urquhart had shrunk unobserved into the corner of a window, near to the seat of the Professors, and no sooner was his name announced, than he had again drawn back and disappeared. There was scarce time to put the usual inquiry of who he was, when a new candidate for attention was summoned. The same simple, unostentatious manner, and aversion to display, which appear in this action, was the result of his general habits and feelings, and not of singular or accidental occurrence. It was in consistence with the other parts of his conduct. No one knew when Mr. Urquhart entered or retired from his class. He had no circle of literary dependants who crowded around him, to receive his philosophical dicta, or his canons of criticism. Yet, to those who observed him, there was something in his appearance in the class, singular and interesting. He had an awkward habit of biting his nails, a practice in him not disagreeable, it was so much of a piece with the simplicity of his look. His head generally inclined to one side, and as he sat it was supported by his arm. This was his usual position while listening to the lecture. As Dr. Chalmers's animation increased, Mr. Urquhart gradually elevated his head, and when he rose into eloquence, you would have seen his arm drop by his side, and his eye steadfastly fixed, looking the orator broad in the face. I know not whether Dr. Chalmers marked these changes in the attitude of his pupil; but if he had, they would have afforded no inaccurate test of the degree to which his eloquence had risen. These incidents are of little value in themselves, but they will convey more truth and effect than any description of the disposition and manners of Mr. Urquhart.

"Of his intellectual character, the most distinguished feature, I would say, was a sound understanding; more clear and judicious, however, than either subtle or comprehensive. Endowed with a mind thoughtful and considerate, he adopted none of the rash speculations and dazzling paradoxes which so often delude the inquirer of his age. Temperate and cautious in the exercise of his own judgment, he was the less disposed to receive the unripe and hasty inventions of others. In a conversational society of his fellow-students, for the discussion of the opinions on moral and political philosophy, that were delivered from the chair, Mr. Urquhart took an intelligent and sometimes active part. The subjects were intricate, and did not admit of an easy flow of conversation. But, such as they were, Mr. Urquhart, when he hazarded his sentiments, generally spoke with clearness and precision. Profound remarks, exhibiting mature knowledge and previous speculative habits, were neither required on such an occasion, nor expected. Plain and natural in his turns of thought, and not venturing beyond what he understood, he escaped those unintelligible extravagances into which more fearless thinkers on intricate subjects not unfrequently fall. If he was unsuccessful in communicating new instruction by his remarks, he pleased from the simplicity with which he expressed ideas that were familiar; and every one eagerly invited and listened with pleasure to Mr. Urquhart as he spoke. There was an air of candour and truth in whatever he said, and the modesty with which he urged his opinions, was only surpassed by the readiness and good nature with which he retracted them when convinced of his error. His name will not soon be forgotten by the members of that society of which, if he was not the brightest ornament by his talent, none was more beloved.

"In his class essays, which, I believe, were among his first attempts at regular composition, there was a correctness of taste, felicity of illustration, and perspicuity in the arrangement of his thoughts, such as is rarely to be found in the early efforts of the juvenile pen. There is often an irregular exuberance in the productions of youthful talent, which it requires years of study to prune into form. The crop of Mr. Urquhart's imagination, if less luxuriant than many, was more free from tares, and more beautiful in its growth. He never blundered into a conceit or extravagance in search of ornament. His mind rested rather upon the broad analogies of things, and converted them into illustrations of his subjects, than upon those nice and secret resemblances which wit discloses in unexpected allusions and metaphors. It was imagination rather than fancy, which he possessed. Though he enjoyed the humour and lighter attempts at wit, of his companions, yet these were fields into which he seldom strayed. His excellencies consisted not in brilliant ornaments of style, or in the higher flights of imagination ; but in illustrations happily conceived, and closely incorporated with his subject. The same simplicity, which was the charm of his manners, and the prevailing feature in his character, was the grace of his compositions. So chaste, and yet so young, was a union of circumstances so rare, that it opened prospects the most sanguine, of future excellence, when his mind should be enriched by knowledge, and disciplined by cultivation."

CHAPTER IV.

Introductory observations — John's return home at the end of his third session — Letter respecting his going to some of the Dissenting Academies — Letter illustrative of his state of mind — Letters — His employments during the vacation — Letter to Mr. Craik — His visit to London — Mr. Adam's account of him at this time — Letters to his father — Engagements during the winter — Letters to a friend — Letter to his brother — Letter to his mother — Letter to a friend — Letter to Mr. Orme — Opposition of his friends to his Missionary devotedness — Mr. Duff's account of him — Testimonies to his literary attainments — Mr. Alexander's account of him — Dr. Chalmers' certificate.

THERE are few things which put the character and principles of a young man more to the test than a classical and University education. He who passes through this ordeal unhurt, has reason to bless the gracious and powerful influences of the divine Spirit. I do not refer at present to the levity of youth, and to the snares of those associations which belong to the state of society in Colleges and classical schools. The danger of infection from the moral atmosphere is, indeed, great. But there are dangers of a different kind, arising out of the studies which chiefly engross the attention, and their powerful, but unperceived influence upon the mind.

The investigations of philology and grammar, though important in themselves, and absolutely necessary as the basis of all correct knowledge, are dry, and often tiresome. The memory is loaded with words and forms of expression, which tend no doubt, to exercise and strengthen it; but do not tend much to the moral benefit of the mind. When from these the scholar passes on to the more elegant studies of the Greek and Roman classics, or even to the polite literature of our own country, how little does he find at all calculated to promote his spiritual welfare! This is not saying enough: how much does he meet with, the tendency of which is positively injurious! The fascinations thrown around vice, the halo of glory with which sin itself is frequently invested, cannot be viewed often, and with great intensity, without damage. The individual who gives his days and nights to the poets and orators of Greece and Rome, must be more than man if he escapes without hurt to his spiritual feelings and principles.

The influence of the exact sciences, and of experimental philosophy, though of a different nature, is still hazardous to a mind which has not arrived at maturity. The absolute certainty of mathematical demonstration, and the sure results of algebraic formula, produce a habit which has proved in many instances very unfavourable to the due appreciation of moral evidence. And the processes of chemistry, and the experiments of physical science, have not been always productive of an increased veneration for the great Spirit who presides over, and pervades all the operations of the universe.

I wish to speak of results, rather than to assign reasons for those results. Whether the evils and dangers referred to are to be ascribed to the weakness and depravity of our nature, or to the imperfections of the systems of education, which are generally adopted, or to both together, does not alter the state of the fact, that our youth cannot receive what is considered a finished education, without sustaining a very formidable trial. How few comparatively can pass through a College, or even an academy, to the work of the ministry, without experiencing a diminution or loss of their spiritual vigour!

To frame a system of education, which would avoid the greater number, or most of the evils, would be a service of incalculable value to the world. But I doubt whether human wisdom, under existing circumstances, is competent to the task. It is no difficult matter to furnish expurgated editions of the classics, and to produce family Gibbons, and family Shakspeares; and those attempts at purifying the foul stream of classical instruction are not to be despised. But while so large a portion of time and thought must be expended in these pursuits, and while a capacity for relishing the beauties, whether of the ancient or the modern classics, is rated so high, I fear that the chief source of the evil will still remain.

The principle on which most systems of education are constructed, is the relation which certain attainments bear to certain temporal advantages. The problem on which they are all founded is, How may an individual, at the least expense, be best fitted to conduct a family, to teach a congregation, to manage a counting-house, or to guide the state? I do not say these are not important questions; they are important, and they are the only questions which the world can ever ask and determine. But surely there are other questions which Christians might be expected to consider. Do not the relations which the pursuits and attainments of time bear to eternity, demand their consideration? Ought what can have little tendency to promote men's interests beyond this world, what in many instances injures those interests, to be the first subject of consideration? Is it quite impossible to frame a system of education, in which all the lines may be brought to unite, in forming the intellectual and moral powers of man, for a state of immortal enjoyment? A system in which every branch shall be deemed important, chiefly as it bears on his eternal condition! A system in which what is showy and superficial, shall be rejected, or thrown into the shade; and what is substantial and useful placed in the fore-ground? A system in which taste shall be less an object than character, and intellect be made subservient to morals? A system in short, which shall have the principles of Christianity for its basis, the advancement of Christianity for its object, and the rewards of Christianity for its end?

I do not conceive such a system to belong only to a region in Utopia. It is perfectly conceivable; but before it can be realized, we must be furnished not only with new principles, but with new men to inculcate them, and with a different state of society to secure their operation. Many as are the evils which we still deplore, much progress has been made during the last thirty years; and before a similar period shall have passed away, it is not too much to expect that the strides of society towards a better state will be still more gigantic.

As the present work may fall into the hands of some who are engaged in conducting seminaries, I hope I shall be forgiven this seeming digression. Considering how many of our youth are seriously injured in the training, how many bitter regrets are afterwards experienced, even by those who do not suffer permanent injury; and how few escape altogether without damage, I can scarcely be required to offer an apology for these remarks. Indeed, though the subject of these memoirs retained his integrity, and passed through his studies without blemish, I know from himself, and from his fellow-students, that "he retained," (I use his own language) "a deep horror of St. Andrew's." He meant, I am sure, no reflection on the place, none on the Professors, and none on his fellow-students. But he considered it marvellous that he got through his academical course without ruin to his soul. In this preservation he was led to admire the exceeding riches of divine grace; but it must appear very extraordinary, that a Christian University should expose its disciples to such hazards. The fact is, the profession is Christian, but the entire process of education is pagan, or anti-Christian. Religion, instead of being the first, the last, and the main object, is subordinate to every other object. The minds both of professors and students, are absorbed in science and literature, as the chief objects of pursuit; and religion, when attended to, is examined rather as one of the sciences, than as the doctrine of God and the path of immortality. While this system is pursued, it is not wonderful that the atmosphere of Colleges should generally be unfavourable to the vitality of Christianity.

Our last chapter brought the subject of these memoirs to the conclusion of the third year of his University course, and the seventeenth of his age. To him it had been a year of great interest, and great exertion. In it he had acquired a large portion of celebrity among his associates, and what was more, he had laid the foundation of some of his most interesting plans of usefulness. We shall now endeavour to trace his spiritual and intellectual progress to the close of his short but useful life.

Returning home at the end of the session, after visiting Edinburgh, laden, not with wealth, but "with honours bravely won," he still appeared the same modest, unpretending youth. His mind was fully occupied with the importance of the Christian ministry, and especially with the necessities and claims of the heathen world. I had the opportunity of seeing a good deal of him during the month of June, which I spent at Perth, and had then many conversations with him about his future plans. I saw the direction of his mind, and was satisfied what would be the issue; but, from his extreme youth, being then only seventeen, I urged upon him the necessity of taking more time to consider the subject, especially as his father and mother were both exceedingly averse to his going abroad. I advised him, as there were then some difficulties in the way of his returning to St. Andrew's, rather to apply to be received into some one of the Dissenting academies at home; knowing, that, if his mind still continued to be set upon the heathen world, the opportunity of gratifying his wishes would not be lost. With this advice he complied, and accordingly addressed a letter to the Committee of the Hoxton Academy, requesting to be received into that institution. His reasons for adopting this line of procedure are well stated in the following letter to his friend Mr. C——:

"PERTH, June, 1825.

"A few days ago I sat down to write you, and wrote about eight pages, which, I thought, with the addition of a few sentences, at present, would make out a pretty respectable epistle. A few days, however, often make a great change in our feelings and our prospects; and I perceive, on looking over the pages I have written, that they are quite unfit for sending at present. The last time I sat down, I wrote, with the full expectation of soon enjoying again the company of my dear friends at St. Andrew's; and I write now under the impression that my lot may soon be cast in a distant part of the island. Mr. Adam perhaps, told you that Mr. Orme is here at preseut on a visit to us. He is a man with whom I have been on the most intimate terms from my very infancy, and one who has ever taken a deep interest, both in my spiritual and temporal welfare. Since ever I have felt anything of the power of religion, I have been accustomed to look to him as my father in Christ, and have ever felt the most perfect confidence in making known to him all my designs and feelings. Last winter I wrote to him expressing my views respecting missions, and my thoughts of devoting myself to this department of the Christian ministry. Since Mr. Orme's arrival in Scotland I have had much conversation with him on this subject, and have received a good deal of information respecting matters in the metropolis. There are some opportunities of instruction in oriental languages to be enjoyed at present in London, which, if neglected now, may be lost for ever. Dr. Morrison remains for *a year only*, to give directions about the study of Chinese; and Mr. Townley remains, it is not certain how long, to teach some of the more important of the Indian languages. Another session, at one of the Scotch Universities, although it might be attended with several very considerable advantages, does not seem to counterbalance the opportunities I have hinted at. I can, in a letter, state the reasons which actuate me in this matter only in a very general way. It is not likely, should I go to London this summer, that I shall engage with the Missionary Society immediately, but rather that I shall enter one of our Dissenting academies, where I shall be able to carry on my general studies at the same time that I have an opportunity of prosecuting the study of the eastern languages. On the whole, I feel in considerable perplexity how to act. I need not tell you that all my feelings are in favour of St. Andrew's, but, I honestly think, duty seems to point in another direction. Mr. Adam seems to agree in thinking it my duty to go to London. I have made this matter, for a considerable time, a subject of constant prayer; and I propose setting apart a day for the solemn consideration of the whole matter, and for the purpose of asking direction from on high. May I entreat an interest in your prayers? These are the circumstances in which we feel most the privilege of a free access to the Father of our spirits; and these are the times when our belief in the revealed declarations of his character, and of his will, come to be tried; and when, if that belief be found real, the revelation of God's character can give the greatest consolation and joy."

With his application the Committee were much pleased, and would have readily acceded to it; but he was rather too young to be received into the house, which was besides, for that period, already full. He was therefore requested to wait for a year, at the expiration of which they would be glad to hear from him again. In consequence of this failure he requested to be admitted into the Glasgow Academy, under the tuition of my respected friends, the Rev. Greville Ewing, and the Rev. Dr. Wardlaw. After some hesitation on the part of the Committee of that Institution, on the ground of his having devoted himself to foreign service, they agreed to receive him. But circumstances changed a little, and it appeared desirable that he should return to St. Andrew's to complete his academical course.

How his mind was exercised in regard to these things will, in part, appear from some of his letters: —

"Perth, July 8, 1825.

"My very Dear Friend — An opportunity is afforded me, by Mr. Machray, of answering your interesting letter, which I am glad to embrace. After you left us, I had a good deal of conversation with my friends, on the subject of my destination; and, having set apart a day for the solemn consideration of the matter, and imploring divine direction, I came to the resolution of making application to Hoxton Academy. The issue of that application determines me to remain another year in Scotland. I received an answer from Mr. Wilson, this week, informing me that the vacancies were all filled for the ensuing session; but that, if I could profitably employ my time for a year, they would have room next year, and better accommodation, as they expect to enter on their new College. In connection with this matter, I have been led to consider more attentively those passages of Scripture, which refer to missionary exertions, and the result has been a deeper impression than ever, of the duty of engaging in this work. It is very true, that much has to be done at home; that there are many here, as my friend Craik writes, who 'can only be considered in the light of more criminal heathens.' But this is a wilful ignorance: they are not 'perishing for lack of knowledge.' And this argument, if carried to its full extent, would stifle missionary exertions to the very end of the world. What would have been the consequence, had the apostles resolved not to leave Jerusalem, till every one of their brethren, according to the flesh, was truly converted? The Gentiles would not have received the glad tidings of salvation to the present hour. This was not the commandment the apostles received, however; and, accordingly, they acted in a very different manner. They were to preach the gospel to all nations, *beginning* at Jerusalem. The nation of the Jews had a claim upon the first preachers of Christianity, which our countrymen have not upon us. They were not only their 'brethren according to the flesh,' but they were also God's chosen nation; and, as such, it was right that they should enjoy a preeminence over all others, in first receiving the proclamation of pardon. But, how did their brethren, the apostles, act even to this favoured nation? They made a full declaration of salvation, through Christ; they made a free tender of the mercy of Jehovah; but, by almost all, this mercy was slighted and rejected. By thus sinning against greater light, these individuals became *more criminal* even than the heathen. Did the apostles, therefore, think that they should not go forth to the heathen, till all these rejecters of the truth were convinced of the error of their ways? No; that very rejection of the gospel, by their countrymen, was a signal for their departure. 'Seeing ye *reject*, &c., behold we turn to the Gentiles.' Had the gospel been proclaimed, in like manner, to *all* other nations, the apostles would have felt it their duty to have laboured assiduously among their brethren at home. But while there remained a single nation on the face of the earth, that had not received the knowledge of salvation, they felt that the parting commandment of their Master was not yet fully obeyed; and, while they lived, they made it their business, more and more fully to execute that command. But their missionary spirit died with them; and, at the present hour, that commandment remains still unobeyed. Is it difficult, in this case, to see the path of duty? Besides, I cannot see, that by preaching at home, we are hastening the coming glory of the church. God has promised, that all shall *know* him. He has not promised that all shall *serve* him. On the contrary, he has said, that he will *gather* his people out of every nation, kindred, tongue, and people; which, evidently implies, that *all* shall *not* be his people. Far be it from me to depreciate the work of the ministry at home. It is a most important work. But still, while there are any sitting in darkness and the shadow of death, it must yield in importance to the missionary field. Besides, who can tell what an effect our neglect of God's commandment, to preach to *all* nations, may have, in causing him to withhold his Spirit from the exertions of Christians at home? I must abruptly conclude. I was struck with the variety of incidents in your last. Let us contemplate much, my dear friend, the grand operations of God to our world; and, let us thus learn to feel our own insignificance, and to merge every selfish consideration in the great work to which we are called."

The progress of his religious sentiments and feelings, the following letters will show.

The first is the letter alluded to, in that to his friend C——, already inserted. It is too valuable to be omitted.

"My very Dear Friend—The receipt of your interesting communication, and of a note from my friend, Mr.

Tait, accompanying a treatise on Confessions of Faith, have been among the most remarkable events in my history, since I wrote last; they have, at least, been almost the only varieties that have broken the regularity and sameness of a ceaseless routine of occupations, repeated with little change or interruptions, day after day. Not that I am displeased, or wearied of my retirement, for I esteem it as a very great privilege. But I preface my letter thus, merely to remind you, that though you, who are a public character, and are surrounded by all the bustle and variety of numerous avocations, have such a body of interesting matter to communicate, that you pant for utterance in the expression of it; and one subject leading to another, the stream of information so enlarges as you go along that the very sheets of paper seem to have foreseen its rising magnitude, and, aware of what was coming, to have extended their dimensions, in proportion as the fund of your information increased—I say, though this be the case with you, you must remember that it is very different with a solitary recluse, who has no companions but his books, (with most of whom you are better acquainted than himself,) and scarcely any engagements but his private studies. But a truce to this trifling. I must proceed to answer your very interesting letter. We may, sometimes, draw illustrations of spiritual things from the most ordinary occurrences in life; and they are not, on that account, the less striking. Your feelings expressed in the beginning of your letter, with respect to your correspondence, struck me as a good illustration of the nature and operation of *faith*. You knew something of the character of a fellow-creature, as much, you thought, as to entitle you to rely upon his veracity. You knew, however, that he was fallible, and subject to change; and yet, on this previous knowledge of his character, you confidently expected the fulfilment of a promise he had made to you. The time of its fulfilment came, however, and it seemed to you to have been broken. You were 'perplexed to account for his silence.' You tried to account for it by some expressions of regret he had used, that he had made the engagement; but you did not think this a sufficient explanation of his failing to perform it. Now, what was it that made you think, even in the face of existing circumstances, that your friend might have performed his promise? It was your faith in his veracity, founded on the previous manifestations of his character which you had observed. Now, let us compare this, or rather, let us contrast it with our faith in the promises of God. Instead of an imperfect guessing at his character, from displays of it, which might generally correspond with what we think its leading characteristics, but which sometimes speak in direct opposition to them; all the manifestations of the divine character we have ever beheld, have been in perfect harmony with each other, all going to establish the grand truths, that the 'Lord is good;' that 'the Judge of all the earth will do rightly:' and, above all, to demonstrate almost from the very nature of the divine existence, that 'with him there is no variableness or shadow of turning;' that he is a God who *cannot* lie. Now is it not very strange, that with these, so sure grounds for implicit confidence, our faith in the divine goodness and faithfulness is so weak, as to permit our being perplexed by any of the dispensations of his providence, however dark and discouraging? You will remark, that this very perplexity is an indication of *a certain degree* of faith; it is a struggling between our confidence in the individual, and the circumstances around us which seem to impeach his character. If this circumstantial proof be very strong, then the perplexity indicates a *very strong degree* of confidence, to enable us to resist the conviction of this strong circumstantial proof. But though, in these circumstances, perplexity does indicate a *very strong* degree of faith; yet it, at the same time, indicates an imperfection of faith. It may require very strong faith to stand in the combat against a very strong enemy: but perfect confidence would do more, it would overthrow the enemy, it would gain the victory. But perplexity implies, that this is not the case. It implies suspense. It implies that we have not come to a decision. It implies that the combat is yet doubtful; that the victory has not yet been gained. Now is it not strange that our faith in a creature, weak as are the grounds of it, should carry us so far? And that strong as are the foundations of our confidence in God, it does not carry us further? — that the one should carry us so far as to land us in perplexity; that the other should not carry us so far as to extricate us from perplexity? Oh! my friend, were we but deeply impressed with a sense of God's all-sufficiency, how much of our unhappiness would be taken away! There would be no murmuring at the dispensations of Providence; there would be no regret on reflecting on the past, but the regret that we had ever departed from God; there would be no fear, on looking forward to the future, but the fear lest we might again break his commandments. Sin itself, from which we can never be wholly freed in this world, would still remain to trouble us; but all those sources of misery which indirectly spring from it would be removed. And by a continual dependence on God, and confidence in him, the power even of sin itself would be continually weakening within us. The firm belief, that God was working in us both to will and to do of his good pleasure, would encourage us to work out with fear and trembling, that part of our salvation which yet remains, even our deliverance from the power of sin. Connected with this subject, that is a striking passage, 'Walk thou before *me*, and be thou *perfect*.'

"But I am awakened from this long reverie, by perceiving that it is near our dinner hour. I sat down in despondency, thinking I should find nothing to say; and resolved by way of making matter, to write a commentary on your epistle. I believe I shall make out pretty well in respect of quantity, if I paraphrase the whole of it at as great length as I have done these first few first sentences.

"PERTH, ——.

"MY DEAR F——: I take the liberty of writing these few lines, in answer to yours. We were glad to hear of your safe arrival, but were sorry to see the same depression spread over your letter, which we had formerly lamented to behold in yourself. You do not say anything particular about the state of your health; we trust, however, that the change of place, and the bustle and excitement of travelling may have (partly at least) removed your nervousness. Circumstances, indeed, seem to be very depressing. But we, my dear ——, have consolations that should bear us up, and even make us glad under the severest calamities. That climax of misfortune, so beautifully described by the prophet, in the verses, 'Though the fig-tree shall not blossom,' &c., has not yet by any means come upon us; and shall our hearts refuse to join in his triumphant expression of gladness, 'Yet will I rejoice in the Lord, and joy in the God of my salvation?' We have a still surer word of prophecy than that which he was instrumental in delivering. We have a surer light to guide our footsteps, and brighter promises to cheer us on our journey. And shall we repine, when all is comparatively smooth and even before us? When we see our way before us and can perceive no difficulty to oppose our progress, we do not need to call into exercise our trust in the promises of God; we do not walk by faith, but by sight. But it is where our way is dark, and there seems to be a lion in the path, that we feel our weakness. It is then that our faith in his promises is put to the test, who hath said, 'Lo, I am with you always.' Is it not strange, that we can believe such promises of support and succour as are written on every page of the Bible, and ever feel discouraged or perplexed? Such a belief, were it perfect, would transform even this world, with all its trials and afflictions, into heaven. Such a faith, however, is unattainable, while we are wedded to a body of corruption, and exposed to the malicious suggestions of the adversary. But though this faith cannot be altogether attained, yet it may be approached to, of which we have some most triumphant proofs in the history of the people of God. But I must stop short."

"PERTH, July, ——.

"MY DEAR C——: It now seems, I think, determined, that I may yet entertain the hope of spending another winter with my dear friends in St. Andrew's; and, as matters have turned out, I feel almost sorry that I did not confine within my own breast, those painful feelings, which the prospect of parting naturally excites. Had the matter been determined otherwise, however, it might have seemed unfriendly and self-willed to have asked no aid in the decision of it from the counsels and prayers of my Christian friends. As it is, the decision is not mine, but has chiefly been determined by circumstances over which I had no control; but which have, I trust, been graciously ordered by him who is the God of providence, and who has promised that *all* things shall work together for our good, if we put our trust in him. In considering what might be the path of duty in this matter, I was a good deal perplexed. Had I not thought at all of engaging in the work of missions, I should not have doubted, that I ought to finish my course at St. Andrew's before entering a Theological Academy. And, on the other hand, had I come to the determination of devoting myself to that work, (especially with the views I have of China as a field of labour,) I should not have hesitated to present my services to the Missionary Society, at present, and thus avail myself of the advantages of personal intercourse with Dr. Morrison. Neither of these was the case, however. It is now about a year since, I thought seriously of personally labouring in the foreign department of the Christian ministry; and although, at a more advanced period of life, twelve months' consideration and prayer might seem sufficient for determining a question even of this importance; yet you will perceive, that my extreme youth altogether alters the case. If my wish to preach the gospel of Christ among the heathen, have in it aught of the romance of a boyish imagination, a few years' thought and experience will extinguish its ardor; but if the Lord has appointed me to declare his name to the Gentiles, and that wish has been implanted in my breast by the Spirit of God, delays and disappointments will but foster its growth and make it yet more vigorous. For these reasons, I could not feel it my duty to make a direct application to the Missionary Society, to study in London under their superintendence. But, on the other hand, the facilities of acquiring oriental languages, which the metropolis presents at present, and which are very uncertain in their continuance, make me anxious to be in London, if possible. After considering the matter in all these points of view, consulting my friends here, and asking counsel and direction from the Most High, it seemed to me my duty to make application to Hoxton Academy, which is intended chiefly for the home department, but which sometimes also receives missionary students. This step, you see, had it been taken, would have given me all the advantages I could wish from an immediate residence in the capital, and yet have left my future destination still a matter of consideration and prayer. The letter I received from the Secretary of the Hoxton Committee, in answer to my application, satisfies me as to the duty of remaining another year in Scotland. Had I not made this application, I might have looked back with regret on the opportunities I had neglected; but as it is, my conscience is satisfied in having done what I thought was my duty; and those feelings are also gratified, which I had to struggle with, in the performance of that duty. Excuse me, my dear friend, for having dwelt so long on this subject. I am sorry that I have spent so much time, that I have little remaining to answer your very interesting and affecting letter."

"PERTH, September, 1825.

"MY DEAR FRIEND — I do not know whether debts of kindness, like other debts, admit of being regularly summed up in a debtor and credit column, and balanced against each other. If so, though you confessed the balance due to me in your last, I fear your punctuality and my negligence have more than reversed the matter, and I am now much deeper in your debt than ever you have been in mine. I will not attempt to offer apologies. I might, I believe, conscientiously spin out some that would appear feasible, but I am always suspicious of the sincerity of a man's sorrow who expresses great contrition for a fault he has committed, which, at the same time, he labours with all his might to extenuate by every trifling excuse that can, or scarcely can be alleged for it. I have been negligent; you will forgive me; and there the matter must rest. I was much struck with the spirit of earnest affection and fervent piety that pervaded your last; and the account you give of the employment of your leisure hours sufficiently explains the greater vividness of your spiritual affections. There is a beautiful action and reaction of our religious feelings and actions upon each other; grace, shown to us by God, prompts us to deeds of charity to our fellow-men; and these deeds, all-imperfect and even displeasing to God, as they must be in themselves from the sin that mingles with the purest of them, are again rewarded by a fresh supply of the favour of our God, which must again lead to deeds of yet more extended benevolence, which are again to meet with a richer reward from the inexhaustible resources of Almighty goodness. It is thus, that he who waters others is watered himself; and of such an individual John Bunyan's paradoxical lines are strikingly true:

"'A man there was, though some did count him mad,
The more he cast away, the more he had.'

I say not these things to flatter you. Even where the richest rewards are given for the most indefatigable labours of love, we must ever remember that no reward is deserved, and the individual should be ready to exclaim, with him who was instant in season and out of season in the duties of his office, and who was conscious that his labours were more abundant than those of any of his brethren, 'Yet not I, but the grace of God that was with me.' I thank you for your very kind admonitions on my weakness of faith. It has much to struggle with in a heart that is but partially renewed; I fear very much that unsanctified confidence which is the most fearful temptation with which the adversary can assail us; a confidence that sin cannot damp; a confidence that, in some cases, the approach of death itself will not destroy, but which will lead its possessor to the very gate of heaven and will only be dispelled when the fearful response is given, 'I never knew you, depart from me ye workers of iniquity.' Then he who has been deceived by its delusive whispers of 'peace, peace, when there was no peace,' shall exclaim in the very paroxysm of astonishment and despair, 'The harvest is past, the summer is ended, and I am not saved!' The consideration of such a case as this, should make us 'examine ourselves, whether we be in the faith.' It is true, that, if we look to ourselves for comfort, we shall never obtain it; but, it is equally true, that, if the gospel is not to us the spring of holiness as well as the source of our comfort, 'we are deceiving ourselves and the truth is not in us.' We must not dread the discovery that we have been making little progress, or even that we have been pursuing a retrograde motion in the Christian course; nor must we smother every emotion of insecurity and danger that may rise on such a review. True, we must not cherish such emotions, and rest in them till they lead us to despair. They must lead us anew to the blood of sprinkling. That which gave consolation when all we could look back upon was an unbroken course of rebellion, will give consolation still; and it is only by such a process, I conceive, that true comfort can be obtained."

During the summer months, besides teaching a Sabbath-school in the neighbourhood of Perth, and keeping his meeting with the young men once a week for conversation on the Scriptures, he diligently pursued his studies and a course of reading. From some memoranda among his papers, I find that he kept a regular account of every day's employment. It commences on the 12th of May, on which day he arrived at his father's. It then lays down the following plan of study and occupation for the future: "To rise at seven o'clock; Greek Testament till eight; walk till nine; breakfast between nine and ten; Hebrew Psalms till eleven; Mathematics till twelve; French till one; Greek till two; English reading till three; dinner, three to four; Latin, four to six; tea, six to seven. Walk," &c.

At the end of September is the following summary of his occupations for the preceding months: "Greek Testament, Matthew to the Epistle to the Romans. Revised one hundred and eighty-four pages of Hebrew Grammar. Read forty verses of Hebrew Psalms. Revised six books of Euclid's Elements; one hundred and twenty pages of Bridge's Algebra; wrote one essay and fifteen letters. Read seventy-two Lectures of Brown's Philosophy; Baxter's Saint's Rest; Gilbert's Life of Williams; Edwards on Religious Affections; Narrative of a Tour to the Grande Chartreuse; Horne's Letters on Missions; Orme's Letter to Irving; fourteen Miscellaneous Discourses."

It is evident, from this statement, that he did not pass his time idly or unprofitably. It does not, however, contain the whole of his employments. Besides what is mentioned above it appears from the daily entries, that he read several of the Orations of Cicero; considerable portions of Homer, Thucydides, &c. He besides met with several interruptions, which repeatedly engrossed most of his time for a number of days together.

The following excellent letter he wrote to his friend Craik, shortly before he went to London:—

"Barossa Place, September 3, 1825.

"My very Dear Friend — I am astonished to find, on looking to the date of your last, that it is so long since I received it: and, probably, if you have been expecting a letter, the time, that has seemed to me like a few hours, may have been felt by you as if longer than it actually is. At least, so I feel. I always think my friends are very long in answering my letters, and yet I find, that, even when I conceived myself most punctual, I am more dilatory than any of my correspondents. That is an apt personification of time, which represents him as a decrepit old man with wings, that are visible only from behind. While we watch his approach he seems to creep tardily along: it is not till he has passed us that we perceive he has been *flying*. I cannot tell you how much I felt on the receipt of your very splendid and very affectionate present. It has become so common, from the higher refinement of our day, in the acknowledgment of the most common-place favour, for an individual to allege that he cannot express his gratitude, that I am almost ashamed to use the much-hackneyed phrase. But, in my case, it is used in simple honesty; and I know you will believe me when I say so. The word 'memorial,' in the inscription, which of course struck my eye before reading your letter, affected me a good deal. I feared it was prophetic of separation, and looked anxiously over your letter for the passage which should tell me that you had got an appointment to some situation which would prevent our meeting in St. Andrew's next winter. I was agreeably relieved from my anxiety by finding in your last page, instead of an account of your fancied removal, a proposal of lodging in the same house with me. And I was pleased to think, that, by calling your present a 'memorial' of our friendship, you meant, perhaps, to remind me of the fleeting nature of our intercourse; which soon, it may be very soon, will exist only in the recollection of the past.

"My alternations of feeling somewhat resembled those of one, who, on returning after a long absence, to the land of his nativity, should ask some passer-by, in pointing to a sepulchral pile before them, whose monument that was which seemed to have been so lately erected, and should be answered by the mention of the name of one whom he remembered as one of the dearest companions of his youth, and in whose company he had yet hoped again to revive the recollection of joys that had long departed, — a feeling, in some respects, more pleasing even than the joys themselves; but whose informer, on perceiving the gloom that had overcast his countenance, should rejoin, not to think that he was dead, he was still alive for whom that monument was intended; he had built it, not like many who in lifetime raise a splendid mausoleum for their dust, as if to demonstrate that infatuated man can be proud even of his frailty; but to stimulate him to greater diligence in the improvement of a season, in which so much has to be done, which, at its longest, is so very short, and which even were it longer is so very uncertain. But whither am I wandering? Excuse a mind that is sometimes too fond of amplifying trifles. I would scarcely write in such a motley strain to any but yourself. If, however, Cowper published a moral poem on 'The Sofa,' I may be excused for moralizing in a private letter, on the word 'memorial.'"

* * * * * *

"Most of Newton's Letters I have read, and those I read with very great pleasure. And, though not perhaps after this particular author that I remember, yet, frequently after perusing such authors, have I shared in the feelings you express; a fear, that the spirit that animated such men is fast declining. Often have I asked myself the question, Is not Christianity the same now as it was in the days of Owen and Baxter, and Newton? and why then is it that we now so seldom meet with 'living epistles of Christ,' such as they were? If *we* do not observe this lukewarmness, the world will. If *we* do not use it as an incitement to greater fervency of prayer for the reviving influences of the divine Spirit, infidels will make their use of it, in drawing from it arguments against the power of religion. I have often thought that I perceived arguments against evangelical religion, far stronger than its opposers have ever adduced; and I have wondered how they could escape the notice of such acute men as we have often had to mourn over among the 'enemies of the cross of Christ.'

I think it is the pious Newton, of whom we have just been speaking, who thinks he perceives in this, the watching of a gracious Providence, lest the mind of a weak believer should be shaken by the corroboration of those arguments from another, which must often have appeared fearfully alarming in his own experience. Were the opposers of evangelical truth, instead of their worn-out vocabulary of opprobrious epithets, to employ fair arguments from the inconsistency of Christians, many of us would be struck dumb. If 'our treasure be in heaven, our heart will be there also.' And if our heart be there, since it is 'out of the abundance of the heart the mouth speaketh,' our conversation will be about heavenly things. How different, however, is the case! On this subject there are two or three very beautiful verses, which I have just read, in a collection of hymns, by Thomas Kelly, (I know very little about the author; the volume I quote them from belongs to a sister of Robert Trail's) in which, although there is no great strength of conception, or beauty of imagery, there are contained some strains of lively piety and Christian feeling, expressed in very simple language. Such, I think, are these verses, paraphrased from, or rather suggested by, Malachi iii. 16. 'Then they that feared the Lord, spake often one to another,' &c.

"'Why should believers, when they meet,
Not speak of Christ, the King they own;
Who gives them hope that they shall sit
With him for ever on his throne?

Is any other name so great
As his who bore the sinner's load?
Is any subject half so sweet,
So various as the love of God?

'Tis this that charms reluctant man,
  That makes his opposition cease:
Beholding love's amazing plan,
  He drops his arms, and sues for peace.

'Twas so with us, we once were foes,
  Were foes to Him who gave us breath;
But he whose mercy freely flows,
  Has saved us from eternal death.

We look with hope to that great day,
  When Jesus will with clouds appear,
A sight of him will well repay
  Our labours and our sorrows here.

Of Him then let us speak and sing,
  Whose glory we expect to share;
In heaven we shall behold our King,
  And yield a nobler tribute there.'

"I cannot help mentioning, that I, last week, received a letter from our friend Mr. T———, very richly imbued with Christian feeling. Political economy, and even church establishments, were fairly cast in the shade; and there was an earnestness of affection, and warmth of feeling manifested, while writing on the grand subjects of our common faith, and expatiating on the endearments of Christian friendship, of which you would scarcely believe our phlegmatic friend susceptible; and with which only *such* subjects could inspire him.

"The account Mr. T—— gives of the employment of his leisure hours, sufficiently explains (to me at least) this increased spirituality of his mind. He had been, for some time, paying daily visits to the 'house of mourning.'

Two of the people he has been accustomed to visit, died during the summer; of none of them he thinks he had hope in their death."

In the month of September he went to London, on a visit to his friend, Mr. Adam; in the course of which, he spent a few days with me, the last of my earthly intercourse with him. The following extract of a letter from Mr. Adam, to me, notices this visit, and some of the objects which occupied his attention during the following winter, after his return to St. Andrew's.

"At the close of the session he persuaded me, before leaving for England, to spend a short time with his friends at Perth, which I did; and before returning again the following winter, I persuaded him to pay me a visit in return, at Homerton. During this visit, he was introduced to Dr. Morrison and Mr. Townley, and openly expressed the wish he had fostered previously in his bosom, to devote himself to missionary labours. We returned to College together, and being linked by a new bond, a common desire to benefit the heathen, we applied ourselves afresh to our general studies, and to a thorough investigation of everything relating to missions. For this purpose we searched the sacred Scriptures, and summed up our inquiries under the head of *precepts*, *prophecies*, *examples*, and *promises*. We also perused Brown's History of Missions; Horne's, Ward's, Milne's, and Judson's Letters; the Lives of Martyn, (which he read repeatedly, and eagerly drank into his spirit,) Brainerd and Chamberlain; Ward's History of the Hindoos, &c. During this winter our Society flourished, and several essays were read, not only by ourselves, but by others, some of whom we believed to be inquiring after the path of duty; and, as I perceived, were not a little influenced by the powerful and affecting manner in which John pleaded the claims of the heathen. With a sedulous attention to his engagements at the College, he found time to visit the sick, to give his assistance at some little meetings formed for the religious instruction of the poor during the week, and occasionally to supply some village stations, where there was preaching on a Sunday. I had forgotten to say, at the beginning of this session he laboured diligently for a time at the Chinese, and actually accomplished, by his unaided endeavours, a translation of the first chapter of John's Gospel. Attention to so many different objects rendered it absolutely necessary that he should soon relinquish the least pressing, and consequently, as I believe, laid it by, and never afterwards resumed it."

In a letter to his father, from London, he gives some account of his visit, and of his future plans. It contains also some remarks on my respected friend, Dr. Morrison, which are so just, that I cannot keep them back. I believe the character and manners of that devoted individual have not been properly understood, and in some quarters have been treated with a degree of unintentional injustice. His long and retired residence in a far distant country, and his absorption in the great object which he has so ardently and successfully pursued, sufficiently account for certain marked peculiarities, which I am convinced had no foundation in any obliquity of temper or disposition. Justice to one of the most enlightened and devoted servants of Christ, which this or any age has furnished, requires that I should bear this testimony, while I introduce the observations of my young friend.

"MARSHGATE, HOMERTON, Oct. 20, 1825.

"MY DEAR FATHER — In company with Mr. Adam I called on Dr. Morrison a few days after my arrival, who received us with that bluntness by which his manners are characterized, which has by some been represented as approaching to rudeness; but which is evidently not the want of kindness, but a superiority to those petty expressions of it which are often used, in our too-refined age, as a covering for coldness and indifference. Neither did I find in Dr. Morrison, as some of our friends had represented to me, an overweening conceit of his own sphere of exertion. What he said of missions, had more in it of calm rationality, and less of enthusiasm, than I should have even expected from a man who had spent seventeen years in a heathen country. Dr. Morrison very kindly offered to introduce me to his students at the Missionary Society's rooms, in Austin-friars, where the Doctor attends three days in the week, to give instructions in Chinese. I have attended there, with a few exceptions, every day since my arrival, and have seen as much of the mode of studying the language as may enable me, should I wish to pursue it, to do so alone. Dr. Morrison has offered me a loan of the books that are requisite, which are very expensive, (the Dictionary alone having been published at thirteen guineas;) and has also made me a present of a small work, which he has just published, entitled the 'Chinese Miscellany.' With these helps, I hope to do something at the language this winter, in St. Andrew's, and should I never make any actual use of it, it will be a good mental exercise. I have not yet called on Mr. Wilson, but intend to do so before I leave; but I think it likely that with my present views, my case does not come within the province of any of the home theological academies. My plan is to return to St. Andrew's, to devote the winter to my ordinary studies, give a little time to Chinese, and more especially, along with my dear friend John Adam, to consider very seriously those passages of Scripture which relate to missionary exertion, as well as to collect from other sources all the information possible upon this interesting subject, and to pray more earnestly than I have yet done, for direction in this particular matter. I thus hope by the conclusion of the winter, so far to have made up my mind as may enable me either to offer my services to the Missionary Society, or to apply for admission to some Dissenting academy. May the Lord direct me! I think you may perceive that my visit to this place has not been to no purpose. There is much general information that I have obtained, which the narrow limits of a single letter do not permit me to communicate; and much more which is of such a nature that it is not very easy to communicate by writing at all; and, on account of which chiefly, a personal visit seemed advisable."

* * * * * *

Dr. Morrison generously presented him with his Dictionary; and the papers which he left behind, sufficiently evince how ardently he entered into the study of that difficult language. He appears to have mastered some of its peculiarities; to have committed a number of its radicals to memory; and to have translated, as Mr. Adam states, the whole of the first chapter of John.

It was during this session that Dr. Chalmers committed to his charge the Sabbath-school, which met in his own house; and I am sure it will not give offence to that respected individual, to find a record in these pages, of the gratitude and affection of his late pupil, for the attentions which were so kindly shown him.

"St. Andrew's, December 6, 1825.

"My Dear Father — The first general meeting of our University Missionary Society was held yesterday. This institution seems now, under the blessing of God, to have weathered all the opposition that threatened at first to crush it, and promises fair to be established on a secure basis, and to extend the field of its usefulness. The dignitaries of our College profess to have quite changed their opinion with regard to it. Dr. Nicol confesses, that the reports we sent him, gave him information that was quite new to him. Last year, we were refused a room in the College, and could scarcely obtain a place of meeting in the town; *now* Dr. Haldane tells us, that the Divinity-Hall is at our service, or any other place which his influence can command. This offer we did not accept, as we had already obtained the old Episcopal chapel, as a place of meeting, which is more comfortable and convenient for our purpose, than any other place we could obtain. Our two principals have not given us fair words merely, but have testified their sincerity, by sending us a donation of a guinea each, with the promise of more on the part of Dr. Nicol. These are triumphs, which the most sanguine advocates of the cause would, a few years ago, have thought it not only ridiculous to expect, but almost foolish even to wish for. With God, however, all things are possible; and it is because we expect so little, and desire so little, and pray for so little on the faith of his promises, that these promises are not more speedily and more triumphantly accomplished.

"I think I mentioned, in my letter to my mother, that I had engaged to teach Dr. Chalmers's Sabbath-school during the winter: my school at Denino, in consequence, is left destitute. I have heard that the children are desirous that it should be begun again. Mr. Adam has commenced his operations, and I have been giving him some assistance. I think it advisable, with my present prospects, that I should engage rather more prominently in such employments, than otherwise I would be inclined to do.

"Dr. Chalmers has been more than kind to me this year: indeed, I feel almost oppressed by his attention. As my school is held in his house, I generally sup with him on Sunday evening, when I enjoy much more of his conversation than at set parties, as he and Mrs. Chalmers are then generally alone. I was very much gratified by a walk I had with Dr. Chalmers, to visit the parents of the children who attend his school. The people in some of the houses, seemed to recognize him familiarly, so that he is probably often engaged in the same labours of love. He thinks such exercises as visiting the poor and the sick, the best introduction to ministerial labour. 'This,' he said, as we were going along, 'is what I call preaching the gospel to every creature. That cannot be done by setting yourself up in a pulpit, as a centre of attraction, but by going forth and making aggressive movements upon the community, and by preaching from house to house.' I mention these remarks more freely, as I think this is a duty by far too much neglected among our Dissenting ministers."

The Sabbath-school which he engaged to teach this winter, in the house of his respected Professor, from whom he experienced invariable kindness, appears to have occupied his attention very closely. In a book now before me, is contained a list of the names of the young persons, with their places of residence. A list of tracts then follows, which belonged to the school library, with Dr. Chalmers's remarks on the character of each. Then a list of tracts, and small books, read by himself, with his own account of their nature and tendency. He has also written out, very fully, some of the school exercises on the Scriptures, which do great credit to his knowledge of the Scriptures, and his tact for communicating that knowledge.

This winter he entered the Natural Philosophy class; and, likewise, attended the Hebrew class. In this language he had before made considerable progress, by the help of some Hebrew books which I had put into his hands. He likewise, as appears from his papers, studied hard at Chinese for some time; and only gave it up from the greater urgency of some other objects.

His mind was now completely absorbed in the contemplation of future missionary labour: and to this object, all his pursuits became subservient. The letter of his friend Adam, shows how much he studied it. The paper book, containing the arrangement of the plan of investigating the subject remains, and contains many extracts from the Scriptures, and from various books, on the subject of missions, and numerous references, which prove how very fully he had examined the matter. It would be very desirable, indeed, if those who offer themselves for this service, were found generally to possess such a knowledge of the work which they profess to undertake. Almost all his letters and papers, from this time, bear upon this subject, and display at once the depth of his piety, the ardour of his zeal, and the large portion of good sense with which he contemplated the service of Christ.

Desirous of obtaining advice, and of engaging the prayers of his friends on his behalf, he applied to those in whose judgment and piety he placed confidence, to assist him. The following is a letter of this kind:—

"My Dear and much Respected Friend—It is now about eleven o'clock on Sunday evening, and I have been engaged almost the whole of the day in public exercises, so that you will be disposed to excuse a hurried letter. I write these lines chiefly to renew my request, that you would favour me with your correspondence on a subject which now most deeply engages my attention; the determination of the sphere of labour in which I can most usefully spend my life, if the Lord spare me, and honour me to do the work of an evangelist. I do not know whether there be any impropriety in my making this request; if there be, you must lay it to the account of my ignorance, and forgive me. Were I soliciting your advice merely for the sake of promoting my own interest, I should feel that my request was stamped with a character of very gross egotism. But I feel that I am the property of Christ, and of his church; and that even my feeble services may have some influence on his cause; and in this view of the subject you will not think me selfish, in desiring your attention to what might at first appear my own private affairs. Almost every person I have conversed with on the matter, urges upon me the duty of attending to the wants of our own country, and assuredly, if our own country were more neglected, or even as much neglected as other lands, I should feel the argument in all its force. I do think that our own countrymen have the first claim upon our attention, and I am inclined to think that the first preachers of Christianity would have declared the message of mercy first to the Jews, even though no express command had been given to preach to all nations, *beginning* at Jerusalem. But I cannot see how the claims of a native land can be stronger to a Gentile, than the claims of their own favoured nation were to the Jewish Christians. On this account, I think we are quite safe in taking the apostles for our example, in their conduct towards their countrymen. They did not wait till every dark corner of Judea was fully evangelized; far less till every heart had been savingly impressed by the truth. It was no argument to them to remain in Judea, that there were many who heard their message, that after all had refused to receive it. On the contrary, this was the very signal for their departure. (Acts xiii. 46; xxviii. 24–29.) I do feel much for the dark places of our own beloved country; but it does seem to me that the evangelical ministers of Britain could, with very little effort, publish the gospel most fully to every individual in the land. And they would do well to examine how far they are not guilty of the blood of souls, in not making more vigorous exertions for the heathen around their own doors. If a pastor of a church cannot do the work of an evangelist, let a separate person be maintained by every body of Christians, for this purpose; or, if each church cannot accomplish this, let a number of churches join in order to do so. I am aware that this is partly done by the itinerant societies, which are now beginning their operations, and I rejoice to see it; but still this is but a very feeble effort, compared with the necessities of the case. I still am inclined to think that the publication of the gospel, as a message of mercy to sinners, is the grand object for which the Christian ministry was instituted, at least it is one of the greatest objects. I do think that even the edification of the body of Christ, yields to it in point of importance. We believe that if a sinner once embraces the gospel, he cannot finally fall away; and even if his progress in the divine life should be slow, we know that in a very few years at the furthest, a full display of the glories of the divine character must burst upon him. Now, whether is it a more important work to rescue a sinner from hell, and place him in this condition of safety, or to antedate, in a very slight degree, the happiness of a future state, in one who has believed? For all our advances in the knowledge of divine truth here must be held insignificant, when compared with the immense addition to our knowledge and our happiness, which we shall receive at that time when the dim conceptions of faith shall be exchanged for the bright realities of actual vision. I beg that you would not understand me as estimating lightly the work of grace in the hearts of believers. It is only when contrasted with the work of regeneration, that I would ever think of it as of secondary importance. But I am not sure that the work of grace would go on more slowly in the hearts of believers, from the attention of the pastors being more called to the work of evangelizing the heathen. I do think in the present day we are apt to trust too much to public ordinances, and I would almost like to see Christians more thrown upon the resources of private devotion, and more direct communion with God. Our knowledge of divine things, to be sure, is small; but oh! that our piety were but equal to our knowledge. I am sorry to be obliged to conclude so abruptly."

His correspondent wrote him an excellent letter in reply to this, which produced another from him, which I subjoin:

"St. Andrew's, February 4, 1826.

"My Dear Friend—I feel much encouraged by your very kind letter. However clear the way of duty may seem to be marked out by our own conscience, still it gives us a much surer confidence in our own convictions, when they are strengthened by the concurring sentiments of our Christian friends, especially of those friends whom we highly esteem. I am not sorry on the whole, that hitherto my friends have all opposed my desire to preach Christ among the heathen. Perhaps it is well that we should have to wade through a good deal of opposition, in making up our mind on a subject of such importance. There is an air of romance which invests the subject of missionary adventure, when first it is presented to the mind of the young disciple; (what Mr. Malan in writing to my friend Mr. Adam, calls 'un trait de l'imagination;') and it is well, perhaps, that this false fire should be damped by opposition. It is a principle, I believe, among the Moravians, 'never to persuade any person to be a missionary.' And perhaps we should still act in the spirit of this maxim, did we even carry it so far as rather to repress than to stimulate the incipient zeal of the candidate for missionary service. For surely if our desire for the work cannot stand against the remonstrances of our friends, we have every reason to think that it would soon be quenched amid the heavy and lengthened discouragements which must be met with in the work itself. If the desire to serve my Saviour among the heathen were merely of *myself*, it is not like the fickleness of my natural disposition to have persevered in it till now, while meeting with so little encouragement. I do trust that the Spirit of the Lord has implanted this desire in my breast, and I know that he will perfect what he has begun. You speak of the difficulties connected with the work of a missionary. I can assure you, my dear friend, that as I have perused the history of former labourers, they have thickened upon my view. It is not to the natural dangers and hardships of the missionary life that I refer. It is not the prospect of encountering the diseases of an insalubrious atmosphere, with a frame that is not very robust, which affects me. If we perish in such a cause, we perish gloriously, and in this respect we 'conquer though we are slain.' There is something sweet in the contemplation of suffering for Christ's sake. 'If we suffer with him, we shall also reign with him.' And 'the more we toil and suffer here, the sweeter rest will be.' These are not the difficulties that I fear. But, I confess, I do tremble when I think of the spiritual dangers, the temptations of a heathen land, where all those barriers are broken down, which are the *only* safe-guards of the boasted virtue of the great mass of our community, and which operate, perhaps more strongly than he is aware, in restraining those evil propensities and worldly lusts, with which even the Christian has to contend. I have been very much depressed to find the instances of apostasy among missionaries, so very numerous; and that some, who, for a long time did run well, were afterwards hindered by 'the lust of the flesh, or the lust of the eye, or the pride of life.' While I look at this dark side of the picture, there is nothing gives me any comfort, but a complete reliance on the faithfulness of Him who has promised that as our day is, so shall our strength be. Oh, for a stronger faith in my Redeemer! a closer walk with my God! I see that *spirituality of mind* is the *main* qualification for the work of a missionary, and this is the very qualification which I feel that I most want. But I believe that He who hath given the desire to serve him, will also give the ability to fulfil that desire. I know that though weak in myself, I am strong in him. And I will rest in the promises of his love. Christ, when he dwells in the heart by faith, can impart of his own omnipotence to weakness itself; for through him, (may the weakest Christian say,) I can do all things. I have been struck with the view you give of the pastoral office, as raising up labourers. It is a view of it which I had not sufficiently considered. When we look intently at one object, it is very probable that other most interesting objects may altogether escape our notice; and so when the mind is much occupied with the consideration of a single object, the very intensity of our attention to it may be the means of obscuring our perception of other objects equally important. Dr. Chalmers has of late plied me a good deal with the same kind of argument for remaining in this country. 'You may render even to the cause of missions,' he says, 'perhaps greater service in raising up labourers by your preaching here.' My reply to this, however, is just a reference to facts. Christianity has been long preached, and many converts have been made in our own land, and the cause of Christian philanthropy, moreover, has been most ably pleaded; but notwithstanding, when labourers are called for, the eloquent advocates of missions shrink back, and scarce any are found to go forth."

Among his papers I find the notes of a speech which he delivered at a missionary meeting at Cupar of Fife, on a Monday evening, in the month of February. It was written late on the Sabbath night preceding, and early on the Monday morning. He walked to Cupar, delivered his address, and returned early the next morning to St. Andrew's. It is full of ardour, and replete with Christian feeling, though perhaps he carries some of his views a little too far. I should have given it in this place, as well deserving of insertion; but being somewhat similar to an address afterwards delivered at St. Andrew's, on the same subject, I omit it to make room for other matter. Such an address by one so young, could not fail to produce a very powerful effect. I pray that those who read it, may feel it equally with those who heard it.

Much as John's mind was engaged with foreign objects, he did not forget those who had a claim upon him at home. His own family, and a few particular friends were the objects of his warmest attachment; and for the salvation of some of them he laboured faithfully with themselves, and wrestled mightily with God. I venture to give the following to his brother, as a specimen of combined fidelity and tenderness of rare occurrence. There is also in that letter, and in the one which follows, to his mother, a manifestation of that exquisite sensibility, which characterized him, and which made his devotion to the work of a missionary no ordinary sacrifice. The prospect of leaving his country and his father's house, was to him one of inexpressible anguish; but the consideration of what was due to the authority and glory of Christ, impelled him forward. With talents not inferior to those of Martyn, he had feelings no less powerful than those of that devoted missionary; and though he was not honoured to follow him in his glorious career, yet as having it in his heart, I doubt not he now inherits with him a portion of his reward.

"St. Andrew's, February 10, 1825.

"My very Dear Brother — I have long thought of writing to you; and, indeed, had a letter half finished a week or two ago. I have at last been able to get a day nearly clear of engagements, and I am glad to spend it in making up a packet of letters for my friends in Perth. I begin with you; and, as I wish, if possible, to get five or six letters written, you will excuse me, if I am more brief than I otherwise should be in writing to an *only* brother. I have often wished, my dear David, to have some closer intercourse with you than I have yet had, on religious subjects, either by conversation or by letter. The latter method is the only one in my power, at present; and, in some respects I think it the most advantageous, as we can express our sentiments both more deliberately, and more freely than we perhaps could in personal intercourse. I hope you will not think me obtrusive in bringing this subject before you. Believing, as I do, that not only a right understanding of the gospel, but also, a real belief of its truths, is necessary to our happiness, either here, or in that mysterious state which is after death, you cannot surely wonder that I should be anxious to know the feelings of my dearest friends, in regard to this important subject. We, my dear brother, have enjoyed very distinguished privileges, in having a knowledge of the gospel from our infancy. But although early religious instruction is a most inestimable blessing, it has also its disadvantages. We, who know the gospel, and whose early prejudices, (the strongest of all prejudices,) are in favour of the gospel, are very apt to rest in our knowledge, or in our attachment to certain religious opinions, as a proof of our faith, and consequently of a state of safety in regard to another world. Now, I think, it is of the very greatest importance, to remember that there can be no *belief* where there is no *feeling*. In the ordinary affairs of life, we are disposed at once to admit, that a man cannot believe anything, without being suitably impressed by it. And how then should we be for a moment deluded into the opinion, that in this one instance, where the truths are calculated to make the very deepest impressions—in this, and in this alone, these truths can be believed without being felt? Would you think me censorious, if I would say, I feared *you* were not a Christian? Would you not be quite startled, if I said I suspected you to be an infidel? I do not mean, my dear David, to make either of these assertions, far less to do so in a spirit of censoriousness. But I will confess to you, that I have an uncertainty of the matter, which fills me with the greatest concern on your account. We start at the name of *infidel*. And we are very apt to think, that a man may be *unregenerate*, and yet very far removed from anything like infidelity. We are very apt to think that there may be such a thing as a half Christian, one who is almost a Christian. But it is silly to be deluded by mere names. The Bible tells us, that 'he who *believeth* shall be saved, and he who *believeth not*, shall be condemned.' We are told of no transition state in another world, half-way between heaven and hell, or nearer the one than the other. No; we must either rise to inconceivable glory, or sink into unutterable woe. The grand question is, *Do we believe the gospel*, or *do we not?* This, and this alone, fixes our after-state. If we believe, we shall reign with saints and angels; if we do not believe, if we have hesitated whether we should receive the gospel or not, if we have been even *almost persuaded* to believe; and if moreover, we have been possessed of all the knowledge and even all the graces that can adorn an unregenerate character; still, notwithstanding all, if matters stop here, we must be condemned throughout eternity, to herd with the very outcasts of society, with blasphemers and atheists, with liars and murderers. This is a very fearful view of the matter, but is it not the view which the Scriptures present? And it is this view of the matter that leads me to fear, and even (I acknowledge) to suspect, that my own brother may be among the number of those who are securely, and even cheerfully, walking on to the pit of endless perdition. This is an awful thought, and I have felt its awfulness. Often have I wept from the bitterness of the thought, that we may soon part never to meet again; and, excepting the prayers I have offered for my *own* forgiveness, the most earnest petitions I have ever presented at the throne of mercy, have been those I have put up for a *brother's salvation*. I believe there is an efficacy in prayer, and I am not without the hope that these prayers will be answered. I have sometimes thought, that I could see that you had a conviction that all was not right with you; that, after all, there was a something in Christianity which you had not experienced. I could remember, that such was the state of my own mind, when the Spirit of God first strove with my rebellious heart, and the hope dawned upon me, that this might be the beginning of his working on your mind. That hope has often been blasted by your indifference, or your open rebellion against God; but, though often blasted, I will still continue to cherish it. The Lord grant that it may be realized. I have written these lines for your own private perusal; and, therefore, I laid aside that veil of propriety, by which, in ordinary life, we are accustomed to conceal our feelings, and I have laid open my heart before you. I do not think you have the hardness to laugh at my concern on your account; but, if even this should be the effect of this letter, still I shall not regret that I have told you all I feel. This letter has been preceded and accompanied with prayer, and part of it has been written in tears. God is sometimes pleased to work by the most insignificant agents; and I am not without the hope, that by the blessing of his Spirit, these confused expressions of a brother's heart-felt desire for your salvation, may be made the means of softening your heart, and leading you to receive the gospel of the Lord Jesus Christ with humility and with joy.

"There is one circumstance, my dear brother, that has especially led me to open my heart before you at present, and to urge thus solemnly and earnestly upon you, the acceptance of the gospel. You have heard, probably, that I have determined to spend my life in preaching to the heathen. I feel that even the innocent pleasures of this life are all of them unsatisfactory; and, in many instances, tend to draw the mind from heavenly objects. And, from all the information I can collect, I am convinced that I can serve my God more effectually, by declaring his name where it never has been declared before, than by repeating the gospel to those who have often heard, and as often refused it. But the thought that I am soon to leave this land, *never to return*, makes me feel it a more urgent duty while I remain, to press the truths of the gospel on the attention of those who are my countrymen; and especially to warn most solemnly, and most earnestly to persuade those who are dearest to me by the ties of nature. *A few months*, my brother, and our earthly intercourse must be for ever at an end. Shall I hope to meet you in heaven? O give me an answer to this question, for on yourself its answer depends. I confess that, in the prospect of leaving my parents, one-half of the great burden that lies upon my mind, would be removed, could I confidently rely on the religious principles of my sister, and especially of yourself, who, in a short time, will be their *only son*, and almost their only earthly protector. There are occurrences that must here present themselves to your mind, which you must know, wound my feelings most deeply in the prospect of separation; but these I will not call to mind. O that the God of the families of Israel may cause his peace to abide upon my father's house!

"You know that my parents feel deeply at the thought of my departure. I am sure, that if they could feel a thorough confidence in you, my brother, it would go far to reconcile them to what I believe to be the will of God concerning me. I know, my dear David, that you are often placed in difficult circumstances; but a belief of the gospel, and a spirit of prayer, will go far to enable you to act calmly and meekly under the most trying circumstances. Believe in Jesus Christ, and look to him, and in looking to him, you will reflect his image; you will become like him. Thus, and thus alone, will you learn like him, when you are reviled, not to revile again; and even when you suffer, not to threaten.

"You see, my brother, I have many reasons for urging upon you these solemn warnings and earnest entreaties. I beseech you to believe in Christ. I beseech you to take his yoke upon you, and learn of him, for 'his yoke is easy, and his burden is light.' I beseech you to learn of him to be meek and lowly. I entreat you to do these things, if you would save your own soul: if you would fulfil the best and most earnest wishes of an affectionate and only brother; if you would, in some degree, alleviate the sorrow of one who is soon to part with all he holds dear on earth; and finally, if you would comfort our bereaved parents, if you would make up the breach which the resistless hand of death has so lately made, and which the imperious calls of duty soon must make again, in that little family which I must try to think no longer my home."

"St. Andrew's, February 14, 1826.

"My Dear Mother — My work of letter writing has taken up nearly all my private time, for two days; and I still feel that there are some who may be expecting to hear from me, to whom it will be quite impossible for me to write. Although I have written to my father, (which I always think the same as writing to you,) yet I cannot think of letting my parcel go, without sending a few lines expressly to yourself. All my friends seem doubly dear to me, since I have thought of parting with them. There was nothing in the prospect of a separation, my dear mother, that gave me greater pain, than the thought of wounding your feelings; and, accordingly, in my late visit, I was very much rejoiced to hear you speak so calmly and resignedly on the subject. Even in this life, God has promised to restore a hundred fold anything we give up for his sake. And I do think, that even these trials in themselves carry a blessing along with them. The prospect of an early separation from all I hold dear on earth, bitter as the thought is, has, notwithstanding, proved to me a real blessing. I have felt an inexpressible dreariness in looking forward, while I think only of the things that are seen and temporal. But then, the very dreariness which seems to hang over my earthly prospects, has led me to look more earnestly to heaven, as my home, and the place of my rest. And, if we can but steadily fix the eye of faith on the heavenly inheritance, the glory of the promised land will shed a brightness even over the gloomiest part of this valley of tears. I know, my dear mother, that you have many trials; and I could wish much to soothe the declining years of that dear friend, who watched over my helpless infancy. I would like to be able to make some return for the anxious hours, and the sleepless nights, I have cost you. This I may never have in my power; but wherever my lot may be cast, I shall never forget the tenderness of a mother's love; never shall I forget the affectionate solicitude which brought you to our bed-side every evening, to see that all was safe with us, ere your own eye could close in sleep; never shall I forget ——. But it is wrong to indulge in this. Let us forget the things that are behind, and rather delight to dwell on the glory and the happiness that are before us. Oh, how highly favoured are we, my mother, with the blessed hope of a glorious immortality! God, it is true, has removed one of your children; and, for His sake, you are called to give up another; but still, though the cup may be bitter, it is a Father's hand that has mingled it. 'Trials make the promise sweet.' You will be able now, more than ever, to enjoy the delightful assurance, that the Lord will be to his people a portion, better than of sons and daughters.

"And again, if we but think of what Christ has done for us, we shall not think any sacrifice too great that we can make for him. He left the bosom of the Father, and emptied himself of his glory, and suffered more than ever man suffered, and died *for us*. Should we not then feel all the force of the argument, which tells us we are not our own, having been bought by Christ, when he gave his blood as our ransom price? Is it not then a reasonable service, to offer our bodies a living sacrifice to him? And then, there is the blest assurance, that if we *suffer* with him, we shall also *reign* with him."

The following is to the afflicted friend, to whom some of his former letters were addressed:—

"St. Andrew's, March 5, 1826.

"My very Dear Friend—You can easily conceive how difficult it is for a young person, enjoying in all its fulness, the inestimable blessing of health, and whose mind is ever actively engaged with one subject or another, all at once to place himself in the circumstances of an aged and long afflicted Christian. Yet this I must try to do, ere I can write in a strain of sympathy with your feelings. But though I cannot enter as I could wish, into your peculiar circumstances, or write with all that closeness of sympathy, or administer that experimental consolation, which the person could, who had seen as much of life's chequered scene, and passed through like trials with yourself; yet there are always some subjects on which Christians feel a common interest, however different their circumstances, and however varied their experience. The great objects of our salvation are alike interesting in youth and in age; in joy and in sorrow; in health and in sickness; in seasons of prosperity, and in the day of trial. What was said by a learned heathen of his favourite studies, (most beautifully, but most extravagantly in his application of it,) might with great propriety be used by the Christian in speaking of the truths of the Bible: "These studies cherish youth, soothe old age, adorn prosperity, and form in adversity a refuge and consolation; at home they are our delight, abroad they are no incumbrance; they are with us by night, they journey with us, and in our country retreat they are with us still." What a pity that worldly men should be so enthusiastic in the praise of their favourite pursuits, while Christians are so dull and careless about objects so much more highly deserving of their love. How few Christians are there who could heartily, and from their own experience, apply to the joys and the consolations of the gospel, those ardent expressions of delight which a heathen philosopher employs in regard to merely human learning. So true is it, that the children of this world are wiser in their generation, than the children of light.

"I should suppose, that to an aged Christian who cannot look for much longer continuance in the church below, the state and employment of the church above must be peculiarly interesting. To all Christians it must be a subject of the most delightful contemplation; but more especially to those who hope to be very soon released from the prison-house of the body. It was the joy set before him, which bore our Lord through the ignominy, and the torture of his sufferings. And surely the prospect of such a glory as is set before his disciples, may well encourage and support them through every difficulty and every trial. It may well reconcile us to suffer with Christ, when we know that this is the sure pledge of our reigning with him. They who have been deepest in suffering for Christ's sake, shall be highest in glory. They who would sit on his right hand, when he is seated on his throne, must drink of the bitter cup which he drank of, and must be baptized with the bloody baptism with which he was baptized. The first disciples knew this, and therefore they were not only patient, but joyful in suffering, and were even apt to run into the extreme of courting danger. They did not count the tribulations of the gospel as trials, to which it was a painful duty to submit; but they regarded them as honours, which it was no ordinary favour to win. 'For unto you it is given, in the behalf of Christ, (says the apostle Paul,) not only to believe on him, but also (higher privilege still!) to suffer for his sake.' It is labour and fatigue which give to *rest* and *repose* their great value. Indeed we have no idea of rest where there has been no previous weariness or fatigue, and the harder the toil, or the more distressing the uneasiness, the sweeter is the rest which succeeds it. I have had little or no experience of bodily suffering, but I find it is these views of the glory that shall follow, which bear me up under the prospect of trials which sometimes burden me with not a little mental distress; and I trust that these hurried remarks may not be altogether useless, in administering some little consolation to you under your lengthened afflictions. May the Lord the Shepherd of Israel guide you; and may his rod and his staff be your comfort, when you tread the dark valley! Do not forget sometimes to pray for

"Your very affectionate brother in the Lord Jesus."

As the end of his last session at college drew nigh, he became increasingly anxious about his future sphere of labour. He addressed two letters to Dr. Morrison, with which the Doctor was much pleased, as appears from his answers; and in the following letter to myself, he discloses all his mind, and intimates his final decision.

"St. Andrew's, March 10, 1826.

"My very Dear Sir — The end of our session is now at hand, and I begin to feel it necessary to determine on some settled plan to proceed upon afterwards. Mr. Adam and myself have made the subject of missions a matter of daily consideration this session; and after deliberately viewing all sides of the question, and candidly comparing the claims of our home population and the heathen world, and earnestly seeking for direction from Him who has promised to be the guide of his people, even unto death, I have come to the final resolution of devoting myself to the service of God among the heathen. I have made the history of missions, and the biography of missionaries, a part of my daily study, for some time, and have perused, I think, nearly all the principal works on the subject. And I am glad I have done so; for it has given me much sounder views of the matter than I had before. There is much in the distance of a foreign land, and the mystery that hangs over the operations that are carried on there; and, above all, in the high and often extravagant eulogiums which the eloquent advocates of missions have caused us to associate with the very name of *Missionary;* there is much, I say, in all this, to produce a false impression on the mind of a young disciple. I remember, when I first united myself to a Christian society, of being much disappointed to find, that Christians, though vastly different from the world, were still weak and imperfect creatures. And so, I had been accustomed to form such a lofty conception of the character of a missionary, that I have been almost disappointed to find, from their history, that they are men of like infirmities with other Christians; and certainly, I have been a good deal depressed to find that many of them were far from possessing that saintly devotedness, and apostolic zeal, which my boyish imagination had attributed to them. Indeed, I have to fear, that there was much of romance in my first thoughts of becoming a missionary; a good deal of what Mr. Malan, in writing to my friend Mr. Adam on the subject, calls 'un trait de l'imagination.' But I trust the detail of facts, which have come under my review, has done much to dissipate this; and has at the same time, impressed me more deeply than ever with the duty of engaging in this department of the ministerial work. The brilliant colouring of romance has faded from the picture; but its outlines seem even more strongly and broadly marked than before. I have not been discouraged by the sufferings of the missionary life; they are borne for Christ's sake. And happy, indeed, are they, to whom it has been given on behalf of Christ, *not only* to believe on him, *but also* to suffer for his sake. Neither do I feel discouraged by the want of success; the expectations of Christians on this subject appear to me very unreasonable. They put forth their little finger to remove a mountain, and are astonished that God does not work a miracle to reward their *great* exertions. But the promise of God stands sure; and though it tarry, we will wait for it. One thing, I confess, has distressed me not a little; it is the prospect of those temptations, before which so many have fallen; but I know it is wrong to fear. The God that enables us to stand in the midst of smaller temptations is able, and has promised to be with us at all times. I see that unwavering faith in God's promises, and closeness of communion with him, are among the main requisites in the character of a missionary. And in these I feel that I am very deficient. O, pray for me, my dear friend, that he who has wrought in me to will, may also fit me to perform it.

"I have had a letter from Dr. Morrison. He recommends an early application to the Society, and even talks of a very early entrance on the work itself. I trust I am ready to engage whenever the Lord will, but I think it is not a recoil from trial, which makes me suppose that prudence might demand my still remaining a considerable time in this country. I am not yet eighteen. After this session I shall have nothing to prevent my engagement in direct preparation for missionary work. I should like to know the state of the Society's arrangements. I was offered a very good situation some time ago, but was afraid it might, in some degree, interfere with my preparations for the work to which I am devoted. I have taught Dr. Chalmers's Sabbath-school for him this winter, as he is engaged otherwise. This has given me the opportunity of very familiar intercourse with the Doctor. I sup with him on Sunday evenings, and have a good deal of conversation with him on the subject of missions, &c. He tries to persuade me to stay in this country, but I do not think his arguments powerful. I have refused to accept of any situation that may occur to him at present, in the prospect of soon offering myself to the Society. On this account I should like you to write soon, if possible, whether the Society can receive applications this summer."

As this letter contains his decision respecting the important work which had so long occupied his attention, perhaps this is the proper place to introduce his concluding address to the St. Andrew's Missionary Society, which was in a great measure the fruit of his own exertions, and which he had cherished with the fondest affection. That address, also, containing his matured views, will afford me the opportunity of making a few remarks on the subject, and on the opposition of his friends to his personal engagement in the work.*

Very far be it from me to write a single sentence that might diminish the force, or detract from the earnestness of this energetic and eloquent appeal.

On the Society to which it was read, it produced a most powerful effect; and on their minutes, they have made the following entry of that impression: "Never probably, in any association, had such an address, on such a subject, been before delivered. To say that it was most eloquent, most solemn, most affecting, the production of a mind of mighty grasp; sedulously and continuously directed to one single object of mightiest import, may convey to those who heard it not, some idea of the impression produced by it."

* See Appendix K.

I trust it is destined to touch the hearts of many, whom the living voice of the author never could have reached. I envy not the understanding, or the feelings of that individual, who can read the address, without experiencing a higher emotion than that of admiration. It is impossible not to be struck with the deep earnestness of the advocate, the cogency of his reasoning, and the affection and simplicity of his manner. Here are "thoughts that breathe, and words that burn," on a subject the most momentous which can engage the mind of man.

Were there any danger of this address producing a general rush into the missionary service, and a desertion of the service at home, it might be necessary to enter some exceptions to certain parts of it. But as long as the love of home and of ease, and various other considerations operate, there is little probability that we shall have to check the fervour of missionary zeal. Perhaps my young friend, however, a little exaggerates the low state of this principle, and represents the deficiency of missionary candidates as greater than it really is. What is chiefly to be regretted, is, the paucity of well educated and gifted men for this work. By far the greater number of persons who volunteer their services, are young men of Christian principle, but whose early advantages have been comparatively few. In this respect, there has, indeed, been some progress of late, but still there is much room for improvement.

Without throwing any reflection on persons of humble life, and limited education, who wish to devote themselves to this work, I do conceive, that in many instances, the failure which has taken place in our foreign operations, may partly, at least, be traced to this source. When a young person, under examination, tells us, that the extent of his reading has been the Bible, Boston's Fourfold State, Bunyan's Pilgrim's Progress, and the Evangelical Magazine; and that, from these and similar sources, with attending missionary services, he has derived all his knowledge of the work in which he proposes to engage, it is obviously impossible, whatever dependence may be placed on his sincerity, to attach any confidence to his knowledge of the nature of the work.

Such a person is perhaps accepted; and, after passing through a hurried and imperfect education, is sent forth to some important and difficult situation abroad. There difficulties and trials assail him, for which he is altogether unprepared, and, after floundering and blundering a few years, becomes either dispirited or ensnared, and effects nothing. Perhaps he has been suddenly elevated to a class of society, in which he had not been accustomed to mingle, and from that circumstance, is exposed to danger, which would scarcely affect persons of another description. It ought not to be concealed, that missionaries labouring in certain situations among the heathen, enjoy advantages which are not possessed by their brethren in the ministry at home; and this circumstance, if caution is not exercised, is in danger of producing great injury to our cause.

As so much reference is made by John in his letters, to the opposition of his friends and others, to his desire to devote himself to the work of Christ among the heathen, I feel called upon to explain the nature and reasons of this opposition, which, I apprehend, he never properly understood. Not having opposed him myself, after I saw his mind was fully made up, my explanation may be received with the greater confidence. As the opposition was not from worldly people, or from religious persons under the influence of worldly motives, the explanation is the more necessary.

I believe then, that opposition arose entirely from two causes, the state of his constitution, and the character of his mind. All who knew him, feared that his bodily constitution would never bear the effects of a warm climate. Though liable to no particular complaint, he was delicate from a child, and incapable of enduring much fatigue or exposure. Of this his parents were most sensible, and hence their decided reluctance to allow him to go abroad. The event proved that their fears were too well grounded.

Other friends connected his mental with his bodily constitution, and feared the labours of a missionary life would soon prove fatal. He possessed a highly morbid sensibility, which rendered him liable to exquisite sufferings, from circumstances that would not have greatly affected more robust and hardy individuals. He was formed for society, and was dependent upon it in a great degree, for his support and capability of acting. This is most strongly marked in many of his letters. In connection with this, the kind of talent which he possessed would have fitted him for eminent usefulness in this country; while his exquisite taste, and various other qualifications, would have been to a considerable extent, lost in a foreign country. I am not disposed to underrate the talents necessary for foreign missionary labour, or to exaggerate the importance of our own, yet I freely acknowledge that I am one of the number, who would have rejoiced that John Urquhart had laboured at home, rather than have gone abroad.

It was too delicate a matter to press these reasons upon

him; but I am sure they are the only reasons which weighed with Dr. Chalmers, Mr. Ewing, and various other individuals, from whom he considered himself as experiencing more opposition than he had been prepared to expect. It is every day becoming more evident that men of a high order of talent in the Christian ministry, are required in this country. The successful prosecution of the work abroad, renders this no less necessary, than the nature of the work at home; and it would augur ill for the cause of Christ generally, were such gifted individuals all disposed to forsake our own shores. Of this, however, there is no great reason to entertain much fear.

I cannot, perhaps, better conclude the account of his progress during this last session at St. Andrew's, than by giving at length several documents with which I have been furnished. It is always more satisfactory to report the evidence of eye and intimate witnesses, than to indulge in general and hypothetical reasonings; and I have found it a very peculiar advantage in conducting this narrative, that in almost every step of the religious life of this interesting youth, I can adduce the evidence of those who were so closely connected with him, that they had the best opportunities of judging; and who were, at the same time, well qualified to form a judgment of him. His friend, Mr. Duff, writes as follows: —

"In the session of 1825-6 his growth in spirituality was quite extraordinary. Literature and science now dwindled, in his view, into comparative insignificancy; they no longer occupied the greatest portion of his time; they no longer possessed exclusive charms; it was sufficient for casting them into the shade, that of them it might be asserted, as of the earthquake and the fire of Elijah, 'that the Lord was not there.' He, no doubt, this session, gained the third prize in the Natural Philosophy class, which from the highly scientific nature of the course, is generally reckoned no ordinary attainment; but this he owed entirely to his real superiority of intellect, as it was gained without labour, without effort, without much preparation. Indeed he could not bear the thought of spending much time on what appeared to him to be but of secondary importance. Christianity now became the *constant* subject of his meditation, the cause of Christ the *constant* theme of his discourse. How to be useful to the souls of men, how to promote the glory and honour of his Redeemer, attracted all his thoughts, and formed the object of his fondest desires. He seemed full of the spirit of the reformer, proclaiming, in all his words and actions, 'None but Christ; none but Christ.' "

Besides the prize in the Natural Philosophy class, referred to by Mr. Duff, he gained a prize in the Hebrew, Chaldaic, and Syriac class, "as a testimony," says Professor Baird, "of my high approbation of his correct and exemplary conduct, and of the many proofs of excellent talents and distinguished proficiency which he exhibited while attending that class."

I should also mention that he attended the Natural History class during the session; and, from some drawings and papers which remain, it is evident that he had made considerable progress in botany. With mineralogy and chemistry he was also well acquainted. The testimony he received from the Lecturer on Natural History is entitled to a place:—

"St. Andrew's, April 29, 1826.

"Mr. John Urquhart was enrolled a student of Natural History in the United Colleges of St. Salv. and St. Leon, at the commencement of the session now closed; and, from the unremitted regularity of his attendance, the interest he took in the course, and the intelligence of his conversations on the subject, I have every reason to believe, that, had there been public examinations, he would have been as eminent in the Natural History as he has been in every class of the United College.

"John Macvicar,
"Col. Lect. Nat. His."

From another of his fellow-students, and indeed his fellow-lodger, Mr. Alexander, I received the following very ample view of his character and talents. The writer, I have reason to know, is well entitled to pronounce his judgment; and all that he says, is at once most correct, as well as judicious: —

"My acquaintance with John Urquhart commenced in the year 1823; but it was not till the summer of 1825 that we became very intimate. When I knew him first he appeared to possess a great flow of spirits, which showed itself more in a perpetual cheerfulness and hilarity, than in any fondness for boisterous mirth. This he seemed still to retain, as far as I could judge, as long as I had an opportunity of conversing with him. Occasionally, however, this gave way to excessive depression, with which sometimes he was dreadfully distressed. During these seasons he was often visited with thoughts, which to his mind, were peculiarly discouraging and terrific; such as doubts of his being a child of God, a fear of losing his senses; and many other equally unpleasant ideas. I have not the least doubt, however, that all these arose from physical causes, and were prognostications of that disease by which his years on earth were brought to a close.

"In November, 1825, it was my lot to come to St. Andrew's to study; and I had the happiness to find myself lodged under the same roof with John Urquhart. Many a happy and delightful hour have we spent together in this room wherein I now sit, — the memory of which is still upon my mind, and it is sweet. Never has it been my lot to meet with one of so sweet and amiable a disposition. Contented with whatever he received, I never heard him utter an angry word, or saw him wear a menace on his placid countenance. He was regular in all his habits, kind and affectionate in all his conversation with those around him; and the estimation in which he was held by those with whom he lodged, was best testified by the heartfelt grief and honest tears with which they received the intelligence of his death. His landlady, for some weeks after, wore mourning, in token of respect for his character and memory.

"His piety was simple and unaffected; and, at the same time, truly evangelical. Deeply sensible of his own unworthiness and guilt, he was humbled before God, and was enabled to lay hold upon him who is the Saviour from all sin. Convinced by his numerous short-comings that he had not yet arrived at perfection, he was taught to cling closer to his Redeemer, and trust in him alone. He was distinguished by a godly, jealous care over his own heart; and was watchful against temptation. Many a time did he deny himself the indulgence of pleasures of which he was naturally fond, just because they might stand in the way of his soul's good. In prayer, he peculiarly excelled. How earnest were his supplications, and how experimental his confessions, every one who has ever heard him can testify. His whole soul seemed to be engaged; and the energy of his expression sufficiently testified, that what he asked, was what he indeed knew and felt himself to want.

"His zeal for doing good was very great. You, sir, already know with what eagerness he sacrificed every prospect of worldly advantage for the arduous and laborious office of a foreign missionary. This was the darling desire of his heart; and, for the attainment of this object, he earnestly and unceasingly prayed. Every work upon Christian missions, every article of missionary intelligence, he anxiously and eagerly perused. He had pondered well all that he might expect to endure; he had looked upon all the dangers and difficulties which lay before him; but his desire was not weakened, and his confidence in the promises of Jehovah was unshaken. So firm was his determination, that he actually commenced the study of Chinese, and spent many an hour of hard study on its recondite symbols. I do not know whether he continued to prosecute this study: I rather think not; as he seemed latterly to have directed his attention more to India than to China.

"But he did not content himself with a mere *desire* to do good, and with forming plans for *future* usefulness; he was also busy in doing what he could for those around him. He was much occupied with Sabbath-schools, and took great delight in communicating instruction to the children by whom they were attended. It was his practice to make them read a chapter, which he explained to them, and questioned them from it. All these questions he previously wrote down and studied, in order that they might be as simple and easy as possible. Indeed, he possessed a peculiar talent for speaking to children, and never failed to secure their attention. The simplicity of his addresses to them may be evinced by the surprise which some of his youthful hearers once expressed, that they should have been able to recollect all that he had said. Nor was he contented with merely speaking to the children on the Sabbath; he made it a point to visit them regularly in their own houses, and to converse with them and their relations there. By these means he secured the confidence of the parents as well as the affection of the children, and was often enabled to speak a word in season to those with whom he met.

"To visit the sick and the infirm was another favourite occupation of my dear brother; to every call of this kind he was ready; and many a time have I known him leave his studies to visit the bed-side of some humble sufferer. On these occasions his conversation was always of a spiritual nature, and it was always his anxious endeavour to direct the mind of the sufferer away from every earthly confidence, unto the 'Lamb of God, who taketh away the sins of the world.' Sometimes in these visits of love, he was kindly received, sometimes he had to endure the suspicion of having some sinister motive by which he was actuated; sometimes he met with intelligence and attention, and sometimes with ignorance and carelessness; but whatever reception he met with, he never failed to repeat his visits: so strong was his desire for the welfare and salvation of his fellow men.

"But, while he was thus attentive to the duties of religion, he was not negligent of those studies for which he had come to this place. On the contrary, I believe there were few of his cotemporaries who studied more closely than he did: certainly, none more successfully. In only one class did he fail to distinguish himself; viz. the Logic Class; but this I am inclined to impute, not so much to any want of ability, as to a distaste for the dull and barren speculations with which the Professor of Logic treats his students. His splendid appearance in the Ethical Class, the year following, proved what he could do; and it was certainly no small achievement to stand first in two separate competitions in a class, perhaps the most numerous and able that ever attended the prelections of a St. Andrew's Ethical Professor. As far as I could judge, his talent lay chiefly in a facility of acquiring languages; and in the elegance, both of thought and expression, by which his compositions were distinguished. There were several of his cotemporaries who took a much firmer and profounder grasp of a subject; but there were few, if any, who could think so clearly, and express themselves with such perspicuity and elegance, as he was able to do. Contrary to what may be inferred from the ease and beauty of his style, his habits of composition were very laborious. Beginning from a rude and imperfect sketch, he, by degrees, filled up the parts and extended the outline. He scarcely wrote a sentence which did not cost him some labour; and, consequently, composition was to him a most fatiguing, and, I may say, irksome exercise. He always set himself to it with reluctance; and, indeed, it was only by the calls of duty that he could be prevailed upon to take up his pen on any subject. I have not seen all his compositions; but the best that I have seen are a series of papers on the St. Andrew's Missionary Society, printed in the 'St. Andrew's University Magazine,' a little work conducted by some of his friends during last session; and an essay on the duty of personally engaging in the work of missions, read before the St. Andrew's Students' Missionary Society; of which he was always a distinguished friend and supporter."

These testimonies are peculiarly pleasant and satisfactory. not only as the expressions of Christian and personal friendship, but as bearing evidence to his holy and exemplary conduct. In him, religion did not appear as a profession, — it dwelt in him, as life, — it attached itself to him as clothing. It was not a holiday, but an every day garb, and was worn with the ease of a natural habit, — not the stiffness of an assumed or foreign dress. There is one testimony more which I cannot withhold, though the name of the respected individual who bears it, has been already repeatedly introduced. No one could know him better than Dr. Chalmers; and no man was more capable of estimating his intellectual and spiritual attainments. The following document presented to John, on leaving the University, does great honour to the heart of the Professor, as well as to the talents of the student.

"St. Andrew's, April 28, 1826.

"These are to certify, that Mr. John Urquhart was enrolled a regular student of Moral Philosophy in the United College of St. Andrew's, for the session of 1825–6; that he distinguished himself highly by his appearances while under examination, and was far the most eminent of his class, for the beauty and eloquence of his written compositions; that he possesses a very uncommon degree of taste and talent for the disquisitions of ethical science; and that altogether, he, as the fruit of great diligence, united with great powers, achieved the credit of being a first rate proficient in the lessons and doctrines of the course.

"THOMAS CHALMERS."

"Mr. Urquhart gained two prizes in this class; one, the first prize, for an essay on 'The Mutual Influences and Affinities, which obtain between the Moral and Economic Condition of Society.' Another, the first prize for essays read in the class during the session."

Perhaps, to some readers, it may occur to ask, did the individual who was so successful in all his academical pursuits, take a degree at St. Andrew's? It appears he did not. If this should excite surprise, I can say in explanation, that multitudes of the best scholars at the Scottish Universities never trouble themselves about the matter; and many of those who take the degree of A. M., never use it. But as I know John was recommended to take a degree, I can account for his neglecting to follow the advice, only by referring his conduct to that instinctive and powerful aversion to human praise, by which he was remarkably distinguished. One of his fellow students, who knew him well, and whose testimony I have not yet quoted, calls my attention to this feature of his character; what he calls, "his total indifference to human approbation. The loudest applause of his instructors and fellow students did not seem to tell on his feelings at all. Had he been susceptible of pleasure from any distinction conferred, it must have shown, when he was singled out, and eminently honoured, by such a man as Dr. Chalmers. Yet, even in this case, he was unmoved. His mind hardly appeared to have a thought for anything, save the good opinion of Him who trieth the reins and hearts of the children of men. He arrived at this heavenly-mindedness, not, I am sure, by any process of acute investigation into the philosophy of our feelings, but simply by ever exercising his affections on those things which are unseen and eternal. His indifference was not the misanthropic stoicism of the philosopher, but the perfect liberty of the Christian."

Whether I am correct, or not, in assigning this reason for his declining to take his degree at the University, the reader, I am sure, will rejoice with me in the evidence of the existence of such a state of mind as that which this extract describes. It is in full accordance with other testimonies, and with all my own convictions. Genuine Christianity does not teach us to despise the approbation of others, or undervalue any useful attainment which may be the object of that approbation. But when it obtains full possession of the mind, it, in a great degree, dislodges those secondary motives and considerations, which constitute the great principles of action in the men of the world. It does not produce meanness or servility; but it produces lowliness of mind. It not only inculcates a spirit of self-distrust and diffidence, and indifference to human glory; but in its very nature induces these dispositions. The individual who feels the charm and the power of a Saviour's love, and who attaches to his approbation all that constitutes the glory of future hope, will not be much concerned for the honours or the applause of this world. Into these views and feelings few have entered more fully and even enthusiastically than the subject of these memoirs. All his letters are illustrative of this state of mind; and his whole conduct was a living commentary on his letters.

CHAPTER V.

Letter to his Mother in reference to his becoming a Tutor in a family of high respectability — Letter to Herbert Smith, Esq. — Extracts from his Journal — Letter to Mr. Craik — Letter — Extracts from his Journal — Letter to Mr. Trail — Letter to his Sister — Letters — Extracts from various letters to Mr. Scott Moncrieff — Letter to his friend C. — Letter to Mr. Herbert Smith — Letter to the Rev. John Burnett — Letter to Mr. Adam — Letter to Mr. Orme — Letter — Letters to his Sister — Letter to Mr. Trail — Letter to Mr. Adam — Letter to his afflicted friend — Letter to Mr. Trail.

PREVIOUSLY to John's leaving St. Andrew's, a negotiation had been carried on, through Dr. Chalmers, with a family of the highest respectability, in which a tutor was required for an only son. It was finally agreed that he should occupy this situation soon after the close of his College course. This arrangement arose, not out of any change in his mind respecting the work of the gospel, but was acceded to, with a view to satisfy his friends, and finally to gain their consent to his becoming a missionary; and also, in the expectation of being able to promote his own improvement by retirement and study. The following extract from a letter to his mother, will explain his motives, the state of his mind, and a few other particulars:

"ST. ANDREW'S, April 15, 1826.

"MY DEAR MOTHER — I am afraid I have kept you in suspense regarding my plans. I have been waiting in daily expectation of hearing something more definite respecting the situation I wrote about.

"Before I heard of this situation at all, I wrote to Mr. Orme, asking his advice how I ought to proceed after this session, telling him my views regarding missions, and particularly wishing to know the state of the Missionary Society's arrangements. I received his answer, and my father's last letter by the same post. His advice was to write to Mr. Arundel, making application to the Society. You know this was the plan I had purposed to myself, and you may guess that I was in no small perplexity how to act. The prospect of benefitting by classes at Glasgow, my extreme youth and inexperience, and, above all, the wish to show my dear parents that I am willing to acquiesce in their wishes as far as conscience will permit, have induced me to accept of this situation. I hope the Lord has been my guide in this matter.

"Accordingly I communicated my willingness to avail myself of his kindness, to Dr. Chalmers, who wrote to Lord Rosslyn immediately. A letter has come from Lord Rosslyn to Dr. Chalmers, this morning, enclosing a letter from Colonel M——— to his lordship, giving some more information respecting the place. Nothing is said about the salary. I do not expect it will be great, as my charge will be very small, and I am to have the liberty of attending classes.

"I told Dr. Chalmers distinctly to state to Lord Rosslyn that I am a Dissenter, and that if I am near Glasgow, I should like to attend Dr. Wardlaw, or Mr. Ewing. Perhaps this may be an objection to my settling in the family; if so, it is better that it be stated now, than afterwards."

Previously to his joining the family, then on a visit at Lord Rosslyn's, at Dysart House, he proposed a short missionary tour in the Highlands, along with his friend Mr. Adam; but he was taken ill in his father's house, and rendered incapable of any exertion for some weeks. While convalescent he wrote a long letter to an old fellow-student, between whom and himself there appears to have subsisted a very endeared friendship. I mean Herbert Smith, Esq., of Egham, Surrey. The testimony of that gentleman, to the amiable, and Christian character of my beloved friend, and to his high intellectual attainments, corresponds with that of all his other associates. To him John gives an account of some of the plans which had been prosecuted at St. Andrew's, during the preceding winter. In this respect it is particularly interesting, and also for the reference to the simultaneous movements in the Universities.

"PERTH, May 11, 1826.

"MY VERY DEAR FRIEND — I was just going to proceed with an account of the St. Andrew's University Missionary Society, (in which you have always taken so deep an interest,) when I was compelled to leave off, through weakness. To resume the subject then — at our first meeting we had not a very large attendance: we presented the different presents of books which had been received from yourself, Dr. Morrison, Mr. Townley, and other friends of the missionary cause. I then read to the Society that part of your very interesting letter, which directly referred to our association; and, I trust, we have profited by the hints it contained. Votes of thanks were ordered to be transferred to those liberal donors who had made such valuable additions to its library. I took the responsibility of communicating to you this expression of the Society's gratitude. I am ashamed to think that it has not been communicated long, long ere now. I cannot go minutely into details. Suffice it to say, that the Society has prospered even more than in the former session. We were kindly permitted to meet in the old Episcopalian chapel. Dr. Haldane at once accepted the patronage of the Society, and offered any room in St. Mary's we might think convenient, as a place of meeting. One thing I think exceedingly interesting, is, that similar societies have now been formed in all the Universities of Scotland, and a kind of simultaneous movement was made this last session, towards a system of general correspondence. Might we hope that this could be extended to institutions of a similar nature, in the Universities of England? In a letter from the Society in the Glasgow University, they mentioned that they had had some correspondence with a Missionary Association in one of the Colleges of America. It were very desirable (and I think it is not impracticable) to see all the pious young men in our great seminaries of learning, united to each other by this great bond of Christian philanthropy. Perhaps you could do something by opening a channel of correspondence between some of the Colleges in Cambridge, and the Scottish Universities. I expect to spend next winter in Glasgow. I could communicate anything from you on this subject, to the Association there, and it would immediately be circulated among the sister Universities.

"15*th*. There is a new system of religious instruction which has been attempted in St. Andrew's this last session, and which I think is a most efficient system for evangelizing large towns. The plan is very simple. We just inquired after some persons residing in different quarters of the town, who were religiously disposed. We called on these, and requested the favour of a room in their house, for a few of the neighbours to assemble in for religious purposes. We expected a little group of eight or ten persons to assemble, but were astonished to find the attendance increase in some of the stations to fifty or sixty. Many of these *never went to church.* We generally read and explained a passage of Scripture, and read some extracts from such books as we thought were most striking and useful. I have some doubt whether a layman in the Church of England could attempt this; but if the laws of the church and the state allow, I think many a Christian would find ample scope for such employment, in the dark places of your towns and villages. You underderstand, we never called it *preaching;* and accordingly Dr. Haldane gave his consent that the young men in the Established Church should engage in the work. Churchmen and Dissenters all went hand in hand, and we forgot that there was any distinction. And this must be the case more universally, ere the cause of our great Redeemer can go triumphantly forward. Tait has already begun similar meetings in Edinburgh, and some have been commenced here. I do think this a most plausible method for getting at that class of the community who do not attend the public services of the gospel. You know Dr. Chalmers's plan is a little different. He wishes the Christian philanthropist to visit every family. The great objection to this plan, in my estimation, is the difficulty of finding a sufficient number of agents. The Doctor's objection to pulpit instructions, when they stand alone, is, that you are setting up a centre of attraction; this will only draw some of the people, some are not under the influence of the attracting power, and they must be dealt with in another way. You must make an aggressive movement towards them. Before setting the plan I speak of in operation, I asked Dr. Chalmers's opinion of it. He gave his decided approbation to it, although he thought the system of individual visitation a better one, if it could be accomplished. This new plan, however, he thought had a much greater efficacy than common preaching, when alone. Instead of setting up one great centre of attraction; it was like carrying about the magnet, and bringing it near to the iron filings.

"P. S. I am not sure where I may be this summer, but a letter addressed to my father's care, will always find me. I could have written a great deal more, but my writing is so bad that I fear when written across, it is quite unintelligible. I wish I had taken a larger sheet."

From this time I shall do little more than make John his own biographer; a journal which he began to keep more regularly and fully than formerly, and a large mass of letters, will enable me to maintain a tolerably connected narrative, without interposing many remarks of my own. To enable the reader to form some idea of his journal, I shall give the first part of it almost entire, afterwards I shall intersperse a few extracts from it, with his correspondence. As he lived for the most part very retired, no extraordinary incidents can be expected; but his steady and rapid advancement towards the heavenly glory is strongly marked.

"Dysart House, June 3, 1826.

"My journal has now been at a stand for nearly a month, and I think I have experienced the bad effects of neglecting it. Hitherto it has been exclusively, or nearly exclusively, *literary;* and, even in that point of view, extremely meagre, a mere catalogue of the number of pages read and written. May I not, with advantage, extend my plan? I think I have profited in my studies, from taking daily account of my progress. Might not this hold equally in regard to other engagements? I have strong objections to the writing down of religious experiences. Perhaps I am wrong in this. My strongest objection is the fear that these papers may meet the eye of another, and that this consideration might influence me in writing. This might prove a great source of delusion to my own soul. But still, perhaps, I am wrong. The conduct of the most eminent servants of Christ is a strong plea in favour of such journals. I am much pleased with the plan of my dear Henry Craik on this matter. I shall attempt something on his system. If I fail, it matters not. I must just relapse into my old brief summary. But to begin. What have I done last month? Left St. Andrew's in the end of April. Spent a fortnight at home with my relations, and my dear John Adam. Unwell nearly all the time, and prevented by illness from an intended missionary expedition to the Highlands. Came here about the middle of May. Felt the dreariness of having no Christian society. Favoured with an introduction to some of the 'excellent of the earth,' Captain Barclay, Mr. Thompson, &c. I have studied very little since I came here, have felt *unsettled.* This is quite wrong. We should ever be ready for duty, and it is our own fault, if, in all circumstances, we do not find abundance to occupy our time.

"*4th. Sunday evening.*—Read one chapter of the Greek Testament. Found my pupil rather backward in his attendance on my religious instructions. Anything connected with the service of the English Church is most relished by the family. Even the Scriptures seem most acceptable when I propose reading the *lessons for the day.* It is right to humour these prejudices, in imitation of him who became 'all things to all men.' I have heard two very excellent discourses from Mr. Thomas and Mr. Aikenhead, respectively. Visited a Sabbath-school, and addressed the children. I have some fear, that these institutions are not, in all cases, productive of the good that might be expected, for want of more efficient modes of teaching. Committing to memory what they do not understand, can profit the children very little. My second proposal, for holding family worship with the servants, has been received with coolness, but not absolutely negatived. The Lord will open up ways of usefulness for me. Read ninety pages of the Rev. Thomas Scott's Life, exceedingly interesting.

"*5th.* A very idle day. I find I cannot study to advantage without a *plan.* I shall lay it down as a maxim, however short time I may stay in any place, to have my hours allotted specifically to different engagements as far as such an arrangement may be practicable. For want of this, I have lost much of the time I have spent at Dysart. Attended a missionary prayer meeting this evening, but was in a very cold and careless frame of mind. I have felt for some days, as if a veil were drawn over the things of another world. I fear I am indulging habits of sloth and luxury. In what am I *denying myself?* Read twenty pages of Scott's Life. Was rather astonished at his idea, (expressed in the narrative after his conversion,) that even when a Socinian, his prayers were '*spiritual enough*' to find acceptance with God. Can a prayer be listened to by God, which is presumptuously offered up without any regard to the Mediator whom he has appointed? When searching after the truth, Scott read none but religious books for three years. Afterwards he returned to general reading, and even felt a pleasure in perusing the classics, and other works of taste. I have read since I came, four hundred pages of Godwin's History of the Commonwealth. He advocates the cause of the Puritans in their political conduct. He dislikes the pompous and persecuting spirit of the prelacy. He seems to like Presbyterianism worse, (as it then existed,) as having all the intolerance of Episcopacy, without its splendor. And he gives unqualified praise to the Independents of these times, as the great champions of unrestrained liberty, civil and religious.

"*6th.* With my pupil three hours in the forenoon. One hour walking, and one hour bathing. This runs away with a great part of the day. I am much pleased with my pupil at present. His disposition is amiable, and his faculties acute. His desire for knowledge is very great. He has been amusing himself to-night in *making a universe* with little balls of wax stuck upon pins. I feel very thankful for a situation, in many respects, so agreeable as the one I occupy. But I feel I am doing little actual service to the cause of my Lord. Read thirty pages of Scott's Life. His prayers for his relations were eminently answered. I have felt this an encouragement to greater fervency in prayer for those who are so dear to me according to the flesh. And yet, the fact that I derive encouragement from this instance of an answer to prayer, is a proof of the weakness of my faith on the promises of God. If I sufficiently believed them, I should not need particular instances of their fulfilment, to encourage me. Can anything be surer than the promise of God? Finished the first volume of Godwin's Commonwealth. Very little conversation, and that exceedingly trifling and general. What can I do, in my present circumstances, for the good of this family? The Lord direct me! Read two chapters of the Greek Testament. Bed at eleven o'clock.

"8*th*. Yesterday I was so fatigued, that I wrote none in my journal; and to-night I have a much better excuse for putting it off, in a very painful headache; but I must cultivate habits of regularity, and write something, however short. Yesterday, I completed my eighteenth year. Hitherto hath the Lord brought me; and, in spite of much wickedness and ingratitude, he continues to bless me. How little have I done! Hitherto I have made my youth an excuse for much inactivity! Will this be an excuse at the bar of God? I have been much troubled these some days, with abominably sinful thoughts. Lord, cleanse thou me from secret faults; and O keep back thy servant from presumptuous sins. Read part of Scott's Life.—Much struck with his remarks on practical preaching, and the unpopularity to which his own system exposed him."

"TENNOCH SIDE, NEAR GLASGOW.

"14*th*. Arrived here night before last.—My journal was neglected yesterday, in consequence of my papers being mislaid.—Left Dysart on Saturday morning, and arrived in Leith a few hours after, where I stayed till Monday afternoon.—A very unprofitable visit.—Some conversations with my kind and respected friends, Mr. and Mrs. Alexander, I remember with pleasure, but scarcely anything else of my friends, whom I had an opportunity of seeing. I feel very comfortable here, and have much to make me thankful to the great Father of our mercies. Although I am disappointed in one great object, (attendance on classes in Glasgow), which I had in view on coming here, yet I trust the Lord has directed me. May I be enabled, faithfully, to fulfil the important duties of my station, and to devote every moment of my time to the service of my God! — Read Shakspeare's Midsummer Night's Dream. — Never read a whole play of this great poet before. Some exquisitely fine passages; and, throughout, the whole admirably true to nature. But how much that is revolting, even to a mind so partially sanctified as mine! Can it be right in a Christian to travel over pages filled with vain imaginations, swearing, and often gross obscenity, in order to arrive at some beautiful passage, which, after all, can only gratify or improve his taste? The pearls are indeed fine, and present a great temptation; but, after all, they are not worth the diving for, or at least, the ocean that covers them is too perilous to be needlessly encountered by so feeble an adventurer as I. Read two chapters in the Greek Testament. What a blessing that we have sublimer and purer joys than those that are afforded by the bright, but transient flashes of unsanctified wit, or the glare of a powerful, yet polluted imagination!

"*Thursday.* — Rose at six — read one chapter of the Greek Testament. I am engaged with my pupil four hours a day, viz. from seven to eight, and from ten to eleven, A. M.; and from one to two, and from five to six, P. M. My books are yet in Glasgow, and this has been an excuse for idleness. Read another play of Shakspeare's. More to disgust, and less to gratify in this, than in the last. I cannot read these plays without being injured by them. Wrote a letter to my dear Nesbit. Received one from my dear father. Have sat a considerable time this evening trying to make verses. Succeeded in manufacturing one stanza. I may say with the Rev. Thomas Scott, 'God has not made me a poet.' And I hope I shall profit from his observation, that he was thankful for never having attempted to make himself one.

"I almost despair of being able to introduce profitable conversation. How difficult to fix that precise line of duty, which timorous indecision dares not approach, and which rash, unthinking zeal is sure to overstep!"

"TENNOCH SIDE, June 30, 1826.

"MY VERY DEAR CRAIK — This is a solitary place. I am all alone. The sweets of friendship, and the joys of Christian fellowship, are to me now associated with the remembrance of the days that are gone. But yet, I am not alone; God is here. And should duty 'command me to the furthest verge of the green earth, to distant, barbarous shores,' *He* is *there* too. The 'communion of the saints,' is, indeed, a delightful privilege; but what is it, when compared with that far higher privilege, which change of circumstances cannot affect; even that 'fellowship which is with the Father, and with his Son, Jesus Christ.' Every shifting scene of life that passes before me, convinces me more and more, that happiness has a very slight dependence on our external circumstances. They may add to it, or diminish it; but they can neither *give* it, *nor take it away*. Mere animal gratification is enjoyed nearly equally by all classes; all are equally subject to disease, and if the rich seem to enjoy more of the good things of this life than others, they only *seem* to do so. Luxury has deprived them of the comforts of life, and has converted its superfluities into comfortless necessaries. Even intellectual happiness, I believe to be more generally and equally diffused, than is commonly imagined. But the truth is, there is no true happiness without the enjoyment of God's favour. How true is it, that '*his favour is life;*' for without it, life deserves not the name; it is but a living death. '*Immo vero, ii vivunt, qui ex corporum vinculis tanquam e carcere, evolaverunt; nostra vero quæ dicitur vita, mors est.*' *We* are more highly favoured than the ancient philosopher who wrote these words. Even here we may have glimpses of the celestial happiness. *Eternal life* is begun on earth. It is true, we may not walk in the freedom of spiritual enlargement, till we have put off these vile bodies; but even within their prison-house there may be many an alleviation of our sufferings; we may be freed from those fetters that galled us sore, and deprived us even of the little freedom which the bounds of a prison-house might permit. We may be gaining new victories over *the devil, the world, and the flesh*, even while here. Let it be our earnest endeavour to maintain this holy warfare within our breasts; and while we drink freely of the fountain of life, let us not forget to present its vivifying waters to that world, which is '*dead* in trespasses and sins.'

"I have been looking over what I have written, and find it is not like a letter at all. But I need make no apologies to you. I am here, nearly eight miles from Glasgow, and have been there only twice. My pupil went there yesterday with the family; and, as there was room for me in the carriage, I went in the morning, and returned in the evening. Of course, I had not much time to see the town. I looked into the area of the college; a fine old, substantial building. Their library, which was the only room I went into, does not seem to be as fine as ours. *Ours!* did I say? But you know what I mean. The cathedral is a venerable building, though somewhat disfigured by modern additions. The statue of our revered Knox stands on a neighbouring hill. Glasgow is blessed with evangelical ministers in all denominations. There is an institution I visited last night, with the plan of which I was very much pleased. It is a sort of religious coffee-room. There is a large hall, where about twenty different religious institutions hold their meetings; and a reading room below, where the Reports and other periodical publications, connected with all the religious societies of the day, are to be found. A book lay on the table, for the insertion of hints, or inquiries on any subject connected with the great interests of Christianity. In this I found some remarks in the hand-writing of 'our excellent Chalmers.' I have had an introduction to the nearest parish minister; but have seen very little of him yet. He told me that his church was much too small for the parish, — and that he believed the greater number of his parishioners were growing up *like heathens.*"

"TENNOCH SIDE, July 5, 1826.

"MY VERY DEAR FRIEND — I begin to feel anxious to hear from some of you, although I believe the agreement was, that I should write first. I am here as much shut out from the world, at least, from what was *the world* to me, as I could be in the deserts of Africa, or the islands of Japan. I write, chiefly to beg you to send me a long letter, — it is all of friendship I can now enjoy. You will not expect much from this wilderness. I have little to write about that can interest you. But why should I say so, when there is a theme, which is ever delightful to the mind of a Christian, and needs not novelty to give it interest. Yes, we have a joy which the world knows not, and which no changes in our earthly circumstances can at all impair. The dearest earthly friends may be removed from us, but there is a 'friend that sticketh closer than a brother.' Here I have no Christian friend; and sometimes my spirits sink very low, when I think on other days. But these are sinful thoughts. 'The Lord gave, and the Lord hath taken away; blessed be the name of the Lord.' Perhaps some path of usefulness may be pointed out to me; but at present, I see little probability of doing anything, except with my pupil. I have been in Glasgow twice. I met Mr. Erskine there, as well as Mr. Ewing, &c. All are against my being a missionary, but I have heard no arguments against it that seem to me at all conclusive. What is doing in Edinburgh? Have you any intercourse with the few St. Andrian friends that are in the great city? Alas! for our little circle. It is now sadly broken up, and we never shall form a little circle again. One of our number is in the south of England, another in the north of Scotland, and all scattered abroad. The fragments of the little community are in Edinburgh. The '*tria*' are there; but, alas! they are no longer '*juncta in uno*.'* But, I hope my lamentations are groundless. Have you no combinations for plans of usefulness either among yourselves, or of a more extensive

* He alludes to the St. Andrew's University Magazine, which had this motto.

nature? Something was talked of when I was in Edinburgh. Has it been accomplished? When do you go to Kirkliston? Let me hear particularly of your operations there. There will be full scope for your most strenuous exertions. Can you suggest to me any practicable scheme of usefulness? Do favour me with a long letter."

Determined not to remain idle, notwithstanding the obscurity and difficulty of his situation, after very considerable exertion, he succeeded in collecting a number of young men together, and for their benefit, prepared a very excellent address. As it fully explains the nature of the meeting which he proposed, it may suggest to some others the importance of making similar attempts, by which great good might be effected.*

About this time he appears to have laboured under severe mental depression. Of the cause of this no doubt can now be entertained. It was, doubtless, symptomatic of the insidious disease which was appointed by God to be the messenger of his dismission. That it was cherished by the intense working of his mind, by his seclusion from that kind of society which was congenial to his feelings, and by anxiety respecting the accomplishment of his much desired object, I feel equally assured. I think it right to give the following extract from his journal, which will explain some of the allusions in his letters.

"*July* 18*th*. Rose at seven. Have suffered excessively to-day from mental depression, and could assign no specific cause for it. I am half-inclined to ascribe it to

* See Appendix L.

the immediate agency of Satan, or some of his emissaries. The Lord has been graciously pleased to restore me to tranquillity; and I remember the former part of the day as I would a terrific dream. I had the opportunity of going in the carriage to Hamilton, and was in hopes that the fresh breeze, and the laughing face of nature, would dispel the gloomy darkness within my breast. But it was all in vain; the malady raged with greater violence, so as almost to make me dread real madness, and to recall to my mind a fearful night of distraction last winter. I have besought the Lord earnestly that this might depart from me; and I believe that I owe my present tranquillity to his gracious condescension in listening to my prayers. I feel, what my pride likes ill to admit, that I am a very feeble creature; weak, not only in body, but still weaker in mind! Is this a fit character for a missionary? In this work I shall soon fail, except the Lord strengthen me. But *even I* may say, 'I can do *all things* through Christ strengthening me.' After all, I have forced myself to go through nearly all my regular studies to-day.

"*Friday.*—Have discovered much to-night of the cursed pride, fickleness, and vanity of my heart. Did those who esteem me most, know me as I do myself, they would abhor me. I do abhor myself. Spent half an hour in prayer, in severe mental conflict. But even for this conviction of sin, I will be thankful. It is well to know the worst, although I fear I do not know the worst yet. '*Who can understand his errors?*'

"I know the remedy; and, blessed be God, despair has not yet barred the way to it, although I fear, from the little effect my *supposed* application to the gospel has yet produced, that I know not how to use the remedy. The

Lord can teach me. The workings of my mind have been severely painful for some days, although in very different ways. Perhaps the Lord has given me over, like his ancient servant, of whom I have been reading, to be tempted of Satan. Has the Mediator 'prayed for me, that my faith fail not?' I will believe that all this is for good. May it lead me to know my own utter weakness, that so I may make the Lord my strength! Then I may say with Paul, 'when I am weak, then am I strong.'"

"TENNOCH SIDE, July 17, 1826.

"MY DEAR TRAIL — I believe, in regard to Christian society, your circumstances very nearly resemble my own: and if, in these circumstances, you feel as keenly as I sometimes do, I know that a letter from an old companion will not be unacceptable, even though it contain 'nothing new.' Accept of my sincere thanks for the notes of introduction you left for my friend and me. I was sorry that my short stay in Edinburgh permitted me to pay but a very short visit to Wellwood Lodge. A Polish missionary was staying there when I called, with whom I conversed a little. I was prevented from accompanying our friend, John Adam, on his missionary tour, in consequence of illness. I believe he enjoyed it very much. I am now fairly settled, within eight miles of Glasgow, removed from every Christian friend who might excite and encourage me; and sometimes I acknowledge I feel very much depressed: but the Lord is ever near. If I feel so faint-hearted here, I know not how I shall endure the living solitude of a city of idolaters, or the extreme dreariness of a savage desert. But, 'through

Christ strengthening me I can do all things.' What plans of usefulness have you set on foot, since I saw you? Can you suggest anything to me, that I can accomplish here? Have you any particular plans in instructing your pupils, which you can communicate, for I feel myself quite a novice in the art of teaching; and I am aware that there is no small responsibility connected with duties, that have such an immense influence in forming a mind which is to exist for ever; and which, in the remotest ages of its eternity, perhaps, is to bear, in some respects, the form of that mould which was impressed on it in the earliest years of its existence. Have you been thinking more of missions? I find everybody dissuades and discourages me, urging the great wants of our own country. I think I feel the claims of our own land as strongly as some who urge them against my plans. But still this does not prevent me from feeling the immense argumentative force of the simple fact, that nothing has yet been done for heathen nations, proportional to their vast extent; and nothing to fulfil the wide command of our Lord. I have had two letters from Captain Felix, pressing on my attention the state of Ireland. By this time, our dear friend Nesbit has applied to the Scottish Missionary Society. I trust that more of our little circle will follow his example. How unfortunate are the debates about the apocryphal question! But why should I say *unfortunate*, as if they could happen without the knowledge of the great Head of the Church.

"18*th*. I have been reading the former part of my sheet which was written last night, and find it is a very dull and careless scrawl. I wish I could send you something better; but the fact is, I have been labouring under very uncommon mental depression, which renders me unfit for doing anything as I could wish. I have had a drive in the carriage to Hamilton to-day, and feel rather better. I know you are never troubled with this sort of affliction, and may be disposed to laugh at it; but I can assure you, it is ten-fold more distressing than bodily disease. The latter often adds to spiritual comfort; the former generally destroys it. But I am ashamed of having said so much about my weaknesses; and assuredly I should not have adverted to the subject, were it not as a plea for an early communication from you. Send me something to cheer and console me. Direct me to the great objects of eternity, and stir me up to do something in the cause of the Lord. Although I am sometimes thus depressed, it is not always so. The Lord has been very kind to me since I came here. I have been *forced* to seek all my enjoyments in communion with God. It is well, when we hasten after other lovers, that He, who will have our whole heart, should hedge up our way. And when he leads us into the *wilderness*, and dries up many a source of what seemed *holy* enjoyment, it is often not to punish, but to bless us, to 'speak comfortably' to us. We do well, my friend, to examine whether the Lord alone be the object of our affections. When surrounded by pious friends, who are ready to praise, or, at least, to esteem us for our zeal in furthering the interests of religion, it is difficult to determine the nature of our motives. Those who went before our Saviour in triumph to Jerusalem, crying Hosanna, &c., were probably afterwards found consenting to his death; and even the boldest and most devoted of his chosen few, 'forsook him and fled.' Are we ready to follow the Lord through *bad* as well as through good report? Have we ever yet been put to the trial? Have you read Samuel

Rutherford's letters? I have been delighted and humbled by the perusal. How much of heaven may be enjoyed on earth, if we will but care to seek for it. I feel that I know nothing yet of Christ, or of fellowship with him. Write very soon to your affectionate brother."

"TENNOCH SIDE, July 22, 1826.

"MY DEAR ANNE—Your verses pleased me much; and with what else I have seen of your first attempts at composition, lead me fondly to hope, that talents have been bestowed on you, which, with due culture, and persevering application, may render you, I will not say *accomplished*, for that is a vain thing, as the term is generally used; but to use an apparently humbler, yet, in reality, far more honourable term, talents that may render you *useful.* I say not this to make you proud, but to humble you, and to encourage you to persevere. You know very little yet, you have much to learn. I may just hint, that in your letter, I can observe a deficiency in one of the MOST REQUISITE of all literary acquisitions. You know what I mean. But in the present case, the hurry in which your letter has evidently been written, is a sufficient excuse. I like your verses. The idea in the fourth verse, I think, is truly poetical. But I would not have you aim at being a poetess, my sister. Make it an amusement if you will, or a means of acquiring correctness and facility of expression, but do not make it your AIM. The most brilliant acquirements are not the most useful. Let me remind you, my dear Anne, that you and I are born to fill humble stations in this world, (and God be thanked, it is so; the humblest are the happiest.) Do not aim, then, at anything above your station. Do not court the society of the rich and the gay; for, *comparatively*, I may apply these terms even to the little sphere in which you move; but choose your companions from those who have the true riches of knowledge, and (if I may add a qualification you may not easily find) *sterling piety*. The *manners* of your companions should not be overlooked; and, by this expression, I do not so much mean the knowledge, or ready repetition of a few *kind-looking* phrases, which even the most *unkind* can learn, as that amiable and obliging disposition, which is the politeness of the heart. In the present state of society, however, a person who wishes to be truly agreeable, will see the necessity of attending to a few of those *forms* of kindness which pass current in the world. I did not mean to write so many advices; but now that I have begun, I will plead the authority, I will rather say, the affection of a brother, as an excuse for adding some more. Let me entreat you to cultivate *domestic virtues*. The Bible bids us not only love and obey, but also *honour* our parents. Be particularly careful to remember this, especially in regard to our dear mother, to whom your little services may now render considerable assistance. Above all, my very dear sister, let me entreat you to remember that we were not made merely to figure for a little on the stage of this passing world. This life is but the infancy of an eternal existence; and yet, here the choice must be made, that shall render all that is worth calling the life of an immortal creature, *perfectly happy*, or *perfectly wretched*. You think you know the truths of the gospel, my sister. Do you feel its influence? Do not be even too sure that you understand the message of glad tidings in the Bible. Many who now think they understand, will find hereafter that they have mistaken its meaning. But, O do remember! it is not enough to understand. Examine whether Christ, and his atonement *alone*, be all your salvation. It is *easy* to *mistake*. We are never more apt to sleep the sleep of a security, from which eternal death alone will awake us, than when guarded from gross temptations by protecting friends, accustomed from infancy to correct, or at least, *seemingly* correct views of the gospel. My dear sister, as you value your happiness, beware of a misplaced hope of heaven. I do not cease to pray that the Lord would make you his own. I should think my prayers in part answered, did I know that you had been constrained to pray with *earnestness* for yourself."

"August 2, 1826.

"My very Dear Brother — They say there is more pleasure in hope, than in actual enjoyment; and, perhaps, this is the reason why I have not written to you sooner. You know I used to have a great aversion to letter writing; but now that it is almost the only kind of Christian intercourse that is left me, you may guess that I regard it with very different feelings. For a week past I have been cheering my solitary hours with the thought, that I was just about to unbosom freely all my feelings to my dear John Adam, (a luxury, which is not the least precious privilege of true friendship), and day after day, some little trifle has seemed a sufficient reason for putting off; while I believed the true cause of the delay has been, the desire to indulge this pleasing expectation a little longer. And now that I have sat down to write, I frankly acknowledge that I have little or nothing to say, — at least, in the shape of news. I left Dysart too late to see you again in Edinburgh, whence I proceeded to this place of exile, where I have now counted five or six tardy weeks of unvaried sameness, excepting one or two visits to Glasgow and an occasional walk to Old Monkland Manse. You know me too well to require me to tell you how I feel, without a single Christian friend near. The harp has been often out of tune; and sometimes, I have feared that its strings were about to break, when the Lord has again tuned it to his own praise. Yes, my dear friend, I have seen much of the deceitfulness of my own heart since I came here. I thought I could leave all, and live happy in a solitary desert, for the sake of Christ. But I find that much of my happiness was drawn from cisterns, and not from the life-giving fountain. And now that the Lord has, in mercy, broken these, to lead me to himself, I have been ready to weep as if my all were lost. I fear I have mistaken love to Christians for love to Christ. I feel more reconciled to this banishment, when I think that it may be intended to wean me from earth, and to fit me more for the missionary life. I have hopes that I may be honoured to be useful to my dear pupil. He is a most interesting boy; in our daily reading of the Scriptures, he makes inquiries which delight me, and sometimes astonish me. All things are possible with God.

"*Monday evening*—The above was written on Saturday night, and your welcome epistle was put into my hand yesterday morning. Your serious charges of carelessness might require to be more seriously met, than in the above nondescript rhapsody, which you see had anticipated them; but too much of my sheet is now filled, to leave any space for apologies. I leave you to make them for me. I am rejoiced at your intention of sending a paper on missions to the Evangelical Magazine. It has a most extensive circulation. My conscience has been sorely reproaching me for my negligence on this subject. I have been partly terrified out of the idea of attempting publication, from the decided opposition our sentiments on this subject have met with, when I have laid them before those, whom I have, from infancy, looked up to as men mighty in the Scriptures. Do not mistake me; my own convictions are by no means weakened. Every prayer deepens their impression. And at times of closer communion with God, a brighter light seems to be shed on the path before me. My own conscience must be my guide; but I have discovered so much of my own fickleness, and weakness of mind, that I do fear to propose my sen iments as rules of conduct to others. 'Instead of being a teacher, I have need that one teach me what are the first principles of the oracles of Christ.' I have only begun to discover my real character; and I honestly believe, that did any of my friends know me as I know myself, they would be utterly disgusted with me, and scarcely believe me a Christian. But what has this to do with the subject? — Much. When I think of myself, a poor weak-minded boy, — the creature of emotion, and almost the slave of circumstances, entertaining opinions different from all my friends in Christ, however strongly they are impressed on my own mind, I have great misgivings when I think of presenting them to others. I am glad to have *one*, at least, who agrees with me. Our comparison of the present generation in our land, to the Jews in the days of the apostles, is very much disliked. The supposition, that we are called to imitate the apostles in going to the Gentiles, Mr. E. thinks *quite enthusiastic*. I like your plan much. It is very comprehensive. I hope it will be admitted, but I hardly *expect* it. I have *no* Christian friends here; but it is all well. I am *forced* to seek closer communion with God. Yes, forced. How just is your idea of the *refuge*. I have been, at times, apt to murmur at being sent here; but I am sure it is for good. I have seen practically illustrated, that man, at his best estate, is altogether vanity. I have seen more of the wickedness of my own heart; but more too of the preciousness and sufficiency of the Saviour. My studies have all a bearing on the Bible; and, I think, I study as much here as ever I have done any where."

"August 10, 1826.

"My very Dear Friend — I am really ashamed of not writing sooner; and yet it has not been for want of inclination. I have been waiting for an opportunity to send; and I write this, expecting that I may be able to send it by Miss Cathcart. It is not often that a day has passed without remembering you before the Lord. Now that I have no Christian friend (indeed no friend at all) near me, I find it, indeed, a delightful exercise, to meet my brethren and sisters in the Lord at a throne of grace. You have been long a prisoner, and I am now an exile. Yes; I am indeed banished from all that I love in this world; and I sometimes think that the Lord may be thus preparing me for the trials of the missionary life, by debarring me the privilege of Christian intercourse. I am often *much depressed;* and this convinces me that I have not yet given my whole heart to God. I think I can see that I have been sent here for good. The Lord often leads us into the wilderness, to speak comfortably to us. He breaks the cisterns we have hewed out for ourselves, to lead us to the life-giving fountain. It is perhaps well for us, when communion with God is our only enjoyment; and so it is with me from necessity.

"I was glad to hear that you had had some little respite, so as to be able to wait upon God in the assembly of his people. How amiable are his tabernacles! What must heaven be, where the Sabbath is eternal, and the temple is the Lord himself! — 'Yet a little while,' (in your case a *very* little while at the longest), 'and he that shall come, will come, and will not tarry.'

"I have been reading Samuel Rutherford's letters of late, and have been much delighted with them. What advances he had made in the way of holiness! I think, in the present day, Christians are apt to be content with too little. There might be more of that knowledge of God and of his Son, which is eternal life, — even in this world, if we would but seek for it more earnestly. It is not enough to enter the strait gate, we must also walk in the narrow way. Sanctification is part of our salvation. And hence it is, that our most gracious Father sees meet to visit his children (as you can testify) with manifold afflictions and temptations, that the trial of their faith being much more precious than that of perishable gold, might be found unto praise, and honour, and glory, at the appearance of Jesus Christ. I doubt not, you can testify that the furnace of affliction is a refining surface.

"My dear friend, I should value a letter from you very much. My experience in the Christian life amounts to nothing more than a discovery of my wretchedness, and a *wish* for something better. I can write little to comfort you, — I can only complain of short-coming. My own deadness and indifference, often make me doubt whether I have yet tasted that the Lord is gracious. I know not anything so calculated to confirm and strengthen the faith of an infant Christian, as the testimony of an aged saint, — especially an aged sufferer, who can tell that all the promises of God are yea, and amen. It is true, our faith should need the aid of no auxiliary evidence, when we have the promise, — nay, the oath of Him who cannot lie. But it does need it. I feel my faith often mingled with distrust. And even when I can say 'I believe,' I have need to prefer the petition, 'Lord, help my unbelief.' If you are so much recovered, as I have some reason to hope, from what I have heard, perhaps you may write a few lines of encouragement to

"Your most affectionate brother in the Lord."

"August 15, 1826.

"My Dear Friend — I thank you for your kind and undeserved letter, and rejoice to hear of your attempt to illuminate the dark places of our own land. I am anxious to hear of the success of your plans. I have been led in the very consideration of the missionary question, to regard more attentively the state of our own country as to religious knowledge. It has been the increasing argument of my friends, against my intention of going to the heathen, that there is much yet to be done at home. The force of this argument, I feel to a certain extent; but I find it is apt to be urged sometimes, by those very persons who are slumbering on as if nothing were to be done at all. There is much to be done at home; and there is need for very vigorous exertion. There are many, in this nominally Christian country, who are quite ignorant of what true Christianity is. This is, indeed, a dreadful thought, when we consider how many *true* Christians are scattered over the land. Take the case of some deadly bodily disease, (an illustration which has been so often put), and think how we should look upon him who could calmly sit still, and see his neighbour or his townsman drop into the jaws of death, while he was acquainted with a remedy, whose application, experience had proved to be a certain cure. Would it be an excuse for this indifference, that an unaccountable prejudice existed against the remedy in question, or that it was one of the fearful symptoms of the disorder, that the unhappy victim imagined himself in good health? Suppose even further, that dispensaries were established through the land, where the medicine was distributed *gratis*, to all who chose to apply. (But, alas! I almost had forgot that in order to complete the analogy here, I must further suppose, that at *many*, nay at the *greater number* of these dispensaries, a *counterfeit* drug was given for the real elixir.) Would humanity think it too much, in such circumstances, to walk from one scene of wretchedness to another, and earnestly recommend to the unhappy sufferers, the use of a specific of such sovereign virtue? Is it true, that a malady is actually raging in our own land, — in our own town, in our own neighbour's house—it may be in our own family, — a malady so dreadful, that the whole sum of human wretchedness, in all its sad forms of bodily pain or mental anguish, can give but a faint idea of it, and is indeed, but one of its *least fearful* consequences? Is it true, I say, that we believe such a fell disorder to be raging at our very doors; and believe, too, that we have discovered a sovereign antidote to its baneful influence, and yet scarce put forth a finger to administer the balm of life to our fellow-sufferers? I do think, my dear sir, that *private Christians* must do more than they do, if they would stand clear of the blood of those who perish around them. They are not called to minister in public, — but might they not do much in preaching the Gospel *from house to house?* In the supposed case of bodily disease, would it be an excuse for indifference or neglect on the part of any one who had the means and opportunity of usefulness, that there were *physicians* in the land, whose *business* it was to attend to the sick? And is not the case quite parallel? I did not intend to fill my sheet in this way; but when I get into a subject, I often find it difficult to leave it. I forget that I am writing a letter, and not an essay. I have attempted to get some people to meet with me here; but there is no village quite near, and it being harvest, it has quite failed in the meantime; but I mean to make another attempt after the harvest is over. I am confined, in the meantime, to private visiting, and *the distribution of tracts.* This, I think, a means of usefulness, which ought to be neglected by none who would attend to the injunction, — 'In the morning sow thy seed,' &c. I have thought a good deal of Ireland of late. It has strong claims; still, I think the heathen have stronger."

"August 16, 1826.

"MY DEAR FRIEND — It has not been forgetfulness, or want of inclination that has kept me from writing sooner. I have often thought of writing; but I feel, that the whole favour of this correspondence is on your side, for I have little to communicate that can be interesting to *you.* My only motive for troubling you with a postage, would have

18

been the hope of eliciting a letter from you in return; and this, I thought too selfish a motive to allow myself to be influenced by it. But, at your request, I will write to you, as the desire to comply with this will be a sufficient apology for an uninteresting letter. I am here quite retired from the world. Colonel M——— sees very little company, and even with that little, I can mix as little as I choose. I dine, *in general*, with my pupil, (at my own desire,) and spend nearly the whole day in my study. This state of seclusion has its advantages and its disadvantages too. There is much time for the study of one's own heart, and for the contemplation of an unseen world. But the mind is apt to prey too much on itself. There is none of that reciprocal sympathy, which is so delightful; which, by dividing our griefs, can almost remove our sorrow; and, by partaking our happiness, does not diminish but multiplies our joy. I have no one here who is like-minded with me; and in these circumstances, my spirits sometimes sink very low. I know this is very sinful, for God is here, and the access to his throne is here as free as in the bosom of Christian society. This, indeed, is my only enjoyment;

"'That were a grief I could not bear,
Didst thou not hear and answer prayer;
But a prayer-hearing, answering God,
Supports me under every load.'

"Sometimes when I enjoy a nearer approach to God, I can, indeed, feel that the loss of Christian fellowship is more than made up; but, in seasons of coldness and indifference, there is none to stir me up, and *nothing* that can give comfort. But it is well that it is so. It is well to be *compelled* to have continual recourse to a throne of grace. How sinful for a Christian ever to think of despondency, with such glorious hopes, and such precious promises to encourage him. But sin will damp the most glorious hopes, and unbelief will render unavailing the most precious promises. Perfect happiness can be attained only by the attainment of perfect holiness: while sin wars in the members, there must be a want of enjoyment. I feel that it is sin which separates between my soul and God. I am sometimes discouraged to think that I have now seemed to myself a believer for a considerable time, and yet I look in vain for a progress in holiness and likeness to God If I have advanced at all, it has been in the discovery of my own utter worthlessness. I *do* feel more than ever, that I am poor, and miserable, and wretched, and blind, and naked. O that the Lord would discover to me more abundantly the riches of his grace, and let me feel more the presence of that Comforter, who is assuredly with me, if I have not received the grace of God in vain.

"I have few opportunities of usefulness here; and this is sometimes a cause of sinful discouragement. I attempted a meeting, which failed, owing to the hurry of the harvest! I have visited most of the cottages near, and distributed tracts, in which employment my little pupil is very willing to assist me. I have discovered one house of mourning, a family that has been much afflicted; there is a willingness to listen to divine things. I went with a person last Sabbath, who preached on an outside stair, in one of the lanes of Glasgow. I confess that it was not without trembling, and some degree of reluctance, that I consented to conclude the service by prayer. The people who gathered around us, I am convinced, cannot be reached in any other way. O! to be willing to be accounted the off-scouring of all things for Christ's sake. I have seen Mr. Burnet, and have promised to take Ireland into consideration, in making up my mind as to the course of life by which I can most glorify God. I still feel the claims of the heathen to be the strongest, although some very highly respected friends here, think I might be more useful at home. I trust my only wish is, to know the will of God."

The following extracts are from various letters, written to his friend, William Scott Moncrieff, in the months of July and August.

"From what you say of your friend, I suppose he has made an engagement with Mr. G——. I trust it will turn out for the mutual benefit of himself and his pupils; indeed, why should I say, I trust? (which is always an expression of some degree of distrust;) we know that all things work together for the good of them that love God. I rejoice to hear of your intended return to St. Andrew's; you must stir up the embers of the flame that has been kindled. There is much to be done, my dear friend, everywhere; and I think every Christian, however obscure, must feel in some degree with the apostle, that there is a woe pronounced against him, if he publish not the joyful intelligence with which heaven has favoured him. It is well that death should sometimes deprive us of a familiar acquaintance, or a dear relative; for the death of thousands whom we have never seen, or at least never known, has been scarcely sufficient to prove to us, that we *may* die; and all the warnings we receive fail of practically convincing us that we *must*. How difficult to conceive the true ratio of the finite to the infinite, of this brief life to that never-ending existence into which it ushers us! And, if difficult to conceive, O, how difficult practically to feel it! There is something delightfully pleasing in the 'little while' (ὅσον ὅσον) of the New Testament, if we are waiting for our Lord; but, if careless and indifferent, or afraid of his coming, how alarming the idea, that 'the Lord is at hand!' Let us gird up the loins of our mind. Let us devote all our time to the service of our Master; 'now is our salvation nearer, than when we believed.' Our friends are parting from us on every side, and we are scattered over the wide world. It is all well; 'this is not your rest.' Let our hopes rest on nothing short of heaven. It is true, that the communion of the saints on earth resembles the intercourse of just men made perfect; but O, what a resemblance! How unlike these grovelling souls to the spirits around the throne! And these corruptible bodies, how vile compared with those immortal forms, which shall be fashioned like the glorious body of the omnipotent Sovereign of the universe! And even our communion with God *here*, how distant, how much interrupted by sin, or obscured by unbelief! How few, and far between the visits of our Saviour's love, when we think of that place where they 'cease not day and night to praise him;' and where they have no need of a temple, for 'the Lord God and the Lamb are the temple thereof.' Let us hold fast our confidence, and run with patience, looking unto Jesus; and, ere a few more years have rolled over us, we shall join that 'multitude which no man can number.'

"You could not have sent me anything more appropriate than Stewart's Discourses on the Advent. You know me too well to need to be told how I felt when separated from you all, and without a single individual to whom I could speak with freedom on the subjects nearest my heart. Mr. Stewart's book I have found a delightful companion. If I can guess at his peculiar views of the Redeemer's advent, through the veil of modesty which almost conceals them, I am scarcely prepared entirely to agree with him. I have been so accustomed to dwell with pleasure on those brighter times to which prophecy seems to point, that the bare possibility that the Lord may come to-day, or to-morrow, seems to blast all these delightful hopes; 'a multitude, which no man can number, must first be gathered out of every tribe, and kindred.' Still, as Mr. Stewart observes, this may be very soon accomplished. Oh, that we may be looking for, and hastening on, the coming of the day of God!

"I have a great dislike to writing letters, but nothing gives me greater pleasure than to receive them. I guess that this is pretty nearly the case with some of my friends, and therefore a consideration of the golden rule should lead me to like the task of letter-writing better. I am most particularly anxious to hear from my friends, since I came to this solitary place; and a friendly letter, always pleasing, will now be doubly sweet. The words, and the looks of friendship I cannot now enjoy. Its written communications are all that are left to me. How unthankful we are ever apt to be! What a privilege is it that we can convey our thoughts to an absent friend! Without the noble invention of writing, a few miles would separate us more effectually from our friends, than half the circumference of the globe can, possessed as we are of this wonderful medium of intercourse. But, after all, epistolary correspondence is but a poor substitute for personal intercourse. We have symbols to express our thoughts, but we have no written characters that can express that peculiar vividness of impression, or tenderness of feeling which is conveyed by the eye, the features, and the very tone of voice of a present friend. The words of a letter are in some respects dead, like the characters that represent them, while the words of the friend with whom we converse, and even the ideas, which these words express, seem to borrow life and loveliness from the lips and countenance that give them utterance. I have been writing several other letters to-day; and I believe that, in all of them, I have been mourning over the loss of friends, and lingering on the recollections of other days. And yet I feel that it is wrong to do so. This is a world of change; and, if our affections are set on any, even the worthiest of the objects that flit before us, our happiness will be but short-lived. If we be risen with Christ, let us set our affections on things above. If we would faithfully serve our Master, we must not look for a life of ease here, or even of enjoyment; we must 'endure hardness as good soldiers of Jesus Christ.' I do little else than study, and walk with my pupil, who is a very interesting boy. I have only been to ride once; I went to call with Colonel M——— at Lord Douglas's, but my horse ran off with me three several times; I was very thankful to have escaped safe, and have not thought it prudent to risk my life in such circumstances since. Colonel M——— promises to get a pony, which I can ride, soon. Let it be our great object in our letters to provoke each other to love and to good works; for all is trifling, that does not bear directly or indirectly on eternity."

"I relish my solitude much better than I did. I am utterly confounded to think of the unnumbered mercies the Lord has heaped upon me, and on the discontented ungrateful feelings, I have often indulged. I have had a long walk this evening, visiting from cottage to cottage, with the view of collecting a few young people to form a weekly meeting. Great backwardness is manifested; and I have but faint hopes of its succeeding. I regret that I had so little Christian intercourse with you, and my other friends, in Edinburgh. I find that the bustle of travelling, and the excitement of new scenes and new circumstances, have a strong tendency to destroy spirituality of mind."

A letter from his friend C., appears to have contained some intimations of a very afflicting and painful nature, respecting the workings of his mind. It produced the long letter, which follows:

"MY EVER DEAR C.—Your last letter was, indeed, a most overwhelming letter, and did I really know any remedy for your mental distress, it were indeed cruel to have delayed so long to administer it. But I have been perplexed and confounded. I have resolved to write and yet tremble to take up my pen. I have delayed thus long, to meditate and to pray. When the spirit of my friend was wounded,—so severely wounded, I feared to take the knife into my own unskilful hand; and it seemed to me wisest to apply to the great Physician of the soul. The more I have thought of your case, the more I feel that it is beyond the power of human relief. I have done all I can. I have entreated Him, who alone can bind up the broken spirit, to send relief. He knows, from dread experience, the depths of temptation; he has experienced the horrors of an hour, when God seemed to have forsaken him, and the power of darkness appeared to rage triumphant. I write in the full hope, that ere now, your darkness has been dispelled by light from above; for it is light from Heaven alone, which can dispel *such* darkness. You see, I have taken a large sheet of paper at your request; but it is only because of that request: for really, I can pretend to give no consolation. I can only direct you to a higher source; but I can do so with the fullest confidence, that there *you will assuredly find it.*

"The metaphysics of natural religion I have studied but little; but if I can judge from that little, it seems to me, that the pretended demonstrations of the immortality of the soul, and the *moral* attributes of God, are little better than proofs how profoundly and ingeniously man can *trifle.* Much solid argument may be expended in the investigation, and many an ingenious method of argumentation discovered. We may have logically refuted, or *appeared to refute*, the objections of an opponent; but when we come to retrace all the steps, we find that no lasting impression is produced, — nothing satisfactory attained. Such discussions seem to me, to end in nothing more than the ingenious and well-calculated moves in a game of chess. We have had some intellectual amusement; and perhaps, too, we may have *won the game*, — but *that is all.* I have lately read the third volume of a novel called *Tremaine*, where the arguments of Clark, &c. seem to me well condensed, and convincingly stated; but the above was my impression on perusing them. By the way, the above is no ordinary novel; it is well worth a reading. The clear, the acute, the *matchless* Brown, seems, *on this subject*, a trifler. Indeed, the dark cloud of mystery which veils the spiritual world, gives us a liberty to imagine of it what we please, and a little ingenuity is all that is necessary to *seem to prove*, what we imagine, in a region wholly unknown. The more we think, the more we are persuaded of the reality of our own fancies, as when we gaze on the shapeless masses of coal in a fire, or on the clouds of a confused sky, our imagination can picture forth the outlines of animals, or castles, or forests, or *any thing*, which seem to grow more and more distinct the longer we gaze. But where have I wandered to? I might have told you in one little sentence, that I have felt these metaphysical reasonings to be as unsatisfactory as you do, who have dived deeper into their profundities. Let me say, however, before leaving this tantalizing subject, that I do think the *existence*, (and *if* the existence, of course the natural attributes of God), abundantly proved by the objects around us. For this, Dr. Brown says, and I think truly, that we have not to search far amid the mysteries of nature, to find proofs; far less to tread the labyrinths of *a priori* argumentation. He who sees not a Deity in the marks and designs displayed in his own body, or in many of the most familiar objects around him, will not be convinced by demonstration itself.

"To leave this then, — How delightful the *facts* of the gospel and the well-accredited testimony of an eye-witness from the world of spirits! But I know the dreadful subject, which is the cause (shall I say, which *was* the cause) of your doubts and your distress. *Millions* created for a moment's giddy pleasure, — and then an eternity of unmingled wretchedness. Ah, my friend, the argument has struck *my* mind too with overwhelming force; and its stroke has cut the deeper, edged, as it has been in my case, (I believe in yours too), with the poignant reflection, that some whom I hold dearest '*according to the flesh*,' seem, at present, to be walking on to the gulf of eternal perdition. But why should I introduce this here? *You* can sympathize with me. Oh, if there is ever a time that this proud heart can think with real delight of its own insignificance and ignorance, — it is, when oppressed by this awfully mysterious subject. When my mind has been darkened by presumptuous thoughts regarding the justice and mercy of the Eternal, the feeble ray of a single twinkling star has seemed like a ray of hope; and the conception of myriads of such worlds, or clusters of worlds, if it has not dispelled the darkness of the soul, has at least given the certain expectation, that *soon it* WILL *be dispelled.* What are *we*, that we should fathom the counsels of the eternal and omnipotent Jehovah? 'Who art thou, O man, that repliest against God?' Has not God revealed to us enough, to warrant this trial of our faith, especially when the express assurance is given, that a time is coming, when we shall 'know as we are known?'

"After writing this long letter, I am almost ashamed of it. I have written, as if I were combating the arguments of an infidel, instead of attempting to console a Christian brother, whom the adversary has been permitted to attack. It would, indeed, be cruel to heal up a cankering wound, ere it had been probed to the very bottom; but I think I am not guilty of this, when I say, that even in that most dismal letter, there are the proofs of a regenerated soul. Peter was given up to the temptations of Satan, that he might be shown his own weakness. Some of the most eminent servants of God have been left to wander even into the dreary regions of atheism for a while, as if to show their own depravity, when unassisted by divine grace. O do not talk of the *unwilling* rejection of a God! All atheists are *wilful* atheists. This, I must believe, while I believe the Bible. God has had some end in view, my dear friend, in giving you up to these dreadful thoughts. I trust he will bring good out of seeming evil, and that this severe trial will lead you to lie more humbly at the foot of the cross, and to put less confidence than ever in the speculations of a bewildering philosophy. Excuse — no, I will not say excuse, I have spoken with the freedom of Christian love. I have not half answered your letter, and yet my paper is quite full.

"Remember me to our dear Nesbit, if he is still with you. The same post that brought your last, gave me the delightful news of another added to our little band of Christian missionaries, our much respected Rentoul. I have had a letter to-day from John Adam, making the very solemn proposal of joining him, in a mission to Madras, to leave this country in two years. Pray for my direction. We return to Dysart in the middle of next month, to be there for some time. I am glad of this, for here I am alone as to Christian intercourse. If I were actively employed in the service of the Lord, I think I could be happy in a desert; but here I do little or nothing. In study, I have done a little; I have read the first book of Samuel in Hebrew; three books of the Anabasis of Xenophon, which seems to throw some light on the style of the New Testament. In Theology, I have studied Paley's Evidences pretty carefully, and Bishop Lowth's Prelections. I have nearly finished Dr. Pye Smith's

Scripture Testimony to the Messiah (a most interesting work, which I beg earnestly to recommend to your perusal), and have just commenced Mosheim's Church History. It is late, but I can scarcely give over writing."

His friend, Mr. Herbert Smith, having proposed to him to assist, and co-operate with him, in some plans of usefulness which he was pursuing, it produced the following letter in reply: —

"TENNOCH SIDE, August 30, 1826.

"MY DEAR FRIEND — If I have delayed a few days in answering your very interesting letter, you can easily guess the reason. Your proposal demanded consideration and prayer. Did I make my own feelings the standard of my conduct, I should, in all probability, without hesitation, have answered your kind proposal with a hearty affirmative. Two circumstances, in my present situation, have contributed not a little to depress my spirits, the want of Christian society, and an exclusion from active exertion in the cause of the gospel. You can conceive then, how delightful to my imagination was the picture of a truly Christian companion, co-operating with me in acts of evangelical usefulness, and exciting me to more zealous exertion. Were inclination my guide, then, you see how gladly I should have embraced your kind offer. But this would have been wrong. In forming any plan, we must not calculate on our own enjoyment merely. The Christian must look to higher objects. His question must be. 'Lord, what wilt *thou* have me to do?' On considering the matter, therefore, in this light, I feel constrained, (in spite of my own longings to comply,) *for the present at least*, to decline *personally* co-operating in your interesting scheme. The difference of our religious sentiments, in *a few points*, has not influenced me in the slightest degree in my decision, except in the single point that it occurred to me, that the fact not of my *being*, but of my *being called* a Dissenter, might probably impede, more than your liberality may allow you to suspect, the promotion of a plan, which, from its very nature, must depend a good deal for its success, on the co-operation of churchmen of all descriptions. Had I thought of accepting, this must have made me hesitate; but as it is, other reasons have determined my opinion, that it is my duty to remain in Scotland for some little time.

"There is a sort of understanding, (although no positive agreement,) that I remain in Colonel Morland's family for a year. I have now been nearly four months. Here I have only one pupil; and, of course, much time for study, which I think invaluable, as I know not how soon my opportunities of study may be past. I am particularly anxious to study closely the original Scriptures, in case of being employed in the very responsible work of translation. This reconciles me to a retirement from active exertion in the meantime, although even in that point, I hope to be able to do a little in the neighbouring cottages. I should feel it cowardly to fly from a station where God has placed me in his providence, perhaps from some gracious purpose, merely because it deprives me of some pleasures, for which the Lord himself knows well how to compensate. The soldier in the camp must not murmur, because he wants the comforts of domestic happiness. To all human appearance, indeed, there is little prospect of my doing anything here, to promote the knowledge of the truth, except through my pupil.

"On the subject of missions, every prayer strengthens my purpose. I am aware of the glare of romance, which fancy may throw round the idea of Christian expeditions to foreign lands; but I have tried to make due allowance for this, and have prayed that a youthful imagination might not lead me astray. The result is, I am every day more and more convinced, that my convictions in regard to this matter, are founded on Scripture. It is impossible, within the limits of a single sheet, to state the grounds of these convictions. I have written something on the subject, which I may, perhaps, have some opportunity of communicating to you in one shape or other. I have taken medical advice, and am told, that my constitution is more likely to stand in a warm climate, than if it were more robust; but no definite opinion can be given on the subject. The same post which brought yours, brought a letter from our friend John Adam, announcing his intention of going to Madras in two years, and asking me to accompany him. This is at present under consideration, and my decision may affect my more immediate plans. My present plans are, if the Lord will, to remain here till May or June next year, and then pay a farewell visit to my dear relations, before leaving them for ever in this life. It is a long time to look forward to next summer; but should you continue where you are, and think I could at all assist you, I may then, by the divine blessing on my studies, be able to give more efficient assistance for a month or two. In the meantime, I shall pray for your success, and perhaps you will have the kindness to let me hear soon how matters prosper."

Various friends interested in the religious welfare of Ireland, having requested him to take its claims on himself into consideration, he wrote the following letter to the Rev. John Burnet, of Cork, which I insert, not only as a part of his history, but to show the comprehensive views he could take of a subject, and how deeply he interested himself in everything which related to the kingdom of Christ: —

"TENNOCH SIDE.

"MY DEAR SIR — I have had but a short notice of this opportunity of sending. The following are the queries that occur to me at the moment: —

"1. What is the proportion of professed Protestants to Roman Catholics; and what the state of religious knowledge and practice among the former?

"2. What the proportion of evangelical ministers in the Church of Ireland?

"3. What the number and character of Protestant Dissenting ministers? I include Presbyterians of course.

"4. Are any Itinerancies undertaken by resident Irish ministers, and to what extent?

"5. What is the number and character of the Hibernian Society's Agents? Are the *readers* also *preachers*, or are they all pious men? Of course, you understand me to mean, as far as our imperfect judgment can decide.

"6. What is the number of the Hibernian Society's schools, and how taught? Are the schoolmasters understood to be pious men? Is religious instruction the *professed* object of these schools, or only common education?

"7. Does the Hibernian Society support any *preachers;* and if so, how many? Are the *two* you mentioned, their agents?

"8. Do the people manifest a willingness to hear? And can you allude, in general terms, to the success that has attended the efforts already made?

"These queries will, at least, show you, my dear sir, how ignorant, perhaps how *criminally* ignorant I am, of the state of the interesting country in which you labour. I could multiply more inquiries, of a similar description; but I think, under these, you may arrange any information your time may permit you to communicate. If anything else should be suggested by these, and your engagements permit, you will have the goodness to mention it. I should be glad to hear *arguments* too, if any particularly present themselves. I promise solemnly to consider the matter before the Lord, and to lay it before such of my companions, as I think, might be fitted for the work. In the meantime, I honestly acknowledge to you, that I feel the claims of other parts of the world to be stronger. I trust my only wish is to know the will of God in this matter. I feel my ignorance and incapacity to judge, but he leadeth the blind by a way they know not. When you see Captain Felix, have the kindness to give him my respects. Excuse this very hurried letter, as it gets late. The Lord bless you in your labours."

While this letter shows his willingness to submit to whatever might appear to be the will of God in regard to the field of labour; it still discovers how much his heart was set upon the great object to which his life had been devoted. In the letter which follows, to Mr. Adam, he gives full scope to his feelings, and refers again to the difficulty of obtaining the consent of his friends.

"DYSART HOUSE, September 17, 1826.

"MY VERY DEAR JOHN — I dare say you expected an answer to your interesting letter long ere now, and have been attributing my silence to my wonted carelessness. But in truth, this is not the case. I was cheered with the prospect of a short visit to Perth, soon after receiving yours, and I thought it better to defer writing till I should know the mind of my friends concerning your very important proposal. My own opinion, excepting in so far as that of my friends and other circumstances might affect it, was fixed almost as soon as I read your letter. With a deep and increasing conviction of the duty of going to the heathen, and with a strong impression of the advantage, and in *my* case, almost the *necessity* of a known and tried companion; this latter circumstance, seemed to me of itself, sufficient to turn my attention to a portion of the missionary field, of which, I confess, I had never before seriously thought. The language of Ruth to Naomi, is the sincere expression of my feelings, when I read your proposal. But notwithstanding this, I do not yet feel quite at liberty to seal the contract, as you express it.

"On consulting my friends I was astonished to find them even more opposed than before. There seemed to be even some disappointment, that I had not, by this time abandoned the idea of being a missionary altogether. Had the impulse on my mind been a mere boyish fancy, in all probability, this would have been the case, exposed as I have been to influences altogether unfavourable. But I trust there is no enthusiasm in supposing, that the impression has been made by the Spirit of God, when time and meditation and prayer, make it deeper and deeper. Still my relations are quite against my views. The first argument is *weakness of constitution.* Most unfortunately I happened to have a little cold on this visit home; and you remember I was rather unwell when you were with us. These trifling circumstances make my friends feel more confident in their argument. I confess that I have felt the force of this objection very strongly; but, after due consideration, it does not seem to me sufficiently strong to warrant the plea of inability to enter on missionary work. I consulted the physician of Colonel Morland's regiment on the subject. His opinion quite coincided with what I had often heard before — that no physician could predict how any particular constitution would suit a hot climate; but, in general, persons of a *thin spare habit* were more likely to stand, than those who were *stouter.* This argument, you see, then, I could get over, but there is yet another, which my parents have strongly urged, and which is of so painful a nature, that were you not my most intimate friend, I should not lay it before you.

* * * * * *

I confess that, all along, it has weighed deeply with me, and has produced a greater willingness to submit to the wish of my friends, in putting off, for a little, the final decision. But we must not be distrustful. All things are possible with God. How far ought these circumstances to weigh with me? I confess, they make me hesitate to give you a decided answer, which else I should do, with all my heart, in the affirmative."

The last letter which I received from him, was dated September. In this letter, he expresses himself with his accustomed affection, and unbosoms to me all his anxieties. Part of it, as well as of the preceding letter, I am obliged to withhold, from motives of delicacy, though it relates to his chief difficulty in accomplishing the acquiescence of his parents in his leaving this country.

"Dysart House, September, 1826.

"My very dear Sir — I know, that of late, the fatigues and anxieties of public business must have pressed on you with more than ordinary severity; and when at home, a few days ago, I heard that in addition to this, you had been visited with bodily distress. In these circumstances, it may seem presumptuous in me to encroach on your time and attention, but I trust you will forgive me. Though circumstances have separated both of us from the place where I was wont to look up to you as my pastor, where our family regarded you as one of their most intimate and most highly valued friends; yet I cannot help feeling, as if these close and endearing relations subsisted between us still. When in perplexity how to act, my mind involuntarily turns to you as the person most fit to direct me; and when any affliction distresses our family, I still seem to feel that we have a claim upon your sympathy, even though I know that you are surrounded by so many, who have *now* stronger claims upon your affection and your friendship. It may be wrong to feel thus; but if so, I must just repeat it — you will forgive me.

"When I wrote last to you, I had the intention of offering myself to the London Missionary Society this summer. The only impediment was the opposition of my friends. I had already refused a good situation, without consulting my father. He was rather displeased. On the offer of a second, I thought it right to submit to his decision. His letter desiring me to accept, and your answer to my last letter, came by the same post. I was a good deal perplexed; but at last, against my own inclination, I submitted to parental authority. I thought this acquiescence might reconcile my parents to my ultimate design, which I still kept steadily in view. In this I am disappointed. They seem to have expected that time and new scenes of life would efface the impression. On a visit home, last week, I found their opposition to my leaving this country more determined than before. * * *

"I will never cease to hope, I will never cease to pray. These are calamities, which my remaining in this country cannot alleviate, and yet they unnerve all my fortitude in the view of parting. Tell me how far you think this trying dispensation of Providenee ought to weigh with me. Mr. Adam writes me, that he thinks of offering himself to the London Society, with a view to a station at Madras. I know the directors do not give the young men their choice as to the station they are to occupy; and, indeed, it would be wrong to do so. I trust I am ready to go to any part of the world, where they think I may be most useful; but still I feel that the presence of a tried and beloved friend would be a mighty stimulus to exertion, and a great solace in trials. He talks of going in two years. Did the directors agree to such an arrangement, when should I be required to come before them? In my present situation, I have only one pupil, so that I have a few hours for study. I have applied pretty diligently to Hebrew this summer; and have studied carefully, Paley's Evidences, Dr. Pye Smith's Scripture Testimony, Bishop Lowth's Prelections. I go on with Mosheim's Church History, and Horne's Introduction. We are, at present, at the Earl of Rosslyn's house here, where we shall continue three or four weeks. I cannot tell what my plans are at present. I am quite confused. I think I shall stay over the winter, at all events, in this family, unless the Lord, by the indications of his providence, seem to point out some other path. I find Lord Rosslyn exceedingly kind and attentive. I trust, the peep I have had at the pomp and luxury of the world, have tended to convince me more decidedly, that it is an unsatisfying portion. My pupil gives me great satisfaction. He has a very good mind. He is only ten years of age, and yet enters with delight into the study of astronomy; philology he is also very fond of. I have conscientiously taught him the doctrines of the gospel. His judgment approves them; and sometimes I have thought his heart was impressed. If the Lord choose him for himself, he may be eminently useful in the Church. His talents, and family connections, open the way to very high stations."

He refers in this letter to his reading, of his diligence in which, abundant evidence remains among his papers. Besides attention to the Hebrew and Greek Scriptures, and to his classical reading, he abridged during this summer and autumn, with great accuracy, Horne's Introduction, Paley's Evidences, Dr. Smith's Scripture Testimony to the Messiah, and Mosheim's Ecclesiastical History. That he was not inattentive to other things, is very evident from his letters.

In consequence of this letter, I wrote to his father some time after, urging the necessity of no longer opposing a desire which seemed so evidently of God, and pointing out the consequences of persisting in resistance. I believe this, and other things, contributed to produce the desired effect; and John was satisfied, that when the time came, he would no longer meet with opposition from his parents. It is gratifying to me to be able to state this; as it must be a source of satisfaction to them now, to reflect that their resistance could have had little or no influence on the cause of his early removal. My answer to this letter, which was delayed in expectation of hearing from his father, he never received. It was written the day on which he died, and was received in Glasgow on the day of his funeral. A few more letters and papers will conduct us towards the closing scene.

"DYSART HOUSE, September 28, 1826.

"MY VERY DEAR FRIEND—I am covered with shame on reading your very kind letter, and especially on observing its date. I will make no apology, but simply beg you to forgive me, and not to attribute my carelessness to want of affection, or even to forgetfulness of one of my dearest friends, and most highly esteemed companions.

"Your letter was, indeed, a refreshing one. Affliction is a blessing; and, I doubt not, that on looking back on the late trying dispensation of the Lord towards your family, you feel it good for you to have been afflicted. Your letter found me grovelling in the dust, wrapt in selfishness, and sunk in depression; brooding over my own vileness, and mourning the loss of privileges I had never deserved; yet, regardless of the inestimable blessings which still remained. Such a letter was quite the medicine for my distempered mind. I forgot myself in sympathizing with your affliction; and the deep impression which a near view of eternity had made upon you, was, I trust, in some degree communicated to myself. O how difficult to keep up a *rational* conviction of the relation between time and eternity! How does our practice give the lie to our profession!

"29*th*. I have been here a fortnight, and am likely to remain a fortnight longer, for which I am truly thankful. Here I am surrounded with Christian friends; and the value of such a privilege I feel more than ever, since I have had some experience of its loss. There is, indeed, an inexpressible heaviness in having no one like-minded. I have temptations here too, but I trust the Lord will uphold me. I am a good deal alone; but I must mingle a little with the society here; and to one accustomed to move in the humblest walks of life, the drawing-room of a peer is not the place to learn humility, or to be more deeply impressed with the realities of an unseen world. Yet, I trust, this peep at the luxury and pomp of the world may be sanctified to me. In what very trifling do the votaries of fashion spend a life, which must determine their condition in that eternal state, into which time soon will usher them! Surely, man at his best estate, is altogether vanity. I have just come from the sick bed of one of the servants, who has been ill since I was here last. He is in a very interesting state; and, I trust has found comfort in looking to Jesus. I am anxious to hear of your brother's parish. I trust the Lord causes his work to prosper. I know you have been active in assisting him. Tell me the nature of your exertions. Herbert Smith was to begin, when I heard from him, meetings like ours in St. Andrew's. Henry Craik and John Brown have commenced them in Exeter. Did you see Henry before he left? You know he succeeded Nesbit, who will be in Edinburgh soon. John Adam means to go to Madras, probably in two years. He proposes that I accompany him. I am in considerable perplexity how to determine. Pray for me, that I may not be left to do my own will. Perhaps you know that W. Alexander, and W. Scott Moncrieff, return to St. Andrew's this winter. What are *your* plans?

"I have been a good deal depressed at the thought of my uselessness. I have done little to promote the glory of God this summer; and in study, I have effected very little. My pupil gives me encouragement. I trust his mind is pretty thoroughly imbued with those precious truths, of which I found him very ignorant. At times he has seemed affected. The Lord deepen and preserve these impressions. Last Saturday night, I was much interested and affected by what he said. In the middle of our usual exercise, he stopped, and said very earnestly, 'Eternity!' Mr. Urquhart, 'eternity! I have had a thought of that which I never had before.' Unwilling to interrupt his feelings, I paused, and fixing his eyes on the fire, he said, in a little, with a tone of deep earnestness: 'Well, I never was impressed till now with the necessity of believing *immediately* on the Lord Jesus Christ.' Such impressions may wear off; but I trust they will return. I am not without the hope, that the Lord may raise up this child to be eminently useful in his church. He is a very original thinker, and pursues science and literature with an ardor that is not common at so early an age. I am not sure whether to address to Edinburgh or Kirkliston. I enclose this to our mutual friend, W. Scott, who will know where to find you. Write soon, and be particular in telling your doings and your plans, to your ever affectionate," &c.

"DYSART HOUSE, October 9, 1826.

"MY VERY DEAR SISTER — I have been long expecting to hear how my father arrived, &c. And I suppose, from this long silence, you expect me to write first. I do not remember what arrangements my father made about writing, when I saw him; but I certainly had the impression, that, as I had more to excite anxiety than you, I had the best claim to have my anxiety first relieved. How did my father arrive? How are you all, in regard to health, &c. How is David, the person about whom I am most anxious? These and a thousand other such questions, I should like much to have answered. I beg that a letter may be sent *soon*, as, for aught I know, we may leave Dysart in a few days. I was much pleased with your letter, my dear Anne, and hope for a frequent renewal of the pleasure I have in hearing from you. You ask me to write to you about religion, and I believe the request proceeds from your heart: for, I cannot think you would allow any motive whatever to make you trifle with sincerity on a subject of infinite importance. You know the absolute necessity of *decision* in this matter. Persons of amiable dispositions are apt to be moulded into the sentiments of those around them, almost without the consciousness that the opinions they have adopted are not their own, and have never had any solid foundation in their own judgment; and, probably, have never made any serious impression on their own heart. We must think and feel *for ourselves*, as *every one* of us shall have to answer *for himself* to God. I have nothing new to write you, my dear sister, on the subject of religion. All my little experience of a deceitful world, and a still more deceitful heart, tends only to confirm me in the belief of those grand truths, which the

Lord has permitted us to know from infancy. When the heart is overwhelmed with guilt, there is nothing can give comfort, but the consideration, that Christ has made a full atonement; and the repeated declarations of Scripture, that, if we believe on the Lord Jesus Christ, we shall be saved. The gospel cannot be believed, till we feel that we are guilty. It is one thing to think of the death of Christ, when we have no apprehensions about our state in a future world; and a very different thing indeed to catch a glimpse of this way of escape, when justice has shut up every other avenue, and the wrath of God seems ready to burst upon the soul, which feels itself to be accursed. Aye, then we can estimate, in some degree the value of a pardon, which the Son of God had to leave heaven to procure; we can then tell something of what is meant by having peace with God; we experience the blessedness 'of the man whose iniquities are pardoned.' Now this guilt and exposure to the wrath of God, is not an imaginary case, into the belief of which we may work ourselves. It is the plain matter of fact. The Bible describes it most plainly, as the state of every son and daughter of Adam. Why then will we shut our eyes to it, and rest secure and contented, without applying to the remedy that has been provided?

"It is the great evil in letter-writing, that we can scarcely enter on a subject, when we are compelled to leave it. Nothing worth notice has occurred since my father was here. I have seen a little more of the folly of the world, and have experienced more of the weakness and worthlessness of my own heart. I have written to John Adam, about Madras, but have not yet received an answer."

"Tennoch Side, October 26, 1826.

"My dear Sister — I believe you owe me a letter; but as I am not very punctual in paying my debts in that way in general, it may perhaps atone for some long delayed epistle, to have sent *one*, at least, before it was due. I often think that my letters are too abstract to interest you, and that this discourages you from writing freely to me. I have seen parts of the country you have never visited, and have sometimes thought of sending you some descriptions of scenery, &c. But really, I have no head for description. Trees, and fields, and rivers occur everywhere; and were I to tell you what I have seen in that way, it would only recall the scenes you yourself are familiar with; for I have not the *tact* of classifying and arranging these elements of natural description, so as to form any distinct picture of a particular landscape. But I have made a journey lately, where there were no trees, no fields; there was a river, indeed, beside us, but fish never swam in it; and in the air, far around, a bird had never been known to fly. After this mysterious introduction, I feel obliged to apologize for my subject. But after all, I can assure you, though you may hear people talk with great contempt of a *coal-pit*, you may travel many a mile in this world of light and sunshine, without seeing anything half so wonderful as the coal mines at Dysart. But this I should have left you to guess, *after* my description; for I fear, after having said so, I shall fail to make you think as I say. Well, to fall upon the subject, without further preface. Having made an engagement, the day before, with my good friend, Mr. Barclay, who conducts the work, and who promised to equip me for the expedition, I repaired to his house early after breakfast. I found only one dress had been procured, which they insisted on giving to me. I wish you had seen us as we set out. You can fancy my slender body, wrapt in a sailor's jacket and trowsers, which had been made for a stout man, and crowned with an immense old hat, which had an irresistible tendency to rest upon my shoulders. After half an hour's walk in this fantastic attire, during which time I afforded some merriment to the natives, and felt now and then a little hesitation on the subject of personal identity, we reached the place of descent. It is a perpendicular shaft, with a wooden partition in the middle, reaching to the bottom. On one side of this partition are placed short wooden ladders, in a zig-zag direction, from top to bottom of the pit. Having each lighted his candle, we addressed ourselves to the work of descending, and were right glad, after some fatigue, and no little wariness, to find that we had reached the bottom. At this spot, we were about half a mile from the shaft where the coals are taken up. Mr. Barclay led the way, with a lantern, and after we had followed for some time, we began to perceive that we had entered a spacious gallery, the roof about twelve feet high. By the glimmer of our candles on the right hand, the wall seemed to be solid, but on the left, now and then appeared a spacious gloomy cavern, which seemed to turn at right angles to the route we were pursuing, but how far we could not tell; all beyond a few yards, was covered with an impenetrable darkness. To let you know more than I did, when surveying these gloomy regions, we were walking in what miners call *the level*, which is excavated in a horizontal direction, (as its name imports) in a line at right angles to the direction which the stratum dips. In this way, a level channel is obtained for the water that accumulates, without passing from the vein of coal, which you will easily perceive, could not be accomplished by running a mine in any other direction. In that case, if you follow the coal, you must descend with the stratum; if you keep a level, you leave the coal. The caverns on our left hand, were the *workings*, which are always wrought upwards; hence we had none on our right hand. On this side *a river* flowed, which was supplied by tributary streams, that issued from the caverns I have attempted to describe, or sometimes by a water-fall, where the roof had given way. Hitherto the murmur of the stream had alone broken the dreary stillness of these caverns, and the feeble rays of our candles had only made visible the darkness they could not dissipate; but now other sounds and sights began to burst upon us; a fire was seen blazing in the distance, and a number of motley faces, which still preserved some colours that could reflect the light, (reflected by nothing else,) danced and gleamed before us like the figures in a magic-lantern. The clanking of chains, and the trampling of horses, were now distinctly heard; and a hollow sound, as of distant thunder, grumbled through the subterranean vaults, as the loaded baskets (I might almost call them wagons) were dragged along. We had now, in fact, arrived at the pit, where the coals are raised by a steam engine; and by that time, I was as much tired with my walk, as I now am in describing it. We had not yet travelled over half the ground; but as the rest of our journey was more expeditious, I hope to make the description more brief. A train of empty baskets were ready to move, in which we made very comfortable seats of straw. Our horse was harnessed, our lights adjusted, and in a few minutes we started at full trot to explore the yet unseen recesses of this endless labyrinth. What we saw here, was just what we had seen before, till we arrived, after travelling another mile, at the place where the men were at work. Here the air was very close, from the smoke of their lamps, and we were glad to make our way back on loaded baskets, though contrary to the laws of those realms. We took no candles in returning, as a lamp is attached to each train of baskets. By accident this only remaining light went out about the middle of our journey, and we were left in darkness, of which those above ground can form no conception. Our horse continued to canter along, as if nothing had happened, at a rate that made it a little difficult for me to keep my seat. In some time, a twinkling lamp again appeared in the distance, on passing which, things went on as before. The baskets we travelled in, are set on wheels, which move on a railway. The horses are in excellent condition, and have very good stables in the mine. They never see the light of day, from the time they are first lowered down. Of our return, I need not describe further.

"When you have read the above confused description, read the twenty-eighth chapter of Job, and tell me if it does not throw some light on the sublime description there. If not, I have failed to represent to you what I have seen. Man can, indeed, do much; but, after all, his power is limited. He can put forth his hand upon the rocks, and overturn the mountains by the roots. He can cut out rivers among the rocks; he can bind the flood from overflowing. His eye seeth every precious thing, and the thing that is hid, he bringeth forth to light. But where shall wisdom be found? God alone knoweth the way thereof; and O, let us thank him with our whole hearts, that what human skill could never have discovered, he has freely made known to us by the gospel. Man can 'bore the solid earth;' but the depth, saith of this wisdom, 'It is not in me.' Man can fathom the ocean and explore its hidden caverns; but the sea saith, 'It is not with me.' In what a pitiable condition is man, with all his boasted wisdom, without divine revelation. O how thankful then should we be, that this precious gift, the gift of heavenly wisdom, is freely offered to all! It is easily accessible to every individual. No careful and laborious search is to be made, ere we can discover it; no difficult task to be performed, ere we can deserve it. 'Say not then in thine heart,' &c. (Read the passage, Rom. x. 8; and the parallel verses, Deut. xxx. 11 – 15.)

"Let us embrace with eagerness and joy, the precious truths that God has revealed to us. Pardon and reconciliation, and spiritual renovation, are the gifts that are offered. They are not to be compared in value to any earthly thing. They have been purchased by the blood of Christ, and are offered to us for nothing. O let us not then despise or neglect these invaluable gifts, which the possession of a thousand worlds could not enable us to purchase!"

"Dysart House, October 13, 1826.

"My dear Trail — Perhaps I should have written sooner, but I trust you will not attribute this delay to want of affection. I have really nothing particular to communicate, except my very sincere thanks for your truly kind and refreshing letter. I trust this will find you a preacher of the gospel, and I am sure, if once all external barriers are removed; the state of those around you, will constrain you to be instant in season, and out of season. You mention having heard from our dear friend Adam; and I suppose, he addressed you on the subject which has taken possession of his whole soul. Have you been thinking more of the missionary work? I feel the argument for personal engagement every day more strong; and if there are times when I have a longing persuasion that it may be my duty to remain at home, they are times when the chilling influence of the world has cooled every holy affection. This convinces me, more than anything, that the matter is of God. Did I tell you, that our friend, Rentoul, has been so impressed with the duty of preaching to the heathen, as to have almost (I trust, by this time, altogether) decided on offering his services to the London Missionary Society? Henry Craik has written me, since his arrival at Exeter, which place he seems to like very much. John Brown and he are making some exertion for the spiritual good of the people.

"I had a letter from Mr. Adam yesterday, who seems to think of Madras as the place of his destination. I suppose he had begun to study Sanscrit when he wrote to you. He goes on with it. I could have wished much to accompany John Adam, but many circumstances seem to demand a considerable delay on my part. May the Lord make me submissive. I know his ways are the best. Generally on looking back, we can see that every step we took was necessary for our welfare, although when we took these steps, all was darkness and perplexity; 'The Lord leadeth the blind by a way that they know not.' It is a privilege even to be blind, if we have such a Leader. Since we came here, the Earl of Rosslyn's family have been all at home, and there has been a good deal of company. Lord Loughborough, Lord Rosslyn's son, was married last Tuesday.

"I feel that the near approach of rank and fashion has a strong, though almost imperceptible influence, in superinducing a spirit of worldliness. Every new scene that opens to me convinces me that the world in which we live is more dangerous than ever I imagined, and every new temptation shows me that my strength is utter weakness. How difficult to learn the lesson of our own utter worthlessness! Experience alone can teach it. O that we may be enabled to look more simply to Christ alone! In him we are complete. Through Christ strengthening us we can do all things. I thank you for your kind present, and for your still kinder advices. Pray for me, that the Lord would uphold me; for I feel that I walk on slippery places. Nesbit will be in Edinburgh soon. W. S. Moncrieff, and W. Alexander, my old companions, are the only persons I know going to St. Andrew's.

"I hope they will be strenuous in their exertions. We return soon to the neighbourhood of Glasgow, where I expect to spend the winter."

"DYSART HOUSE, October 16, 1826.

"MY VERY DEAR FRIEND — I have just been conning over your very interesting letter, by way of foraging for my own pen, for I fear this will be a very barren and uninteresting letter. Every line of your epistle is filled with what is interesting, so that I scarcely know what to allude to first. The first thing that strikes me is, that the date of this letter is exactly a month later than yours, which was the time fixed for our dear Nesbit's leaving you. I trust he has left you, else I shall be denied the pleasure of an interview with him, as I pass through Edinburgh for Tennoch Side, the end of this week. But, by the way, when your letter was written you did not know I had left that part of the country. It is now about five weeks, since Colonel Morland's family came to Dysart, and on leaving our former residence, I was permitted to pay a visit to Perth, which was doubly sweet to me, from having been removed for a time from all who were like-minded. One thing I was much disappointed in, my parents showed a more determined opposition than ever to my going to the heathen. I had hoped that, by this time, they would have been quite reconciled, and I had formed my plans accordingly. I have now no plan. I am waiting till the Lord, by his providence, point out the way to me. Even my dear John Adam recommends delay in my circumstances. I fear he must leave me behind him, for I suppose, to be qualified to go with him even as an assistant, I should require to be in London immediately. But it is well that we should have our plans frustrated. God has marked out the way for us already, and it is very presumptuous in us to try to mark it out for ourselves. I feel that the present is very apt to be overlooked, in laying schemes for the future, and the opportunities of usefulness that daily present themselves, are apt to be neglected in the imagination of still more favourable opportunities that are to come. This is evidently a device of Satan's. How many precepts have we in Scripture to guard us against delusion!

"Since I have been here, I have seen a good deal of what is called *the world*. Lord Rosslyn's family has been at home, and there has been a good deal of company.

There is a fascination about rank, and fashion, and gaiety, and splendor, which has an almost imperceptible influence even on the heart that is conscious of their utter vanity. The smile of the world is more dangerous than its frown; and the kindness and attention of those who are called great, have a strong tendency to lead away from the simplicity that is in Christ. This I have, in some degree, experienced.

"I do not know whether I ever wrote anything about my pupil. He is a boy of a very affectionate and amiable disposition: and if I am not mistaken, he has an intellect of no ordinary cast. But he has been quite spoiled, he has never been accustomed to obey anybody, and has never been punished for a fault. Of course, you can see, in such a case, I have a good deal to try me, but yet I have encouragement too. He has been several times a good deal impressed with the doctrines of the gospel, and though these impressions may wear off again, at present they give encouragement to hope and pray, that the heart which has been influenced by them, may be, sooner or later, entirely subjugated to the Lord. I rejoice to hear of your exertion in your neighbourhood. Persevere, my dear friend. I mean to renew my efforts to have a meeting near Tennoch Side. Give my affectionate regards to John Brown. I am glad to know, that, practically, he has given up his peculiar tenets. I am not in a condition for writing on Mr. Grove's pamphlet at present, as it is some time since I read it, and I have not a copy here with me. I feel in a very peculiar manner towards Mr. Grove, though I have never seen him. I would travel a good way to meet with him. Give him my respectful and affectionate compliments. I will not send any expression of affectionate regard for my dear Nesbit, for I indulge a hope of seeing him in Edinburgh. I like the general outline of the Hamiltonian System very much. I have adopted it so far in Hebrew, as to take all the assistance I can from our English translation, at the same time examining the grammatical structure of each word. Pray for me, my dear brother. I have need of your prayers, for I am in a very cold and lifeless state. Ever, my dearest Henry, yours most affectionately."

"Tennoch Side, November 16, 1826.

"My dearest Friend — For some time back, I have *every day* been thinking of answering your very kind letter. I had actually sat down some days ago, but finding I had nothing of importance to communicate, I felt unwilling to break, without a cause, upon your very valuable time. But I cannot resist the pleasure of conversing with you for a little, for it is now some time since I have talked with a Christian friend.

"You know I have been a wanderer since I wrote to you, and perhaps it may amuse you to give some account of myself! But I have such a memory. I had forgot that I had written to you from Dysart. In passing through Edinburgh I saw Scott and Tait, and Alexander, of whom, the last alone has returned to St. Andrew's. I have heard that Rentoul intended going, but not from himself. Alas, poor St. Andrew's! I am anxiously expecting a letter from Alexander. Craik left Edinburgh without giving any account of the Missionary Society's book, which he had as secretary; and I had great difficulty in compelling Alexander to write about it. By the way, I have heard Duff is returned. I trust he will be staunch and zealous. I mean to write to him soon. Since I am in the way of giving news, I may mention, that I had a letter the other day from our old friend Hoby, accusing both yourself and me of not writing. He has 'pitched his tent,' as he expresses it, at Weymouth, being disappointed in his attempt to find a settlement near the Metropolis. His letter breathes a strong missionary spirit. 'It is impossible,' he says, 'to think of going *now;* but would to God I could find a more extended sphere of usefulness among the heathen, than I am likely to find here.' This, in part, I do not quite understand, for it would appear, that there is abundance of work at home, for those who *cannot* go to heathen countries.

"I am back to my hermitage, and have been here for three weeks. All around is more dreary now than ever; and, in other respects, external circumstances are no better than they were, and yet I know nothing of that strange dejection which pressed so heavy on me before. I wish you would destroy anything I wrote to you then; as, if I wrote as I felt, I must have appeared to you little other than a fool or a madman. I cannot help thinking, on looking back, that I was afflicted with a lighter species of the most dreadful malady that can visit a rational being. I do in earnest thank the Lord that I now enjoy not only health of body, but that littled valued, but highly precious blessing, soundness of mind. I cannot say that the advice of your last letter did not damp me a little. But you are right, I must wait till the Lord direct me. If you must go without me, I think I can bear it. All my experience tells me that I want a tried friend to lean upon, (a sentiment by the way, which you strangely misinterpreted in a letter to Scott;) and such I hoped you might be to me. But I see my error, I must lean upon Christ. I am more convinced than ever that happiness depends little on what is without. O, for a closer walk with God! for this alone, in any circumstances, can give true enjoyment. I have seen a good deal of the gaiety of the world since I saw you. It is all vanity. I have learned that lords and ladies are just men and women. It is probable that we return to Lord Rosslyn's at Christmas, to remain some time, so you see I am quite a pilgrim. 'We have no abiding city here.' That reminds me of a delightful month at Homerton, and of many a change since."

"Tennoch Side, November, 1826.

"My dear Friend—I trust you continue to enjoy, in some degree, the measure of health and freedom from pain, which you did when I last had the pleasure of seeing you. But the uncomfortable weather we have had for some time, almost forbids me to think so. Whichever way it is, I know that you refer it to the Lord, who doth all things well. It is in kindness that he afflicts, and it is in kindness too, that he sometimes gives a short respite from suffering. Perhaps it is in such seasons that the benefit of affliction is most felt. In the midst of severe distress, the most serene mind must be agitated; and it is difficult to feel that the Lord afflicts, because he loves us. In such circumstances David was beginning to fear that the Lord had forsaken him; it was only by escaping from himself, as it were, that he could find comfort. 'This is my infirmity,' said he, 'I will remember the years of the right hand of the Most High;' or, as some translate it, 'the *change* of the right hand of the Most High,' that is, his varied dispensations, in dealing with his people. But when severer suffering is for a while removed, there is often a holy calmness that pervades the soul, and the remaining affliction, instead of ruffling the mind as before, has a soothing influence; and, like the exercise of fasting, melts the whole soul into willing submission to the divine will. It is with bodily affliction, in some respects, as it is with the diseases of the mind —

"'When the wounds of woe are healing,
When the heart is all resigned, —
'Tis the solemn feast of feeling,
'Tis the Sabbath of the mind.'

"This sacred repose I am sure you have often felt, and have thought the trouble well worth the bearing, which yielded such peaceable fruits. Such seasons are the earnests of that rest which remaineth for the people of God. It is an acquiescence in the divine will that causes this holy calm within the breast. How sweet and sacred must that *rest* be, which remaineth for us! Then all the dispensations of God will have wrought together in producing *perfect resignation* to the will of our Heavenly Father. Surely this must be perfect peace. Let us welcome, then, all that fits us for such a state of holy enjoyment. *All things* work together for our good. You will excuse me for writing on a subject of which I may be supposed to know little. True, I have had little bodily affliction; but I have not lived eighteen years in such a world, without tasting the bitterness of sorrow. You know some trials that have pressed heavily upon me. You have been long severely afflicted, and if anything I can write can suggest any consolation, I shall esteem it a high honour to have been permitted to minister to one of the saints."

"Tennoch Side, November 30, 1826.

"My dear Trail — The important subject of your letter has been much in my thoughts, and often in my prayers since I received it. I have felt a reluctance to write, from a feeling of the deep responsibility of influencing you in so momentous a matter, and from a consciousness of utter unfitness for the task you impose on me. On many accounts I am not the person to advise you. The book of Providence is often difficult to interpret, and I will not pretend to offer an opinion on the particular passage of it, you have laid before me in your own history. We do well to remember, however, that the devil can quote from this declaration of the divine will, as well as from his written word, to give effect and plausibility to his temptations. Perhaps we can never be sure that we interpret the divine Providence aright, in deciding a doubtful question of duty, except when the mind has been duly exercised by prayer, in regard to the subject connected with the particular event, or chain of events under consideration. If the mind thus prepared has a particular bent, which is favoured or not opposed by external circumstances, I think in such a case we have rational grounds for supposing that prayer has been answered, and the desired direction has been given. Since supernatural communications have ceased, I see not how prayer can be otherwise answered. And there is no scope for the working of enthusiasm in obeying this inward impulse, when we limit it by the declarations of Scripture, and confine it to those points of conduct which as you observe, are left undetermined by the sacred word. This is the course you have pursued, I doubt not. It is the course I have tried to pursue. The Lord will direct us, my dear Trail. He who has made the path plain hitherto, will direct us still. I am tired of laying plans, they have been so often frustrated. After all, I see that I have been ever too anxious about the future, and all such anxiety is useless, for the Lord will lead the blind by a way that they know not.

"My views with regard to missions are still much the same. The gospel is for mankind, for the world; and why should one little island contain *nearly all* the messengers of peace? The little success in some parts is no discouragement, nor does it even show that men had run where they were not sent. Remember the first attempts in Otaheite. Consider the continent of Asia. John Adam remains in London, preparing, I suppose, for India. I say nothing of Rentoul, as I hope you have met him at St. Andrew's; if so, remember me very affectionately to him, also to Duff, and W. Alexander. Craik and Brown remain in Exeter. I have not yet heard of Nesbit's arrival in Scotland. I am anxious to hear how matters go on in St. Andrew's this winter."

He wrote, in the month of November, a paper on "Fiction as a Medium of Religious Instruction," which was inserted in the Christian Herald, a periodical work, published in Edinburgh.*

* See Appendix M.

CHAPTER VI.

The commencement of his last illness — Extract from his Journal — Letter to Mr. Tate — Letter to Mr. Craik — Letter to his father — Letter from Mr. Ewing to his father — Letter from Mrs. Ewing to the same — Letter from Mrs. Ewing, giving an account of his illness and death — Letter from Miss Cathcart on the same subject — His death — Letter from Dr. Chalmers to his father — Lines addressed to John by a friend — Concluding observations on his character and death.

THE time now drew nigh, when my beloved friend was to be removed from this delusive and suffering world, to the 'unsuffering kingdom' of his adorable Lord. For that state of ineffable bliss, he had been for a considerable time preparing, under the discipline of Providence, and the sanctifying grace of the Redeemer. In knowledge, he had far outstripped his equals of his own age; in zeal and devotedness, he occupied the front rank of a chosen band of youthful associates; and in the feelings and exercises of humility, he lay lower than the lowest. The measure of his spiritual stature was now completed, and the full reward of glory was made ready for him, by Him whom he loved. I feel myself incapable of describing the closing scenes, and shall therefore leave them, in a great measure to be told by others.

From a child, he gave evidence of possessing a constitution of peculiar delicacy, which was, therefore, liable to be affected, both mentally and physically, by many causes, which do not operate powerfully on persons of a robust and hardy temperament. The symptoms of a morbid depression, which appeared during the summer of 1826, were only, I apprehend, the harbingers of the fatal attack, by which he was appointed to be removed from this world. I fear it was not discovered in time, that the brain was the origin of his complaints; the intense and unceasing action of the mind, proving too powerful for his delicate bodily frame. In the mysterious arrangements of Providence, it would seem, that whatever arrives very early at perfection, is destined to be soon cut off. Premature growth is generally followed by a premature end. The case of Urquhart is very similar to those of Durant and Kirke White; and the inimitably beautiful lines which Lord Byron applies to the latter, are, I conceive, equally applicable to my young friend. It is singular, that the passage to which I refer, was transcribed by him into a scrap-book, entitled, "Extracts in Poetry, from various authors," only a short time before his death.

"Oh! what a noble heart was here undone,
When Science' self destroyed her favourite son!
Yes! she too much indulged thy fond pursuit,
She sowed the seeds, but death has reaped the fruit.
'Twas thine own genius gave the fatal blow,
And helped to plant the wound that laid thee low.
So the struck eagle, stretched upon the plain,
No more through rolling clouds to soar again,
Viewed his own feather on the fatal dart,
And winged the shaft which quivered in his heart.
Keen were his pangs, but keener far to feel,
He nursed the pinion, which impelled the steel:
While the same plumage that had warmed his nest,
Drank the last life drop of his bleeding breast.

The last entry in his journal describes the commencement of the attack, which terminated his earthly career, and gives a most delightful view of the state of his mind. "The ruling passion," his devoted attachment to the missionary cause, appears strong even in death. To be withdrawn from this work was the only thing which excited his regret, or extorted the expression of painful feeling; yet, even in regard to that, his mind appeared perfectly subdued.

"December, 1826.

"*Wednesday* 13*th.* — An excessive languor and weakness has prevented me from studying regularly this week. Had a long conversation with the gardener, last night, whom I find to be a very shrewd man. He is quite a Scotchman. The contrast, in point of intellect, and acquired knowledge, between him and the English servants in the family, is very striking. Yet they have travelled a good deal, and have nearly one-third of the day at their own disposal. His knowledge has been picked up in his own cottage, and those around it. He argues well on the doctrines of Christianity; but, I fear, as is the case, alas! with many of our countrymen, the head is engaged more than the heart.

"14*th.* Rose to-day at a quarter to eight. Read half a chapter of the Greek Testament. Second chapter of Joshua in Hebrew. Dr. Cokely called to-day, and pronounces my illness an affection of the liver. This has distressed me a good deal, as it may unfit me for the East, which I have long contemplated as the scene of my labours. But the Lord knows what is best. If he hedge up the way, I *may* not walk in it. I *would* not, if I might.

I begin a course of medicine on Friday, which, I pray God may bless, for the restoration of my health; that my body may be fitted for his service. If this be not his will, I know, that the destruction of this body will perfect the soul, and fit it for a higher, and a holier service, in the heavenly temple.

> "'O most delightful hour by man
> Experienced here below;
> That hour which terminates his span,
> His sorrow and his woe.'

"*14th.* Not so weak this morning, but able to accomplish little in the way of study. Prepared and attended my meeting. This is always a refreshment. I was enabled to speak with earnestness and feeling on the mercy and the justice of our God. My breathing a good deal affected to-night in walking. Though the night is wet, I feel better since I have been out."

How delightful it is to find, that to the very last, he laboured in his Master's service, and seemed to derive fresh strength from doing the will of God.

To his friend Tate, he wrote the following interesting letter, on the 19th of December: —

"TENNOCH SIDE, December 19, 1826.

"MY DEAR BROTHER — This world, through which we are passing, is a desert, and no wonder that its dreariness should depress our spirits. Our souls too are suffering under a loathsome disease; and if we are sensible of its loathsomeness, no wonder that we sometimes abhor our ownselves. But the desert through which we travel, leads to our home, and we have an all powerful remedy for the disease that preys upon our souls. True, sin will struggle on, and the old man will fight for the mastery, as long as he may, but we shall soon leave the wilderness, and all its sufferings, behind us. Strange that we should ever wish to linger. You remember that beautiful hymn; —

'There is a land of pure delight,
Where saints immortal reign;
Infinite day excludes the night,
And pleasures banish pain.

There everlasting spring abides,
And never-withering flowers:
Death, like a narrow sea, divides,
This heavenly land from ours.

Sweet fields beyond the swelling flood
Stand dressed in living green:
So to the Jews old Canaan stood,
While Jordan rolled between.

But timorous mortals start and shrink
To cross this narrow sea,
And linger, shivering on the brink,
And fear to launch away.

Could we but climb where Moses stood;
And view the landscape o'er;
Not Jordan's stream, — nor death's cold flood,
Should fright us from the shore.'

"I had a letter from our dear Craik, a few days before I received your last. He talks of being a missionary. Brown and he think of Ireland. I should think them well fitted for debate, especially Henry. I fear some one must be found to supply my place among the number of intending missionaries. You know that I have not been bent from what I thought the course of duty, by the arguments of men; but now God has spoken in a way which I think, (but I am not sure,) is decisive. I have been sickly for some weeks, and it turns out to be inflammation of the liver. I have been taking the usual course of mercurial pills for some days, and the Doctor orders the side to be blistered to-morrow. I wished to write before I am quite laid up, chiefly to request you to tell me all about St. Andrew's when you return. I hoped to have visited it soon, but the Lord has determined otherwise. Pray for me, that whether death or life be in this cup, the Lord may enable me to drink it with cheerfulness. Remember that I am literally in a land of strangers. Not a single Christian friend to whisper consolation, none to whom I can pour forth the feelings of my soul. Remember me very affectionately to my dear Rentoul, in whom I feel a very peculiar interest. My old companion, William Adam, I expected to have heard from. I have others, in my mind, but I am wearied. My chief pain is in my right arm and side. Do not speak of my illness at St. Andrew's, as the report might reach home, and I have not yet written."

Whether the means resorted to, were those best suited to his case, I pretend not to say; but while a partial recovery was effected, the disease would seem still to have gone on. To his esteemed friend, Craik, at Exeter, he wrote at different times, the following letter: —

"Tennoch Side, December, 1826.

I have to thank you, my dear brother, for two affectionate letters, since I wrote last. Your last was a letter of mourning, and yet it refreshed me much, and comforted me. It was but a day or two after, that I had a letter from our dear friend Tait, breathing the same strain of lamentation for worldliness, and panting after a closer walk with God. We are all one family, my brother, and what wonder that the feelings of our hearts are *one*, while banished from our home, and wandering amid dangers, fighting with powerful enemies, and surrounded by strangers who know us not, or who know us only to hate us. But let us take courage. 'The night is far spent, the day is at hand.' Weeping may endure for a night; but joy *will* come in the morning. It is not always by light, and faith, and joy, that the Lord answers prayer for spirituality of mind. There is great truth in that hymn of Newton's, —

"'I asked the Lord that I might grow
In faith, and love, and every grace;
Might more of his salvation know,
And seek more earnestly his face.

I hoped that in some favoured hour,
At once he'd answer my request;
And by his love's constraining power,
Subdue my sins and give me rest.

Instead of this, he made me feel
The hidden evils of my heart;
And let the angry powers of hell
Assault my soul in every part.

Lord, why is this? I trembling cried;
Wilt thou pursue thy worm to death?
''Tis in this way,' the Lord replied,
I answer prayer for grace and faith.

These inward trials I employ,
  From self and pride to set thee free;
And break thy schemes of earthly joy,
  That thou may'st seek thy all in me.'

"Why does God leave us *so long* in a world of sin? Why were his ancient people forty years in travelling through the wilderness? Why are we exposed to so many temptations? It is because he will not only deliver us, but will show us the horror of that state, from which we have been delivered. And the more we know of our own vileness, shall not our praise be the louder, when we join in that glorious anthem, 'Unto him that loved us?'

"I have been a mourner too. New circumstances have presented new temptations, and the Lord has shown me my utter weakness. Once, I thought my heart could not be viler than I knew it to be; but God has led me, as he did his prophet of old, from one scene of iniquity to another; and when I have thought that now I have seen all, he has opened some secret place within my breast, and showed me 'greater abominations still.' Nor am I sure, that I know yet the depths of iniquity that are within me. How easy to pass among men as pious and holy! They compare themselves among themselves. You talk about passing the Rubicon, my dear brother. The river of death is the Rubicon. Not till we have passed *it*, shall we be completely freed from the world, and from its cares. I say this, because I remember feeling, as I think you do. I thought, did I decidedly give up the hope of worldly honours and comforts, by deciding on the missionary life, I should no more be harassed by the cares, or allured by the vanities of earth. But it is not so. To think much of the Saviour is the only way to be made like him. I like much your plan regarding Ireland. I do think your talents, and also those of our friend Brown, are quite of a cast for it. It has been urged much upon *me*, but you know well I am not the person for such a scene. You ask me concerning *my* plans. I have no plan at present. If Colonel Moreland goes to Edinburgh in April, I may probably stay a little longer with him. Some information I got to-day, has distressed me a good deal, as it makes me fear that I shall never be fit for a warm climate. I have been drooping and sickly for some weeks. To-day, the doctor has come from Glasgow, and pronounces my illness an affection of the liver. He thinks there is no inflammation, and that a course of medicine will remove this attack. I am able to go about, though not very fit for study, and have merely a slight pain, like rheumatism, in my arm and side. Rentoul, Alexander, Duff, and Trail, are in St. Andrew's. From John Adam, I have not heard since I wrote you. My meeting here is confined to young people, thirteen or fourteen attend. There is no village. They come from scattered cottages. Of course, I do not preach, I talk to them. My meeting with them always refreshes and invigorates me. We go, perhaps, to Dysart, at Christmas. I may, perhaps, have an opportunity of visiting St. Andrew's."

"This is Christmas-day, and it is well for me the family have not moved. John Adam has written me lately; he is well, and goes on with his plan of preaching occasionally.

"The other part of this letter was written a considerable time ago; but I thought it better, since I had mentioned my illness, not to send it off, till I should see what the issue might be. Decided symptoms of inflammation soon appeared; but I am glad to say, that the Lord has blessed the means employed to remove the disease. At least, we think so at present. You must excuse me for not writing more, as I am excessively weak. I have ate very little, and have been allowed to eat nothing nourishing for some time. Add to this, that I have had a good deal of medicine, and a blister on my side, and you will not wonder that I am much reduced. I can add no more at present, but that I am ever your friend and brother in the strongest bonds."

The last letter he wrote was to his father, though the painful event that so soon followed, was then little anticipated.

"TENNOCH SIDE, December 27, 1826.

"MY DEAR FATHER — Christmas is past, and I am afraid you will be expecting me. This is the reason, I suppose, that my many letters have produced no answers. The family do not go to Dysart; and, in my present circumstances, that has been a great blessing to me. I may venture to tell you, now that I am better, that I have had rather a serious illness, inflammation of the liver. I had been very weak for some time, loathing food, and oppressed with a pain in my arm and side, which I called rheumatism. Mrs. Moreland had the kindness to send for the doctor of the regiment, who prescribed great abstinence; the blue pill to be taken every night; and, lastly, a large blister for the right side. It has pleased God to bless these means for the removal of the disease. Of course, I am very much reduced. I have been treated with as much kindness as if I had been at home, by the house-keeper especially, who always dressed my blister, and watched me like a mother. I could not have looked for such kindness in a land of strangers. The Lord can raise up friends wherever we are; but I have had no Christian to whom I could open my heart. But the Lord is here. With love to all, I am ever your affectionate son."

This letter was written when he must have been very ill, as he found it necessary to leave Colonel Moreland's on the second or third of January, with a view to return home. He got as far as Glasgow; and, under the hospitable roof of Mr. Ewing, received that kind welcome, which had invariably been shown him, from the first period of his acquaintance with that excellent family. The following letters, addressed by Mr. and Mrs. Ewing, to his father, are important, as they show the progress of the complaint, the means which were employed to arrest it, and the deep interest which they took in the amiable sufferer.

"GLASGOW, January 5, 1827.

"MY DEAR SIR — I am sorry to inform you, that your son came to us two days ago, rather in a poor state of health. I suppose he must have informed you, some weeks ago, of his having pain in his side, for which the regimental surgeon, (who seems a very respectable man,) ordered a course of mercury; that is now finished, but seems to have reduced our young friend to a state of great weakness. Nevertheless the doctor says he sees no cause for alarm, as there is little or no fever in his pulse; but there is no getting him to follow advice in taking his food. This the doctor thinks will prevent him from recovering strength till he can go home, which he thinks he may do, if he gets into the coach, and takes a little warm brandy and water once or twice on the road. At Tennoch Side, he became hypochondriac, and would eat nothing till it was out of season. We hoped he would have cheered up a little here, from conversation and nourishment; but I am sorry to say we are disappointed. I think it my duty, therefore, to beg, that if possible, either you or his mother will come here in the beginning of the week, to endeavour to prevail with him to take nourishment, and to consult with his medical attendant what is best to be done. The doctor declares he sees nothing but the flatulency of an empty stomach that should prevent him from eating. After all, I shall not be surprised if he propose going to-morrow by the coach, for he did so last night, but not till the places had been all taken. Yet, if he persist in neglecting his food, he cannot get better. I grieve to write thus, but we are quite at a loss, for we cannot urge him; and he does not appear to be at present a good judge in his own case. I am writing without his knowledge, for when I proposed it before, he refused to let me."

"GLASGOW, January 5, 1827.

"MY DEAR SIR — Since writing to you in the forenoon, Mr. Ewing (who has been obliged to go to the church-meeting) thinks I should write to go by the seven o'clock coach, by which you might expect your son, to say he has never spoken of it again this day at all; and that though his pulse is down, we do not think him better, and feel at a loss how to manage him. The doctor says he should not lie in bed, but we cannot persuade him to make any exertion. The doctor says he must eat, and it is almost by compulsion, and never but when one of us in a manner insists and holds it to him, that he takes anything. We hope, therefore, you will come, as the doctor assures us he is quite able for the journey. We should feel it quite distressing to let him go alone, and shall feel very anxious till you come. At the same time let me assure you, we have not concealed any circumstance from you. The doctor says his pulse is seventy-two only. He appears to me, as I have seen people, highly hysterical. We are sorry to give you all this anxiety, knowing what must be felt for such a son; but we feel it a matter of duty, and doing as we would be done by. Lieutenant-Colonel Moreland called to-day with the doctor; all that family seem to have paid him uncommon attention."

His father, it may be supposed, lost no time in proceeding to Glasgow; but before he could reach it, the most melancholy progress had been made by the fatal disease. Other medical aid had been called in, and that which had been supposed to be an affection of the liver, was discovered to be an affection of the brain, on which an effusion had taken place, which accounts for the comatose state into which he had been sinking for some days, till at last it had deprived him of all consciousness, and left no hope of a recovery.

My esteemed friend, Mrs. Ewing, who watched his dying bed with a mother's anxiety, has furnished me with a full and interesting account of his last days, which, together with the additional information supplied by her valued relative Miss Cathcart, who also acted the part of a tender nurse, the reader I am sure, will be pleased to receive in their own words, although their letters contain a slight repetition in some particulars.

"Glasgow, April, 7, 1827.

"After Colonel Moreland's family returned at the end of October, I think from Lord Rosslyn's, young Urquhart was only one Sabbath with us, and then said he had been a good deal troubled with his stomach. When Dr. Marshman was here, I wrote to ask him to meet him at dinner. He wrote, I might guess his disappointment at not being able to come seven miles to see him, when he had gone to London to see Dr. Morrison. The surgeon of the cavalry told me he had had a threatening of inflammation of the liver, for which he had given him Dover's powders, and blue pill, but this Mr. Urquhart had mistaken for a course of mercury. He came in here on the Wednesday preceding the one on which he died, and seemed very weak and much worn out with the drive; but told me he was now quite free of pain or complaint, except weakness and sickness when he took food. He said he had been so very ill, that though he never was insensible, he had felt what he never had before, that he could not pronounce the words he wished to say. He appeared to me highly nervous, and till his illness took a more serious turn, I had the idea which the medical attendant confirmed, that it was a hysterical case, from weakness. Both the surgeon and himself thought he was able for the journey to Perth, but he was persuaded to stop till the Friday, and take one day's rest. No ticket was to be had providentially for Friday: for we should have attributed his illness and death to the journey, had he gone. But it is very probable, though the ticket had been got he could not have been conveyed to the coach, as we could never get him to set up after the Thursday night; though he told the doctor he was better, and that he had had five hours' sleep. His pulse also was better that day. That night, however, we thought him worse, and got a careful sick nurse, in whom we could confide, to be in his room all night. It was two next day when the surgeon called, and when I told him that he ate and drank what we gave him, but stared at us and did not speak, he left me abruptly, and ran up to his room. I followed instantly, being alarmed, and on examining his eyes and trying him in every way to make him speak, he requested more assistance, and told us what the other medical man confirmed, that it was a very bad case of suffusion on the brain. His head was shaved, leeches applied, and then a large blister over his head, and one on his neck. He continued quite insensible that night and next morning, and the medical gentleman then thought it was hastening to a close. His father arrived at eleven, but John did not know him when first he came. When Mr. Ewing came in from the forenoon service, it struck me there was more intelligence in Mr. Urquhart's face, and I begged of him to come up and speak to him, and pray; which, to gratify me he did, for he had no hope himself, thinking I fancied I saw what I so eagerly wished. Mr. Ewing spoke a few sentences on the hope of the gospel, as suited to one in the near prospect of death, and the glory, honour, and immortality, that were treasured up in heaven for those whose trust was in the Lord Jesus Christ; and then prayed for him as seemingly near death. You may believe I watched narrowly the effect of this, and observed him exceedingly agitated and affected. When Mr. Ewing finished, his hands, which he had not moved for many hours, I saw him endeavouring to disengage from the bed clothes, and therefore I raised the clothes; when he stretched out his hand and pressed Mr. Ewing's, and smiled. Mr. Ewing said, 'Do you know me?' When he said, 'Do not I know Mr. Ewing?' I went for his father, and he knew him and named him. After this he lay above an hour quite motionless, but apparently to me in meditation and prayer. At the end of that period, he observed and named me, and said, 'My mind is quite calm now.' I said, I trust your hope is fixed on the Rock of Ages. He three times replied in a most impressive way, 'Yes; my hope is *fixed* on the *Rock of Ages.*' I went on speaking for a little in the same way, saying, You will find it 'a sure foundation;' that Christ is able to save to the *uttermost;* that he is *a very present help* in trouble; that the hope set before us in his blessed gospel, is a *glorious hope.* His weakness seemed not to permit him to say much, but he repeated the emphatic words in each passage, in a tone of exultation I think I hear yet, and with a countenance beaming with delight. Knowing the state of insensibility from which he seemed newly recovered, I felt a kind of half fear at his only repeating what I said, and stopped; when he went on himself with two or three passages, importing the full triumph of faith. But now I remember only one; it was, '*I know* that nothing shall separate *me* from the *love of God,* which is in Christ Jesus *my Lord;*' but it is impossible to convey an idea of the tone and manner. It made all in the room weep abundantly except myself; I was thankful I could command my feelings, on his account. We were not aware till afterwards, that his mind had, during the illness before Christmas, been extremely depressed; and that it was on expressing that to his young friend, that the beautiful lines were sent that were something like prophetical of his state before death. I send you Jane's letter to Miss Young, which will supply anything else he said while able to speak. From that time till within an hour or two of his death, and long after he ceased to speak or see, whenever he heard Mr. Ewing's voice, he ceased his moaning or laborious breathing, to listen; or when any of us repeated a passage of Scripture. When the medical men returned at four on Sabbath, expecting to find him very near a close of his sufferings, they were very much astonished at the change in his sight, and restored understanding and speech; and though they would not say they could give us hope, they said symptoms were better, and that he must not be excited by speaking, but kept very quiet. This slight hope was kept up all Monday, and we went to bed that night (leaving two to watch him) with stronger hope; but at four in the morning his attendants came for me on his being greatly worse. At four in the afternoon of Tuesday, he was increasingly worse, and then death was so evidently near, that both Miss Cathcart and I sat up till after four, when I was compelled to lie down for two hours, from worn-out strength. When I returned at six he was evidently weaker. His last hour was while we were at breakfast. Miss Cathcart would not leave the room, and I just entered it to see the last breath drawn by the dear young saint.

"You will remember first introducing him to my husband, and I have often thought we owed to the fondness of that interview excited in both to each other, the honour

God granted us of having him to minister to in his illness and death. He came first to this house when he arrived in Glasgow, and we secured by that, what any other family would have done, that he should always come to us; and so eager were we to have him, that when Mr. and Mrs. Matheson and children were with us, after fixing we should ask a bed for him from our kind neighbour Mrs. Smith, we put up a bed for him in the little dressing-room. I send you the letters of Dr. Chalmers, and Mrs. Moreland, &c., and you know the universal testimony to his worth, and talents, and piety, and engaging manners. If there is anything further you wish on this subject that I can supply, it will give me satisfaction. I cannot but hope the Lord will bless the memoir to many souls. Surely such a bright star has not, in the short space it was seen, reflected all it was lighted up for, of the glory of God."

The following is Miss Cathcart's letter, to which Mrs. Ewing refers: —

"We have witnessed a very painful and solemn scene, in the death of that dear child of God. Mr. and Mrs. Ewing felt it an honour to administer to his comfort; and it was a privilege to myself attending him, which I trust will benefit my own soul. Much mercy was mixed with the trying dispensation. It was most providential a ticket in the Perth coach could not be had; and when Mr. Urquhart seemed to regret it, Mr. Ewing said there was a Providence in all these things; in which he directly acquiesced. In all his wanderings, not a murmur or complaint was heard. When he was collected and prayed aloud, it was most delightful to hear him pouring out his heart to

God in such humble and scriptural language. I wish the self-righteous had heard him declare that if he got where he deserved he would be in hell-fire, and that he had nothing to plead but the mercy of God, through the righteousness of Christ. At times, when unable to speak, he appeared sensible, by the placid smile on his countenance. When Mr. Ewing was praying, and when he mentioned any of the cheering promises in the gospel to believers, Urquhart would say, 'Yes! yes!' with great emphasis. At one time when his poor father asked the state of his mind, he replied, 'in perfect peace, stayed on God,' and repeated a second time, 'stayed on God.' One morning he asked me if his father was up. I asked him if he wished to see him; he replied, 'Yes.' When he came he said, 'John, do you know your father?' to which he replied, 'I know my father;' and then Mr. Urquhart said, 'I hope you know your Father in heaven, who, I trust, has prepared a mansion for you.' I think the sweet youth said, 'I believe there is.' At another time when nobody was in his sight, I heard him say, 'Come, Lord Jesus, come quickly.' When alone in his room, but not that he could see me, he said, 'Who is there?' I went to his bed-side, and said, Miss Cathcart, thinking he might not know my voice; he replied, 'When did you come here?' I said I have been with you all the time you have been ill here, and I feed you with what you eat; he said, 'I am happy to have my friends with me.' I replied, you have a Friend who sticketh closer than a brother; 'Yes,' he added, 'Jesus Christ is a friend who sticketh closer than a brother; but all the Lord's people are interested in each other.' At times when we did not think he knew us, he showed us he did by naming us, or holding out his hand, and ex-

23

pressed anxiety for Mrs. Ewing fatiguing herself, by different times saying, 'My beloved Mrs. Ewing, lie down beside me.' The most heart-rending scene I ever witnessed, was on the Tuesday night before his death. Mr. Urquhart came into the room, and at the bed-side gave up in prayer his son to the Lord, when all the yearning of the afflicted parent was expressed, and the submission of the Christian exemplified. Some present thought John sensible and agitated, but I was so much distressed myself that I did not observe. The poor father is much to be pitied, who says he has lost his child, son, friend, counsellor, and comforter. My friend Mrs. Smith's husband, told me he had never been at a funeral where such a feeling of regret was shown. The sick-nurse and the servants paid him the greatest attention, and many tears they shed for him. He told us how very kind Colonel and Mrs. Moreland had been to him; also that the housekeeper had been quite like a mother to him during his illness."

His death took place on Wednesday, the 10th of January, 1827, when he was only eighteen years and six months old. His career was short, but interesting, useful, and glorious. However mysterious it may appear to us, it was doubtless well with him; and Christ, who was gain to him in life, proved to him gain in death also. His course was calm, holy, and consistent; its termination was peaceful and happy, It was improved by Mr. Ewing, on the following Lord's day, from Psalm cxvi. 15. "Precious in the sight of the Lord, is the death of his saints." It produced, among many others, the following letter from Dr. Chalmers, to his father:—

"St. Andrew's, January 15, 1827.

"My dear Sir — I cannot refrain from offering my condolence on the late melancholy bereavement, wherewith it hath pleased a mysterious Providence to visit you. I received the intelligence, by a letter from Mr. Ewing, which I circulated among the numerous friends and acquaintances of your son in this place. His death has created a great sensation among his fellow-students, by whom he was held in the highest reverence and regard; which feelings were shared also by the Professors; several of whom I heard expressing their utmost regret, and affirming him to be the most distinguished, in point of ability and good conduct, of all the disciples who ever attended them. I yesterday communicated the afflicting intelligence to the children of uy Sabbath-school. They both knew and loved him, he having taken charge of their religious instruction for one session of College. They were evidently affected by the melancholy news.

"To your Christian mind, there is a far richer consolation than that which is afforded by the report, or the remembrance of his first-rate talents; talents which would have raised him to the highest summits of learning and philosophy, had he not wished to consecrate them all to the service of his Redeemer. Your best, and most precious comforts, under this heavy dispensation, are to be drawn from the consideration of that faith, by which he was actuated; of that grace which animated his heart and adorned his history; of that glory, for the enjoyment of which he was so ripened and prepared; in a word, of that promise, that they who sleep in Jesus, shall meet again in that country, where sorrow and separation are alike unknown.

"Few parents are called to sustain so severe a loss as you have now done; but with few, very few indeed, is the loss tempered by such precious alleviations.

"I am, my dear sir,

"Yours, with sympathy and regard,

"THOMAS CHALMERS."

The following lines addressed to him by one of his correspondents, were, indeed, sadly prophetical of the event which so soon after took place. They are simple, and beautifully descriptive of the feelings, not of the writer only, but of his friend, and strikingly applicable to his last closing scene.

2 TIMOTHY iv. 6.

"The Christian Pilgrim bid depart,
Departs without a sigh,
Fear can no longer chill his heart,
Or sorrow dim his eye.

In Heaven's own garments see him stand
On death's much dreaded shore,
He gazes on the promised land,
And seems already o'er.

We saw him oft betray a fear
As near this flood he drew;
But now a willing pilgrim here,
He kindles at the view.

A ray hath broke from Canaan's land,
Across that sullen flood:
It bids him quit his mortal strand,
And onward march to God.

He marches on, for now his eye
 Hath lost life's lurid ray,
As suns which quit a clouded sky
 To shine in brighter day.

Oh could we catch a moment's view,
 Of what he now must know,
Sorrow would fill our spirits too,
 To linger thus below."

I feel as if I had now filled my allotted task; and that it is better to draw this narrative to a close, than by attempting anything in the shape of character, to deprive the reader of the impression, which the facts themselves, and the concluding scene, are fitted to produce. But I cannot abstain from a few concluding observations.

To me, the undertaking has been one of a very painful, and, at the same time, pleasing nature; partaking as much of the mixed feeling, which the poet describes, as "the joy of grief," as anything which has ever engaged my attention. How much I loved him, I have not ventured, nor will I now venture to express. That he was entitled to it all, and to more than all, I am well convinced. If I felt towards him all the affection of a father, he repaid it with all the tenderness and confidence of a son. I feel as if the world had become, by his death, less an object of interest to me than it was; but I trust I have also been made to feel, in common with many of his devoted friends, that the attractions of a better world have been multiplied and strengthened, by his removal thither.

Afraid to trust myself in describing his character and attainments, lest my personal feelings might be supposed to have too powerfully influenced my judgment, I have interspersed the opinions and testimonies of others, with my own statements, and the papers of the deceased. These testimonies I have not nearly exhausted; nor is it possible for me to convey an adequate idea of the extent to which he was beloved and admired by all who knew him. The sweetness of his natural disposition, and the bewitching simplicity of his manners; the soundness of his judgment, and the fertility of his imagination; the ardor of his pursuit of science and literature, with the variety and accuracy of his attainments, rendered him one of the most extraordinary individuals of his years. When with these, are combined his extensive knowledge of the mystery of redemption, and of the sacred volume; his simplicity of aim, with the fixed and intense ardor of his zeal; his love to the souls of others, which made him ready to lay his learning, his talents, his genius, and his life, at the foot of the cross, and to abandon the country where he might have shone and triumphed, for scenes of foreign labour and suffering; the eminent spirituality of his mind, the consistency of deportment, and maturity of character and experience, at which he arrived, I need scarcely add, he presented an uncommonly rare assemblage of natural, acquired, and Christian excellencies. Of the truth of this representation, every reader has now been furnished with the means of judging for himself; and I safely leave with him the conclusion to be drawn.

His Christian character is that on which the mind now reposes, with the greatest satisfaction. As it regards his other attainments, "literature has failed, tongues have ceased," and "knowledge has vanished away." What he was as a linguist, and a mathematician, might have been of importance, had he lived; what he was as a believer in Jesus, is the only thing of importance to him now. He has attained to the perfect state, and experiences a high degree of that felicity, which he could so well describe, and which he so earnestly panted to enjoy.

"If I might be allowed," says a correspondent, to whom one of his last letters was addressed, "to say anything, from the acquaintance I had with him—and there was scarce a day, last winter, in which I was not some time with him—I would say of him, as his biographer said of Henry Martyn, 'A more perfect Christian character I never knew.' Like Martyn, indeed, it might be said of him, 'His symmetry in the Christian stature, was as surprising as its height.' I never saw a finer example of 'a living sacrifice;' he seemed, indeed, to reckon himself not his own, but bought with a price, and, as such, he was entirely devoted to the glory of God. Nor did he care what perils, or sufferings, he underwent, if so be that that object might be promoted. In this cause, even death did not appal him. I remember well, when he thought of China as a scene of missionary labour; and when he was told that the government positively prohibited the missionaries from preaching in that country, he said, he should conceive it his duty to transgress this prohibition; and if his death was the consequence, let it be so; the blood of a missionary sometimes advanced the cause, as much as his long life and labours. Think of such devotion in a youth of eighteen, whose rare talents and unquestioned Christian character, gave him the fairest prospect of usefulness and comfort in his native land, while they would have infallibly secured to him the admiration and affection of all who knew him. He was eminently spiritually-minded. No one ever felt more the burden of indwelling sin, and never did captive exile long more earnestly to be loosed, than he did for deliverance from its taint and its power. Hence he dwelt much on the holiness of heaven. It was the theme, he has often assured me, of his refreshing meditation, when his mind was depressed, as he looked forward to the perils, and sufferings, and privations, which he might be called to undergo in this world. I remember one day, while I was with him, his telling me, that while reading the Scriptures that morning, on this his favourite subject, his mind was so wrapt in contemplation, that he forgot, for the moment, where he was; till, when his consciousness returned, on looking into his own heart, polluted with sin, and then into the world around him, 'lying in the wicked one,' he burst into tears. He was possessed of much tenderness of spiritual feeling, and was most vividly impressed by every Scripture truth which he received. In one respect, much of the same mind dwelt in him, which was in Christ Jesus: he felt much for his brethren of mankind, and his heart bled for the condition of those who were not in Christ; yet was he possessed with the keenest indignation at iniquity, and every exhibition of it provoked his holy abhorrence. His was a character most exquisitely formed for Christian friendship. Possessed naturally of the most amiable dispositions, they were rendered still more so by the Spirit of God which dwelt in him. In his friends, he encouraged the most unbounded confidence; and his was a heart, into which, when distressed or disgusted, they could unbosom every thought which grieved them, and find a balsam for every wound. I speak not this at random. I know it from sweet experience."

I cannot conclude the memoir of my beloved friend, without once more soliciting the attention of the reader to the prominent feature of his religion and of his religious character, — his devoted zeal to the glory of Christ in combination with the salvation of men. It is obvious, that, to diffuse the knowledge of the gospel in the world, constituted his life and happiness. The subject pervades all his papers, runs through all his letters, and at length, entirely engrossed his thoughts. In his case, it was nothing assumed or professed, but something growing out of the very principles of his faith, and constituting a chief element in his religion. He had no conception of Christianity, apart from the love of extending it. That which constituted its glory, in his eyes, was its perfect adaptation to the wants and wretchedness of men; and the more he knew the evil, and the better he became acquainted with the remedy, the more powerfully he felt the obligation to preach the gospel to every creature.

His devotedness, therefore, was not so much an act of obedience to a law, as the operation of the great principle of the new economy, and of the new nature, LOVE — grateful love to God, and compassionate love to men. Hence the calmness and rationality, as well as the ardour of his mind, in reference to this great subject. He did not regard himself as making an unreasonable sacrifice, though to certain consequences he was acutely sensible; or as called to a work of a peculiar and unprecedented nature; but merely as discharging a common obligation, and engaging in a service which ought, in one way or other, to be attended to by every disciple of Jesus. He felt that much had been forgiven him, he therefore loved much. As he grew in spirituality of mind, he grew not only in deadness to the world, but in indifference to those literary and scientific pursuits in which he was so well qualified to excel, and in his admiration of the superior excellence of the knowledge of Christ Jesus his Lord. He despised them, not because he was ignorant of them, or because they were beyond his reach; but after he had subdued the difficulties of the ascent, and had their loftiest summits full in view! Even then, he did not disregard them as worthless, but as less worthy than another and a higher object. While the laurels, which he had so honourably won, were yet fresh and unwithered on his brow, he laid them at the foot of the cross, and with high Christian magnanimity declared, "that what things were gain to him, those he counted loss for Christ."

When I speak of his indifference to the pursuits of philosophy, I mean not to say that he neglected the cultivation of his mind, or that he turned aside from any of the paths of learning and science which he was capable of exploring. I only mean to say that he pursued them no longer for their own sake, for the gratification which they afforded, or for the earthly rewards which they might have secured. They became subordinate, in his mind, to an ulterior object. In as far as they might fit him for more eminent usefulness, he considered them important, and studied them with diligence and unconquerable determination.

To the ardour of his spirit in the acquisition of the qualifications which he felt to be necessary for the service of Christ, and the intense working of his mind in regard to that service itself, I have no doubt he fell a sacrifice. Many an individual has been a martyr for Christ, who has not expired on a gibbet, or suffered at the stake. Zeal for the glory and the house of God is a consuming principle. It burnt up the Saviour himself, and it has brought to a speedy termination the career of many a disciple. Such, I feel assured, was the case of John Urquhart. His feelings became morbid; but this was the result of weakness of body, rather than of any improper or undue exercise of the mind. The sensibilities of his nature were indeed refined and excited by his Christian principles, till they became too powerful for the bodily structure on which they operated. But this reflects no discredit on Christianity. It only illustrates the weakness of man, and the disproportion of his powers to the magnitude and the lofty enterprise of the gospel. Granting that it killed the individual, it only follows, that the event is mysterious, not that a loss has been sustained. That the reward of the sufferer is secured, we have the best reason for believing; and that gain, rather than damage, may arise to the cause of the Saviour, eternity will enable us to discover.

Did the present state terminate the being and the bliss of man, we might well be discouraged by the occurrence of such early deaths, from cultivating our intellectual faculties. The uncertainty of enjoying them for any length of time is so great, that the labour of the cultivation might seem disproportioned to the result. But if all intellectual and moral worth shall find place and scope in the eternal world, the case is very different. No mental attainment can be lost. The language and the literature, and the science of heaven may be different from all that we have known on earth; but the capacity which grasped the word and the works of God in this world, and which was improved by the influence which is from above, will operate in proportion to its strength and its spirituality on the things of eternity.

If the reader is young, and enterprising; if he possesses talents, and if those talents are cultivated; let me submit to such an individual the consideration of the example, and the lessons recorded in these memoirs. I mean the example and the lesson of high devotedness. For what purpose has God endowed you with his gifts, and blessed you with his grace? What is your proposed field of glory or enterprise? Have you devoted your life and your talents to Christ, or to the business and the ambition of this world? Are you a Christian? Then is there one object placed before you, and one course marked out for you to follow. "None of us liveth to himself." Every Christian is Christ's property and Christ's servant. The service of Christ, the glory of Christ, and the salvation of the world, are as much the interest of the weakest believer as they were that of the apostle Paul. Every Christian owes his all to the Redeemer; and Paul could owe no more. We may not be honoured to preach the gospel, or to die for the gospel; but to live and die to Christ is the honour and privilege of all his saints. The life which is consecrated to his service, and the talents which are devoted to his glory, will be found the happiest, and, in the end, the most productive. It may be short, it may be long, as the will of God shall determine; that is not our concern, and ought not to cause our anxiety. But it ought to be our anxious and unceasing desire, that, "whether we live, we may live unto the Lord; or whether we die, we may die unto the Lord: that, whether we live or die, we may be the Lord's." We are constantly reminded, by the events which occur, of the truth of the Scriptures: "All flesh is as grass, and all the glory of man as the flower of grass. The grass withereth, and the flower thereof falleth away." While these things humble us, and remind us of our sinfulness and our mortality, we still have hope. "We are cast down, but not destroyed; we are sorrowful, yet always rejoicing:" for, "while the world passeth away, and the lust thereof;" we know that "he that doeth the will of God abideth for ever."

APPENDIX.

A.

AN ESSAY ON THE NATURE AND DESIGN OF THE MISSION OF THE SAVIOUR ON EARTH.

WHEN we look around us on the broad field of nature, and contemplate the numberless beauties of the universe, we are struck with the great power and glory of God, as the Creator and Preserver of all things.

When we turn over the page of history, and reflect on the ages that are past, and more especially when we trace the various wanderings of the favoured descendants of Abraham, we are still more impressed with his goodness and wisdom as the God of providence.

When we turn to the inspired volume, and behold the just and perfect nature of the law, which he has there announced to us, we are led to adore his perfect justice and holiness as the great Lawgiver.

From these sources we may deduce many of the attributes of God, and form some conception of his moral character; but there is a darkness which envelopes it, which not one ray of mercy irradiates; there is a cold gloom which hangs around it, and which is not enlivened by one spark of love.

It is only through the atonement that we can behold him as the God of mercy; it is here that he is emphatically styled the God of love. It is only as he appears in the person of the Saviour that we dare approach unto him; it is only here that he condescends to be called "Immanuel, God with us."

Here the darkness and uncertainty through which we viewed him, are dispelled, and life and immortality are brought to light by the gospel. Here mercy and truth meet together, righteousness and peace embrace each other.

The nature and design of the wondrous scheme of redemption are beautifully and simply described to us by Jesus Christ himself, who tells us, that "God so loved the world, that he gave his only begotten Son, that whosoever believeth in him should not perish, but have everlasting life."

Here man is represented as perishing; for God gave his Son, that whosoever believeth in him should *not perish;* by which is evidently implied, that man, previously to his believing in the Son of God, is in a perishing condition.

We would first then consider the perishing state of mankind which called for the intercession of the love of God; and which is the state of every sinner before he believes in the Saviour.

Here we would remark, that God did not create man in this perishing condition; he brought it upon himself. In the beginning, God created man in his own image, that is, with a moral character in conformity with his own, with a heart pure and holy, and abhorring iniquity. In this state of holiness, and at that time when man was morally able to keep the commandments of an infinitely pure and just God, his Creator, as a pledge of his attachment to himself, desired him not to eat the fruit of a certain tree in the garden in which he had placed him; and at the same time warned him, in the most solemn manner, of the consequences of his disobedience. "In the day that thou eatest thereof, thou shalt surely die."

In defiance of this awful warning, the first of mankind put forth his hand and broke the commandment of that God who had bestowed upon him every blessing. In consequence of this transgression, a state of things took place, in which every descendant of Adam has been utterly unable to keep that law which God was pleased to reveal to them. This law is of necessity in accordance with God's own character, — perfect, — promising life to every one that abideth in all things that are written in it, to do them; and at the same time declaring, "The soul that sinneth it shall die." Such a law is the only one which could be given by a perfect God. Man had undergone a change: he was now become unable to keep any of the commandments of the Lord; but because man had fallen, the law of God was not to be suited to his depraved capacities. Such an adaptation would have argued change in the Lawgiver, — in Him who knows no variableness nor shadow of turning. This law every individual of the human race has broken times and ways without number. We all, like lost sheep, have gone astray. All have sinned and come short of the glory of God.

This, then, was the state of our fallen race; we had all broken God's law, and were exposed to its just condemnation. A holy God could not wink at sin, nor a just God forgive iniquity:—it behoved that satisfaction should be made, or that the whole human race should be given up to endless destruction.

Such satisfaction man could not make; he could not even perform his duty, much less atone for the sins he had committed.

None of the blessed spirits before the throne could give for us the satisfaction required; they were all bound, as well as we, to render perfect obedience for themselves at every moment of their existence, and could, therefore, perform no supererogatory duty to atone for the sins of others. Since then man had sinned, since he could render no satisfaction for himself, and since no created being, however exalted, could render it for him, there was but one alternative: it was necessary that the required satisfaction should be made by the Judge himself, or that man should be consigned to endless punishment.

This is the condition alluded to in the passage we have quoted. It was when man was in this state, when he had made God his enemy by his multiplied transgressions, that that very God against whom he had offended, "so loved the world, that he gave his only begotten Son, that whosoever believeth in him should not perish, but have everlasting life." Yes! at that very time when all that was dear to man seemed lost for ever,—when there seemed to be no way of escape, — when there was no eye to pity nor hand to help, — even then God said, "I have found a ransom." His eye pitied, and his right arm wrought salvation. No sooner had man fallen from his innocence, than God declared to him that "the seed of the woman should bruise the head of the serpent." This was the first of that lengthened series of prophecies regarding a future deliverer, which terminated in the coming of our Lord Jesus Christ. It was through faith in his name, as foretold in those prophecies, that the people of God were saved, who lived before his coming; it is through faith in his name, as manifested in the gospel, that more sure word of prophecy with which we are favoured, that believers are saved now; and through faith in his name also shall the elect be saved unto the latest generations. "For there is none other name under heaven, given among men, whereby we must be saved."

The design of the mission of Jesus Christ, we conceive, consists chiefly in two things: — the one is usually denominated our justification, the other, our sanctification. The first of these consists in our freedom from wrath, as the punishment due to our sins; being that part of the atonement which reconciles our forgiveness with God's justice, that through which he can be just and the justifier of the sinner who believeth in Jesus.

The second, or our sanctification, is that which fits us for enjoying eternal life in the presence of God; being that part of the scheme of redemption which reconciles our reception into favour, with God's holiness; that through which he can be of purer eyes than to behold iniquity, and yet hold communion with the most polluted sinner who believeth in Jesus.

We have already shown that no less a being than God could atone for sin; but we must now remark that as man had sinned, so the law required that man should suffer. It was for this reason chiefly, we conceive, that our Saviour took not on him the nature of angels, but took upon him the seed of Abraham, being thus fitted in the estimation of the law to atone for the sins of man. Having therefore in due time appeared in the flesh, and sojourned a considerable time on earth for an example to his followers; the time drew nigh when the sentence of the law should be fulfilled in him who knew no sin; when he, who was God over all, blessed for ever, and who thought it no robbery to be equal with the Father, should be made a curse for us.

The sentence of the law was death; it behoved therefore, that the substitute should bear that sentence, — and he did bear it in its fullest extent. He bore our sins in his own body on the tree, and thus magnified the law, and made it honourable. While hanging on the accursed cross, the Son of God exclaimed, "It is finished; and he bowed his head, and gave up the ghost." Then was justice satisfied,—

it had wreaked its vengeance on the person of our Surety; and thus as many as believe in him, are saved from the wrath to come.

While he thus obtained our justification on Calvary, our great Redeemer also made provision for our sanctification. While he was yet with his disciples on the earth, he promised to send to them "another Comforter, even the Spirit of truth." To sanctify the heart of the believer, and to assimilate his character to that of God, is the peculiar office of the Holy Spirit. Sanctification is not, like justification, attained at once; it is a progressive process. When a sinner believes in Jesus, his justification is completed, he is entirely freed from the punishment due to sin; but he is then only partially freed from the influence of sin itself. The work of the Spirit is only begun in his heart. That work, however, will still go on; day by day he will increase in love for holiness, and hatred of sin, though it will never be completed on this side of the grave.

Such, we conceive, is the design of the gospel, and such the means employed to accomplish this design. We shall now attempt to show the fitness of the means for the end.

We have already seen that the law was not adapted to the fallen state of man, nor indeed could be, so long as God was just; but "what the law could not do, in that it was weak through the flesh, God, sending his Son in the likeness of sinful flesh, and for sin, condemned sin in the flesh; that the righteousness of the law might be fulfilled in us, who walk not after the flesh, but after the Spirit."

To man in his fallen and depraved state, the gospel is most admirably adapted. In calling upon a sinner, it does not address itself to his generous feelings; it does not appeal to his gratitude, and say, "Can you any longer remain in disobedience to that God who has done so much for you?" "Can you any longer love sin, when you see its awful consequences in the death of the Redeemer?" The force of such language could only be felt by a renewed mind; such language were addressed to an unregenerate sinner in vain.

In his mind there is no generous feeling; it is wholly selfish. In his mind there is no impression of the love of God; there can, therefore, be no corresponding emotion of gratitude. How then, does the gospel address him? Is there yet any principle left in his depraved mind, which may be impressed by its declarations? Yes, there is such a principle, it is this very selfishness by which we have characterized him, it is a love of self, a desire of self-preservation, a desire, when he sees his danger, to escape from the wrath to come. "What shall I do to be saved?" is the language of every sinner in this condition. It was for such characters that the gospel was intended, and it is to such that it holds forth its most gracious invitations. "Believe on the Lord Jesus Christ and thou shalt be saved." "Come unto me, all ye that are weary and heavy-laden, and I will give you rest."

If, through the blessing of the Holy Spirit, the sinner be led to this refuge, he immediately experiences a heavenly joy, a peace which the world knoweth not. To this joy succeeds love. His heart is now in some degree sanctified, and hence, he is in some degree capable of receiving impressions of holy love; the emotion of gratitude is excited in his bosom, and he loves in return. He feels that the debt of love which he owes is far greater than he can ever pay: and his language now is, "What can I do too much for him that died for me?' It is no longer a selfish principle which influences his conduct; he is now resolved to live not to himself but to Him who died for him, and who rose again. It is not now we apprehend merely through the fear of future punishment, or even through the hope of future reward, that he avoids sin, and follows after holiness. He has now acquired a new nature, which cannot take pleasure in iniquity. He is not indeed, freed from sin, for then he were perfectly happy; but it is now the object of his abhorrence, and he is looking anxiously forward to the time, when it shall no more break in upon his enjoyment.

Thus we have attempted to give a cursory sketch of the nature and design of the mission of our Saviour; we have endeavoured to show how he reconciled the forgiveness of sinners, and their reception into favour, with the justice and purity of the divine character; and also the fitness of the means employed for this purpose, and the wondrous change produced by them, upon the character of man. And now let the reader solemnly ask his own heart, "Am I a partaker of the mercy here exhibited?" "Have I been led to commit my soul to the keeping of Jesus?"

On the result of these questions depends our eternal happiness. And in this important inquiry let us not deceive ourselves; "A tree is known by its fruits." If our character does not correspond with the precepts of the gospel, whatever we may think, we have not believed it. And if we thus find that our belief has been merely nomi nal, let us seek God before it be too late; let us come to him in the way which he has appointed while it is called to-day; let us recollect that "now is the accepted time, and now is the day of salvation." Let us remember that every moment we put off, our hearts are acquiring an additional degree of hardness; and let us take warning from the declaration, that "He that being often reproved, hardeneth his neck, shall suddenly be destroyed, and that without remedy."

But, if we do experience something of that joy and love which the gospel describes, and have thus reason to think that we have believed in the Son of God; let us not be content with what we have already obtained; let us forget the things that are past, and press onward to the things which are before, for the prize of our high calling in Christ Jesus. Let us recollect that there is no standing still; that if we are not growing in holiness and spiritual strength, we must be falling back. Let us beware of thinking that the contest is over, as though we were already perfect; let us remember that sanctification is a progressive work; that it is not to be attained in a single day, or a single year, or in a series of many years, nor ever *wholly* attained, so long as we remain in this world of sin.

As a means of attaining greater degrees of grace, let us look to the Saviour and reflect on his finished work; the more we think on his sufferings, the more will we hate sin, which was the cause of them! The more we reflect on his love to us, the more will we love in return; for "we love him, because he first loved us." With our love, our holiness will increase, and we shall be the more assimilated to his glorious character; and consequently, we shall the more largely partake of that happiness which is enjoyed by him in full perfection. The subject of the love of God as exhibited in the atonement, is infinite, and will be the theme of our praises through eternity. But though never able fully to comprehend, yet may we ever be learning more of the height, and depth, and breadth, and length of that love which passeth knowledge.

B.

DR. CHALMERS.—THE ST. ANDREW'S MISSIONARY SOCIETY.

Perhaps an apology may be necessary for again calling the attention of our readers to a subject which may be supposed by some of them to have already occupied too prominent a place in the pages of the University Magazine. It is not, however, to the general subject of missions that the following observations refer; but to an institution, which, for several reasons, is highly deserving of our attention. The meetings of the St. Andrew's Missionary Society are conducted by one of the most distinguished men of the present age; and one who is both an *eleve* and a Professor of our own University. After alluding to Dr. Chalmers, it is scarcely necessary to add, that the perfect originality of the plan of procedure in the public meetings of this society, furnishes the subject with an additional claim upon our regard. We feel quite ashamed, indeed, that we have not ere now given a more detailed account of these highly interesting meetings. Our only excuse is, that we have felt unequal to the task. When any subject is treated in an ordinary manner, a brief summary of leading ideas may be sufficient to suggest a pretty accurate conception of the whole; as a well executed sketch may give a just enough idea of a common painting. But should we attempt to give any adequate conception of the rich and expressive diction, and the living imagery of Dr. Chalmers's style, by a meagre outline of his ideas, it were something as if a mere dabbler in the fine arts should hold up his own rude and imperfect sketch of some masterpiece of the pencil, and pretend thereby to afford a just representation of that original, in which every lineament gave grace and beauty, and every touch gave life. This, therefore, we shall not attempt. Our object in these remarks is to give some account of Dr. Chalmers's plan of procedure, which we think might be extensively adopted in meetings of a similar nature, with very considerable advantage.

Dr. Chalmers is, in the widest sense of the word, a Philosopher; and philosophy is his companion wherever he goes. He has here succeeded in introducing her into a place, where, it must be confessed, she has but seldom appeared hitherto, and where her friends expected, least of all, perhaps, to find her, the meeting of a Missionary

Society. If we have been at all able to guess at the scope of Dr. Chalmers's general plan, from the few of these meetings we have had the pleasure of attending, he appears to us to have taken a most interesting view of missionary operations. He seems to regard the history of Christian enterprise among the heathen, as a wide field of observation, from whence we may gather, by induction, some very important truths in reference to the Christian religion. Accordingly, while interesting selections are read from the periodical accounts of different missionary societies, the inferences that may be legitimately drawn from the facts there recorded, are set forth by Dr. Chalmers in paragraphs of his own composition, occasionally interspersed with extemporaneous explanation. These serve to connect together the extracts that are read, and thus give to the whole the air of a continuous and well arranged discourse, where some important doctrines are advanced, which are proved as well as deeply impressed on the mind by an appeal to very striking historical illustration. Apparently from a desire to give a more distinct view of the different spheres of missionary labour, Dr. Chalmers seems to wish to confine his attention to the operations of one body of Christians at a time. At those meetings which we have had the opportunity of attending, during this and the preceding session, the facts which have formed the ground-work of Dr. Chalmers's observations have been gleaned chiefly from the accounts of the Moravian missions. We have been informed that, during the summer months, the Church Missionary Society, and the Baptist Missionary Society, have also shared his attention.

The facts connected with the Missions of the United Brethren, that Dr. Chalmers has brought forward, have given rise to some investigations concerning the great principles of our faith, which must prove interesting, not only to the supporters of missionary societies, but to every one who feels any concern in the cause of genuine Christianity. Some of these inquiries are so interesting, and lead to results of such paramount importance, that we shall refer a little more particularly to those facts which tend to their elucidation.

The United Brethren have been at once the most successful, and the most popular of all missionaries. And it may be interesting to examine a little more closely into these two characteristics of the Moravian missions. And, first, as to their success. — What has been the cause of it? What are their views of divine truth? What has been the mode of their instruction? And in their discourses, what are the truths which they bring most prominently forward? It is well known that, on this very subject, there is a division of opinion among the teachers of Christianity in our own land. One would think that a careful examination of facts might lead to a satisfactory determination of this question.

Some theologians are of opinion that a few of the leading truths of the gospel, such as the atonement of Christ, and the other doctrines that are inseparably connected with it, should hold a most prominent place in their public instructions. Others, while they may admit that these truths are contained in the Scriptures, and as such are to be received by us as matters of faith, are yet of opinion that they are a little too mysterious for the common people, and assure us that they think themselves far more likely to promote the cause of religion and virtue, if, instead of chiming on a few theoretical dogmas, they attempt to enforce on the attention of their hearers, those divine precepts, which embody the principles of a morality, the purest and most perfect that the world has ever known.

Now, on perusing the accounts of the Moravian Missions, we find that, on this very subject, a most interesting experiment has actually been made. These two systems of religious instruction have been successively brought to bear upon the same people, while their circumstances remained the same; and therefore the experiment may be deemed a fair and decisive one. What renders the case still more interesting, is its great simplicity. There are no disturbing forces, so to speak, to confuse or embarrass our calculations in this highly important question of moral dynamics. The subjects of the experiment were savages in the very lowest state of degradation, and therefore we have no allowance to make for any state of preparation that might result from previous knowledge. If it appear from the facts to which we shall refer, that the declaration of those doctrines generally deemed too abstract to produce any practical effect on the popular mind; the doctrines, viz.: of the total depravity of all mankind, of the vicarious suffering of the Son of God, —of justification through belief in his atonement, and sanctification through the emission of the Holy Spirit; if it appear that the simple declaration of these truths has wrought efficiently to the moral and economic renovation of the most ignorant, and the most barbarous of the human species; then it follows *a fortiori* that these are the doctrines which when preached in our own country, are most likely to prove effectual in producing uprightness, sobriety, and godliness throughout our own enlightened community.

To come then to the facts. The scene of the experiment was the inhospitable region of Greenland; and the moral and intellectual condition of the inhabitants was even more barren and dreary than the scenery with which they were surrounded. Here the only plausible system of instruction seemed to be to attempt to teach the savages those truths which are of a preliminary nature. Accordingly, the missionaries set to work most assiduously, in telling the Greenlanders of the being and character of a God, and of the requirements of his law. However plausible this mode of instruction may appear, it was patiently continued in for *seven years*, without producing even the smallest effect on those hearts which ignorance and stupidity had rendered almost inaccessible. The first conversion, (as far as man was concerned), may be said to have been accidental. Some Southlanders happened to visit the brethren, as one of them was writing a translation of the gospels. They were curious to know what was in the book, and on hearing read the history of Christ's agony in the garden, one of the savages earnestly exclaimed, "How was that? Tell me it once more; for I also would fain be saved." But it would be foreign to our purpose to enter into a minute detail of facts. We refer those who may wish to inquire more particularly into this most interesting passage of ecclesiastical history, to the original accounts,* which may be found in the library of the University Missionary Society. Suffice it to say, that some time after this remarkable conversion, the brethren entirely changed their method of instruction. "They now directed the attention of the savages, in the first instance, to Christ Jesus, to his incarnation, to his life, and especially to his sufferings."† This was the beginning of a new era in the history of the evangelization of Greenland. Conversion followed conversion, till the missionaries could number *hundreds* to whom the message of God had come, not in word only, but also in power. There is still one objection that may be

* See Brown's History of Missions, vol. i. p. 294-298. Crantz's History of Greenland.

† See Brown's History of Missions.

made to the inference drawn from these facts, and one which at first sight appears very plausible. It may be asked, How do we know how far the first mode of instruction employed by the missionaries, although it produced no immediate benefit, may not have prepared the minds of savages, for receiving with intelligence the truths that were afterward declared to them? To this we answer that previous to the preaching of the gospel, the savages do not seem to have been so much interested in their teachers, as to give them a fair hearing; and they surely could not be influenced by instructions to which they had never listened. But even were this a doubtful matter, the first conversion in Greenland is a splendid proof of the way in which the simple truths of the gospel seek their way to the human heart, unpioneered by any preliminary instruction whatever.

But, quite satisfactory as this experiment is, still, did it stand alone, we might justly be charged with a rash induction, in drawing a general conclusion from premises so limited. But it does not stand alone. The Moravians have attempted the conversion and civilization of men of almost every country and of every condition; and their uncommon success is borne testimony to, by all who have visited the scenes of their philanthropic exertions. Amid the snows of Greenland they have planted their little villages of comfort and happiness; and the eye of the traveller has been refreshed, as it lighted on some spot of luxuriant verdure, which their hand has decked out in the midst of an African desert.* And, wherever success had attended their endeavours, whenever they tell of a single addition to the number of their converts, it is to the preaching of Christ, and of him crucified, that they attribute it all. Indeed, if we inquire into the reason why the Moravians have been more successful than other missionaries, we find that the distinguishing peculiarity of their preaching consists in this, that they dwell more simply and more constantly, on the love of Christ. In all parts of the world their mode of teaching has been nearly the same, and the change which their instructions have produced, upon men, the most diverse in their character and circumstances, is a beautiful illustration of the divine efficacy which accompanies the simple preaching of the gospel. Under the instruction of these simple, and often uneducated men, the roving and unrestrained savage has been led

* See Barrow's Travels.

to abandon his irregular habits, and to cultivate the decencies of civilized life. Under their instruction, the North American Indian has been divested of his barbarous cruelty, and has even been known to suffer the most palpable injustice, and the most inhuman treatment from his countrymen, without an attempt, or even a wish to revenge. And, finally, under their instruction, the degraded, and almost heart-broken slave has been led to bow to the scourge of his insulting oppressor, with a meekness and submission, which the religion of Jesus alone could inspire.

These are facts ; and facts are far more eloquent than words. We leave them to make their own impression.

We are aware that we may seem to have dwelt too long on this one illustration; but the paramount importance of the subject is a sufficient excuse. Almost every extract that Dr. Chalmers has read, has tended to demonstrate the vast superiority of that mode of Christian instruction which is generally termed *evangelical.*

After dwelling so long on a single illustration of Dr. Chalmers's method of conducting the business of these meetings, we could have wished much in the present paper, (and more especially as this is the last opportunity that may now be afforded of so doing), to have gone on with a more general account of the numerous interesting topics that have been discussed during the course of the doctor's prelections. There is still one point, however, regarding the missions of the United Brethren, which we should be most unwilling slightly to pass over. And we are the less sorry, that we have been led, in these detached sketches, to confine our attention exclusively to one or two points in the history of missions, inasmuch as we have all along expressed it to be our design, to draw the attention of our readers, not so much to the subject of missions, as to those important truths which the experiments of Christian philanthropy may have tended more strikingly to illustrate, and more firmly to establish.

We have said of the United Brethren, that they have been at once the most successful, and the most popular of all missionaries. We have, already, at some length, inquired into the causes of their success; it now remains, that we briefly advert to the subject of their popularity.

We have already seen that the peculiar views of religious truths which these Christians entertain, are not such as generally meet with very high admiration in the world; and any person who has just glanced at their writings, must know, that the way in which they express their sentiments, is not very highly calculated to please the ear or gratify the taste of general readers. Certainly, at first sight, it is not very easy to conceive how the very persons who dwell most exclusively on those doctrines of the Bible, that are known to be most revolting to mere men of taste, should at all have attracted their attention, or gained their esteem. And yet it is a notorious fact, that by men in power, in the colonies where they labour, the Moravian missionaries are very highly respected; while, among men of taste at home, they have become the objects of an almost sentimental admiration. The explanation of the matter which Dr. Chalmers has given, is at once simple and satisfactory. It is just this: The thing has had time to work. And those very principles which themselves are so generally nauseated by men of science and literature, have effloresced into a beauty and a luxuriance which command the esteem, and excite the admiration of all.

When the man of taste reads in the accounts which these missionaries give of their success, such sentences as these, "Our Saviour continues to bless our feeble testimony, concerning the atonement which he has made for sinners;" "The Lord graciously owns our feeble endeavours, and accompanies with his blessing the preaching of the word of the cross," * (and these are fair specimens of the whole strain of their writings;) in all probability, the sneer of mingled pity and contempt curls upon his lips, or he turns proudly away with loathing and disgust. But when the same individual is told of smiling villages, and cultivated fields, starting forth as if by magic, in the midst of a barren wilderness, when he hears that those whom he had been wont to rank, in point of intellect, with the inferior creation, are now disciplined in the elements of general knowledge, and skilled in the endowments of the arts, when he beholds the wandering marauders of the desert associated in little communities where peace and order reign in every breast, and comfort smiles upon every family; his whole soul is enraptured by the realization of those very scenes, the mere imagination of which has given to poetry and romance, their chief and loveliest attractions.

* Periodical Accounts of the Missions of the United Brethren.

Indeed, so different are the emotions excited in the mind of a man of taste, by the contemplation of the principles which are at work, and of the effects that are evolved by their operation, that he cannot be brought to believe that there is any such close connection between the result, and that which is alleged to be the cause of it. He will not admit that a state of things, so truly worthy the admiration of every benevolent and right thinking mind, could ever have been the result of a mode of operation so despicably weak and unphilosophical. And so biassed is his judgment by former prejudices, that no form of evidence, however strong, can ever compel him to the belief that those scenes of happiness and prosperity, which have so charmed his fancy, can at all have anything to do with the canting weakness, or the severe austerity of a system, which, far from thinking it capable of introducing order and comfort, where confusion and misery had reigned before, he had always been wont to regard as that which damped the hilarity, and embittered the pleasures of those who were weak enough to become the dupes of its hypocritical promulgators, even in happier lands. Accordingly, in the broad day-light of the strongest evidence for the contrary, it has been most confidently asserted, that the success of the Moravian missionaries is not at all to be referred to those causes to which themselves have ascribed it. The celebrated traveller, Barrow, who visited the stations of the brethren in South Africa, gives the very highest testimony to the success of their operations; but the nature of their operations themselves, he most grossly misrepresents. *Their* system he contrasts with one, which he is pleased to call that of the "gospel missionaries." "Instead of preaching to the natives," he informs us, "the mysterious parts of the gospel, the Moravians instructed them in useful industrious habits; instead of building a church, they erected a storehouse. Their labours were crowned with complete success." * In a paper on Barrow's work, in the Edinburgh Review, as well as in another article in the same periodical, on Lichtenstein's Travels, the same high commendation is awarded to the Moravians, for the wisdom manifested in their plans, and the same gross misrepresentations are made in regard to the *nature* of these plans.† In the last

* Barrow's Journey in Africa, p. 381.

† Edinburgh Review, vol. viii. p. 434 – 438, and vol. xxi. pp. 65, 66.

mentioned article we are expressly told that the Moravian brethren "begin with civilizing their pupils, educating and instructing them in the useful arts." We are not sure whether this reviewer was the original inventor of the oft-repeated objection to missions in general, that "you must civilize a people before you can Christianize them." But if he was, it is most unfortunate for his theory that he happened to stumble on the operations of the Moravian missionaries, in order to support it; for never has the objection met with more triumphant refutation, than in the successful labours of these devoted philanthropists. The author of the review meant to compliment the Moravians; but they felt insulted by his eulogium, and were the first to come forward and deny his assertions.

Here, then, is a very high testimony to the efficacy of evangelical religion. A person unacquainted with the hidden mechanism, is delighted with the visible effects which are produced by it. He begins to speculate on the principles in which such results must have originated. He forms a theory of his own, agreeable to his own previously acquired modes of thinking, and proceeds forthwith to compliment those who had acted on so excellent a plan, and who had demonstrated its efficacy by the beautiful system which they had caused to emerge from it. The workers behind the scenes, now come forward, and tell him that he has quite mistaken the matter; for they have been acting on a system altogether different. Our speculator is not only disappointed to find that his own theory receives no support from the facts under consideration, and may not, for aught that he has yet seen, merit the high eulogiums, with which he has thought fit to honour it; but he is confounded to discover, that he has been unwillingly bearing testimony to the merits of a plan at variance with his own; and that the system to which his high eulogiums are now most legitimately transferable, is one, which he has all along been accustomed to declaim against as irrational, and to despise as unphilosophical.

C.

ESSAY ON THE DIVISIONS OF PHILOSOPHY.

THE first which I shall give, is the essay read at the commencement of the class, and which has been repeatedly referred to already. At this time it must be remembered the writer had not enjoyed the benefit of Dr. Chalmers's course. It had only then begun. The subject is difficult, the paper is short; but the statement is most luminous, and the illustration uncommonly beautiful and felicitous.

In considering this subject, the question has very forcibly presented itself to us, "Why, in the physical department of philosophy, have the divisions and sub-divisions been carried to such a degree of minuteness, while in the moral department, they are comparatively few?" Not, we conceive, because in the latter the field of observation is more limited, or the materials more scanty than in the former; (for quite the reverse of this we believe to be true,) but chiefly because the latter is involved in the darkness of mystery, which entirely obscures many of those lines of demarcation, which even in the former, are not very strongly delineated.

Let us suppose, in illustration of this, that a man wholly unacquainted with the classifications of philosophy, looked around on an ordinary landscape. There are traces of such marked distinction between some of the objects, and such strong points of resemblance between others, that he could not fail to make some general arrangement and classification of the whole. He would at once distinguish the land from the water, and the green herbage from the naked rock, and the houses from the trees, and the animate from the inanimate objects that surrounded him. If we further suppose that while he was thus gazing on the scene, the shades of night began to gather around him, it is easy to conceive how many of the nicer lines of distinction which were before so apparent, would now become dim and undiscernible; how the sky would seem to mingle with the ocean; and how the herbage, and the trees, and the houses, and the animals, would be involved in one dark shade of unvaried sameness; and how, where he could before point out many a division, and many a sub-division, two or three grand lineaments, and these but faintly perceptible, would be all he could discern within the whole range of his survey.

And thus it is with the two grand divisions of philosophy; the philosophy of matter, and the philosophy of mind. In the one we have to do with an external world, where all is luminous and distinct; in the other we have to do with the busy world within, where all is seen as through a glass, darkly. Need we wonder, then, that the one has been far more minutely divided and sub-divided than the other?

Accordingly we find that while mental science has been divided into three parts, viz., Logic, Rhetoric, and Moral Philosophy, the divisions of physical science amount to at least ten times that number.

But not only are the divisions of mental science few, but few as they are, they have been confounded together. And this we think has arisen, not so much from that obscurity which envelopes the whole subject, as from the intimate connection with each other of its different departments.

There is here a distinction, which we would notice, between the physical and mental sciences, that while the materials of the former are widely scattered over the whole face of nature, and seem not to be connected by any common tie, those of the latter have all a reference to a single object — the human mind. It is thus, that, as among the members of the human body, there exists among all the departments of this latter science, a common sympathy, if we may so speak; so that if one suffer, all suffer with it; if one is injured, all are injured. And it is this very close connection which has been the cause of their being confounded together.

To illustrate this, let us suppose that war has been declared against one of two confederate states, and that the inhabitants of the other come promptly forward, to defend the territories of their ally, and that after they have succeeded in beating off the enemy, they still linger in the country, and become gradually so amalgamated with the original inhabitants, that in process of time the two peoples are confounded in one.

Now this, we think, is just what has happened with regard to the moral and intellectual philosophies. Distinctly separate, yet nearly allied; the attack which Mr. Hume made upon the one, struck, though indirectly, at the very vitals of the other, and the champions of moral science wisely took the alarm. It was then first, that with a laudable zeal, they overstepped the limits of their own domain; and had they returned when tranquillity was restored, they had done well. It is not for going forth to meet a common enemy that we censure them, but because when that enemy was defeated, they still lingered in a foreign land, and forgot to retire within their own peculiar territories.

ESSAY ON THE ANALOGY WHICH SUBSISTS BETWEEN THE OPERATIONS OF NATURE AND THE OPERATIONS OF POLITICAL ECONOMY.

On the 31st of the same month he read another essay in the class, on one of the topics of Political Economy, around which the fertile genius of Dr. Chalmers has thrown a fascination and a splendour, of which the subject was not previously supposed to be susceptible. How thoroughly his pupil was imbued with the ardent spirit of his professor, this essay most powerfully illustrates. Every reader will form his own judgment of the argument. Of the composition of the paper, and the beauty of the illustration, there can be but one opinion

It has been said by some writers of natural history, that an antidote to the venom of the serpent is to be found within the body of the animal itself. We know not whether there be any truth in this assertion; but if there be, that must surely be a very beautiful mechanism by which those very organs which produce a deadly poison, produce also a remedy for its fatal effects; and surely that arrangement is a display of the most consummate wisdom by which the efficient cause of an evil is also the efficient cause of its cure.

Now there is a principle very much akin to this, which exists in almost all the operations of nature, a principle to which nature in a great measure owes that constancy for which she has been so greatly admired. The principle we refer to is this, — That an operation of nature whenever it arrives at that stage in its progress, where its effects would begin to be detrimental, by a very beautiful constitution of things, gives rise to an operation of an opposite tendency, and thus works out a cure for those very evils which itself seemed to threaten. Thus, were we unacquainted with the workings of nature, and did we behold the sun, day after day, shining on the earth with unclouded splendour; and did we perceive that, day after day, in consequence of this the soil was becoming more parched; and did we further know that, without moisture, vegetation would cease, and the fruits of the earth could not come to perfection, — we might well look forward with the most dismal foreboding to what would seem the inevitable consequence. But how would our fears give place to our admiration of the Creator's wisdom and goodness, when we were told that that sun which we were thus contemplating as the cause of so much misery, was at that very moment gathering by the influence of his rays, the waters of the ocean, and suspending them in mighty reservoirs above us, which would again gently descend over the whole surface of our earth, and thus refresh the drooping plants, and give a new impulse to the economy of vegetation. There is another very beautiful instance of the operation of this principle. When any particular region of the earth begins to be overheated, the air is rarefied, — it consequently ascends; the cool air which is around, rushes in to supply its place, and thus does a refreshing breeze blow over that land, which had else been in a short time rendered uninhabitable.

And now to apply this to the subject before us. In the operations of political economy, as well as in the operations of nature, there is a beautiful constancy; and it is truly wonderful to think what a rough handling a nation will come through, and with what hardihood she will endure it; to think how famine and pestilence, and foreign war, and internal commotion, will successively lay hold of her; and how she will escape from their grasp, and in a few short years will be nearly what she was before she was subjected to it. And as the operations of political economy resemble the operations of nature in their constancy, we think they also resemble them in the cause of this constancy; and we shall try to illustrate this by an example or two.

Thus, in every country there should be a certain relation between the produce and the population; and it is interesting to observe how the constancy of this relation is maintained, through all the changes to which a nation is exposed.

Let us suppose, for example, that by improvements in tilling the ground, in the rotations of the crops, &c., the agricultural produce is increased, and thus the constancy of the relation between the produce and the population is for a time destroyed. There is in this instance a superabundance of produce, or what is the same thing, there is a deficiency of population. Now let us see how the original relation between them is again restored. The agricultural produce being increased, more corn is brought to market, and the demand, in the first instance at least, remains the same: the consequence is, corn is cheapened. The cheapening of corn again puts more of the inhabitants in a condition to support a family; marriages take place earlier, and the population is increased; and thus is the deficiency made up, and the proper relation between the produce and the population again restored.

But it must be evident to every one, that were the population thus to go on increasing indefinitely, the proper relation would soon be more than restored, the ratio would become reversed, and instead of a superabundance of produce, there would soon be a redundancy of population. But here, too, may we behold the beautiful effect of that arrangement, by which the remedy for the evil is involved in the evil itself. As the population has now increased, the demand has also increased: but in this latter instance the supply has remained the same; the natural consequence of which is, that the price of corn rises. It is now of course more difficult to support a family; marriages are discouraged, and thus does the very increase of population, as soon as it comes to that point where its further increase would be detrimental, actually bring a check upon itself.

Again, from various causes we sometimes see an old manufacture abolished. And here there would seem to be a great and immediate evil; a vast number of operatives are thrown out of employment. And yet, if we consider the subject attentively, we shall find that here, too, as well as in the example already adduced, the evil, if let alone, will remedy itself. And wherever we thus see an old manufacture abolished, may we with confidence predict that the wealth which supported that manufacture, will either give rise to a new one, or will so divide itself among those that yet remain, as to give a new impulse to each. And thus will the evil be remedied, and that class of the community which have been thrust from their old occupation, will either find employment in a new manufacture, or will be parceled out among the manufactures that yet remain. There is still as much food for them in the country as before, and all that they will suffer will merely be the temporary inconvenience attending a change of employment.

Were one of the mouths of the Nile to be stopped up, that river would not discharge less water into the ocean than it did before. The water which used to flow through that channel, would at first, it is true, flow backwards; but it would not continue to do so, nor would it even remain stationary; it would seek another direction, and it would either overflow the banks, and hollow out a new channel for itself, or it would divide itself and flow to the sea, through the channels that yet remained. And here, by the way, would we advert to that political delusion which would magnify the importance of any one branch of manufacture or commerce. The waters of the ocean would not be diminished by one drop, because they had ceased to receive the tribute of that stream. So long as the same body of water continued to flow on from the fountain head, so long would the monarch of waters know no diminution in his resources. And it were well if our statesmen, as well as our operatives, could perceive that the manufacture does not *produce* either the taxes in the one case, or the wages in the other; that it is merely the channel through which they flow; and that so long as the national ability remains the same, neither the revenues of the state, nor the wages of the operatives will suffer one iota of diminution by the decay of any one branch of commerce or manufacture. We do not say that in such an event there would be no loss at all; but we do affirm that ultimately the loss would not be sustained by the government, nor by those employed in the manufacture, but by the public at large.

To return to our illustration. That particular branch of the Nile might have added much to the beauty of the scenery on its banks, and might have ministered in a high degree to the enjoyment, and even to the comfort of those who dwelt among them; and the stopping up of its channel would be felt by them to be a very serious inconvenience. And thus, too, the particular branch of manufacture might have furnished an article which contributed very much to the enjoyment or the comfort of the public; and in so far its decay might be felt as a very calamitous event. But still our remark holds true, that ultimately the operatives will not suffer; that ultimately the state will not suffer; that in this respect the evil will remedy itself; that if the stream of public wealth flow not through that channel, it will seek out another, and that if there be a temporary stagnation till the new outlet be formed, it will be compensated by the more than usual rapidity of the current, when it has cleared away the obstructions.

We hope the two examples we have adduced may have been sufficient to illustrate that constitution of things, by which an evil is made to remedy itself, and to show how the operation of this principle serves to regulate the vast machinery of a nation, and to give a constancy and a steadiness to all its movements. And we would now ask to what should the discovery of this lead us?

We might have concluded *a priori* that that God whose goodness is over all his works, while he regulated all the changes of nature, and maintained an unvarying constancy in all her operations, would not leave to chance, or to the guidance of mere human wisdom, the regulation of those principles on which depends the temporal happiness of his rational creatures. And when in the workings of these principles we discover that same constancy which distinguishes the operations of nature, and the same means employed to preserve that constancy; and when we perceive, further, that all this may go on independent of our knowledge, and most certainly does go on independent of our direction; should it not go very much to strengthen the conclusion? Let us acknowledge then, that there is here the working of a mightier agency than man; and let us ascribe that constant hardihood with which a nation survives all the changes that pass over her, to the care and the wisdom of that same Mighty Being, "who causeth the vapours to ascend from the ends of the earth: who maketh lightnings for the rain; and who bringeth the wind out of his treasuries."

The concluding paragraph is a beautiful instance of the prevailing disposition of the writer's mind, and of the happy ease with which he could connect every speculation and exercise with his leading and darling subject. His mind traced the hand of the benevolent Creator in all his operations, whether of nature or of providence. He beheld and adored his wisdom, both in the uncontrolable and efficient laws of the universe, and in the frame and constitution of society. What affected his own mind, he was desirous should affect the minds of others; and "out of the fulness of his heart, his mouth spake." Yet there is no thrusting of the subject forward. It is not only presented in all its importance, but with the grace and modesty which could not fail to command respect and attention.

Not satisfied with his labours in the several classes which he attended, he took an active part in a Literary Society, consisting of the young men attending the University; and at one of its meetings, held on the 11th of December, he read an essay, or delivered a speech, on the following subject: —

THAT KNOWLEDGE GIVES ITS POSSESSOR MORE POWER THAN WEALTH DOES.

It has been said by Lord Bacon, that "knowledge is power," and the same thing has been asserted of wealth by Mr. Hobbes. And with both these statements we perfectly agree. The very nature of our present debate presupposes the truth of both. The question this evening is, "Whether does wealth or knowledge give its possessor more power?" Now we do think that there is a great deal of vagueness in the terms of the question; and we do anticipate, from this, a good deal of misapprehension, and a good deal of wrangling about words and definitions, when, after all, the disputants may be one in sentiment. There are various views that may be taken of the question; and we shall first consider it in its strict and literal interpretation; and in this view, we think, there can be little or no debate at all. The very fiercest of our opponents, we should think, will allow, that wealth, altogether apart from knowledge, can accomplish nothing at all; for a certain degree of knowledge is necessary to the right application of wealth. An idiot might lavish the most boundless fortune, and after all be further from his point than he was before. On the other hand, we frankly confess, that knowledge, altogether apart from wealth, can accomplish but little, since a certain portion of wealth is necessary to carry our plans into execution. The fact is, that, to accomplish anything of importance, they must go hand in hand, knowledge must devise the plan, and wealth, in general, must furnish the means to carry that plan into execution. To knowledge and wealth may we justly apply the language of Sallust, when speaking of the mind and the body: "Utrumque per se indigens, alterum alterius auxilio eget."

But even in this view of the subject there are some things which knowledge can do altogether independent of wealth, though we know of none that wealth can do altogether independent of knowledge. Thus, with a mere knowledge of the power of the lever, (a machine so simple that it may be had for nothing,) I can raise a very great weight; a thing to accomplish which, wealth might have been lavished in vain.

But there is another view of the subject, and we think the most correct of all, in which wealth itself may be said to be the result of knowledge, and, consequently, all the power which is attributed to wealth may be referred to knowledge as its ultimate cause. And, that this a correct view, a very slight attention to the subject will convince us. Let us look to that country which is sunk lowest in the depths of ignorance, and we shall invariably find that that country too is sunk lowest in the depths of poverty and wretchedness; and that, on the other hand, that country which stands highest in the scale of knowledge, stands highest also in the scale of wealth. And if we just consider how much commerce is indebted to the invention of the compass, and the discoveries of astronomy, and how much manufactures owe to the invention of machinery, and how much their productive powers are thus increased, we shall come to the conclusion, that almost, if not altogether, all our wealth is the result of our knowledge. Most justly then, viewing the subject in this light, might we turn the weapons of our opponents against themselves, and make their every argument, for their side of the question, to tell most powerfully against them on our own.

But this, though the most just and philosophical view of the question, is evidently not the view that was intended to be taken of it: for it is a view that resolves the question itself into an absurdity — a view, which, if the framers of the question had taken, they would never have framed it at all. And though we could thus take the advantage of our adversaries by disarming them, and then by those very arms, compelling them to surrender, we are not reduced to such a shift; we can meet them upon more honourable terms.

We shall therefore attempt to show, that, even in the more loose and ordinary interpretation of the question, knowledge gives its possessor more power than wealth does. And, as the word *power* is very general and undefined, we shall take two modifications of it; viz., mechanical power, and political power. By the mechanical power of knowledge, we mean that power which it gives us over inanimate nature; and, by political power, that power which it give us over our fellow-men; and from both these acceptations of the term, we shall try to show, that knowledge gives us more power than wealth. First, with regard to its mechanical power. We would remark here, that two agents may both be capable of performing the same thing, and yet the power of the one may very much exceed that of the other; and in such a case we must estimate their relative power by the effort which it costs each to perform the thing in view, and we shall find that the power is inversely as the effort. Thus I may be able to lift a weight with my little finger, which a child can do only by exerting his whole strength, and in this case I am said to have more power than the child, because the effort it costs me to do the same thing is not so great. Now, we shall take a case analogous to this where something is to be done, and where knowledge and wealth may be said to be the agents, where we have a distinct view of the way in which each performs it.* Wealth performs the task, but it is with such an effort as almost drained the coffers of even Roman resources. She builds a gigantic bridge across the valley, while knowledge accomplishes the same object by simply laying a pipe along the ground. When we compare the vast and imposing fabric of an ancient aqueduct with the simple, and withal, undignified

* The problem is to carry water across a valley.

apparatus of a modern water-pipe, we cannot fail to be struck with the ease and simplicity with which knowledge can perform that which it costs wealth such an effort to accomplish. And one would think, that in viewing these proud remains of Roman wealth and Roman ignorance, a feeling of the painfully ludicrous would stifle our rising admiration of their sublimity, and that the very grandeur of their structure, when compared with their design, would remind us of

> ———————"an ocean into tempest wrought
> To waft a feather, or to drown a fly."

But though, in the present instance, wealth, by the mightiness of the effort, may seem to rival knowledge in solving the problem, there are many instances were she is left far behind, and cannot by the very mightiest efforts, come up with knowledge.

By the assistance of knowledge, we are enabled almost by a touch of our finger, to raise the most immense weights, and may almost be said to weigh the mountains in scales, and the hills in a balance. By her assistance can we scour the unknown regions of ether, and penetrate the still more secret caverns of the deep. By her assistance too, can we guide a floating city over the main, and turn it at our will by a little helm. By her assistance, too, can we impress the very elements into our service, and make the winds our messengers, and the water and the fire our slaves. And by her assistance, too, can we give to inanimate objects all the vigour of animal life; thus creating for ourselves a Behemoth, whose bones are brass, and sinews bars of iron; thus making him our slave, and forcing him to prepare for us those necessaries and conveniences which formerly we obtained by the sweat of our brow. Such is the power of knowledge; and, till our adversaries can give us instances of the power of wealth, which can be compared with them, we think that we have gained the question.

We intended next to have treated of political power; but we shall first hear refuted the arguments we have already adduced.

None of my young friend's Essays have pleased me more than the one, which is now to follow. It was read to the moral class, on the 10th of January, 1825. The subject afforded a favourable opportunity of introducing the evangelical system, and that opportunity was not neglected. But there is more than the introduction of the system—there is a beautiful exposition of it, in which the writer steers clear of the selfish system of Sandeman on the one hand, and the ultra-spirituality of some of the American divines on the other. The one does not sufficiently distinguish between *self-love* and *selfishness;* the other treats man as if he were a being capable of merging all his personal feelings and interests, in a vague and undefined idea of God, and of holiness. The Scriptures never require us to lose sight of our personal interest in the divine favour; but they never urge it as the principal or the only plea, that we should do the will of God. They bring us, as is here well stated, under the influence of the great principles which govern Deity himself; and thus combine the perfect enjoyment of blessedness, with the perfect exercise of benevolence.

AN ESSAY ON THE SELFISH SYSTEM.

We are told of the Emperor Nero, among his other unnatural actions, that no sooner was his appetite so satiated with one course of gluttony, as to refuse more food, than he again fitted himself in a most revolting manner, for renewing the round of sensual gratification. Of another individual we are told that such was his dread of future disease and death, that he sat continually in one scale of a balance, with a counterpoise in the other, and that it was his constant employment to watch the deflections of the beam, and most studiously to preserve the equality of the balance, so that he never took food till his own scale ascended, and stopped eating as soon as the equilibrium was restored. As the motives which induced each of these individuals to take food are evidently very different from each other, so are the motives of both strikingly different from those which in this matter actuate the great mass of mankind. Of the first individual we would say, that pleasure was his object, and that he took food merely as a means of obtaining this pleasure. With regard to the second, again, we would say that it was self-love that dictated his extraordinary conduct; that he took food, not like the other, for the sake of gratifying his palate, but purely from a consideration of the posterior advantages which would thence accrue to him. With the great mass of mankind, again we would say, that hunger is the primary and ruling incitement; that they eat not in general to gratify their palate, and far less from a consideration of any posterior advantage; but chiefly for the purpose of satisfying their appetite. Food is not used by them as the mere means of obtaining something else, it is itself the primary and terminating object of their desire.

From these familiar illustrations, we think we may discover the difference between self-love, and the more special affections of our nature. The chief distinction seems to be, that the latter terminate in some external object, while the former uses that object as a means of promoting some plan of future interest. Of all the characters we have mentioned, only one seems to have been actuated by self-love, he who took food from a sense of the beneficial effects which would follow. It may be thought, that Nero, too, was actuated by selfishness, inasmuch as he used the food as a means of obtaining something else; but on a close examination, we shall find that it was not the love of self, but the love of pleasure, which was his actuating motive; that if he had any regard to self-interest, his conduct would have been altogether different: that he was in fact pursuing a line of conduct in direct opposition to all that self-love would dictate. We may here just remark by the way, the wisdom displayed in this constitution of our animal frame. Our Creator has not left us to discover that without being invigorated by food, and refreshed by sleep, our bodies could not long subsist; and thus, from a principle of self-love to attend to the taking of food and repose, as duties which it was necessary to perform, in order to self-preservation: but He has endowed us with special affections; with a desire for food and sleep when the body requires them: just as he has given us a sense of injury, and a feeling of resentment, to preserve us from the injustice of our fellow men.

Now in morals there are facts analogous to those which we have just mentioned, with regard to our animal frame. As there is a desire for food altogether apart from any future consequences; and as there is a more immediate pleasure, and a more remote advantage which attend the satisfying of this desire,—so is there a motive to the performance of a virtuous action, altogether for its own sake, and apart from all its consequences; and there is also a more immediate pleasure, and a more remote happiness attending the performance of such an action. As it has appeared that there are different motives which may induce us to take food, so are there different motives which may urge us to the performance of a virtuous deed. The abettors of the selfish system seem to have erred in confounding these together, or rather in making the one motive of selfishness swallow up the rest.

It may be true that much of the seeming virtue of our world must be put to the account of selfishness; and much of it, too, to the account of sentimentalism; and yet, is it true, that virtue may be followed for her own sake; that she has a native grace and attraction of her own, altogether independent of the pleasure and the happiness which follow in her train.

In the illustration which we took from our animal nature, we felt it difficult to adduce a solitary instance where selfishness was the actuating motive; and there one would think it impossible to confound, unless designedly, self-love, with the more special affections; but in the moral world, alas, the case is different. Here are thousands who perform virtuous actions, altogether from selfish motives, for one that follows virtue for her own sake. And when we find that many seem virtuous in their outward conduct, who care not to swerve from the path of rectitude, if they can but do it unobserved; that the merchant who would shudder at the thought of forgery, or any such gross and palpable crime, can yet in his every day transactions, impose on those he deals with, and indulge in a thousand little and unperceived deceits; and when we find that this is a true delineation of the moral character, not of one in a city, or even one in a family, but of the great bulk of our species, — need we wonder that, from such a view of human nature, some should have come to the conclusion that all virtue is the result of selfishness, or rather that there is no true virtue at all?

But all this is easily accounted for by the fact, that a blight hath corrupted the moral scenery of our world; and it just tallies with what we are told in the book of revelation, of the total depravity of our whole race.

If, then, there were a system which professed to be able to renew our nature, and to restore us to our original purity, we should most confidently expect that the disciples of such a system should follow virtue, not from any selfish principle, but simply and solely for her own sake. There is such a system, by which these expectations have been fully realized, — even the system of evangelical Christianity. We know that it has been asserted, that here, too, self-love is the actuating motive; that the disciples of this system are influenced in their conduct by the hope of reward, and the fear of punishment; but if we rightly understand this system, the assertion is most false. It is true that the evangelical system makes its first appeal to our self-love, or otherwise it could not have been adapted to depraved and selfish creatures; but it is equally true that the virtue to which it leads, is of the most pure and disinterested nature. The way in which this is accomplished, is, we think, well illustrated, in the case of that young man who was couched for a cataract in the beginning of the last century, and whose case so much interested the philosophers of Europe. To induce him to submit to the operation, his friends told him of the loveliness of scenery, and of the pleasure to be derived from gazing on beautiful objects. — Such reasoning had no effect, — *he* could form no conception of beauty; they were in fact addressing a special affection which did not exist. An appeal was made to his self-love, he was told of the advantages to be derived from reading, and this we are told, proved effectual. And thus it is that the gospel addresses itself to man. It might tell him of the loveliness of virtue, and the deformity of vice; and well do we know that such reasoning would prove utterly powerless. True, he has a faculty for perceiving moral beauty, just as the blind man has an eye; but as in his case, too, there is a thick film spread over it. True, the most depraved of our race can distinguish virtue from vice, and perceive a rightness in the one, and a wrongness in the other, just as many blind people can tell the light from the darkness; but just as they cannot perceive that harmonious variety of colour and shade which constitutes the loveliness of natural scenery, so cannot the unrenewed mind perceive that which is so emphatically termed the "beauty of holiness." The same appeal which proved effectual in the case of him who was blind, is also effectual in the case of fallen man, — an appeal to self-love. The Bible can tell him of the future punishment of sin, and to the whispers of his own conscience it can add the voice of its authority, in telling him that he is a sinner: it can constrain him to cry out, "What shall I do to be saved?" and to such a question it can give a most satisfactory answer. If he is thus led to accept of its terms, he no sooner does so, than the film which obscured his moral vision is removed. He is now in some degree restored to the lost image of the Godhead, and can therefore perceive an independent beauty in virtue, and an independent deformity in vice. It is not now, we conceive, from the hope of heaven, or the fear of hell, that he is virtuous; it is because he loves holiness that he follows after it; — it is because he hates sin that he flees from it; his attachment to the one, and his recoil from the other, will still continue to strengthen: and even now, all weak and imperfect as they are, do they proceed from a principle similar to that which determines the choice of Deity himself.

Little do they understand the evangelical system, who urge against it the plea that the virtue of its disciples is a virtue of selfishness. So far is this from being the case, that let but self-love be the principle that regulates our conduct, — let but the hope of reward, and the fear of punishment be all that prompts us to virtue, and the reward itself will never follow. Some there have been, who from this principle have refrained from many of the vices, and even from many of the innocent enjoyments of life, — who have been ingenious in inventing self-torments here, that they might escape eternal punishment hereafter; but yet, is the character of such virtue, and the final judgment which shall be passed upon it, most truly de- bed by the poet, when he exclaims,

"What is all righteousness that men devise?
What, — but a sordid *bargain* for the skies?
But Christ as soon would abdicate his own,
As stoop from heaven to sell the proud a throne."

D.

THE DOCTRINE OF A GRADATION IN REWARDS AND PUNISHMENTS; AND AN ATTEMPT TO APPLY IT TO THE SUBJECT OF MISSIONS.

In all those descriptions of the final retribution which are given us in the Bible, our attention is called to two great divisions of the inhabitants of our world: namely, "Those who shall go away into everlasting punishment; and those who shall go into life eternal." But, though there be thus one grand classification of our whole species, where the line of demarcation is very broad and very strongly marked; yet in the same description, do we find an account given of minuter sub-divisions, whose bounding lines are not so vivid, but which imperceptibly shade into and blend with each other. And we think ourselves fully warranted to suppose, that there will be different degrees of glory on the one hand, and different degrees of punishment on the other; and that these will be determined by the privileges we have enjoyed on earth, and the degree to which those privileges have been improved or neglected. He that had gained ten pounds was made ruler over ten cities; he that gained five, over five cities. And again, "That servant which knew his Lord's will, and prepared not himself, neither did according to his will, shall be beaten with many stripes; but he that knew not, and did commit things worthy of stripes, shall be beaten with few stripes. For unto whomsoever much is given, of him shall much be required; and to whom men have committed much, of him they will ask the more." But this doctrine of a gradation in rewards and punishments has been thought, by some, inconsistent with the Scripture doctrine of justification by faith; and inconsistent with the free and unmerited nature of that reward which shall be given to those who are thus justified. Were the glory promised a fair return for our well-doings, there might then be some force in the objection; but when we consider, that, after we have done all that we are commanded, (and, who is there that can boast of having done so?) we are still unprofitable servants; and when we consider that sin mingles with our best services, which cannot, therefore, be pleasing to that God who cannot look upon iniquity but with abhorrence; we shall perceive, that this view of the final retribution, far from being at variance with the grand and fundamental doctrine of the gospel, magnifies it and does it honour; inasmuch as it is the imputed righteousness of Christ, which imparts to our actions all in them that is pleasing, and all that is acceptable to God.

The doctrine of the cross is represented in the Bible as the foundation, and the virtuous actions of believers as the superstructure which is built upon it; the latter, deriving all their strength and all their stability from the former: standing upon it, and falling in utter impotency to the ground as soon as it is removed. "For other foundation," says Paul, "can no man lay than that is laid, which is Jesus Christ. Now if any man build upon this foundation, gold, silver, precious stones, wood, hay, stubble; every man's work shall be made manifest, for the day shall declare it, because it shall be revealed by fire; and the fire shall try every man's work of what sort it is. If any man's work abide, which he hath built thereupon, he shall receive a reward. If any man's work shall be burned, he shall suffer loss; but he himself shall be saved, yet so as by fire."

There seems, then, to be a connection between the degree of active exertion here, and the degree of reward hereafter; and also a connection between the degree of suffering here, and the degree of glory that shall follow. "He which soweth sparingly," says Paul, "shall reap also sparingly; and he which soweth bountifully shall reap also bountifully." And the same apostle assures us, that "our light affliction which is but for a moment, worketh out for us a far more exceeding and eternal weight of glory."

Of the truth of these remarks, we have a very beautiful illustration in the mediatorial character of the Son of God. His was a life of the most strenuous exertion; it was his meat, and his drink to do the will of his Father. His, too, was a life of the most unparalleled suffering. He was emphatically "a man of sorrows, and acquainted with grief." And as he suffered more than any one of his followers, as his visage was marred, more than any man, and his form more than the sons of men, so shall his glory far exceed that of any of those whom He condescends to call his brethren. It is the connection between his unwearied exertion and his reward; the connection between his sufferings, and his glory, that we especially advert to. Paul tells us that it became him "by whom are all things, and for whom are all things, to make the Captain of our salvation perfect through suffering." And it is after giving an account of the humiliation of our Lord, that the apostle adds, "Therefore, (on which account) God also hath highly exalted him, and given him a name which is above every name." But it may be thought that though these remarks hold, in their fullest extent, with regard to Him who was without sin, and who could demand, as his due, that reward which was but a fair compensation for his faultless accomplishment of the work which was given him to do; yet that they are wholly misapplied with regard to those whose very best services are polluted and mingled with sin. It is true that we can make no demand, that we have no plea to urge at the hands of justice, that our very salvation from wrath is a matter of purest mercy, of free and unmerited favour. But yet it is true, that "God is not unrighteous to forget our work and labour of love;" and we are assured that if we suffer with Christ, we shall also reign with him.

We shall first, then, consider it as a *privilege* to be permitted to labour in the cause of Christ; and we shall advert to one or two of the ways in which we can share in his sufferings, and consequently be made partakers of His glory. First, then, Jesus Christ was a martyr. He sealed his testimony with his blood. And hence the promise, "Be thou faithful unto death and I will give thee a crown of life." And hence the willingness, nay, the eagerness of the first disciples to gain a martyr's crown. Yes, there was a time when the followers of Him whom Pilate crucified, were proud to show their attachment to their Master, at the expense of life itself. But those days of fiery trial are gone. And too much cause have we to fear, that the spirit of martyrdom is gone along with them. That spirit of fervent love to God, and of devoted attachment to each other, which so distinguished the early Christians, as to draw forth the applauses even of their enemies, is gone with the persecution which was the cause of it; and there hath come in its room a spirit of cold and heartless profession; a spirit of animosity and dissension among those of whom once it was said, "Behold, how these Christians love one another." The test of faithfulness unto death you cannot now make. In our land at least, the voice of persecution has long been silent. But though your faith cannot now be thus tried in reality, did you never in imagination bring your Christianity to this test? After having read of the unwavering constancy of a Hamilton, or of the still more recent sufferings of a Wishart, whose memory yet lives so palpably in all that is around us, did you never ask your own hearts the question, "Would I have acted thus?" And in the glow of enthusiastic feeling, have you not thought with the generous and warm-hearted, yet self-confident apostle, that you were ready to follow your Master to prison, and to death? Like Peter, you may indulge in the romantic thought of your attachment, and your constancy; without, like him, having your feelings tried by the test of stern reality.

But, though the crown of martyrdom is now placed beyond our reach, and in this particular we can no longer drink of the cup which Jesus drank, nor be baptized with the baptism which he was baptized with, is there no other way in which we can suffer with Christ, and consequently reign with him? Is there no other feature of the Saviour's character, whose resemblance we can yet trace upon our own? There is such a feature, one of the most prominent in all the mediatorial characters of the Son of God. Not only was he a martyr, he was also a missionary. He came on a mission to our world. He came to preach the gospel to the poor. He was sent to heal the broken-hearted, to preach deliverance to the captives, and recovering of sight to the blind, — to set at liberty them that were bruised, — to preach the acceptable year of the Lord. It was for this that he left the bosom of the Father. It was for this that he emptied himself, and took upon him the form of a slave. It was for this that he exchanged a throne of glory for a manger, and the praises of sinless angels for the revilings of sinful men. And it is in the same cause that the missionary now goes forth, leaving father and mother, and houses and lands.

It has often struck us that those very objections which are now urged against the preaching of the gospel to the heathen, might have been brought with equal plausibility against the first preaching of the gospel to our world. When you have heard the opposers of missions argue about the insufficiency of the means for the end in view, and in support of this objection, proudly appeal to the fact that little has yet been accomplished, did it never occur to you, that such, in all probability, would be the reasonings of those who opposed the ministry of our Lord and his disciples?

Just picture to yourself a few poor and illiterate men, with nothing that was imposing in their outward appearance, sometimes without a place where to lay their head, and sometimes eating of the ears of corn, to satisfy their hunger. And when your imagination has filled up this outline of apparent meanness and poverty; just think of the mighty revolution which they professed was to be brought about by their instrumentality, and you may conceive the sneers of philosophic pride with which these professions would be contemplated. You may well conceive what would be the feelings of the literati of the day; how they would remember the vain attempts of a Socrates and a Plato, and all the master spirits of antiquity, to reform the manners even of their own countrymen; and how they would laugh at the pretensions of an illiterate tradesman, the son of a common mechanic, who professed that the system which he taught should one day be acknowledged by the whole world. So much for the apparent insufficiency of the means for the end.

But mark, this was not all. Think again of the little success which seemed to accompany his preaching, think of the few followers whom he had gathered round him, after spending thirty years in the scene of his labours. And think of the inconstancy of these few, when the day of persecution arrived. The followers of Socrates stood by him, when he drank the fatal cup; but the disciples of Jesus forsook him and fled. Think of his death as a common malefactor; and then can you wonder, if even the most devoted of his followers, thought all was over; and if, in the bitterness of their sorrow, they confessed to the unknown inquirer that their hopes had died with their Master, but that once they "trusted that this had been he who should have redeemed Israel?"

But the opposers of missions tell us, that here the means, though apparently inadequate, were not so in reality; that the men were inspired by the Spirit of God. We immediately answer them, by applying the very same argument to the operations of the present day. The means, though seemingly inadequate, are not so in reality. We mean not to say that missionaries are inspired; but we do mean to say, that the Spirit of God accompanies their labours. He who gave the command, "Go ye into all the world, and preach the gospel to every creature:" gave also the promise, "And lo, I am with you alway, even unto the end of the world."

But this has been a digression from our original design, though we hope not a useless one. We go on to remark, that as there are special promises for the martyr, so are there for the faithful missionary. And as there was a time when the disciples of Christ were eager to wear the crown of martyrdom, so was there a time when the pretended soldiers of the cross were eager to gain the reward which is promised to him who shall leave all for the sake of Christ. There was a time when the inhabitants of Europe rushed with one accord, to fight in what they deemed, but falsely, the cause of the Saviour. So great was the enthusiasm, that in that army there mingled men of every rank, and of every condition; the high and the low. There might be seen the crown of royalty, and the coronet of nobility, and the crested plume of knighthood, towering above the humbler array of the surrounding multitude; and there, too, might be seen the peaceful banner of the cross, floating above those who were soon to imbrue their hands in the blood of their fellow-men. That was an age of zeal; but it was also an age of ignorance. The present is an age of knowledge: would it were also an age of more fervent zeal. The true soldiers of the cross are now going forth to fight; but they wrestle not against flesh and blood. And they have buckled on their armour, but it is not a material armour; and they have taken their arms, but they are not carnal weapons.

But they fight against principalities and powers, against the rulers of the darkness of this world, against spiritual wickedness in high places. And they have taken unto them the whole armour of God, even the shield of faith, and the breastplate of righteousness, and the preparation of the gospel of peace. And they are armed with the sword of the Spirit, even the word of God, which is mighty through God, to the pulling down of strong-holds. The faithful missionary is the true soldier of the cross. It is he that hath left father, and mother, and houses, and lands, for Christ's sake and the gospel; and to him is the promise of a hundred-fold in this life, and in the world to come, life everlasting.

But as the labours and the sufferings of the missionary resemble those of Christ, so shall his reward resemble that of our glorified Head. For what is the reward of Christ? Is it not the souls which he has ransomed? In the prophecy of Isaiah, God is represented as thus making a covenant with his Son —

> "If his soul shall make a propitiatory sacrifice,
> He shall see a seed which shall prolong their days.
> And the gracious purpose of Jehovah shall prosper in his hands.
> Of the travail of his soul, he shall see (the fruit) and be satisfied.
> By the knowledge of him shall my servant justify many;
> For the punishment of their iniquities he shall bear.
> Therefore will I distribute to him the many for his portion.
> And the mighty people shall he share for his spoil."
>
> LOWTH.

This was the joy that was set before him, for which he endured the cross, despising the shame.

And what is the reward of the minister and the missionary? Is it not the souls whom they have been the instruments of saving? "For what," says Paul to the Thessalonians, "for what is our hope, or joy, or crown of rejoicing? Are not even ye in the presence of our Lord Jesus Christ at his coming? For ye are our glory and joy. Thus is it that if we attain unto the kingdom of heaven, the souls which we may have been instrumental in saving here, will in that day be as a crown of glory around us; and yet along with ourselves, form part of that brighter crown which shall beam around the head of our glorified Redeemer: as in our solar system, the satellites revolve round their respective planets, and yet are with them borne in their mightier orbits around that brighter luminary which is the centre of the whole.

There is such a thing as being saved, yet so as by fire; such a thing as being least in the kingdom of heaven: and even this is a thought of highest ecstacy; but there is a thought more ecstatic still. It is the thought of an abundant entrance, and an exceeding great reward, and a crown of glory that fadeth not away, and a splendour like the shining of the stars in the firmament. Yes, to emit the faintest ray from that dazzling crown, which shall ever encircle the head of the Saviour, is a thought far too glorious for human conception; but there is a thought more glorious still, — to blaze forth, the central gem of one of those brilliant clusters, — to add to the glory of the Redeemer's diadem, and yet have around us a coronet of our own.

Hitherto we have considered it as a privilege to labour, and to suffer, for the sake of Christ; we come now to consider it as a duty. Hitherto our attention has been directed to the glorious reward of those who shall avail themselves of their privileges; we come now to consider the condemnation of those who shall neglect them.

We doubt not but there are some who would give a willing assent to all that we have advanced; but who, notwithstanding, would not be actuated by these remarks, to a single deed of Christian philanthropy. They think that it may be all very true, that a crown of glory is reserved for the martyr and the missionary; and that a distinguished place in the kingdom of heaven will be given to those who have been unwearied in their zeal, and patient in their suffering, for Christ's sake and the gospel's; but for their part, they have no such ambitious views, they are well content if they can but get to heaven at all; they like to steal quietly along with heaven in view, and not to make too much ado about religion. They think it right, indeed, to be religious; but they like not those who are religious over much. They do well in saying that they disapprove of ambition; we know not that even with regard to heavenly things, this desire of greatness is ever in any shape countenanced in the New Testament. But it is not the reward itself which these individuals dislike, it is the suffering, and the self-denial which lead to it. And too often is such reasoning employed as an excuse for treating with the most listless neglect, all that has a reference to the extension of the kingdom of our Lord.

But there is one circumstance which has always struck us most forcibly in reading those allegorical representations of the final retribution which are contained in the Bible — a circumstance which tells most fearfully against that class of individuals to which we have alluded. And it is, that while a greater or a less reward follows the improvement of our talents, the simple neglect of these, subjects us to a greater condemnation than if we had never enjoyed them. While those servants who had gained by the talents bestowed upon them, received each a suitable reward, that servant who had gained nothing, not only received no reward, but was ordered to be cast into outer darkness, where shall be weeping and gnashing of teeth. And in that sublime description of our Lord's, where the final judgment is brought so vividly before us, the condemned are not accused of positive crime, but of conduct altogether of a negative nature. And when the Judge pronounces the fearful sentence, "Depart from me, ye cursed, into everlasting fire;" he does not add as the cause of their condemnation, "Because ye imprisoned me." It is "because I was an hungered, and ye gave me no meat. I was thirsty, and ye gave me no drink. I was a stranger, and ye took me not in; naked, and ye clothed me not; sick and in prison, and ye visited me not." Not only then should we consider as a matter of high and distinguished privilege, that we have been endowed with talents, but also as a thing of deep and fearful responsibility.

There are various talents which have been entrusted to our keeping. Some of us may have received more, and others less; but we shall have all to render an account according to that we have, and not according to that which we have not. There is one talent which we have all of us received, and that, too, a talent of no common value; even that Book which maketh wise unto salvation. This wisdom is within the reach of every one of us; and this wisdom it is our duty to send to those who have it not. Or it may be, that, in that day there may be some who have been less highly favoured than ourselves; but who have more diligently availed themselves of the privileges they enjoyed; who shall bring against us the accusation; "We were hungering and thirsting after righteousness; and ye supplied not our wants."

It is in vain for any one of us to say, that we can do nothing in the cause of evangelizing the heathen. We may be able to give but little to support the external mechanism; but there is something more required in this mighty work than the mere outward apparatus: even that quickening principle, which of old breathed life into the dry bones of the prophet's vision; and which even now, is exerted in bidding those live "who are dead in trespasses and sin." The Holy Ghost is the gift of prayer. It may be, that we can give but little to the support of the outward means; but we can all pray for that life-giving principle, without which, these means will be employed in vain. It may be, that we cannot ourselves go forth to reap; but we can, at least, "pray the Lord of the harvest to send forth labourers into his harvest." But there are some of us who can do more; to whom there has been entrusted the talent of this world's wealth. This is an element, my friends, which is absolutely necessary to the carrying on of the cause of Christ on earth. It is a talent which we have received from God; and yet how little of it is employed in his service. Can it be, that so many millions are annually embarked in the uncertain speculations of this world's merchandise; and that a few thousands are all that are employed in the service of Him who is the rightful owner of all that we possess? Can it be, that so many are willing to lend on the treacherous security of this world's contracts; and that there are found so few who are willing to lend on the security of His word who cannot lie, and who hath promised a hundred-fold in this life, and in the world to come life everlasting?

But there are some of us who have received talents of a higher order still; talents which might enable us to engage personally in the work of missions; even those mental endowments, which, with the teaching of the Holy Spirit, might qualify us for preaching to the heathen, the unsearchable riches of Christ.

It is altogether vain to assert, as some do, that great mental powers cannot be profitably employed in preaching to the heathen. It is true, there may be some exceptions; but in the general, we know no office in the church of God where the very highest mental attainments can be more beneficially employed, than in the office, all despised as it is, of the Christian missionary.

Mental endowments are gifts, which more than any other, perhaps, have been alienated from the service of Him that gave them. And it will not be the greatest condemnation of by far the greater part of those who have received them, — that they have wrapt them in a napkin or buried them in the ground. Not only have they been withdrawn from the service of God; but far too frequently have they been employed in the service of his enemies.

This is the kind of assistance which is most wanted at present in the missionary cause. It is not work that is wanting; it is not wealth to carry on the work; it is labourers.

It was not the hope of rendering any considerable pecuniary assistance to missions which induced some of our number to attempt the formation of this society; it was the desire of cultivaing a missionary spirit among ourselves. We remembered, that from the Halls of Cambridge, there had gone forth the zealous and devoted

Martyn; and that a sister University had sent forth a Brown and a Buchanan; and we were not without the hope, that even from this remote and hitherto lukewarm corner of our land, there might be found some to imitate their honourable, though despised, example.

This may serve to explain to you why we have already laid out so great a portion of our funds in procuring the lives and the writings of some of the most distinguished of our missionaries. And we are sure, that there are few who can peruse the diary of a Brainerd, or a Martyn, without being animated with something of that devoted spirit which animated these illustrious servants of our God.

But we fear, lest it may be thought by some, that these remarks savour too much of selfishness; that we have held up as an incitement to exertion, the hope of glory, and the fear of condemnation.

Well do we know, that if the love of Christ constrain us not to live not unto ourselves, but to him that died for us, then all other inducements will be utterly powerless. But in this age of antinomian delusion, when religion has, among one class of our community, been transformed into a thing of definitions and cold speculation; and, when, among another, it has dwindled into a thing of mere feeling and poetic sentiment; we deem it right to bring forward those passages of the Bible which bear most directly upon our conduct.

For how often in these days of cold and heartless profession, do we meet with those who have the most perfect knowledge of all that is orthodox, and all that is Calvinistic; who can argue most ingeniously about all the dark and doubtful points of theology; whose heads have been stuffed with the dogmas and the disputations of a speculative divinity; but whose hearts have never been reached by the melting declarations of the gospel.

These are willing to talk and debate about religion; and they are willing, perhaps, to speculate about the possibility or impossibility of their salvation to whom the glad tidings of the gospel never came. But if, on the ground of the uncertainty of the question, you urge home upon them, the duty of sending instruction to the heathen; and if you but mention Bible or Missionary Societies, immediately are they ready to silence your every argument by their usual cant charges of fanaticism and enthusiasm.

How often, on the other hand, do we meet with those whose religion is not indeed so cold, but altogether as lifeless; with those who are loud in the praise of benevolence, and who are ever saying to the poor, Be ye warmed, and be ye fed; whose tenderest emotions are excited by the recital of some tale of imaginary woe; but who would think the lofty dreams of their sentimentalism degraded by being brought in contact with what they reckon the grossness of real life. And how lamentable is it to think, that, in this class of individuals, we can sometimes meet with those who can talk, and who can write, the most pathetically about the misery and the degradation of the heathen; and who can yet demonstrate by their own deeds, that the religion of the Bible has even less influence upon themselves than the mock morality of the Koran on the followers of Mahomet, or the fables of the Shaster on the deluded votary of Brahma.

This admirable essay, with another, which will afterwards come in, illustrates more powerfully than any description of mine, the character and talents of the writer. His knowledge of the Scriptures, and the ease with which he reasons upon them, are extraordinary in a boy of his years. Human teaching could not have produced such excellence as is here displayed. The subject is a difficult, and, in some respects, an original one; yet he discusses it like a person familiar with it, and who had devoted to it, the leisure and the application of years.

It affords the most decisive proof that his zeal was not the sudden excitement of passion, or that temporary and often violent heat, which is put forth by a young convert: which is sometimes in the reverse ratio of the light which is possessed; and, therefore, as ephemeral in its duration as it is unproductive of solid benefit to the individual himself and to others. It is good to be zealously affected in a good thing. But it is always desirable that zeal should be according to knowledge; and that the flame should be clear as well as ardent. Such was the case of my young friend. His warmth arose from those doctrines which he so well understood, and the influence of which must ever be powerful on those who really believe them. The love of Christ to himself, brought along with it, the most devoted gratitude in return. And perceiving that the manifestations of Christ's love, in devoting himself for the salvation of the world, are recorded, not only to be the foundation of our faith towards God, but to be the example and the excitement of the same principle in us, he felt called upon to give his talents and his life to the same cause. Is this fanaticism? Then was it fanaticism which led the Son of God to give his life a ransom for many. It was fanaticism which sent the apostles round the world on a mission of benevolence. It was fanaticism which influenced the confessors and martyrs of primitive times to sacrifice all things for their Master's sake, and "for the elect's sake, that they might obtain the salvation which is in Christ Jesus with eternal glory."

It is far easier on Christian principles to defend the utmost degree of self-devotion in the work of disseminating the gospel, than it is to defend the sincerity of men who call themselves Christians, and yet remain cold, selfish, and worldly. For the highest ardour — for what may be even called the extravagance of zeal, it is easy to find not only an apology, but a justification in the principles and hopes of the gospel. But it is passing strange, that men should conceive themselves to be Christians, while they "live to themselves," and are equally regardless of what is due to consistency, to the honour of Christ, and to the claims of a perishing world. It is not necessary that every Christian should become a missionary to the heathen, but it is necessary that every Christian should consider himself the Lord's, and that he is as much bound to propagate the faith of Christ, as were the primitive believers. No obligation lay on them which does not devolve on us; and it is only in as far as we adopt their maxims and imbibe their spirit, that we can expect at last to share their reward.

There is reason to fear that the New Testament doctrine of future rewards and punishments is very imperfectly understood by many Christians. They use the terms, heaven, eternal life, the crown of glory, and other corresponding expressions, in a vague and indefinite manner. Their hopes and expectations seem to be exceedingly low, and to produce a proportionately feeble influence on their minds and conduct. Christianity is not sufficiently their life; and, hence, they find it necessary to repair too much to other sources of enjoyment.

With them, the escape from future punishment, and the possession of heaven, considered as a state of entire freedom from suffering, is the *ne plus ultra* of hope. The idea of a scale of reward scarcely enters into their mind, much less that this scale will be regulated by the degree in which the character is in this world conformed to that of Christ. Hence the satisfaction with themselves which is felt even when much that is evil exists. Hence the indifference to eminent degrees of labour, self-denial, and holiness, which so generally prevails. And, hence the little attention which is paid to some of the most interesting views of future glory which the Scriptures present.

The doctrine of grace is thus unconsciously perverted by many. They seem to think that doctrine not only at variance with human merit, but with degrees of glory proportioned to the degrees of Christian excellence. They regard the arrangements of eternity as so arbitrary that they have little or no connection with the transactions of time. They imagine that the thief on the cross will not only be saved, but may shine with as bright a lustre as the apostle of the Gentiles. Is not this forgetting that the forgiveness of the kingdom of heaven is a very different thing from the rewards of that kingdom? The former having a reference to the evil which is common to all, necessarily places all in the same state; the latter having respect to what is good, or to positive conformity to the will of God, must be proportioned to the degree in which it exists.

In this constitution there is not only a recognition of the principle of grace, but a very high display of it. To the merit of the atonement, and to the influences of the Divine Spirit, we are indebted for all our positive goodness, and for the acceptance of all our services. To his own gift, therefore, we are previously indebted for all our hopes of distinction in his heavenly kingdom, and to encourage the highest possible cultivation of the benefits which he bestows, and of the opportunities of usefulness which he presents, he graciously engages to reward every attempt to glorify his name. The idea of merit is for ever excluded by the infinite disproportion which obtains between the service and the reward. We are so treated as to be left through eternity with a perpetually increasing and accumulating debt, to the infinite grace and love of God.

It is impossible to entertain this idea of future glory, without experiencing its elevating and stimulating effects. It is not necessary to restrict it to missionary labours; nor was this the object of the writer, in this admirable essay. It applies to all the branches of Christianity; and to all the engagements of Christian enterprise. In whatever way an individual may most fully live to the Lord, most entirely exercise the self-denial which the gospel inculcates, and most clearly evince the hallowed nature of his principles, he may receive the promised boon. Urquhart believed that a missionary life was the course in which he might most satisfactorily and honourably discharge his obligations to the Saviour, and deserve his approbation. Believing this, he devoted himself to it, and only parted with his determination thus to glorify his Redeemer, with life itself. With him these views were not a beautiful speculation, but living and efficient principles. They influenced his studies, his dispositions, his pursuits. They raised him above the low ambition, and the petty warfare of the earth. They fixed his hopes on the enjoyments of a purer region; and stimulated his exertions by the prospect of a crown of incorruptible glory.

E.

ESSAY ON THE DISTINCTION BETWEEN PRODUCTIVE AND UNPRODUCTIVE LABOUR.

That there is some distinction between what Dr. Smith calls productive, and what he terms unproductive labour, we think every one must allow; and that it consists in this, that the former produces something which the latter does not produce, it must, we think, be as readily admitted. The question comes to be, "What is the something?" If all that Dr. Smith means by this distinction be, that the one produces something which is tangible, while the produce of the other is something too ethereal and too evanescent to be laid hold of, we perfectly agree with him. We think his distinction a very just, but at the same time a very useless one; and, in our opinion, he might as well have amused us by a further subdivision of labour, according as its produce was hard or soft, liquid or solid. But this is not Dr. Smith's meaning; and, on appealing to his definition we find, that he founds this distinction on the supposition, that "the one sort of labour adds to the value of the subject on which it is bestowed; and that the other has no such effect; that the one produces a value, the other does not." The distinction seems now to turn on the meaning of the word value; and, on referring to a former definition to explain the present one, we do not find much light thrown on the subject. We are merely told of a value in use, and a value in exchange. If we take the latter of these and apply it to the subject under consideration, we shall find that the one kind of labour produces a value just as much as the other; for the musician receives his subsistence in return for his labour in playing tunes; just as much as the tailor does, in return for his labour, in making clothes. But it may be said, that Dr. Smith terms a certain kind of labour unproductive because it produces no value in use. But this cannot have been the cause of the distinction; for, while on the one hand this objection does not apply to all the kinds of labour which he has termed unproductive, it, on the other hand, does apply to some of those which he has denominated productive.

The terms wealth and value seem to us to be very indefinite; and to depend very much on the circumstances and the taste of the individual in reference to whom they are mentioned. The clothing which is so valuable to the inhabitant of Europe, would add nothing to the comfort of the naked inhabitant of New Zealand, and would consequently be of little value to him. And the antique vase which would be so highly valued by the curious antiquarian, may be thoughtlessly destroyed by the less refined peasant who digs it up.

Thirty or forty years ago, a stock of shoe-buckles would have been an addition to the real wealth of this country; at present, they would be valuable only for the material which composes them; and those who should now be employed in working them up, instead of adding, would, in fact, detract from the value of the subject on which their labour was bestowed. We have therefore the definition of value or wealth confined between two limits, and we shall come to a sufficiently correct, if not a sufficiently comprehensive notion of what that is which constitutes wealth or value, if we can but discover what that is which existed in these shoe-buckles thirty or forty years ago, and which does not exist at present. They are as substantially material now as they were before. Were they manufactured, there would be as much labour wrought up in them as ever, and the only change that we know of, that has taken place with regard to them is, that they were in fashion then, and they are so no longer; they cannot now minister to the enjoyment of the community. So that we must conclude, that these commodities, or any other commodities whatever, which are the produce of labour, form a part of the wealth of a country, just because they minister, in some way or other, to the convenience or enjoyment of its inhabitants; and because, since they are the produce of the labour of man, they must have an exchangeable value, if there be any demand for them.

Now it seems to us remarkably unfair, that of two men, whose labour has precisely the same effect on the wealth of the society, the one should be denominated a productive, and the other an unproductive labourer, merely because the labour of the former is realized in some material commodity, while that of the latter is not; that, of two men, for example, the object of both of whom it is to minister to the enjoyment of society, by furnishing them with music, he who makes a musical instrument should be called a productive labourer, while he who performs upon that instrument, and but for whom it could have no value whatever, is stigmatized with the epithet of unproductive.

By Dr. Smith it is asserted, that the former of these individuals produces a value, while the other does not. Now, if in this respect there be any difference at all between them, it seems to us to be, that the one needs materials to work upon, while the other does not; that the one merely adds to the value of what was valuable before, while the other creates a value altogether; that the maker of the instrument merely increases by his labour the value of brass and wood, and other exchangeable commodities, while the performer on the instrument gives a value to the unbought air of Heaven; and on this account, were we to make any distinction, should we deem the labour of the latter to be much more productive than that of the former.

But it may be said that this is a mere cavilling about words. It must be remembered, however, that words are the symbols of ideas, and that the sign necessarily affects the thing signified. The very distinction against which we have been arguing, seems to have confused the views of our great author through the whole of his chapter on labour. After having once associated, with a certain kind of labour, the idea of unproductiveness, he seems ever after to have contemplated it with an evil eye, and to have loaded it with the burden not only of its own faults, but also of those which did not belong to it.

Through the whole chapter there seems to run a confused notion of a subsisting connection between expenditure and the support of unproductive labour, and a connection, on the other hand, between the employment of productive labour and the accumulation of stock. And thus it is that Dr. Smith attributes to the supporting of unproductive labour all those evils which are the result of prodigality and extravagance.

It is some indistinct idea of a connection between the employment of productive labourers and the accumulation of capital which Dr. Smith entertains, where he tells us, that "a man grows rich by employing a multitude of manufacturers, while every body knows that a man may waste his whole fortune in the purchase of manufactured commodities; and thus, far from growing rich, may ruin himself,— just by employing a multitude of manufacturers."

The same confused ideas seem to have clouded our author's understanding, when he wrote the following sentences:—

"Whatever part of his stock a man employs as a capital, he always expects it to be replaced to him with profit. He employs it, therefore, in maintaining productive hands only. Whenever he employs any part of it in maintaining unproductive hands of any kind, that part is from that moment withdrawn from his capital, and placed in his stock received for immediate consumption."

If a person worth 1000*l.* can employ it in two ways, he can either on the one hand, employ it as a capital, either directly, or through the medium of the bank; or, on the other hand, he can use it as a stock reserved for immediate consumption. In either of these ways I can employ it in supporting indifferently either productive or unproductive hands; and it does not appear that my success or my failure will be at all necessarily influenced by this circumstance. If I use it as a capital I may choose to embark it in some manufacturing or mercantile speculation, and thus employ productive labourers; or I may become the manager of a theatre, and thus take into my service a number of unproductive hands. And this last scheme may be just as profitable, or even more so than the other.

On the other hand, I may use the whole of my fortune, or too great a part of it, as a stock reserved for immediate consumption; and, if I do so, I shall most certainly go to ruin, whether I spend it in the employment of productive or unproductive hands. In such a case it will not be the direction, but the amount of my expenditure, that will bring me to beggary.

But it may go far to demonstrate the absurdity of upholding the distinction between productive and unproductive labour, if we can show that one of those whom Dr. Smith most unequivocally sets down among his unproductive labourers, can be transferred without any change in his occupation from the service of the spendthrift to that of the capitalist; for we shall thus prove, first, that he has become a productive labourer, as Dr. Smith tells us, that "that part of the annual produce of the land and labour of any country which replaces a capital, never is immediately employed to maintain any but productive hands." It pays the wages, he says, of productive labour only.

Now, let us suppose that a musical amateur has so impoverished himself by maintaining a full band of performers for his own entertainment, that he finds himself almost ruined by his extravagance; but that rather than give up this his favourite amusement, he resolves, with the wreck of his fortune, to set up an opera, and offers to retain in his professional capacity still, those performers who had hitherto ministered to his private enjoyment. And, we may suppose, still further that they accept of his terms, and that matters go on so well, that he recruits his fortune by the profits of this speculation. There does not seem any thing very improbable in all this, — the difficulty is to reconcile it with Dr. Smith's chapter.

These men are now supported by capital, and therefore are productive labourers; but they are musicians, and therefore are unproductive labourers. Again; they ruined their employer, and therefore a man may grow poor by employing unproductive labourers, but they have also again enriched their employer; and therefore a man may accumulate capital by employing unproductive labourers.

There does not seem then to be any real distinction between productive and unproductive labour; and even supposing that there is, there seems to be no good reason for Dr. Smith's idea of a necessary connection between the employment of unproductive labour and expenditure, or between that of productive labour and the accumulation of stock.

Dr. Smith seems to have gone on with the popular idea, that wealth consists only in material commodities, without much consideration; and the wonder is, not that in one or two instances his acute understanding has been misled, but that in by far the greater number he has so successfully succeeded in clearing away the mists of popular prejudice and error.

Even with regard to the definition of wealth, it seems to have been our author's own opinion, had he kept by it, that it was not confined to material objects. Had Dr. Smith but remembered his own aphorism, that "every man is rich or poor according to the degree in which he can afford to enjoy the necessaries, conveniences, and amusements of life;" and had he, by his usual train of reasoning, generalized this proposition, by applying to the whole community what may be said of every one of its members, we should in all probability never have heard of productive or unproductive labour.

F.

ON WRITTEN LANGUAGE.

The acknowledged priority of spoken to written language, appears to us a very decisive argument for the divine origin of the latter.

Among those who hold that language is a mere human invention, there have been two opinions, some maintaining that substantives, or the names of external objects would be the words first invented, and others holding that verbs or words expressive of the mutual relations of objects, must have existed anterior to these, as an individual would not think of naming an object, until he had been in some way or other affected by its properties. On either of these hypotheses, it seems to us very obvious, that it would occur much more readily to the mind of a savage to represent his ideas by forms than by sounds. If he wished to particularize any object that was near, he would point to it; and if he wished to express the relation between any two objects, he would, in all probability, point first to the one, and then to the other; or, if the objects were movable, he might express the same idea by bringing them into actual contact.

Were these objects removed from his view, so that he could no longer express his idea by pointing to them, the most natural resource that could occur to him, would be to produce, if possible, a resemblance to the objects, and now to point to these, as he had formerly done to the objects themselves.

As there are comparatively few objects that utter sound; and as the sounds cannot be distinctly imitated by human voice; and, as on the other hand, all external objects have a form which can in general be easily represented, it would probably occur to him, that to delineate the absent objects would be the best method of representing them. If he wished to express some relation existing between two objects, he would express the idea as before, by representing the symbols of two objects in a state of contact.

Thus, had man been the inventor of language, we should have expected that at first men would have expressed their ideas by written symbols accompanied by gestures, and now and then perhaps by the utterance of such articulate sounds, as evidently resembled the idea they intended to express. But quite the reverse of this is admitted by those who maintain that language is of human origin, and while they do not deny that a slight degree of civilization is necessary before men begin to express their ideas by symbols, which bear some resemblance to the objects they are intended to represent, these philologists are guilty of very gross inconsistency in attributing to the most barbarous savages, a discovery of a much higher order, even the discovery of spoken language, where ideas are represented by sounds almost entirely arbitrary.

On this subject, as on most others, men of different parties seem to have run into opposite extremes. Some of the advocates of revelation, thinking they perceived it clearly declared there, that language is of divine origin, jealous of the least infringement on the authority of the sacred volume, have attempted to prove the unqualified proposition, that language is the gift of God. A hold has thus been given to their opponents, as it is evident from the very nature of the expressions, that many, if not most of the words in every language have been invented by man. The mere philologist again, in attempting to philosophize on language as a mere human invention, has landed himself in the absurdity of attributing the sublime discovery of the power of speech, to an age confessedly too barbarous to make the much more simple discovery of symbolical language. Revelation and sound philosophy in this case, as in all others, are at one. Language was originally the gift of God, and no doubt, for a considerable time, the same language. It may have been a language of the simplest kind, and in all probability was so. And yet, although there had been no multiplying of the languages of the earth, and the passage of Scripture in reference to this bears another signification which has been sometimes assigned to it, that "God confounded their works;" still we say, from this one original tongue, there may easily have emerged all the languages on the face of our earth. When we consider the great changes that have taken place in modern languages in a comparatively short time, how easy would it be for a language to be entirely changed, when there was almost no communication between different countries?

On the supposition that language is of human origin, we should be inclined to favour the former of these hypotheses, although we confess, from the very able treatise on this subject which was delivered a few weeks ago from our Humanity Chair, we had almost been led to give the preference to the latter. Place a number of children in a room by themselves, say the advocates of the first hypothesis, and the first thing they would set about, would be, to give names to the objects around them. This, however, say those who hold by the other supposition, suppose that the children have been previously acquainted with language. Were it otherwise, no child would give a name to an object, until it had, in some way or other, affected his own person, and then he would name the object from its felt effects. Thus, it is said, he would call fire *the burner*, water *the cooler*, &c.

There is a difficulty, however, connected with this hypothesis, notwithstanding its plausibility, which would lead us, were we at all inclined to think language a human invention, to give the preference to the other. Before the child could make his companions understand what was meant by the name *burner*, he must have first communicated to them the meaning of the verb *to burn*.

* * * * * *

In the discussions of Political Economy, the subject of ecclesiastical establishments necessarily finds a place. Dr. Chalmers naturally and properly discusses them in his prelections. Though unacquainted with the arguments employed in his lectures to his class, those who have read his volumes on "Christian and Civic Economy," cannot be altogether ignorant of his views. Those volumes I have read with some attention, and greatly admire the ingenious and often conclusive reasonings of their eloquent and candid author on many of the points which he discusses. But I do not hesitate to say, that on his own principles as a political economist, he begs the question in regard to civil establishments of religion; he assumes what he ought first to have proved, and reasons on premises not sufficiently established. And, if certain data laid down by himself be incontrovertible, the defence of such institutions is, in my opinion, rendered impracticable. If bounties and drawbacks are invaribly injurious to commerce; if chartered companies and monopolies are destructive to the natural operations of enterprise and labour: if fair trade, and fair competition, ought to be allowed and encouraged in regard to all other things, I do not perceive how religion should be excluded from the same benefit. With the religious question I have here nothing to do; that rests on different principles, and must be met on different grounds. But I am not the only person who wishes most ardently that Dr. Chalmers would fairly meet the subject on its true merits as a question of Political Economy. He will forgive me for saying, in this public manner, what I know to be the opinion of many of his own pupils, as well as of others, that he is called upon to do so: for, if his politico-economical principles should be once firmly fixed in this country, they would do more to lessen and destroy the faith of the country in the necessity and beneficial tendency of church establishments, than any other thing.

I am led to make these observations, by finding among the papers of my young friend, a fragment on this subject, which refers to the views and reasonings of Dr. Chalmers, and which shows, while it shows no more, that they had not produced conviction on his mind. The truly catholic spirit of the writer is strongly marked; and I can only regret that the paper was left unfinished.

ON RELIGIOUS ESTABLISHMENTS.

In the history of nations, we often find that those states which had been united in the closest alliance by the approach of some common enemy, have no sooner succeeded in their efforts to repel him, than there have again burst forth between them those ancient feuds and dissensions which the common danger had for a while extinguished. And such too has been the case among different sects of Christians. The doctrines of Christianity are of such a nature, that in order to experience their efficacy we must judge of them for ourselves. They cannot, like algebra and political economy, be transmitted unaltered from one mind to another. All those who give sufficient attention to a mathematical problem, however varied may be the conformation of their minds, will come exactly to the same conclusion. Such truths are not affected by the peculiar conformation of the mind through which they pass. But it is quite the reverse with the truths of Christianity. And, accordingly, though we may find many whose philosophical or political creed agrees in every iota, yet we know not if there can be found any two Christians whose theological views entirely coincide. Were every one to resolve to hold communion with none but those whose theological creed in every point coincided with his own, there would in all likelihood, be in the Christian Church, nearly as many sects as there are members.

They are only the externals of Christianity, however, about which Christians are divided; concerning those grand doctrines which distinguish it from every other religion, they are perfectly agreed. In times of persecution, accordingly, we find, that their petty differences are forgotten, and they rally with one accord to defend the bulwarks of their common faith. And no sooner was our land favoured with the inestimable blessing of religious toleration, than religionists began to be divided into different sects or parties. This of itself, however distressing it may appear at first sight, we consider as a matter of rejoicing, rather than regret.

There seems to be a final cause in even this imperfection of our Christian knowledge. There is a generous emulation thus maintained in the walks of Christianity, and a greater provoking of one another to good works, than if all were perfectly agreed. But there is a spirit of sectarianism, which, in this state of things, is too apt to break forth among all parties, — a desire to magnify those matters about which Christians differ, and thereby to forget those sublimer truths concerning which they are agreed.

It must be matter of regret to every one of a really catholic spirit, and who has the interests of genuine religion seriously at heart, that so much has been said, and so much has been written about the merest trifles in the externals of Christianity, while those who have been keenest in the controversy have frequently been forgetful of those grander truths, which imparted to the matters about which they were contending, all their weight and all their importance. Insignificant and unimportant, however, as we believe these matters to be, when compared with the vital doctrines of Christianity; yet, viewed abstractly, or, in comparison of earthly things, we deem them of the highest and most serious import. While it seems most imperiously our duty to attend to the spiritual things of religion, it seems equally our duty not to neglect those external regulations which are intended to preserve the purity and spirituality of our faith.

Of all those inferior points about which Christians disagree, the question of religious establishments is perhaps the most important. We confess that, from our education, all our prejudices have been against church establishments; and it is, perhaps, on this account that that powerful argumentation, which has appeared so luminous and so satisfactory to others, has failed to produce upon our mind the same effect. It has very much enlightened, but it has not convinced us. We waive, at present, the consideration of any religious establishments that have ever existed, or of our national establishments as they exist at present.

* * * * * *

ON THE LOVE OF FAME.

"And seekest thou great things for thyself?" &c.

JEREMIAH.

I HAVE often thought it peculiarly interesting to compare that morality which is to be found in the systems of ancient philosophy, with the morality which is contained in the Bible; to see the heart of man still reflecting, though dimly and imperfectly, that image which was stamped upon it at first; to observe the harmonious accordance which obtains between the law that is written in the heart, and the law which has been revealed to us by the Spirit of God, and thus to identify that God who hath formed the heart of man, with that God, who, in times past, spake unto the fathers by the prophets; and who hath in these last days spoken unto us by his Son.

Some of these theories of the ancients are so beautiful, and so perfect, that we are apt to feel disappointed that their practical influence was not extensively and powerfully felt. But we shall not wonder at this, if we consider how difficult it is to arrest the attention by abstract truths; and how little of practical efficacy there is in such truths, even when most fully apprehended. To cultivate any feeling, we must not look to the feeling itself, but to the object which naturally excites it. And in this point of view we may behold the vast superiority of the Christian religion, to every other, as a system of practical morality.

Here the abstract principles of natural religion are embodied in facts: and all that we have to do is to direct the attention to these facts, and the proper state of feeling is the invariable and immediate result.

But not only are the symptoms of the ancient philosophers deficient in practical efficacy; they are even imperfect as theories of morality. Pure and elevated as they appear, when viewed abstractly and in themselves, they cannot stand a comparison with that purer system which has been given us by revelation.

To most of the precepts which are given us in the Bible, we can find some counterpart in the writings of heathen philosophers; but there is one virtue which we hesitate not to say, is more frequently inculcated in the Bible, than any other, for a counterpart to which you may search the whole writings of ancient philosophy, and find nothing that bears to it the most distant resemblance. Never did there come from the pen of a heathen, sentiments like those contained in our motto: "Seekest thou great things for thyself? Seek them not." It is a very striking fact, that, in the language of Greece and Rome, there is not a word to express humility as a virtue: those words which are generally used signify rather meanness, and that crouching to power, which is the feeling not of a humble, but of a dastardly spirit. On the other hand, pride and haughtiness were considered as the concomitants of prowess and bravery; and hence the heroes of ancient poetry are generally furnished with an abundant portion of both.

Yes, that vice which we inherit from the author of our misery, lurks too successfully in the recesses of the human bosom, to be discovered by the light of reason alone; it requires a more searching scrutiny to drag it from that place, while it has taken up its abode in the inmost penetralia of our souls. In the present depraved state of the human heart, it is difficult to distinguish between those desires and propensities which may have once been pure, but which, at the fall, were perverted; and those which are radically evil, and which could not have existed in the heart of man, in his state of original purity. Without hesitation, we would class pride in the latter division, as a feeling altogether of demoniacal origin; and which could not exist in the mind of a pure and holy being.

But though we can thus give a most unhesitating deliverance with regard to this vice itself, there are some of its modifications about which we cannot pronounce so decidedly. The desire of fame, and the desire of power, and all that is described in our text by the seeking after great things, have so often been declared by our theological writers to be innocent, if not laudable propensities, that we almost feel as if it were presumption for us to give it as our opinion, that they are inimical to the spirit of true religion.

It may be true, that such feelings existed in the bosom of our first parents, before their expulsion from the blissful abodes of Eden; and that they vied with each other to gain the favour and applause perhaps of their God. And it may be true, that there is among the angels a generous emulation, to provoke each other to good works; but still we think it true, that in our present condition, it is extremely dangerous, if not sinful, to give way to this propensity.

It may be argued, indeed, that the love of praise operates as a very powerful principle in restraining many of the fiercer passions, and that without it the moral world would soon become a scene of wild confusion and disorder; but in the same manner might we plead for anger and selfishness, and even avarice itself. These are all very powerful checks in restraining many of our grosser propensities, and to them we are indebted for many of the decencies which adorn civilized society; but who would make this a plea for their virtuousness?

There is one circumstance which makes the love of fame a very dangerous propensity; it is the very low standard of virtue which generally prevails in the world. Were the standard a perfect one, then would the case be different. He only would be praised, who was truly virtuous, and the love of fame would be identical with the love of virtue. But this, alas, is not the case. The men of the world have fixed on a standard of virtue convenient for themselves; and whoever by his actions goes beyond this standard, tacitly pronounces condemnation upon them, and most assuredly will meet with their hatred and disapprobation. It is thus that the most virtuous in all ages have been met with ignominy and contempt. And it is thus that this deference to the opinion of the world has diverted many from the conscientious performance of what they knew to be right.

Thus, even in a worldly point of view, and considered merely as an abstract question in morals, would we consider the opinions of our fellow-men a most improper standard whereby to regulate our actions. But when we add yet another element, and consider the subject as it bears upon our religious character, — when we consider it not only as it affects our duty to our fellow-men, but as it affects our duty to God, we shall feel that to make the praise of men the standard of our conduct is still more dangerous.

The love of praise is, perhaps, an original principle of our constitution; and if it be, then it were vain to attempt its annihilation. Nor is this required of us. All that we are bid to do in the Bible, is to give it a new direction. And the condemnation of the Pharisees of old, was not that they loved praise, but that they loved the praise of men more than the praise of God.

We know of no feeling in our constitution which is stronger, which is more difficult to overcome than the love of fame, or the love of praise, for we hold them to be very nearly the same. So strong is it, that it is capable of carrying us through the greatest difficulties and dangers, of enabling us to persevere in the most unwearied exertion, and urging us onward even to death itself.

What is it that animates the breast of the enterprising traveller, in his laborious researches?

*   *   *   *   *   *

G.

DISCOURSE ON 2 CORINTHIANS IV. 13.

"We having the same spirit of faith, according as it is written, I believed, and therefore have I spoken; we also believe, and therefore speak."

There is a common proverb, that "the truth should not be always told." In other words, that it is not always a good reason for speaking that we believe. Although apparently at first sight a little paradoxical, this saying will be found like most other proverbs, to embody the wisdom of very extensive experience.

There are some truths which concern only a few individuals, and in which the rest of mankind have no interest whatever. If there be nothing absolutely wrong, there is at least something very trifling in publishing such matters. And you cannot, perhaps, pitch upon a character more universally despised, than that of the busy-body or the tell-tale. Yet each of these deservedly detested characters, could, perhaps, allege in excuse for all his silly conversation, that he spoke because he believed.

There are other truths which, it would be not only idle and improper, but which it might be cruel, or even criminal to promulgate. That man could have but little tenderness or humanity in his disposition, who should assiduously relate the disgraces, or the crimes of a departed parent, to the surviving children; and we would not hesitate to pronounce it a breach of the second great commandment of the law, to expose to public view the defects in the private character of our neighbour. You are aware, indeed, that the latter action not only is a palpable transgression of the law of God, but comes under the cognizance even of human jurisprudence. Truth is a libel; and it would be no excuse in a court of justice, for the defamer of his neighbour's good name to affirm, that he had published only what he had good ground to believe.

You perceive then, that the quality of the motive which Paul affirms to have actuated him in his public speaking, and in his writings, must depend upon the character of those truths, which he so assiduously proclaimed. If they were truths which concerned only a few individuals, or which, if they had a reference to all, were of comparatively insignificant importance, then it was folly in Paul to labour so hard, and to suffer so much to proclaim them; and, notwithstanding all the cogency of his reasoning, and the sublimity of his eloquence, we should, in such a case, be tempted to concur in the opinion of the eastern ruler, that after all he was but a learned madman.

If, again, the truths which Paul preached tended only to harrow up the feelings of mankind, and to destroy what might be but early prejudices, but yet prejudices with which those whom they influenced had associated all that they held dear as patriots, and all that they thought sacred in religion: if these truths tended only to bring to light evils that had long been hidden, and which had even by the common consent of mankind been carefully concealed: if, finally, they tended only to demonstrate to mankind that their wisdom was folly, and that their boasted virtue which they had hoped would open for them the gates of heaven, not only was altogether unable to expiate their crimes, but was itself too much tainted with impurity to find acceptance before God: if this alone was the tendency of the truths which Paul preached, it was more than folly — it was cruelty to proclaim them. Better far for the world, they had never been promulgated.

But I need not tell you that the doctrines which Paul preached were of a far different character.

It is true that they directly tended to produce all the seeming evils I have been describing; but God be thanked, this was not their only tendency. True, the feelings of the decent and the virtuous among mankind would be harrowed up, when they were classed with the vilest of their species, and told that they had been wearing but the mask of virtue; that the hidden man of the heart was utterly polluted; that God had concluded all under sin, and that therefore, all are under condemnation. True, the prejudices of the Jews, with all their associations of patriotism and sacredness, must have been shocked at being told that the descendants of Abraham were no longer God's chosen nation, but that the Gentiles were become fellow-heirs with them of the promises. True, the apostle's preaching was, to the Jews, a stumbling-block, and to the Greeks foolishness; but this was not all, or I repeat it, the apostle was guilty of the greatest cruelty. But unto them who believe, both Jews and Greeks, it was the power of God, and the wisdom of God.

In order then to show that the simple belief of the truths of the gospel is sufficient reason for preaching them, and preaching them, too, with all the unwearied diligence and fervent zeal which characterized the preaching of the apostle Paul; and at the risk too, of all the losses and persecutions to which his ministry subjected him, we shall attempt to show,—

I. The perfection and excellency of the New Testament dispensation.

II. We shall also attempt to show, that the belief of the gospel is not only a sufficient reason for preaching it, but that it is the *only* right motive which can lead an individual to the choice of the ministry as his occupation.

The perfection and excellency of the New Testament dispensation may perhaps be most strikingly illustrated by contrasting it with less perfect discoveries.

We remark, then, that the doctrines of natural religion, (with a very few exceptions,) are so very dark and confused, as scarcely to warrant, and by no means to encourage its promulgation as a system, on the part of those who embrace it.

By the light of nature, it is true, we can clearly perceive the existence and some of the attributes of Deity. It is not to the doctrines of natural religion, taken individually, but to natural theology itself as a system of religion, that the foregoing remark is applicable. Had God never revealed himself to us by his Spirit, or by his Son, still we might have known something of his character from the works which he has made. And in contrasting the declarations of God's word with the language of his works, we conceive that men of different parties have fallen into opposite extremes. The mere philosopher would wish to convince us that nature speaks so audibly, and so unequivocally of her Sovereign, as to render all supernatural declarations of his will unnecessary; while, on the other hand, it must be confessed, that the advocates of a written testimony from above have sometimes, through a wish to magnify the importance of the communications of God's Spirit, depreciated that testimony which his works undoubtedly bear to the character of their great Creator. It is our wish to steer clear of these extremes; and, in attempting to do so, we cannot follow a safer course than that which the written testimony itself points out.

"The heavens declare the glory of God, and the firmament showeth forth his handy-work. Day unto day uttereth speech, and night unto night showeth knowledge. There is no speech nor language where their voice is not heard. Their line has gone out through all the earth, and their words to the end of the world." The invisible things of our Creator, even his eternal power and Godhead, are thus clearly seen from the creation of the world — "being understood by the things that are made."

So far the voice of nature utters a clear and decided declaration; and so far, those who have listened to no higher testimony, are reprehensible if they speak not what they believe, or what they would believe did they attend as they ought to the evidence around them. But when we attempt from these few isolated, though important truths, to form a system of religion — something that may satisfy us as to the relation in which we stand to the powerful Being who created the world, how very imperfect does all our knowledge appear — how unsatisfactory all our conclusions — how dark and fearful our prospect of futurity!

The ancient philosophers of Greece and Rome could clearly perceive, that there was one great Author and Governor of all things — a Being of inconceivable glory, and of infinite power — and therefore a Being widely different from those contemptible deities which the impure imagination of their poets had feigned, and which the perverted judgment of a degraded populace had accepted as the objects of their worship. They must thus have perceived that idolatry was not only a folly but a crime, and, in so far, they were guilty for not promulgating the truths they believed; and, in so far, they are liable to that fearful curse which is denounced against those who "confine the truth by unrighteousness."

But it may go far, perhaps, to palliate, though it cannot atone for their crime, that, when they attempted to carry out their own speculations, they were landed in most unsatisfactory conclusions; and if they attempted to guess, when they could no longer determine with certainty, their conjectures of futurity must have been only those of terror and despair. Not only must they have been convinced from the wondrous objects around them, of the power and glory of God, but from the conscience within them — that monitor which whispers approbation to all that is good, and so loudly and bitterly condemns what is evil; they must have been impressed with the belief, that He, who gave them such a constitution, must himself be a lover of righteousness, and a hater of iniquity. The voice of that monitor, however, they must have been conscious they had often disobeyed; and the thought cannot fail to have struck them, that in so doing, they had offended Him who had placed that monitor within them. They must thus have arrived at the conclusion, that they had forfeited the favour of him whom his works declared so mighty and so glorious. If they risked the thought of another state of being where they should be brought into the more immediate presence of an offended God, how fearful must have been the prospect! If God were just, they must abide his righteous indignation; and if he were unjust, the prospect was not more pleasing. Here was a very fearful dilemma, and yet this was the legitimate conclusion into which their inquiries must have landed them. We do not say, that all, or any of the ancient philosophers arrived at this conclusion; but if they did not, it was because, dreading the result, they shrunk from the inquiry.

Now, with such a revelation as this, what encouragement was there to promulgate their opinions? They could not come boldly forward with the great apostle of our faith, and say, — "We speak because we believe." All with themselves was darkness and doubt; or if their conjectures amounted to probability, it was a probability of the most fearful kind; they felt that their opinions landed themselves in no satisfactory conclusions; or if they did seem to point to any one conclusion more decidedly, it was one of the most appalling nature, — even that the whole world were exposed to the anger of a justly offended God.

This view of natural religion may serve to explain to us how the philosophers of ancient times were so enlightened, while the multitude around them were sunk in the most degraded ignorance. They did not think the truths they possessed worth promulgating, far less worth suffering for. Socrates, that prince of heathens, dashed the arrow of martyrdom away from him, when it had been as easy for him to have gained it as to have refused it, disclaimed the honourable charge that was laid to him of despising the abominations with which he was surrounded, and even by his latest breath giving the order that the idolatry of his country should be sanctioned by his name.

They like very well to start objections, or even to throw the most insolent aspersions on the truths of Christianity; but when you ask them what they would substitute in its place, they can give no satisfactory answer. They are, in the true sense of the word, sceptics; they have no settled opinions. Infidels they are, too, — they doubt, — they disbelieve.

You see, then, that with such knowledge of God as his works can give, there is little encouragement to promulgate that knowledge — to speak, because we believe. We might more strikingly illustrate this, by contrasting the inactivity and easy carelessness of mere worshippers of nature in spreading what they profess to believe with the ardour and the self-denial of the apostles of our faith. Where, among the great and the wise, who have made reason their god, do we find an instance of suffering for conscience' sake? Or, if a very few such examples can be adduced, — where do we find a single instance of martyrdom for the cause of truth? But I am almost forgetting that this part of my discourse is only an illustration; and is merely intended, by the darkness of its representation, to mark with a clearer outline, and paint with stronger colouring, that glorious dispensation under which we live.

But between the twilight darkness of nature, and the full blaze of that light which shines forth in revelation, there are many intermediate shades of brightness; and besides that dispensation of mercy under which we live, there is many a supposable way in which a perfect Being might have treated his rebellious dependants. You will excuse me, if, in order to illustrate, still further, the perfection and excellence of the Christian revelation, I dwell on some of the supposable revelations which the Deity might have made to us.

I am aware, that, to some, this may seem a very circuitous method of treating my subject, and I may appear to be continually hovering round the point I would be at, without ever actually reaching it. But it seems to me, that there are two methods by which a clear conception of any object may be presented, either by directly describing what it is, or by contrasting it with what it is not; just as the painter may delineate any object, either by actually colouring what he wishes to portray, or by encircling it with a ground of a colour different from its own. Unquestionably, both in the case itself, and in the illustration, the former method, in most cases, is decidedly preferable; but it is as unquestionable, that there are few instances in which the latter method is more advantageous. Such an instance, I conceive, is afforded by the subject which I am now attempting to set before you. You have all heard of the gospel again and again; and with its peculiar doctrines, and the blessings which flow from them, you are intimately acquainted. Since you know, then, what the gospel is, I have hoped to throw some additional illustration around it, by contrasting it with what it is not. We all know what a blessing health is, — but how much more highly do we prize this blessing when just recovered from some painful disease. To return, then, from this digression, I remark,

The revelation of God might have been only a revelation of wrath.

Indeed, this is the kind of revelation, that, from any previous knowledge of the divine character, we should have expected. I have already attempted to show, that, if natural religion points to any conclusion this is that conclusion; that God is just and holy, and that man by his sin has offended him. The word of God, we should expect, would sanction the declarations of his works, and would clearly reveal what they had but faintly indicated. And, accordingly, it is so. Revelations of God's word do not give the lie to the testimony of his works. They speak one language, though the one utters its declarations with a voice more audible and distinct. Instead of a reflection of God's character from his works, we have now a clear manifestation of that character in his word; but it is the same character which both assign to him; both declare him to be holy, just, and good.

Instead of the dictates of conscience, we have now the precept, clear and express, written by God's own finger. And instead of the conclusion to which natural religion might have led us, that, since God is just and holy, sin must be punished, we have now the express declaration annexed to the law by Him who wrote it, — "The soul that sinneth, it shall die."

Instead of the fearful conjectures of natural religion, we have now a still more fearful certainty, — that, since all men have manifestly sinned, all have to look forward to eternal condemnation. It is true, some have objected, that, if none can keep the law of God, it is surely inconsistent with his goodness to have given so strict a law. We might answer such objections with the apostle's argument, — "Nay, but who art thou, O man," &c. But we need not make such an appeal to God's sovereignty. An imperfect law would have argued a lawgiver imperfectly holy. So that either holiness and goodness are incompatible with each other, or the strictness of the law of God is consistent with his goodness.

If there was little encouragement to promulgate the doctrines of natural religion, still less would there be to promulgate the doctrines of a revelation so fearful as this. In that case there is uncertainty, or at best, fearful conjecture; but then it was but conjecture, and the powerful influence of hope bore the minds even of those who half believed it, above its fears. But here there is nothing on which hope can lay hold. Here is no conjecture; it is certainty, and certainty the most overwhelming, even "a certain fearful looking for of judgment, and fiery indignation."

Such is the revelation we might have expected from Heaven; and had God thus dealt with us according to our deserts, in all probability this world, as it now is, would never have existed. The very first breach of God's law must have immediately incurred the full weight of the curse; for, it were absurd to talk of a state of trial in regard to those whose certain destiny was everlasting destruction. But supposing, for a moment, that the world did exist under such a dispensation, as it exists now, and rebellious man were permitted to live a few short years as the ungodly now do, in forgetfulness of God, and careless security; the question presents itself, — Supposing this fearful revelation of God's wrath to be made known to some individuals, would it be right to promulgate the dreadful truth, — to speak, because we believed? We conceive not. That there would be no encouragement to do so is abundantly manifest. For if it be no enviable duty to communicate to a criminal the sentence that condemns him to the suffering of temporal death, it were assuredly a fearful task to publish the death-warrant of a world doomed to eternal perdition.

But, we conceive, were this revelation known to a few, it would be the greatest cruelty on their part to publish it; it would be tormenting before the time. Could it indeed be hoped, that by the revelation of God's wrath against all iniquity, men would be led to see the evil of sin, and would be kept from sinking deeper in destruction; then it might be merciful to proclaim it, inasmuch as we might thereby hope to alleviate the punishment which we could not prevent. But who, that knows the mind of fallen man, does not see that quite the reverse of this would be the case? This announcement of the Divine justice would call forth a fresh display of the corruption of his rebellious subjects, who would thereby plunge still deeper into the abyss of perdition. There are instances even now in the world, of some who have despaired of mercy, and none do we find more hardened against their God, or more proudly eminent in rebellion. They gather strength from despair, and they dare the Almighty to his face. Their language is, "Evil, be thou our good. Let us eat and drink, for to-morrow we die. — Let us enjoy while we may, the pleasures of this life, and then sink into endless misery." Rather than rouse such a spirit as this, would it not be better to let men slumber on in ignorance of their fate, till destruction itself awoke them from their slumbers?

Under such a dispensation, it is very obvious, an office, analogous to the ministry, could never have existed. If these fearful truths were known to a single individual of our species, he must thereby be rendered perfectly wretched, even in this life, and would be led from the depravity of his nature, to curse the justice of Jehovah, and to sin with a high hand against his God. It is, therefore, altogether impossible to conceive that such an individual should publish these appalling truths from a sense of duty, or a conviction that it was right, whatever might be the consequences, to publish the will of God; and we can see no other motive that could lead him to divulge the awful secret, but one of the most devilish malignity,—even a wish to steal from his fellows their envied ignorance, and make them as wretched as himself. Such cruelty were it, to break the slumbers of a malefactor, who, on the night before his execution, should dream of pardon, and think himself restored to his family and his friends, to tell him that his fancied happiness was all delusion, and to recall his thoughts to the fearful realities before him.

There is an anecdote of an Indian Brahmin, which may throw some light upon this subject, and with which some of you may be acquainted. You are aware that the priests of India think it the greatest crime to destroy animal life, and accordingly live entirely on herbs. It is said that one of our countrymen, in arguing with one of these Brahmins, in order to convince him of the falsity of the doctrines he held, in regard to this matter, showed him by a microscope that the stems and leaves of the herbs on which he lived, were covered with hundreds of minute, yet living sentient creatures. This was ocular demonstration, and it could not be resisted. The priest had placed his hopes of happiness on his fancied innocence, and now that the enormity of his crimes was laid before him, his peace of mind was destroyed, and all his hopes of enjoyment were blasted. It is said, that after continuing thoughtful for a considerable time, he earnestly inquired of the other on what terms he would part with this wonderful instrument; and having at last with considerable difficulty, obtained possession of it, he dashed it into a thousand pieces. It had broken his peace of mind, he said, but never should it destroy the peace of another.

This anecdote is generally adduced as affording an instance of bigoted attachment to former opinions, even when convinced of their falseness. But we view it in a very different light; we think that the action displays a dignified benevolence. Had new hopes of happiness, founded on more rational principles, been substituted in the room of those which he now perceived to be so groundless, then it would have been cruelty to have allowed his countrymen to dream of happiness that could never be realized; but the alternative was not between delusive hopes and rational expectations of enjoyment, but between a dream of happiness and the certainty of woe.

And just so, had the gospel never reached our earth, but only a revelation of God's perfect holiness and justice, it had been better far that men should be permitted, while here, to dream on of a heaven they were never to enter, than to tell them beforehand of the punishment it was impossible to escape, and thus to add to the sufferings that soon were to burst upon them the dire forebodings of misery, in some cases more dreadful even than the misery itself.

But let us turn from these terrific suppositions to the glorious reality. It is not a message of condemnation which we are commissioned to bear to our fellow-men. The tidings that have reached us from on high are " glad tidings of great joy." That fearful revelation, indeed, which we have just been considering, is still true, and has been revealed to us from heaven, but, God be thanked, it came not alone; and the dread nature of that condemnation which it reveals, serves but to cast a brighter lustre around the offers of that mercy which promises a free pardon to all who will but accept of it. In all the revelations God has made to us, mercy is the prominent feature. Mercy even anticipates justice, and it is a striking fact that man was never let into the fearful condition into which his sin had brought him, till deliverance was promised. There was no room left for the workings of despair; for the curse was not pronounced upon the rebellious representatives of our race till God had pledged his word that the seed of the woman should bruise the head of the adversary who had seduced her.

This mercy has been obtained for us in a way that natural religion could never have anticipated. There could be no hope that any being, however powerful, could stay the arm of offended omnipotence; neither could there be any rational expectation, although such an expectation some have chosen to indulge, that, by a sort of amiable weakness, which creatures sometimes indulge, a shrinking from infliction of punishment which justice demands, the Deity should screen us from the misery we have entailed upon ourselves, even though his justice and his holiness should suffer by his compassion. "God is not a man, that he should lie, nor the Son of man that he should repent." He had declared that death was the inevitable consequence of transgression; and his mercy, far from giving the lie to his justice, confirms the sentence of the law: for in the dispensation of the new covenant, that truth has its most striking illustration; that, without a due satisfaction to injured justice there can be no remission of sin. It is the Lawgiver, the Judge himself, that has offered us forgiveness. And his character, as our Saviour, is in perfect consistency with his character, as our righteous Judge. "The Lord saw that there was no man, and he wondered that there was no intercessor, therefore his own arm brought salvation unto him, and his righteousness it sustained him." God sent his Son into the world, but it was not, as well might have been expected, to condemn the world, but that the world through him might be saved. Thus a free offer of pardon is made to the whole of a condemned world; and had the simple truth of redemption through the sacrifice of Christ to every one that believeth, been all that had been revealed, this of itself would seem enough to answer all the circumstances of our lost condition. Could any one be acquainted with such a truth, and not speak what he believed? Is not the simple belief of such a doctrine enough to account for all the trials and privations that have been undergone by the evangelists of our faith, in order to promulgate the knowledge of this treaty of reconciliation between a rebellious world and its offended Sovereign?

But though this free offer of mercy seems at first sight to be suited to all the circumstances of fallen man, we shall find, on further inquiry, that were this single doctrine to constitute the whole of the dispensation of mercy, the plan would be incomplete, and the Son of God might have come into our world, and died for our sins, and yet have suffered and died in vain.

Man, by his fall, became a sinful being, and as such, he has a dislike to every holy principle. We have already remarked, that a revelation of God's wrath against sin would tend only to harden him in his depravity, but it is a still more striking proof of the depth of human depravity, that even the offers of mercy are contemptuously refused. Instead of the tone of indignation in which God might have addressed us, he has chosen to speak in accents of mercy, saying, "Look unto me, and be ye saved, all ye ends of the earth." He condescends even to reason with, to warn us of our danger, and to entreat us with more than a father's tenderness. "Turn ye, turn ye, why will ye die!"

But the terrors of God's law, and the gracious invitations of his mercy, and the earnestness of his warnings, and the tenderness of his expostulations, fall equally powerless on the ear of infatuated man. He will not be saved.

You see, then, the necessity of the doctrine of divine influence, to render the gospel dispensation altogether complete, and suited to all the peculiarities of our lost estate. Without this influence, not a single individual would accept the proffered mercy of heaven.

But supposing a single individual, or a few individuals, did accept the testimony, you can see that there would be no encouragement to proclaim it to others. At first, indeed, if the message were truly believed, there would be an ardent wish to communicate to others the inestimable blessing, and the confident expectation that all would cling to the terms of mercy as soon as they were offered. But how soon would the zeal of the supposed evangelist be damped, to find that the offers of forgiveness were turned from with loathing, and treated with contempt. How soon would he abate his ardour, and exclaim, as he sat down in despair of benefitting his fellow-men, "I have laboured in vain; I have spent my strength for nought and in vain!"

To make a new application of an illustration sufficiently trite: Were a building in flames, and had you succeeded in making an easy communication between the ground, and some part of the tenement where the noise of voices indicated that there were human beings within; you would naturally suppose that your benevolence had effected its purpose. You would never dream that the inmates would need to be persuaded to escape for their life. But did you, in the prosecution of your benevolent purpose, actually ascend to that part of the building whence the voices issued, there is nothing absurd in the supposition, that you might find the inmates to be a company of bacchanalians, who, in the phrenzy of intoxication, were alike ignorant of their danger, and regardless of your entreaties. It is possible, that all your warnings might be answered by the infatuated laugh of intemperate mirth, or even by the insolent attack of some furious debauchee, and thus might you find that all your efforts were vain; and even after having made all the preparations for their deliverance that seemed necessary, you might find yourself compelled to abandon them to their fate. And so it is with the men of this world, in regard to the everlasting destruction that is hanging over them. They, too, are "drunken, though it be not with wine; and they stagger, though it be not with strong drink." "The spirit of a deep sleep has been poured out upon them, and their eyes have been closed."

You perceive, then, that without the pouring out of the Spirit of God, in order to turn the hearts of our apostate race, all the apparatus of a Saviour's incarnation, and sufferings, and death, might have been spent upon our world in vain. But, God be thanked, the system of mercy is complete in all its parts, and suited in every respect to the circumstances of our case. The promise of the Spirit has been given, and in every individual who is turned from darkness to light, we have a standing proof that the promise is fulfilled.

Such is the system of truth, which, as Christians, we profess to believe. If we do not belie our profession, we believe that every individual of the millions that inhabit our globe, or that have dwelt upon its surface ever since the beginning, has transgressed the law of Jehovah. We believe that by the most stupendous sacrifice, even the humiliation and death of one of the Persons of the Godhead, the punishment that is due to our deeds has been averted, and unlimited pardon procured for the whole human race. We believe, however, that in order to profit by this general deed of amnesty, which the Sovereign of heaven and earth has issued, there must be a distinct reception of the terms of forgiveness on the part of an individual criminal; and, coupled with this belief, we are aware of the fact, that, though it is now eighteen hundred years since an express Messenger from heaven published this treaty of reconciliation in our world, comparatively few have welcomed the gracious message, and at this moment three-fourths of the population of our globe are in utter ignorance that such a message has ever come.

Do we believe these things, my brethren, and shall we not speak what we believe? Is there not a duty entailed upon every Christian, as far as it is in his power, by the belief of these great truths, to publish them to his fellow-men? And is there not a woe pronounced against every believer, if, in as far as he has opportunity, he preach not the gospel? It is not necessary to the preaching of the gospel that we pass through a preparatory course of science and literature, or that we be commissioned to do so by our fellow-men. Nor is it necessary to the preaching of the gospel, that we ascend a pulpit, or be surrounded with any of the apparatus of ordinary parsonship. It is not necessary that our address be made to a public assembly at all. Nor is it even necessary, ere we open our mouth to our fellow-men, that we work up a laboured systematic discourse. These things may accompany the preaching of the gospel, but they are by no means its necessary accompaniments, and it is hard to say whether this lavish profusion of human preparation, and worldly pomp, has not in many instances robbed of their native dignity and impressiveness, those sublime but simple truths which manifestly appear — "when unadorned, adorned the most." The preaching of the gospel, as imperative upon every Christian, needs not the aid of deep meditation, or of human scholarship. It consists in the simple communication to others of the simplest truths. We may preach to the little family circle as we sit in the house, or even to the solitary companion as we walk by the way. The simple belief of the gospel is all that is necessary to give us a title, and even to lay us under an obligation, to preach it in the sense which I have explained. David believed, and therefore he spoke! Paul believed, and therefore he spoke! and every Christian, having the same spirit of faith which dwelt in the Psalmist and the Apostle, should be able to adopt their language, and say, I also believe, and therefore speak. And if, my brethren, the same spirit of faith is working in us, it has not been the choice of our profession that has laid us under an obligation to preach the gospel; but the previously felt obligation that has led us to make choice of our profession.

If we can conscientiously give it as the reason for our proclaiming the truths of Christianity, that we speak because we believe, our conduct will be necessarily modified by the motives that actuate us; and our preaching shall be of a very different kind from that of the mere mercenaries of the church, or even from that of those who make their regular Sabbath-day exhibitions merely from a sense of professional duty.

In the first place, I remark, that our motive will regulate *the time* of our preaching.

If it be merely the wish to perform decently the duties of a minister, which is our ruling motive, then we shall, in all probability, be content with working up during the week, as much matter as will enable us to make on the Sabbath, two or three speeches, of the ordinary length, according as the custom of our predecessors, or the taste of our congregation may demand. If a parish be entrusted to our care, we may in all probability add to this the yearly or half-yearly visitation of a few of our parishioners; and if we be set over a dissenting congregation, we may, perhaps, contrive, without much risk (if our discourses happen to please the taste of our hearers;) of being thought inattentive to duty, to neglect the duty of visitation altogether.

But if we speak because we believe, — if it be a decided conviction of the truth and importance of the doctrines of the gospel, and an experimental proof of their soothing and sanctifying influence on our own mind, which inspires us from a principle of gratitude to our God, and compassion for our fellow-men, with the desire to devote ourselves to the service of God in the ministry of his Son; then our preaching will not be a thing of set times, or formal exhibitions. We shall not, indeed, despise the established order of Christian worship; the principle that actuates us will lead us to become "all things to all men, if by any means we may save some." We shall thus be glad to seize those opportunities when the commandment of God, and the laws and customs of our country have assembled many together for the purposes of religion; but our preaching will not be confined to the public exercises of the Sabbath, but according to the very solemn charge of the apostle, we shall be instant in preaching the word, in season and out of season, and in imitation of his example we shall not only speak as we have opportunity in the public places consecrated to devotion, but also from house to house. And even the ordinary intercourse that we carry on with our fellow-men, our correspondence with friends at a distance, and our conversations with companions who are near, will alike be consecrated to those grand objects to which our own selves are devoted.

But our motive will not only regulate the times of our preaching, it will also determine *the mode* of our preaching.

If we believe that the great object for which the gospel was sent into our world was to effect the pardon and moral renovation of man; and if we believe what the Scriptures assure us, that this is chiefly to be effected by faith in a few simple elementary doctrines, we shall dwell much upon these doctrines, and ever make them the theme of our discourse.

If we are assured that he who believes in Jesus Christ shall be saved, we shall determine, like the early promulgators of the faith, to know nothing among men, but Jesus Christ, and him crucified: we shall not preach ourselves, but Christ Jesus the Lord, and ourselves the servants of all, for Jesus' sake.

If, again, we believe that the same Spirit which breathed life into the dry bones of the prophet's vision, must still exert his vivifying energy, ere a single sinner can be raised from a death in trespasses and sins, to newness of life; and if we further believe that the Spirit is the gift of prayer, we shall be ardent in our supplications at the throne of grace, for the out-pouring of that mysterious influence, which, though itself unseen, is so visible in its effects, and without which the most splendid eloquence, and the most cogent reasoning can absolutely effect nothing.

Finally, our motive will also, to a certain extent, determine *the sphere* of our labours.

If we believe that there is one broad line which separates men into two distinct classes, — those who believe, and those who do not; those consequently who have obtained pardon, and those who are still under condemnation—we shall esteem it a matter of infinitely greater importance to lead an individual across that boundary, than to lead an individual who has already past it a few steps further on in his progress. The building up of believers is, no doubt, a most important work; but still we cannot help thinking, that it must yield in importance to the work of conversion.

H.

ON NATURAL RELIGION.

In the Bible we are told, that, at the final judgment, all men will be made the subjects of an equitable moral reckoning. But we know, from the history of our species, that there have been, and that there still are in the world, thousands who have never had access to that revelation from Heaven with which we have been favoured. It becomes then an interesting inquiry, how far the natural light of reason can render men the fit subjects of a moral reckoning; and how, in such a condition there can be any distinction between the godly and the ungodly. In that record, which hath come from Heaven, it is said, in reference to such individuals, that "God hath showed unto them that which may be known of himself, because the invisible things of him from the creation of the world, are clearly seen, being understood by the things that are made, even his eternal power and Godhead: so that they are without excuse." In other words, it is affirmed that those who have never had access to any direct communication from Heaven, are yet accountable for their deeds, inasmuch as the existence and the character of God may be gathered from the works which he has made. And it is thus that there may be a distinction between those who have been led by these dim intimations of his presence, to grope, though in the dark, after their Creator; and those, who, notwithstanding these intimations, "have said in their heart, that there is no God." When God looked down from heaven upon the children of men, it was to see if there were any that did understand, — if there were any that *did seek after* God.

The evidence for the existence of a God is so manifest in all his works, that there have scarcely been found any people, however ignorant and degraded, who have not recognized, in the objects that are around them, the traces of a designing and intelligent Creator. The marks of design are evident in the combinations and processes of inanimate nature. We can see them in the harmonious revolutions of those vast globes which compose the universe. We can see them in the varied operation of those elements which are at work upon the surface of our earth; in the regular succession of summer and winter, spring-time and harvest. We behold them in the descending shower which refreshes the soil, and in the ascending vapour which feeds the mighty cisterns from whence that shower was poured. And still more palpably do we recognize the traces of intelligence in the structure and physiology of the vegetable kingdom. In those roots which fix the plant in the soil, and collect for it its nutritive juices; in those tubes by which these juices are conveyed through all its various branches; in those leaves which cover and protect the infant bud, and die away again when the seed is ripened; in those autumnal breezes which scatter the seeds on the bosom of the earth, there to spring up in their turn, and to become distinct members of the vegetable family—in all this varied conformation of parts, and succession of agents, can we distinctly perceive the adaptation of means to an end; an adaptation which must have been the result of contemplation and design. But it is in animated nature that we have the most striking proofs of the existence of an intelligent Creator. In the structure of the bodies of animals the marks of design are so manifold, that the simple enumeration of them would far exceed our limits. In the structure of the eye alone, they are sufficiently numerous for our purpose. It is arched over with an eye-brow to carry off from it the moistures of the head. It is furnished with an eye-lid, which washes and moistens it, which covers it in sleep, which protects it when awake, spontaneously shutting on the approach of danger. Its optical adaptations are still more striking. It has its levers, which shift backward and forward, and which, without the will, or even the knowledge of him who possesses it, suit themselves to the distance of the object on which he gazes. In like manner, by the enlargement or contraction of its orifice, does the eye adapt itself to the degree of light that is around it, by a mechanism which baffles the imitation of human ingenuity, and even mocks the scrutiny of anatomical investigation. Nor is the internal physiology of animals less indicative of design than the external organization of their bodies. We might enumerate, as examples, the preparation and distribution of the various secretions, which either moisten the eye, or which lubricate the joints; or which supply that stream of circulation whose ebbings and flowings are the mystic indication of animal life; in short, all the varied and multifarious processes which are going on in the laboratory that is within us.

These are but a few of the indications inscribed upon the face of nature, which point to nature's God. And it were indeed strange, if man, with all these evidences of design, should never think of an intelligent Designer. Nor has it been so. All have recognized these proofs of a Divinity. The most ignorant and barbarous nations on the face of the earth, have imagined for themselves (however degrading and incongruous their imaginations may have been), some great and intelligent Being who made the heavens and the earth. It is not among the rude and ignorant sons of barbarism, that we are to look for those who have denied the existence of a God. Atheism is an unnatural crime; and we must look for its manifestations chiefly among those who have been bewildered by the speculations of an unnatural philosophy.

The natural attributes of God seem to follow as corollaries to the demonstration of his existence. Every one must admit, that, if there be a Being who made these heavens, and this earth, and all that is in them, he must be a Being of infinite might. We at once conclude, that He who gave the sea its bounds, that it should not pass his decree, must be very powerful; that He who counts the number of the stars, and guides them in their courses must be very great; that He who binds them to their orbits by the simple law of gravitation, must be very wise.

So far our way has been smooth and even, and the steps of the demonstration have been of easy ascent; but it is when we begin to consider the moral attributes of Deity, that we feel our progress impeded by many obstructions. It is here that we begin to perceive the insufficiency of the light of nature. It is when we begin to look around amid the works of God for the proofs of his goodness and his justice, that we feel ourselves bewildered and confounded. Yet some proofs of these there must exist independent of that revelation which God has made known to some of his creatures, or we cannot see how those who have never heard of this revelation are at all accountable for their actions. For aught that we have yet proved, He who formed with such exquisite skill, and such infinite power, these heavens and this earth, may after all care nothing for the beings he has made. He may sit in cold abstraction upon the throne of his majesty, regardless of the intelligent creatures he hath formed. He may have required nothing at their hand, and in consequence it may not be their duty to render aught to him. Or, he who reigns over the monarchy of the universe, may, notwithstanding his greatness, and his power, and his wisdom, be a demon of malignant influence; and however fearful our situation under such a conjecture, it may be our duty to resist his every commandment. In order that all men may be accountable before God, even natural religion must furnish some clue to the ascertaining of these uncertainties. And we conceive that it does so, though not in the way that has usually been represented.

It has been usual with the expounders of natural theism to sum up all the misery that is to be found in the world, and having placed it in counterpoise with the happiness which we also find there, to pronounce the Deity benevolent or malignant as the one scale or the other preponderates. They have represented to us the many hours of health we enjoy for one hour of sickness; and the many different circumstances that must meet ere we can enjoy one hour of ease. And they have told of the happiness of the inferior animals, and have instanced the countless shoals of happy ephemeræ which dance with joy in the meridian sunbeam. Now we can see that this is an argument for comparative benevolence, but we cannot see it to be an argument for perfect goodness. It proves that our Creator is not a devil, but it does not prove him to be a God. It may be true that we enjoy hundreds of hours of health for one hour of sickness; but why this one hour of sickness? Our natural theist should remember too, that health is not all that is necessary to constitute happiness. Why is it that not a day passes over our head, but brings with it something to mar our enjoyment, some painful affront, some boding fear, some disappointed hope? And when they point to the happiness of the inferior creation, they would do well to remember the ravages of death. Do they forget, that for those numberless myriads of insects which sport so blithely in the noontide sun; myriads as numberless have, since He made the circuit of the heavens, struggled in the throes of dissolution? Why this mixture of misery with happiness, if God be altogether benevolent?

These objections did not fail to present themselves to the minds of our academic theists, and accordingly they have made an attempt to meet them. They have feigned for themselves some delightful region beyond the grave, where there will be happiness without alloy, and where the miseries of life will be merged and forgotten amid the joys of a blissful eternity. We say, "have feigned for themselves;" for, on coming to examine their grounds of belief in the existence of a future state, we find that the opinion has no foundation but in the assumed goodness of the Deity, the very point they have employed it to prove. But passing for the present this defect in their reasoning, we cannot see how a futurity of happiness, though established on the surest evidence, can at all make out their case. The question still recurs, Why a state of mixed enjoyment at all? Why a single moment of imperfect felicity under the government of a benevolent God? Would it be deemed a sufficient excuse for the cruelty of an earthly parent to his infant son, that when that son had grown to manhood, the father had done all in his power to promote his happiness? And can it be thought a sufficient vindication of the character of him who is called the Father of our spirits, that although he hath made us miserable upon earth, he will not make us miserable in heaven?

Notwithstanding this anomaly in the moral government of God, and notwithstanding the weakness of the reasoning on which the argument for his goodness has been founded, there is a strong intuitive belief in the minds of his intelligent creatures, that God is good and that the Judge of all the earth will do rightly. So strong is this inherent faith in the divine goodness, and so abhorrent to the mind of man is the thought of a malignant God, that rather than accede to the monstrous proposition that the Divinity is wicked, men have chosen to struggle against the most palpable demonstrations of their senses, and have acceded to the equally monstrous proposition that there is no Divinity at all.

Whence springs this deep-rooted and almost universal belief in divine benevolence and justice? We conceive it to be the result of that constitution of our nature by which conscience has the supremacy in the kingdom that is within us. It seems a just conclusion, that had he been a spirit of demoniac malignity, or of aught but perfect righteousness, who built our frame, he never would have placed within us a monitor to reproach us for our vice, and to whisper approbation to our deeds of virtue.

This seems the only satisfactory evidence, independent of revelation, for the moral perfections of the Deity. It does not resolve the anomaly of his moral government, but it may lead to the resolution of it. It does not satisfy, but it may stimulate to inquiry. And who can fix the limit which must bound the discoveries of the pious inquirer on this subject, who has nought but the glimmering of nature's light to guide his footsteps? Even he may come to perceive that there is an indissoluble union between vice and wretchedness, and that the misery which exists in our world is casually connected with the moral evil which is also found there.

But this same constitution of our nature, which proves the moral attributes of God, tells us also of our connection with him, by revealing to us what he hath required of us. And thus it is that all men become, to a certain degree, acquainted with the law of God, and are consequently the fit subjects of a moral reckoning. It is thus that "the Gentiles not having the (revealed) law, are a law unto themselves: who show the work of the law written in their hearts, their conscience also bearing witness, and their thoughts the mean while accusing, or excusing one another?" If a man thus perceive the moral perfections of God, and if he compare his own doings with the requirements of his conscience, he must find that he has come short of the law of God; and he will wistfully look for a way of reconciliation.

This is the state in which natural religion leaves its votaries; but, unfortunately, it is not the state in which academic theists have usually left their disciples. They have been desirous of solving those difficulties in which their science places them, and they have done so by making a most degrading compromise between the goodness and the justice of the Deity, by representing God to be such a one as ourselves.

There are two grand desiderata in which natural religion lands its disciples. The one is to effect a reconciliation between the benevolence of the Deity, and the misery that exists among his creatures. The other is to effect a reconciliation between the mercy and the justice of God, in the pardon of those who have transgressed his law. The solution of these two desiderata, constitutes the grand design of that revelation which God hath given us. And it is thus that the humble disciple of natural religion is in the best state of preparation for the faith of the gospel. He is there told, that the misery which exists in our world, is the fruit of moral evil: that "by one man sin entered into the world, and death by sin; and so death hath passed upon all men, for that all have sinned." There, too, he is told of a Mediator, who hath suffered in the room of the guilty, and he can thus perceive how God is just, yet not at the expense of his goodness; merciful, yet not by a degrading compromise of his justice.

This revelation has made manifest all that relates to ourselves, but it has not made manifest all that relates to God. With regard to the second desideratum, (the way of our acceptance with God), it is clear and perspicuous: but with regard to the first, (the reconciliation between the divine goodness and the misery of his creatures), it has thrown a light across the darkness, but it has not perfectly illumined it. It has shifted the difficulty, but it has not entirely removed it. It tells us that misery is the result of moral evil; but with regard to the origin of evil, it is altogether silent. It answers the objection, "Why does he yet find fault, for who hath resisted his will?" by reminding us of our ignorance, and our weakness; "Nay, but, O man, who art thou that repliest against God?" The Bible was not intended to present us with a full development of the divine character; but only to make known to us so much of that character as affects our own acceptance with the Deity. It was not meant to be a sun from whence might emanate a full illumination to reveal every object around us, but it was given us as a lamp to guide our own footsteps through the darkness of nature. The Day Star, it is true, hath arisen upon us, and "our path is as the shining light, which shineth more and more unto the perfect day;" but the day itself hath not yet dawned. Here we see as through a glass, darkly, and know but in part: but we look forward to a period of clearer revelation, when there shall beam forth upon us a brighter display of the Divine attributes in all their harmony. And then shall we see "face to face, and know even as we are known."

I shall be excused from giving my opinion of this production, when I quote the following sentence annexed to it, in the handwriting of Dr. Chalmers:—"An Essay of surpassing worth, as have been all the other compositions of its author in the Moral Philosophy Class."

I.

PRIZE ESSAY ON THE MUTUAL INFLUENCES AND AFFINITIES, WHICH OBTAIN BETWEEN THE MORAL AND THE ECONOMIC CONDITION OF SOCIETY.

With those who wish to prove from natural religion, the existence of a state of retribution, beyond the grave, the unequal distribution of rewards and punishments in the present life, has always been a favourite argument. Such individuals have usually placed before us, in strongest colouring, that success which sometimes crowns the fraudulent schemes of the vicious; which they have rendered doubly impressive, by contrasting it with those unforeseen calamities, which so often, in this world of uncertainty, crush the most strenuous exertions of aspiring virtue. In order to reconcile this seeming injustice with the assumed goodness of the Deity, they argue that there must be some future state of existence, where a recompense shall be rendered to the virtuous for all his sufferings on earth; and where that vengeance, which has been long delayed, shall at last overtake, and utterly overwhelm the vicious.

Now, though we perfectly agree with those who thus reason, and think that their conclusions are most legitimately deducible from the premises, yet we cannot help the conviction that they have somewhat overstrained their argument, and that in their zeal to prove that the present life is but a state of probation, they have sometimes represented the moral government of God in our world, as more deranged, and further from equity than actually is the case. Notwithstanding all that has been advanced to the contrary, we think we are entitled, from the strongest historical evidence, to believe that the proverb, though not universally, yet very generally, holds true, even when we confine our regards to man's present existence, that virtue is her own reward, and that vice involves its own punishment; or, in other words, that there is a very intimate connection between a man's moral character, and his economic circumstances. Idleness and vice are, with few exceptions, the harbingers of disease and misery, while sobriety and industry seldom fail to procure for their possessor, respectability and comfort. So that we shall in general find, that if a virtuous man come to ruin, it is not because of, but in spite of his virtue; and that on the other hand, if a vicious man prosper, it is not because of, but in spite of his immorality. And these remarks are not only consonant to experience and sound philosophy, but they also receive additional confirmation from the announcements of revelation, which ever describes moral evil as the sole cause of all the misery that is to be found in our world; and which holds out to him who is obedient to its precepts, the promise of the life which now is, as well as of that life which is to come.

But if these remarks hold, generally, with regard to individuals, they are still more universally true when applied to nations. An individual may get rich by fraud and injustice; but we know of no vice that can aggrandize a nation. Some unforeseen calamity, on the other hand, may overwhelm the most virtuous individual; but we know not of any obstacle which can impede the rising greatness of a country, whose inhabitants are sober and industrious, and which is governed with justice and liberality. So that we may safely aver, if not of individuals, at least of communities, that there is a very close and intimate connection between their moral, and their economic condition.

To point out a few of the mutual influences and affinities which obtain between the moral and the economic condition of mankind, will, therefore, be the object of the following observations. And we shall consider the subject; First, As it may be illustrated in savage life, and in the subsequent progress of a community from barbarism to refinement. And, secondly, In its relation to civilized society.

The most degraded condition in which we can suppose human beings to be placed, and that in which man most nearly resembles the animals of the inferior creation, is that condition in which there is no mental culture, no moral instruction whatever. As this is the lowest condition in which a community can be placed in point of morals, so is it the lowest in point of economic comfort. The untutored savage comes into the world, and feels himself actuated by certain appetites and passions, which, as he has never been taught to restrain, he makes it his sole employment to gratify. His present wants occupy so much of his attention, that he seldom thinks of making provision for those that are future. His subsistence, therefore, consists entirely in the spontaneous productions of the earth and the sea; in the animals which he can succeed in capturing, and in the scanty fruits which the soil may produce without the labour of human hands. The latter are so insignificant that they can scarcely be taken into account; and accordingly, we find, that fishing, and the chase, constitute, in general, the sole employments of nations sunk in this lowest state of barbarism.

Nothing can be more uncertain, however, than the returns which such occupations yield; and the savage has too little foresight to make the success of one expedition compensate for the failure of another. If he catch a deer, he does not think of laying up part of it against the emergencies of future bad fortune, but proceeds forthwith to gratify the voracious appetite of himself and his family, which has in all likelihood, been whetted by long fasting, or by a long succession of scanty meals. After he has thus profusely wasted his whole stock of provisions, he must again fast, perhaps for days, or support existence by means of the few miserable berries which the woods can afford him, till another deer falls in his way, when the same scene of gluttony takes place, and the same course of misery follows. If another has been more successful than himself, his sense of justice is by far too weak to deter him from satisfying the cravings of a famished appetite at whatever expense. He will not hesitate to fight with his enemy for the sake of the animals he may have caught, or even, in some instances, to murder him for the sake of the horrid repast which his flesh may furnish. A want of the necessaries of life is said to be the cause of those bloody contentions which are ever bursting forth among savage tribes. And the cruel and merciless nature of that warfare may be imagined, where the contest is not, as among civilized nations, for some imaginary honour, or for some disputable territory; but, where the prize of victory consists in the flesh of the vanquished. It is only necessary to take into account the element of population, in order to complete this revolting picture of human wretchedness. If the savage has not foresight enough to provide for his own wants, it is not likely that he will be more careful to provide for the wants of his family. In such a state of society there can be no moral restraint to keep the population within the bounds of an uncertain and scanty subsistence: these bounds, however, it cannot exceed, and we may look for the positive checks which restrain it, in those extirpating wars to which we have already alluded, as well as in the licentious and impure habits of savages, and in those famines and pestilential diseases which are occasioned by their wretched mode of life.

In this state of things we may suppose that some savage, who had often experienced the miseries of extreme want, bethinks himself of laying up part of the provisions which he has caught to-day, to insure against the uncertainty of to-morrow's expedition. We may suppose that he feels the benefit of this new arrangement, and that, in consequence, he continues it. There may thus originate in the mind of the savage, a sense of property. Savage, though he be, he is yet man; and on man, even in this most degraded of all conditions, may that rule of universal application have some influence, "As ye would that others should do unto you, do ye even so to them." From a feeling of attachment to his own property, and a wish to defend it from the attacks of his neighbour, may he learn to have respect for the property of others; and thus, from a sense of property, may there emerge a sense of justice.

This, however, is an important step in the progress of morality; and we shall find that it is immediately followed by a step as important in the march of economic improvement.

An example has been shown of the good effects of foresight, and property is now in some degree regarded; it therefore becomes a general custom among the savages to hoard up the overplus of a successful hunting or fishing expedition, in order to insure against future emergencies. By and by they perceive, that, if they can but keep the cattle which they take, alive, they thus acquire a kind of property, which not only furnishes a safeguard against future want, but which has also this peculiar advantage, that it is continually increasing. In a little time they find that this live stock, which is kept at home, multiplies so rapidly, as not only to enable them to bear out against the failure of a single expedition in fishing or the chase, but to render them independent of fishing and the chase altogether. Though they can now live without engaging in the toils of their old occupations, and are no longer obliged to roam through the woods in search of subsistence, yet they are by no means idle; their increasing flocks and herds demand every day more and more of their attention. Instead of hunters and fishers, they now become shepherds; and, to a state of most degraded barbarism, there now succeeds the pastoral condition, greatly more improved indeed than the former, yet still very far removed from a state of perfect civilization.

The pastoral condition is one that has been a favourite theme with the poets of every age and nation; and in their writings it has been pictured forth as a state of purest simplicity and most perfect innocence. Green fields, and flowing streams, and cattle browsing upon their banks, furnish indeed very beautiful imagery for poetry, and naturally lead us to imagine how simple, and how innocent their manners must be, who are conversant with objects so pure and so peaceful. But there is a fearful contrast between the face of external nature, and the heart of man. The curse that was pronounced upon the ground, hath still left many a lovely trace of Eden behind it; but that withering blight which hath gone forth over the face of our moral scenery, hath left scarce a vestige in our world, of primaeval sanctity and justice.

Notwithstanding all that has been said or sung about the happiness, and the innocence of the pastoral state, it seems to stand in the scale of morality and civilization just where we have placed it, at a very small distance from the grossest barbarism.

When once a number of savages have turned from the ruder occupations of fishing and the chase, to the tending of cattle, they find that the fodder of the place where they dwell is soon consumed. They are thus obliged to proceed in search of new pasture ground, which again is soon exhausted and left in its turn. In this wandering condition they find it necessary to form little bands or tribes, both for the purpose of self-defence, and also to enable them to extirpate or expel from their territories, the inhabitants of such districts, as may seem most fit to be converted into pasture ground for their cattle. The morality of these pastoral tribes seems much akin to that which is generally to be met with in a band of highwaymen, who must necessarily keep up some semblance of justice among themselves, but whose business it is to plunder everybody that does not belong to their gang. This character but ill accords with that which is assigned to them in the high-wrought descriptions of pastoral poetry; but unfortunately it is their real one. Mr. Malthus, in his work on population, describes the Scythian shepherds, as actuated by a most savage and destructive spirit; and as an exemplification of this, he tells us that "when the Moguls had subdued the northern provinces of China, it was proposed, in calm and deliberate council, to exterminate all the inhabitants of that populous country, that the vacant land might be converted to the pasture of cattle."

The economic state of pastoral nations, seems quite as miserable as their moral condition. There is still but little of prudential restraint to confine the population within the limits of subsistence; and still the checks, as in the case of utter barbarism, are vice, and famine, and pestilence, and war.

It is long before, by that gradual process of improvement which is going on in every society, the morals of such a people are so far improved, as to give security sufficient for carrying on the operations of agriculture: and it is still longer, perhaps, before by their establishment prejudices are so far removed, as to induce them to change the employment of the shepherd for that of the husbandman. But when once this period arrives, improvement advances apace. The land begins to yield a rent to the landlord. The principle of the division of labour begins to operate. New inventions are consequently made, and the productive powers of labour are almost infinitely increased. A knowledge of science and the arts is disseminated, and then follow in their train all the blessings of civilization and refinement.

This process, tardy as it is, seems to be the natural one, by which a society advances from a state of barbarism to a civilized condition, and through the whole of it may we behold how the *moral* and the *economic* blend together, and mutually influence and affect each other. And it is a fact, not the least deserving of our notice, in this beautiful process, that though the moral and the economic are mutually subservient the one to the other, yet it is the moral, generally speaking, which takes the lead. Where, by the gradual progress of improvement, a change is effected in the moral condition of a community, it is instantaneously followed up by a corresponding change in its economic condition. And not one step can be taken in the path of economic improvement, till the way has first been prepared by the advancement of a purer morality. This fact, we apprehend, if properly appreciated, would lead to the solution of a problem in economic science, which has long engaged the attention of every genuine philanthropist. It is a melancholy fact, that a very large portion of the human family are still sunk in the depths of utter barbarism, or but a few steps removed from it: and the problem is, — to civilize them. We are aware that nature herself would accomplish the task in the lapse of ages, but the question is, cannot we hasten her operations? It is extremely natural to suppose, and, accordingly, it has been the opinion of most of the philosophers of our day, that the way to solve this important problem, is to begin directly by teaching the barbarians the arts of civilized life. If, however, there be any truth in our remark, that the moral precedes and paves the way for the economic in the natural progress of society, there is a very strong presumption that we must observe the same order, when it is our wish to hasten this natural progress. And if this be the case, we should be prepared to expect, that the plan we have mentioned, however well it promised as a theory, would prove unsuccessful when brought to the test of actual experiment. And it has accordingly proved so. A class of men, who have ever stood among the foremost in the enterprises of philanthropy, have made an attempt, upon this plan, to civilize the Indian tribes of North America: but so far as we have heard, their efforts have proved unsuccessful. Nor need we wonder that such has been the result of their operations. However zealous they may have been in their endeavours, they have been working at the wrong end of the lever. The way one would think, were, first, to elevate the moral feeling of the barbarian; and then, having thus paved the way for economic improvement, to superinduce those instructions which might hasten the progress of civilization and refinement. On this plan, too, the experiment has been tried, not in one country, or among savages of one disposition; but the arena of its operations has been chosen from every latitude in either hemisphere of our globe, — from the frozen regions, encircled by the Northern Sea, to the distant islands of the Southern Ocean: and wherever the experiment has been fairly tried, it has been universally attended by a greater or less degree of success. And yet, strange as it may seem, the originators of this plan have been laughed at as enthusiasts; and they who have devoted their lives to carry it into execution, and who have told of its success, have been reviled as hypocrites and liars. And that, not because the plan has failed in its operations, or because there has not been sufficient evidence of its success, but because of the seeming insignificancy of the means by which this mighty work is achieving. It is because they are not the philosophers of this world who are its executors, but those whom the philosophers of this world too often despise. It is because they are not the manuals of philosophy which have guided its operations, but that book which philosophers have too frequently rejected.

But we shall be very much deceived, if we imagine that all that can be done for a country, is to civilize it; and that, after this has been effected, the comforts of this life are secured to every individual within its borders. Such, indeed, is the vast increase in the productive powers of labour, that the very lowest member of a civilized community, has a greater command over the comforts of life, than the prince of any savage nation. But even in a civilized community do we find much of economic wretchedness. After we have succeeded in solving the problem, "to civilize a society," there still remains to be solved another economic problem of the last importance; and one which has long occupied the attention of philanthropists, both in our own and other civilized nations. It is to elevate the condition of the poor.

In the attempts which have been made, in our own country, to solve this problem, and in what we consider the only effective method of accomplishing this task, do we think that we have several beautiful illustrations of the way in which the moral and the economic mutually influence and affect each other; and to this subject, therefore, we propose chiefly to direct our attention in the remainder of this essay.

After the division of labour has allotted to each individual his peculiar employment, and stock has been accumulated, and land appropriated, the inhabitants of every society are divided into three grand classes.

The first consists of those, who, by the labour of their hands, work up commodities both for their own consumption, and that of the other classes, and are thus the originators of the whole wealth of the society. The second class consists of those, who, in virtue of a capital, which either they or their progenitors have accumulated, are enabled to furnish the labouring class with the implements of their industry, and to support them till the produce of their labour finds a market: and who, in return for these important services, lay claim to a part of the produce of their labour. The third class consists of those who, in virtue of a possessory right, lay claim to the earth, that great implement of industry, and who derive a revenue by lending out this implement to the other classes.

On taking an abstract view of these three classes, we should least of all expect, that that class should be the poorest which furnishes the wealth of the whole society. Experience, however, teaches us that that class of the community who do most, are the worst rewarded; while they who do little, are in comfortable circumstances; and they who do least, are overflowing in wealth.

It has, accordingly, been almost universally the custom to declaim against landlords and capitalists, as if they were the authors of all the misery which exists among the working classes: as if it were their avarice and their injustice which had wrested from the most useful class of the community, that wealth which their own hands so laboriously had earned. But it is not the landlords who are the authors of this misery; it is not the capitalists who are the authors of it: in very deed, it is the labourers themselves who are the authors of it. Were but their manners virtuous, and their habits prudential, they might bid proud defiance to their haughty superiors, and might refuse to treat with them but on honourable terms. They, and not their employers, are the arbitrators of their wages. But it is the vices to which they are wedded, which, like the false mistress of Samson, have betrayed to their enemies the secret of their strength: it is their own improvident habits which have brought them down from that lofty vantage-ground which else they might occupy, and have placed them at the mercy of their employers: it is their own over-grown numbers which have reduced them to the point of starvation, and have thus compelled them, like the inhabitants of a blockaded city, who are hard pressed by the horrors of a famine, to submit to any terms, however humiliating, which their masters may be pleased to hold out.

This miserable condition of the working class, when contrasted with the ease and affluence of the other two, may not appear so anomalous, if we but consider the matter a little more attentively. There are comparatively few who are born heirs to fortunes or landed property, and still fewer who acquire either, by dint of their own exertions; but, on the other hand, many who lose both by carelessness or extravagance. The working class is thus, not only naturally by far the most numerous, but is continually exposed to the overflowings of the other two. It requires an effort to resist the force of the current, which carries downward, and the most strenuous exertions seldom prove successful in the attempt to move upward against it. The demand for labour, however, is necessarily limited; and it is the eager competition which takes place among labourers, for subsistence, which is the cause of the miserable condition of the working classes.

This misery has attracted the notice of our legislators, and an attempt has been made, on their part, to relieve it. But in this attempt they have committed the same error as those philanthropists whom we formerly mentioned as having made an unsuccessful effort towards the civilization of the North American Indians. They have wrought at the wrong end of the lever. They have not adverted to the fact, that it is moral derangement which is the cause of economic misery; and that, therefore, in every improvement, the moral must take the precedency of the economic. Their experiment, accordingly, has hitherto not only failed, but has tended to aggravate the evil which it was meant to cure.

The greatest expedient by which it has been attempted to relieve the misery of the working classes, is that system of legalized charity, which is enforced, by what are usually called, the *poor laws* of England. We give credit to the benevolent feeling which prompted the enactment of those laws. It was a zeal in the cause of philanthropy which dictated the measure; but, unfortunately, it was a zeal not according to knowledge. Our legislators seem, in this instance, to have acted like that physician, who should administer water to allay the thirst of a patient in a dropsy, and thereby increase the virulence of the disease, for the sake of giving the sufferer a few moments of temporary relief. When the Parliament of England framed the system of English pauperism, they were guilty of two inadvertencies. In the first place, they did not advert to the nature of the evil which it was their object to cure; for, had they but discovered its cause, they would at once have perceived that it was their business to set to work in a very different way; to remove, if possible, the cause of the evil, with the full assurance that the removal of the evil itself would be the necessary consequence; and aware, that while the cause of the evil continued in full operation, all their attempts to remove the evil itself would prove utterly vain. In the second place, they forgot that that same compassion which dictated their well-meant exertions, was not confined to them alone, but glowed as fervently in every English bosom. The first of these things our legislators did not perceive, or they would have conducted the business in a very different manner. The second, they did not advert to, or they would never have proceeded a single step in the business at all.

The present system of English pauperism has been productive of two very great evils, arising from these two inadvertencies of its originators. In the first place, it has prevented the operation of those effectual remedies which nature has provided for the relief of existing misery. And in the second place, it has contributed very much to add to the numbers of the wretched.

The first and greatest of those remedies which nature has provided for the relief of existing misery, is the relative affections. The filial and parental affections are perhaps the strongest and most universal instinct we know of. They have been implanted in us by a wise Creator, for the most important ends, and were we altogether deprived of them, society could not exist. They are not confined to man alone, but are shared with him by all the tribes of animated nature; so that, to deprive him of these affections were to sink him below the level of the inferior creation. Yet this, to a certain extent at least, is the effect of English pauperism. It is the helplessness of tender infancy and childhood, and of decrepit old age, which calls into action, with all their vigour, the family affections. The poor laws, however, have provided both for the helplessness of youth, and the infirmity of age, and have thus contributed to burst asunder the strongest and tenderest ties of our nature. Nor is this an assertion that is unsupported by facts. There are instances in which a parent has actually disclaimed his own children, and has told the overseer of the parish that it is none of his business to provide for them; that the parish must find work for them, or support them, if it cannot.

If the poor laws have extinguished those natural affections which subsist between members of the same family, we cannot expect that they have left uninjured those mutual sympathies which reciprocate between the inhabitants of the same neighbourhood; far less those more distant expressions of kindness which descend upon the wretched from the coffers of the rich.

But were this all the mischief the poor laws had done, there might still be found some to advocate the cause of pauperism. It might be argued for this system of legalized charity, that if it has destroyed the natural remedies for existing misery, it has substituted in their place an artificial remedy, equally effective; that a provision for the distressed is still as sure as before, though it flows through a different channel.

It were but a silly excuse for complicating a clock or a watch with a great deal of intricate mechanism, that the additional work had the wonderful property of rectifying those defects of which itself was the cause, and that the instrument answered its end every whit as well as it did before. But even such a defence, weak as it is, cannot be advanced for English pauperism.

The evils which we have mentioned, are, after all, but the least which pauperism has effected. Not only has it prevented the operation of those remedies which nature has provided for existing misery, but it has actually increased this misery. Its regulations, by insuring against the wretchedness which they generally occasion, have thrown down those barriers which naturally restrain from vice and imprudence. Imprudence qualifies an individual for receiving parish support; and vice, at least, does not disqualify us. For the first of these positions there is sufficient evidence in the fact, that single persons, when the overseer has refused to enrol them on the list of paupers, have flatly told him, that if he do not give them the usual parish allowance, they will go away and marry, and thus compel the parish to support, not only themselves, but also their families. Of the latter position, that vice is no disqualification, we have a most palpable illustration, in the case of an individual, who on the overseers refusing to give him any support at all, on the ground of his possessing some property of his own, most impudently threatened to go to the next ale-house, and there spend his all in dissipation, in order that he might more effectually burden the parish by compelling it to give him a full allowance.

But the greatest mischief of all, perhaps, of which pauperism has been the cause, is, that it not only adds to the numbers of the miserable, by destroying the prudential habits of a great part of the community, but that it deteriorates the economic condition even of those whose confirmed habits of sobriety and industry have withstood its baneful influence. The composition of wages with parish allowance, is perhaps the most mischievous part of all this mischievous system. If our legislators did mean to give the poor a title to legal support, it were better far, that in every instance, they had made the parish allowance sufficient to maintain the pauper entirely, and that they had never had recourse to the ruinous experiment of compounding this allowance with the ordinary reward of labour.

In this case all the evils we have already mentioned, would no doubt have followed, but there is one very great evil, which would have been in a great measure prevented, the reduction of the wages of the independent part of the working classes.

In the present state of things, let a man be ever so industrious, and ever so sober, and ever so prudent, it is absolutely impossible for him to better his condition, so long as pauperism sends forth her myriads of labourers to compete with him at any price, however low, which the employer may choose to offer. It is true, that the working classes have the power of regulating their own wages; but it is not one individual, or a number of individuals, who can effect this. It requires a combination of, at least, a very considerable portion of the labouring community; and to this most desirable of all ends, pauperism presents a most insuperable obstacle.

But we have, perhaps, entered too much into detail, in enumerating the evils of a system, with regard to whose mischievous tendency, every body seems now to be perfectly agreed. It requires not now a well argued representation, to convince people of the evils of pauperism. It has long been felt, experimentally, to be the scourge of our nation. The question is not now, — Should the poor laws be abolished? but, — Can they be abolished with safety? And, if so, How is this most desirable end to be accomplished? It must be palpable to every one, that the poor laws of England are now so enwoven into the very constitution of society, and so amalgamated with the manners of a very considerable portion of the people, that a sudden repeal of them would be an experiment attended with the most dangerous consequences. There is every reason to fear, that were the Parliament of Great Britain, by a single act of their authority, at once to disinherit every pauper of his wonted allowance, the result might be nothing less than a rebellion; and that the precipitancy of such a measure could scarce fail to land us in all the horrors of internal commotion. In attempting the cure of a disease so virulent, and which has its seat so deep in the constitution of the society, the greatest care must be taken, lest, in the attempt to extract the part that is diseased, we pierce the very vitals, or let flow the life-blood of the body politic. If pauperism is ever to be abolished, it must be by a gradual process. The abolition of the poor laws must be the work. not of a day, but of months and of years.

It must, in fact, be a work of prevention, rather than of cure. It were cruelty, — it were madness, to snatch their wretched pittance from the present dependants on the vestry. The present race of paupers must be permitted to die away, in the quiet possession of their rights: and it must be made the main concern, not to cure the evil which exists, but to prevent the evil which threatens.

The whole system of pauperism may, we think, be illustrated by the case of a machine, which has gone into disorder, and whose errors are attempted to be rectified by one who is unacquainted with its internal mechanism. We shall suppose that the machine is a watch, and that, from some cause or other, it does not keep time. The most palpable method of rectifying this error, which would occur to one that was ignorant of its cause, would be, to move backward or forward, as the case might require, the hands on the dial-plate. But it would soon be evident, that this was but a temporary remedy, and that the index of the watch, in a short time deviated as far as ever from pointing out the real hour. Temporary, however, and withal troublesome as this remedy undoubtedly would be, it might come, by frequent repetition, to have at least the semblance of efficiency. And yet might it happen, that this continued application of external force to the hands of the dial-plate, was, all the time, doing violence to the internal mechanism of the watch; and thus, instead of diminishing, was continually increasing the real cause of the evil. Let us now suppose, that the watch is put into the hands of one who is intimately acquainted with the construction and arrangement of all its parts; and let us try to perceive, wherein the method which he takes to rectify its movements, differs from that which the first individual pursued. The existing error, he will treat just as it had been treated before: he will apply an external force to the hands of the watch. But he will not be satisfied with this. He will search amid the intricacies of the internal mechanism, for that which has been the cause of the error; and it may be by a slight touch of the regulator, he will effectually prevent the recurrence of the error in time to come.

Now it has thus happened with the vast engine of the community: its mechanism has been deranged, — and without searching for the cause of this derangement, it has been attempted to rectify it by the application of an extraneous remedy. This remedy was found to effect only a temporary cure, and accordingly it was frequently repeated. It is now found, however, that this continuous application of external force, has tended to derange more and more the internal mechanism of this mighty engine. So fearfully has the evil increased, that every one now perceives that some new method must be adopted. But there is a dread, lest, if we all at once give up this external rectification, which confessedly, however, is every day augmenting the cause of the evil, this mighty machine may go into utter disarrangement. There is then a dilemma, and either alternative seems attended with the most dangerous results. The only way, which seems at once safe and effectual, is to proceed, as in the case of our illustration; to treat the existing evil as it has been treated all along, but to prevent the future evil, by an alteration in the inner mechanism of the machine. And it is interesting to observe, that the analogy holds still further. As in the case of the watch, a very slight alteration of the regulator may be sufficient to counteract a very great deviation from the truth in the hands of the dial-plate; so, in the case of a community, the cause of the economic misery which exists among the working classes, is, after all, but slight, and consequently can be easily removed.

From these observations, it appears, that there are two grand points which must be kept in view, in any attempt to abolish the system of English pauperism. First, that the abolition of the system should be so complete, that no future amendment might be required; and yet, that in the second place, it should be so gradual as to cause no sudden disrupture. We may just briefly remark, without entering into details, that both these points may be attained by a mode of policy similar to that which has been employed with regard to the enclosure of English commons. It is interesting to observe, how, on the abolition of pauperism, the relief which nature has provided for misery, begins again to operate; and those numerous fountains of benevolence, which had been frozen up, under its cold and cheerless influence, again begin to flow. And still more interesting is it to observe, how soon our population will shake off that lethargic indifference about the future, which the provisions of legalized charity so long have fostered; and, how soon prudential restraint will again reduce the numbers of a community, whose overgrown size has been the great cause of their misery.

But we are not so sanguine in our expectations, as to suppose that the abolition of pauperism would procure for the working classes, all the ease, and all the comfort, we could desire to see them possessed of. We assuredly do suppose, however, that by its abolition, a mighty obstacle would be removed which at present destroys the effectiveness of those means which are employing to accomplish this most desirable end. It is well, perhaps, that the evils of pauperism are continually increasing; for this is a circumstance which ensures it speedy abolition. The system cannot work much longer. Things must soon come to a crisis. And what our legislators are now unwilling to do, at the instigation of reason, they will soon be compelled to perform by the power of an irresistible necessity.

Besides the system of pauperism, there are yet two other obstacles which have hitherto stood in the way of those philanthropic exertions which are now making in every quarter, for elevating the condition of the working classes. The first is, the law against combinations of workmen, for the purpose of raising their wages. The second is, the want of a small capital among the operatives, to enable them to stand out till their masters may accede to their terms. Happily the first of these obstacles is now removed; and an attempt has been made to remove the second, which bids fair to prove successful. For the repeal of the combination laws, the labouring classes are indebted to the enlightened policy of the present age, which has at length taught our legislators, the absurdity of compelling an individual, in a country which boasts of its liberties, to sell his labour at a price which can barely supply him with the necessaries of life, and all for the purpose of keeping up the wealth and the dignity of his more affluent fellow-countrymen. For an attempt to remove the second obstacle to which we have alluded, our operatives are indebted to a zealous and philanthropic minister of the Church of Scotland.

This gentleman has succeeded in establishing, in his own parish, and in several other parts of the country, those admirable institutions, which are now beginning to be generally known, by the name of Saving Banks; institutions where the humble shilling of the labourer is received, with as much thankfulness, and tendered back to him when demanded, with as much promptness and affability, as is the most valuable deposit of his wealthy employer. It is a very remarkable coincidence, and one which augurs well for the future prospects of the labouring classes, that these two circumstances should have occurred, as if to give them every opportunity of profiting by their elevated standard of enjoyment, just at the time when, by means altogther different, it was in contemplation to elevate that standard. These means are now beginning their operation; and there is reason to expect, that the opportunities of moral and scientific instruction will soon be patent to every individual in the society. Among these means, we might enumerate our schools of arts, and our reading societies for the instruction of the old; and our parish and Sabbath-schools for the education of the young.

These are institutions which have already been productive of the most salutary results, and of whose beneficent influence we may yet hope to behold more visible manifestations written upon the face of our country. By their instrumentality may we hope, even within the short period of our life-time, to see the balance of society more equally poised, — to behold our landlords retrenching a few of their more extravagant superfluities, in order to supply more liberally, with the comforts and conveniences of life, by far the most deserving class of the community.

On the whole there seems something like the dawning of a brighter era in the history of our world. Whether we listen to those cheering reports, which are daily arriving from the friends of religion and philanthropy abroad, or direct our regards to the animating prospects of our home population; we cannot help thinking, that we already descry the visible approach of a period which has long been expected by the Christian, as well as dreamt of, and longed for by the infidel philosopher; a period, which, by the plenty and the happiness that shall be showered down upon every family, and by the fidelity, and the justice, and the benevolence, that shall animate every bosom, will outvie the high-wrought descriptions of a golden age, which poetic fancy has imagined.

We, at least, who believe in the divine inspiration of the Bible, can look forward with joyful anticipation, to that time, when, in the language of the prophecy which has foretold its coming, "the knowledge of the Lord shall cover the earth as the waters cover the channel of the deep." And then, under the influence of that pure and elevated morality, which Christianity shall universally diffuse, might we confidently predict, that the economic condition of society shall assume a brighter aspect than ever yet it hath worn, since that day when man was driven from the blissful bowers of his first inheritance, and was condemned to earn his bread by the sweat of his brow. Then shall those private animosities and heart-burnings, which now embitter the joys of social intercourse, be for ever extinguished: and then, too, shall the tribes of the human family forget those quarrels, which so long have been the scourge of this fair world; "nation shall not rise up against nation, neither shall they learn the art of war any more."

"St. Andrew's, April, 1825.

"A truly admirable essay, replete with sound judgment, and felicitous illustration; and announcing itself, at the first glance, as worthy of the highest prize.

"Thomas Chalmers."

K.

ADDRESS TO THE ST. ANDREW'S UNIVERSITY MISSIONARY SOCIETY, ON THE DUTY OF PERSONAL ENGAGEMENT IN THE WORK OF MISSIONS.

I am tired of arguing with the opponents of the missionary cause. It is my intention this evening to address myself to those who profess to be its friends.

I can easily conceive a mind so biassed by prejudice, as to take a distorted view of every argument that can be adduced on this, or indeed on any other subject whatever; or, a mind moving in such a sphere as never to have had these arguments fairly presented to it; and, therefore, I am by no means disposed to speak roundly of all who refuse to lend their aid to missionary societies, in a tone of unequivocal condemnation. But, I do confess. I cannot imagine a mind which has deliberately weighed the arguments, and candidly considered the facts of this important subject, still refusing to embark its energies or its influence in some way or other, in the work of evangelizing the nations of the earth. Indeed, the cause of missions has already met with such able defence, and the arguments of its opponents have been so often refuted, that they themselves seem to be almost sick of the very sound of their oft repeated objections. And, more than this, as if to show that the subject is quite impregnable, even at those points which the adversaries have never assailed, the advocates for the *promulgation* of Christianity, like the advocates for the *truth* of Christianity before them, have even brought forward fictitious objections of their own invention, in order to demonstrate with what perfect ease such objections could have been met, had the adversaries of the cause adduced them. And truly, after the champions of the missionary cause have done their part so well, it seems altogether needless still to keep up the debate with those who seem determined to resist the appeals of the most cogent reasoning, and even to set at nought the authority of human testimony. For of those who persist in denying the efficacy of missionary exertion, it may in truth be said, that they "will not believe the great work which the Lord is working in these days, even though a man declare it unto them." Surely, then, we cannot justly be charged with a want of charity, when thus compelled to the belief that after all, this pretended opposition of judgment on the part of our adversaries, is nothing but a screen for the coldness and indifference of their hearts.

I turn, therefore, altogether at present from those who oppose these exertions of Christian philanthropy, and address myself to the friends of missions. I address myself to you, who, by being the members of a missionary society, profess yourselves the advocates and supporters of this benevolent scheme; and, more especially, to those of you who, by entering on a course of study preparatory to the duties of the Christian ministry, have thereby professed to devote yourselves unreservedly to the service of God, in the gospel of his Son.

And I do not address you, my friends, for the purpose of again repeating those unmeaning compliments that are wont to be presented to the subscribers and office-bearers of missionary societies, at such meetings as the present. I do fear that there is too much of the tone of this world's flattering adulation in the public language of our missionary assemblies. The doctrine of this essay may be unpalatable, but I believe it to be true, that the members of missionary associations have absolutely done nothing, when we consider the high demands of a cause whose object is the spiritual and moral renovation of a world. Neither do I address you for the purpose of picturing forth in the colouring of romance, the high devotedness of missionary character, and lofty achievements of the missionary life. This has often been done already; but like most other poetic descriptions, while it has excited the imagination, it has failed to influence the conduct. It may have caused him who listened, to indulge in some fairy dream of exile and martyrdom for the sake of his religion and his Saviour; while all the while it is quite possible that not only he, but even the very person who drew the splendid picture, may have remained altogether unimpressed with the sober convictions of a duty his imagination had set forth in such glowing characters. In reality, this has been the case. One cannot help wondering, that of the many who have pleaded so earnestly for the cause of missions, and have declaimed so eloquently concerning the high dignity of the missionary enterprise, so few have been found who were willing to go forth to the combat. It seems to me, that while the enemies of missions have altogether despised and vilified the missionary office, the advocates of missions have erred in the other extreme, by regarding it with somewhat of a sentimental admiration, and by describing it rather as a work of supererogation than of duty.

We have been too much accustomed to regard the missionary life as an undertaking of most extraordinary magnitude, and as reserved for a few of the most daring and devoted spirits in the race of living Christians; and thus we easily succeed in pushing from ourselves the duty of personal engagement. But we should do well to view the matter apart from this borrowed splendour, which, by its glare obscures rather than brightens the object of our contemplation. After all the greater part of the work must be accomplished by ordinary men. And I am persuaded, if we but take a candid and sober view of the case, we shall begin to suspect that the matter *may* come home in the shape of duty, even to ourselves. Great, as are the sacrifices the missionary makes, they are but small when we take into account those sublime truths which we believe as well as he. And it is of the very deepest importance that we should bear in mind that those very sacrifices are represented in the Bible, not as the fruits of an overreaching faith which may fall to the lot of, but here and there, a mind of apostolic endowment; but as the test of simple discipleship itself. "If any man come to me and hate not his father and mother, and wife and children, and brethren and sisters, yea, and his own life also, he cannot be my disciple." If by these, and the remarks that follow, I can impress the mind of any one of you with the duty of engaging in this great undertaking, let me warn such an individual of the delusion of putting such convictions away from him on the ground that this is a work far too high for him to engage in; or under the deceitful impression that his shrinking from such an enterprise is a sign merely that his faith is weak, and has not yet acquired sufficient strength to warrant his engaging in a work of such difficulty and self-denial. If the words of Christ be true, which I have just repeated, to shrink from duty, even in the face of all the trials that present themselves in the contemplation of the missionary life, does not argue a weakness of faith merely, but a want of faith. The man who is not ready to part with country and even life itself, at the bidding of his Saviour, is not worthy of the name of a disciple.

Now were it not that the minds of all of us, in regard to this subject, are under the influence of most overpowering and bewildering prejudices, I am sure I should only have to lay before you the present state of missionary operations, in order to convince you of the duty of taking the question into most serious consideration: Whether you may not be called to engage in this work of evangelizing the heathen. You give your assent to the duty of sending the gospel to pagan countries, and by your subscriptions you profess yourselves willing to co-operate in the accomplishment of this grand object. And so far, you have done well. You may have thought you were doing all that was in your power for the furtherance of the great design, and you may have never once suspected that there was any call for greater services on your part. But if I can convince you, that there is such a call, then, on the simple score of consistency, you are bound to listen to it, and to obey it. For, if this matter demands our attention at all, it demands our deepest attention; if it has a right to our services at all, it has a right to our most devoted services. If you are not prepared to make greater sacrifices in this cause than you have ever yet done, when manifestly called to do so, then the little you have done will only serve most clearly to condemn you. Others, who deny the importance, or disbelieve the efficacy of the missionary project, may have some plausible excuse for standing aloof: they are at least consistent with their own profession. But, assuredly, it does convict us of singular hard-heartedness towards our fellow-men, if our zeal for their conversion can carry us the length of giving up a few paltry shillings, which were not surrendered, it may be, at the expense of a single comfort, and our zeal can carry us no further. We might pardon, though we could not defend, the incredulity of the individual who would not believe that some family near was in a state of starvation; but we should utterly detest the sordid avarice and unfeeling apathy of the man who by giving something, should just show us that he gave credit to the tale of suffering, and who yet, by the worthlessness of the trifle which he gave, should let us see that the wretchedness of his neighbour had made no suitable impression on his heart.

Now, I say, there is a call for much more devoted services on your part, than you have ever yet rendered in the work of evangelizing the nations. If we are disposed to estimate the prosperity of the missionary cause from the sums that are annually poured into its coffers, we should indeed augur well of its success. But you are aware, that after all, *money* is but a subordinate part of the apparatus. It may be the main-spring of the machine, but it is not the machine itself. The agents, who go forth to the work, are the effective part of the mechanism. And what avails it, that we have obtained a good moving power, if there be no machine to set it in motion? A good will to the cause of missions has been on the increase, but there is every reason to fear that the spirit of missionary zeal is on the decline. It has grown more fashionable of late to subscribe to missionary societies: in consequence of this, the revenues of the different societies have been so increased, as would enable them to extend their plans, could they but find a sufficient number of zealous and devoted agents. But such is the languishing state of missionary zeal, so little is there of what Horne would call "a passion for missions," that it is with considerable difficulty the present stations can be supplied; and, in such circumstances, it is altogether vain to talk of extending the plan of missionary operations.

When first the proposal was made to send the heralds of salvation to the ends of the earth, the Christian world received the proposal with eagerness and joy. A splendid equipment was fitted out, and many were desirous of sharing the honours of the victory that was so confidently and so ardently anticipated. But the novelty of the missionary enterprise is gone; and it would seem that the spirit of undaunted chivalry which a scheme of such lofty sublimity, and such disinterested benevolence, at first excited, has languished, and well nigh expired under the heavy pressure of those difficulties and discouragements which an actual experiment has brought to light.

The Scottish Missionary Society is in want of labourers; the London Missionary Society is in want of labourers; the Church Missionary Society (to the shame of the churchmen of England be it told) have for some time been compelled to gather the missionaries, whom they send forth, from the other countries of Europe. And, to sum up all, even among the Moravians themselves, so famed for the devotedness of their missionary zeal, that spirit of other days, which could brook slavery and death for the sake of Jesus, would seem to have died away. Of them, it once could be said, that, no sooner was a missionary station vacant, than there was an eager competition who should have the honour to supply it; for then it was counted an honour, for the love they bore to Christ, to succeed to a dreary station, amid eternal snows, or to fill the places of those who had fallen by the murderous hand of the savages for whose sakes they had left their country and their home. But now there is a difficulty in finding persons willing to go even to stations of ordinary comfort and ease. In this state of matters, what avails the increase of missionary funds? Do you not feel that there is a loud call for something more than mere subscriptions? And to whom can this appeal be made, but to the members of missionary associations? And on whom can it be urged home, more forcibly than on those who have professed to surrender the whole energies of their minds and their bodies to the promulgation of the religion of Christ?

This is a statement of facts, and such a statement, I am sure, would be quite sufficient to call forth the willing offer of his services, from any one who believes in the efficacy of missionary exertion, and who is not tied down by some peculiar circumstances to his native land, were it not that the mind is driven from its convictions of duty, by prejudices and affections, the strongest that can influence our nature — and I will even say, the purest that can oppose the will of God. Accordingly, I have found in my own experience, that even those who are most liberal in their donations to missionary societies, and most active in spreading among their friends a spirit of good will to this work of Christian philanthropy, immediately abate their ardour, and turn upon another tack, so soon as the duty of personal engagement is pressed home upon themselves, or even upon any of their near relations. Those who are most strenuous in their arguments for the general cause of missions, instantly start objections to the proposal of themselves becoming missionaries. A thousand plausible arguments immediately present themselves. Our own country has much higher claims upon us, all are not yet converted here. Besides, the success of missionaries has not been very great; and we think we can do more good by remaining at home. Such arguments, when in the mouth of an opponent to the general cause of missions, none so forward to answer, or so eloquent in refuting as they; and yet to the very same refuges do they betake themselves, when we merely carry out a little further, and make a new application of their own previous assertions.

Nor do I at all wonder at this, though I cannot apologize for it. The ties which bind us to our country and our home, cannot be so easily broken. The love which we bear to parents, and sisters, and brothers, and a whole circle of affectionate friends, is perhaps the strongest passion that has its seat in the human breast; and Christianity, far from impairing, refines and strengthens the attachment. The land which gave us birth, and where our fathers lived before us, and the companions of our youth, and the affectionate guardians of our tender infancy, are objects which most, of earthly things, deserve our love. There is but one, and only *one Being*, in the universe, whom we are commanded to love with a stronger affection. It is little wonder then, that when feelings like these—so strong, that no time or distance can ever efface their influence; and so pure, that piety itself imparts to them a tone of deeper tenderness—that when feelings like these exert an opposing influence, even the most devoted

Christian should be startled at the first proposal of a duty which speaks destruction to them all.

It is on this account that I feel the statement of facts I have laid before you, may not be sufficient to call forth your services to the work, which loudly calls for them, and in which you profess to take an interest. It is only on this account that I feel that the statement I have made needs to be enforced by arguments. For I believe, that to a mind which could take an unprejudiced view of the matter, no reasoning would be required to convince him of the urgency of the appeal, and no argument, however strong, could add to the force of the simple statement.

I feel, however, that it is necessary to reason with you. And the main argument on which I would insist, is founded on the commandment of our Saviour; "Go ye and teach all nations," This has often been repeated by the advocates of missionary exertion; and though it may thereby have lost something of its freshness, it has yet lost nothing of its force. I consider it still the strong hold of the missionary cause. But I am inclined to take a more extended view of the precept. Not only do I look upon this little verse as the great foundation on which all arguments for missions must be received, — but as the only scriptural authority which we can have for preaching the gospel at all. I can conceive many other inducements, which lead men in our own land to profess, or pretend to be ministers of God. But I believe, that every truly Christian minister in the land, must rest the whole authority of his commission on this and similar commandments. Now you must all perceive the bearing of this argument. It places our own country exactly on the same footing with the other nations of the earth, — and it makes the work of the missionary abroad, and the minister at home, one and the same work. *The world is the field;* and the preaching of the gospel is the work to be accomplished. And it is only in as far as Great Britain is one of the "*all nations,*" specified in the terms of the commission, that we have any warrant from scripture to preach the gospel here. Grant me but this view of the subject, and the question comes home with irresistible force. How comes it that all the labourers should have contrived to cluster together in one little corner of the vineyard? What special order has been given by the Lord about this little island on which we dwell? Or, in what does the vast superiority of its claims consist? It is nothing to my argument, that in this country, an ecclesiastical establishment has poured forth its benefices over the land, and has connected with the profession of the Christian ministry, the comforts of civilized life, and the enjoyments of a refined society, — or the opportunities of literary and scientific retirement. With the hirelings that have crept into the church, at present, I have nothing to do. Neither is it any thing to me, that numerous sectaries with which some of us may be connected have spread themselves over the land, and are struggling for the superiority. I have no sympathy with the outcry that is made by each rival party, about the interests of *their cause.* I know of no cause that demands the homage of our hearts, and our services, but the cause of Christ. Now, strip our country of these, and other accessory distinctions, which I think all of you will admit, should have no control in giving it a higher claim upon our Christian services, and then tell me wherein it differs from other lands, in as far as the scriptural argument for the preaching of the gospel is concerned.

I am persuaded, that with all our knowledge of geography, we are accustomed, from irresistible prejudices, to rate the extent and importance of our own country much too high. Now, in order to dissipate this delusion, and give the subject a more manageable appearance, let us try if we can take a reduced sketch of the world, diminishing every thing proportionally, just as a land surveyor finds it convenient to draw upon paper a reduced representation of the estate which he has been measuring.

Let us imagine, that instead of the world, a single country had been pointed out by our Lord as the field of action. And, since we are most familiar with our own land, let us just suppose that the particular country specified, was the island of Great Britain: and that, instead of the command to go forth into all nations, and preach the gospel to every creature, — the order had been, to go throughout all the counties of this island, and preach the gospel to every inhabitant. I find, that on a scale which would make the population of Great Britain represent that of the world, the population of such a county as Mid Lothian might be taken, as a sufficiently accurate representation of the population of our own land.

In order then, to have a just picture of the present state of the world, only conceive, that all who had received the above commission, somehow or other, had contrived to gather themselves together within the limits of this single county. Imagine to yourselves, all the other divisions of Scotland and England immersed in heathen darkness; and that by these Christians, who had so unaccountably happened to settle down together in one little spot, no effort was made to evangelize the rest of the land, except by collecting a little money, and sending forth two or three itinerants, to walk single-handed through the length and breadth of the country.

I shall be told, however, that illustration is not argument; and so distorted have our views been on this subject, that you will be disposed to think this a perfect caricature of the matter. But I deny that this is an illustration at all. It is merely a representation, on a reduced scale; and I believe you will find it to be a correct representation of the state of the world. It is no argument against the conclusions of the practical mathematician, that his calculations have had to do, not with the very objects or doctrines themselves about which he determines, but with proportional representations of them which he has delineated. The very same thing holds here. And if you but grant the correctness of my representation, then the deductions made from it are every whit as conclusive, as if our minds could so expand, as to do away with the necessity of the representation, and could gather their conclusions with as much ease from the consideration of the objects themselves about which we reason.

You will permit me, therefore, to argue from the representation a little further.

Were I to ask you what, in the case we supposed, you would imagine to be the duty of the ministers who had clustered within the limits of a single county, when their commission embraced every county in the land; you would at once reply, that they ought to spread themselves over the face of the country, till every corner of the field shared equally in the benefit of their ministrations. Now I am almost afraid to transfer this question from the representation to the actual case before us. Not, but that I believe I might most legitimately do so, but because I feel that I cannot carry along with me the sympathies of the Christian world. In fact, I am arguing at present for a much humbler effort, than the fair answer to such a question would land us in. To return to our ideal field of operation, let us suppose, that even the little band of itinerants began to fail, and a difficulty was found to recruit their numbers. Let us suppose, that the funds collected were sufficient to send forth more, if any could but be found who were willing to go. Let us try if we can fancy any thing in the shape of an excuse, which our professed evangelis s could allege, for still refusing to quit the little territory to which they had all along so pertinaciously adhered. Some might say, they did not think it was the proper time to go forth. You might meet them with the unlimited command of their Master, and especially his promise, to be *always* with them in the work to which the commandment called them. Others might say, they did not think those who had gone forth already, had taken the right plan, and might even urge, in support of this, that actually the two or three preachers who had been sent forth had not yet converted the country. The direct reply to such, would be, — The error of another is no apology for your disobedience. It is only a louder call to you to fulfil the command of your Lord, by some plan which will be more agreeable to his will. Such excuses might be framed by those who had never co-operated in the little effort that had been made. But can you conceive, that those who had given their entire consent to the plan itself, and had been zealous in sending forth others, could have any imaginable excuse for shrinking back, when their personal services were called for? Let us try if we can invent any. They might tell us, there were yet many within the little sphere they had allotted to themselves who were yet unconverted. They might bear witness to their own negligence, by telling us, that actually there were still some within their own sphere of action, to whom the message they had received from the Lord, had never been fairly delivered. They might express their apprehension, that if they began to go forth over the face of the country, the little spot which they had hitherto cultivated with so much care, might hereafter be overlooked in the wide field which lay before them, and come to be altogether neglected. And some might even have the effrontery to tell us, that they quite felt the urgency of the call, to go forth over the face of the country; but for their part, they had rather stay at home, and persuade others to go.

You feel that there is something ludicrous in the very description. There is such an utter discrepancy between the command

and the professed obedience of it; between the work to be performed, and the scantiness of the means that are expected to accomplish it; between the obvious call of duty, and the frivolous excuses by which they are evaded. Now, would this were but an imaginary picture; but it must recommend itself to all of you as too true a representation of the present state of the world, and of the kind of obedience which the disciples of Christ render to the last command of their Lord and Saviour.

I have thus tried to set before you, and illustrate my main argument, that the world is one field, and consequently that every minister of Christ should be ready to go to that part of the field, wherever it be, which stands most in need of his services. You must perceive that we have taken it upon ourselves to circumscribe most unwarrantably the limits of our commission; and that in these days nothing adequate to the fulfilment of our Lord's command has so much as been attempted. I have pressed upon you the loud demand that there is at present for labourers, in order to maintain even the comparatively feeble effort which the Christian world has of late put forth; and you perceived that the objections to this appeal just hinted at, appeared sufficiently frivolous. I am aware, however, that on these, or similar objections, the whole force of your refusal to obey this call, must rest; and, therefore, I feel it necessary to take each of them singly into more serious consideration.

I shall say nothing concerning the argument that the heathen are not in a fit state for receiving the gospel, and other similar objections. These are adduced only by the opponents of missionary societies. I take it for granted at present that I am addressing those who give their full assent to the duty of sending the gospel to the heathen, and who give their decided approbation to the plans that are in operation for the accomplishment of this grand object. The arguments which I mean to consider at present, are those which are urged by the supporters of missionary operations, when a demand is made for their own personal services. Among the most prominent of these, is the assertion, that all are not yet converted in our own land, and therefore our own country has the first claim upon our regard. The terms of the argument are very true, but the conclusion drawn from it I believe to be false. It is a lamentable fact, that so many in our own land are not under the power of the gospel.

But why? In by far the greater number of instances, because they will not come unto Christ that they may have life. Have they not had the message of mercy proclaimed to them, and what more can the messenger do? Have they not been plied, Sabbath after Sabbath, with the call to repent and believe the gospel, and if they still remain impenitent, what more can man accomplish? Can we hope to do more than apostles, with all their miraculous powers, and their unwavering faith, could effect? When the gospel was declared by those extraordinary men who had trod this earth in the company of their incarnate God; and who, after he left them, were visited with the supernatural endowments of his Spirit, — the account of their success is, that "some believed the things which were spoken, and some believed not." And as long as the Scripture doctrine of election holds true, it will still be found, wherever this gospel is proclaimed, that some will receive the message, and some will most obstinately reject it. Far be it from me to adduce the doctrine of election as a reason why we should ever cease to ply with all our earnestness, and admonish with all our tenderness, the most hardened unbeliever, or the veriest scoffer at sacred things. But I am quite warranted in adducing it, in order to show the fallacy of the expectation, that we shall ever be able, by any concentration of our energies to any sphere however narrow, to convert *all* who dwell within these limits, to the truth of the gospel. We do well to consider whether by such expectations we be not opposing the purposes of God. He has given us no reason to indulge the hope that he will choose his people exclusively from our nation, although that nation has been favoured very highly. He has said that he will take one of a city and two of a family; and it is said of the redeemed in heaven, that they have been gathered "out of every kindred, and tongue, and people, and nation."

But it may be said, that I am not giving a fair view of the case, for that very many in our own land have never had the message of mercy fairly proclaimed to them. This is too true, and a disgrace it is to the ministers, and even the private Christians of Britain. How easily might the numerous evangelical ministers of the land, or at least the evangelical ministers among the dissenters who are hindered by no ecclesiastical authority from preaching the truth where they think it has not been fully declared: how easily, I say, might they dispel the ignorance that yet darkens the spiritual atmosphere of this enlightened country? But, after all, I do not feel the force of this claim when weighed against the claim of those who are literally perishing for lack of knowledge. I do believe that every inhabitant of our land has heard so much, as makes him utterly inexcusable if he be ignorant of the way of acceptance before God. If he sits under a minister who perverts, or but imperfectly declares the gospel, he has the standard of truth in his hand, and by the Bible he can, and he ought to try the doctrine, whether it be of God. If he have not a Bible himself, he has seen it in the possession of others, or at least he has heard that there is such a book, which many believe to be a revelation from Heaven. And, finally, even in the haunts of the most abandoned depravity, where ignorance and wickedness may have spread a gloom as dismal as the darkness of paganism itself, even there the wretched inmates are still reminded of a God and a Saviour; if by nothing else, yet by the weekly return of a day of unusual stillness, and by the oft repeated and well known invitations of the Sabbath bell. But when you urge as an excuse for remaining in this land, that some within its borders are yet ignorant of the terms of mercy, do you, indeed, mean to wander from parish to parish, and illumine every dark corner on which the light of truth has not yet shone? Or will you venture, where none have dared to venture before you, within the receptacles of vice and infamy, to proclaim the tale of a Saviour's sufferings to those who may have never heard of his name? If you will not, or cannot do these things, then this argument is no argument for you.

Closely connected with this objection, that all are not yet converted in our own land, there is the apprehension lest a spirit of missionary zeal should damp the spirit of exertion at home, and that our own country should suffer from our attention to foreign lands. The spirit which excites this apprehension for the eternal welfare of our countrymen, deserves the highest commendation. But depend upon it the fear is quite unfounded. I am quite willing to allow that our kinsmen according to the flesh have the first claim upon our Christian sympathy. It is true that, as the messengers of Christ, and as far as the command of our Saviour is concerned, the world is all before us, and no country has any peculiar claim upon our regard. But as men who are linked to those around us by bonds so strong as those of relationship, and all the other connections which form the cement of civil society, there is no doubt something very peculiar in the claims of our native land. To true patriotism I am willing to allow all the eulogiums that poets and orators have heaped upon it. The love of our country is a very noble affection. But there is a thing which has been misnamed patriotism, which consists not so much in loving our own country, as in despising and disregarding every other. But surely it but ill accords with the liberal sentiment of the present age, to despise any brother of the human family, because he has not sworn allegiance to the same sovereign with ourselves; or because, forsooth, he happens to be separated from us by some river and mountain, or imaginary political boundary. Time was, when in our own little country, every petty chief was a monarch; and whatever may be the associations that romance has gathered around these olden times, every generous mind must look back with detestation and disgust on that narrow-minded spirit of clanship, which could tie down the affections of an individual to the few families that happened to bear the same name, or to serve the same lord with himself, and which pronounced him the noblest of his clan, who hated with the deadliest malice the whole world besides. But what is this pretended patriotism but the dross of this same detestable spirit. We surely have not need to be told in this age of enlightened liberality, that God has made of one blood, all nations that are on the face of the earth. And if the spirit of the age cannot reclaim us, Christianity at least should reclaim us from such bigoted narrowness. A spirit of true patriotism is in perfect harmony with a spirit of the most extended liberality. Your benevolence must overflow the narrow channel, ere it can dilate itself over a wider surface. Just tell me of a man that he is a general philanthropist, and I can immediately conceive of that man, that his family and social affections are stronger than those of other individuals. There may be exceptions to this rule, it is true; for it is quite possible to find monsters in the moral world, as well as in the natural. All I assert is, that it is the general tendency of an extended benevolence to unite us in closer affection than ever, to those objects which have a nearer relation to us. And, indeed, in the late extension of our Christian philanthropy to other lands, this principle has been most beautifully illustrated. Whence sprung our tract societies, our school societies, our itinerant societies, and the other institutions that are now in operation for instructing the ignorant of our own land? They have all originated in the impulse that was given to Christian philanthropy, by the formation of the Missionary Society. The stream of Christian benevolence, when it sought its way to the ends of the earth, first filled and overflowed the reservoir that had contained it. The very consideration of the case of those who were further removed from them, made the Christians of our land take a deeper interest in the situation of those who were connected with them by stronger ties. It is on this account that I would have you to extend your views still further, till not only would I have you think of our country as a little spot, when compared with the world, that so you may feel the close relationship that exists between ourselves and our fellow-countrymen; but I would have you think of this globe itself, on which we dwell, as but one among the myriads that travel with it in their mighty journeys, through boundless immensity. And then will you begin to feel that the whole human race forms but one little family in the universe of God. We shall thus yet forget those little distinctions which the ambition and avarice of man have made upon the face of our globe. We shall feel ourselves to be denizens of this earth, and the inhabitants of the universe. We shall feel that we are united to our fellow-men by stronger ties than the indefinite relation which subsists among all the creatures of God. Are we not united by the ties of a common nature? Are we not involved in a common calamity, in that we have forfeited the favour of our God, — a calamity which, for aught we know, may have happened to our race alone, of all the families of the universe? And is not a common pardon offered, and has not a common Saviour died for us all?

I have thus tried to answer the objections that spring from an overweening partiality to our own country, and from the ignorance and unbelief that still exists there. But by far the most triumphant answer to all these arguments is founded on the authority of apostolic example. Paul the apostle had a much stronger attachment to his country than any modern patriot can boast. He wished himself even accursed from Christ, for his brethren's sake, and yet he gloried in being the apostle of the Gentiles. But there were feelings stronger than patriotism, that bound the early disciples to the land of their fathers; feelings which none but an Israelite could experience. Their country was the favoured land of heaven. Their countrymen were the chosen people of God. And if any may urge as an excuse for lingering in the land of their nativity, that all their countrymen had not yet embraced the gospel, assuredly the apostles and early evangelists might have used this plea. But far different was their conduct. They thought it enough to have fairly offered the terms of mercy to their countrymen, and when some rejected the message which they delivered, so far from thinking this a reason why they should still remain, they considered it as the very signal for their departure. They thought that those who had never had the offer of God's favour, had now a prior claim upon their regard; and they addressed their countrymen in such language as the following: "It was necessary that the word of God should first have been spoken to you; but seeing ye put it from you, and judge yourselves unworthy of everlasting life, lo, we turn to the Gentiles."

There is still one other argument, perhaps the most plausible of all, against engaging in the work of missions, and to which I beg very briefly to advert. It is, that in the present state of matters, we can do more good at home than abroad. A minister in this country, it is said, may make as many, and sometimes more converts, than the missionary in a heathen country. And the question is triumphantly put, whether the soul that is converted at the distance of some thousand miles from our land be more precious than the soul which is converted in our own neighbourhood; and whether it be not a matter of as great thankfulness and joy that a soul has been delivered from a state of self-delusion, though living in a country called Christian, as that a heathen has been turned from idols to serve the living God. The argument has a great semblance of fairness, but I think we shall find it to be unsound.

In the first place, it is not true, that in general the success of ministers at home is greater than that of those who labour in heathen lands. And, secondly, though it be allowed that the conversion of a soul is not more acceptable to God, because of the place where the conversion is wrought, yet there is much in the case of those who first turn to the Lord from a nation of idolaters, that may well fill our hearts with unusual joy and thankfulness, inasmuch as these are the *first fruits* of a hitherto uncultivated field, and may be regarded as the earnest of an abundant harvest. In the same manner, you can easily conceive, how a few grains of wheat, though comparatively little worth in a cultivated country, might acquire an immense value in a new colony, where no other seed could be obtained. Besides, there is much in preparing the way. We are not to suppose, that the conversion of a world is to be the work of one generation. The ground must be cleared, ere we can so much as sow the seed, and this must be a season of toil, and difficulty, and discouragement.

You would perceive the fallacy of the objection now under consideration, in almost any case but the one before us. Let us suppose an accommodation of our Saviour's parable of the vineyard, to the present circumstances of the world. Imagine to yourselves all the husbandmen to have settled down in one little fertile corner of the vineyard, and to have left all the rest with the soil unbroken, covered with briars and thorns, and trodden down by the beasts of the forest. When called to account for their negligence, you may conceive them to answer: "Our fathers have planted vines, and they have yielded fruit luxuriantly; and we truly thought, that we were acting best for your advantage, in choosing that spot for our labours, where the fruit was most abundant." Who would not see, in such a case, that their own ease had been consulted, and not their master's interest? And who could help the suspicion, that they wanted to press into their own cup of the overflowing vintage?

I have thus tried to set before you the present state of the missionary cause, and the loud call which there is for efficient labourers. I have stated to you the great argument, that the world is one field, and that our Saviour's command is not fulfilled, so long as the distribution of his ministers over this field is so very unequal. And, finally, I have tried to answer some of the objections that are made to personal engagement in the work.

The matter, some time ago, presented itself very forcibly to my own mind, and I felt that it at least demanded my serious consideration. As I have proceeded with my enquiries on the subject, the difficulties seemed to have gathered thicker on the prospect, but the convictions of duty have grown stronger too. The arguments for personal engagement, seem to me to have acquired the strength of a demonstration. I have, therefore, resolved, with the help of God, to devote my life to the cause; and I have only solemnly to charge every one of you, who are looking forward to the ministry of Christ, to take this matter into most serious consideration.

Some of you may think that I have not satisfactorily answered the objections which may be urged against personally engaging in the work, and other objections may possibly present themselves to some of you. But I ask you, seriously to examine whether there do not lurk under these objections, a want of devotedness to God, and a secret love of the world. Why is it that there is an eager competition for the ministerial office in our own land, where a comfortable salary is annexed to the preaching of the gospel? And why is it that the love of country can be overcome, whenever any worldly advantage is to be gained? But when the gospel is to be preached where there is no reward, but the reward of winning souls to Christ; and no honour, but the honour that cometh from God; there alone the ranks of the labourers are thin, and there deficiencies can with difficulty be supplied. I mean no uncharitable insinuations respecting your motives, but I ask you, if too much reason has not been given for the outcry that has been made against priestcraft, by the worldling or the infidel!

Do not think I wish to press you into this service. It is a maxim, which much experience has taught the Moravians, never to persuade any man to become a missionary. I have laid the matter before you, and I leave it with your own conscience, as you soon must answer before God.

I have the happiness to mention to you, that your respected secretary, of last year, has given himself to the work; and I know that there are some present who have felt the urgency of the call.

I am not without the hope, that even from this unnoticed association, a little band of devoted labourers may be raised up, who shall carry the name of their Saviour to the ends of the earth, and shall meet in another world, to receive that high reward, which is reserved for those who have left father, and mother, and sister, and brother, and houses, and lands for Christ's sake, and the gospel's.

* * * * * *

L.

ADDRESS TO A SOCIETY OF YOUNG MEN, WHOM I WISH TO MEET WITH ME, ONCE A WEEK, FOR RELIGIOUS INSTRUCTION.

As I have called you together, my friends, with only a very general intimation of what we propose to do at these weekly meetings, it may be necessary before we enter on the regular exercises, briefly to explain to you the design and nature of the association, which we are met this evening to form, and the motives which have induced me to attempt its formation.

You know that the age in which we live is very gloriously distinguished by the exertions which are making for the religious improvement of the whole world. In former ages, Christians seem to have had so much to do in providing for their own spiritual comfort, and fleeing from the hand of the persecutor, that we cannot wonder if they thought but little of the wants of others; or, thinking of them, could do but little to relieve them. In these ages of ignorance and bigotry, the flame of Christian benevolence was damped, but its fire was not wholly extinguished; and when civil and religious liberty were again restored, it burst forth with fresh and undecayed vigour, from the grasp of that oppression which had for a while restrained its energy. In these days, and in the happy country in which we live, we see the principles of the gospel of peace left (to a certain extent at least) to their own free operation, no longer adulterated so much as formerly, by the allurements of human ambition, and no longer in any degree restrained by the threatenings of human power. You live in a neighbourhood that may remind you of other days; "*The battle of Bothwell Brig*" is not yet forgotten. May it be remembered only to inspire us with thankfulness, that we need no longer to *fight* for our religious privileges; but can each of us sit under his own vine, and his own fig-tree, none daring to make us afraid. At length men have happily begun to see, that carnal weapons are altogether unfit, either for the defence or furtherance of a kingdom, which is spiritual; and the happy effects of unrestrained liberty of conscience, and freedom of discussion, are universally felt and acknowledged, by those who differ most widely in almost all other opinions. In these circumstances, we see that spirit of Christian philanthropy again awakened in the breasts of modern Christians, which glowed so fervently in the hearts of the early believers. The effects of religious liberty on the revival of Christian benevolence, must forcibly strike those of you who are at all acquainted with the history of philanthropy, during the last fifty years.

Within that short period, many institutions have been formed, most diversified indeed in their modes of operation, and in the more immediate purposes for which they are intended, but all having for their grand and ultimate object, the glory of God, and the best interests of man. These institutions do not confine their operations to one country or to one class of individuals. The field of their benevolent exertions extends over the whole habitable globe; and they embrace within the range of their benefits, people of almost every rank and every condition. We might enumerate among those intended for the temporal and religious improvement of our own countrymen, Bible Societies, whose operations are also extended to other nations, whose object is to furnish with the word of God such as could not, or would not otherwise obtain it; Home Missionary Societies, for sending the preachers of that word to such as are without the range of an evangelical ministry; Religious Tract Societies, for breaking down religious publications into a suitable form, and furnishing them at reduced prices, to encourage an extensive circulation; and had we time to extend our attention to those institutions which have an especial regard to the temporal welfare of our fellow-men, you know well that we might introduce a lengthened list of charitable institutions, of which not the least interesting, or the least important, are those Mechanics' Institutions, which are now forming in the most populous parts of the country, and which bid fair to make the labouring classes tread upon the heels of their superiors, in the walks of science and philosophy. But our business at present is with religious institutions, and we remark, that besides those we have mentioned, which are especially designed for those who are grown up to manhood, we have also Sabbath-schools, with all their appendages, for the religious instruction of children.

While these institutions embrace a field so vast, and a variety of character so diversified, we cannot wonder if there should be some peculiarity of disposition or circumstances to which the operations of none of them are specifically adapted. Such a peculiarity, I conceive, is to be found in the case of young people of our own age. We are, generally speaking, too young to sympathize with the religious feelings of the old; and on the other hand, we are too old to submit to the discipline of institutions which are intended for the instruction of children.

When I say that we are too young to sympathize with the religious feelings of the old, let me not be misunderstood. Far be it from me to say that we are too young to feel interested in the preaching of the gospel; or even too young to unite ourselves to a Christian Church, and to unite in the most sublime and delightful exercises of the Christian sanctuary. If there be any age more suited than another for receiving impressions of an unseen world, and boldly declaring ourselves on the Lord's side, it is surely that age when the affections are warm, the conscience not yet seared, nor the heart hardened by the deceitfulness of sin. What I mean to say, is, that many of us are not yet old enough, or may not think ourselves old enough to talk familiarly of religion with our parents and their associates, to enter into their views, and to sympathize with their feelings. Their trials, their temptations, their besetting sins, and even their pleasures and their hopes in this life, are all different from ours. There is a reverence about age that forbids too great familiarity: we feel more at ease when talking to those of our own age; and especially on the subject of religion, we feel a reserve when conversing with those who are much older than ourselves. From the conversation of the young again, this most important subject is often banished by mutual consent, as something gloomy; or at least too serious for youth, and that may with great safety be put off to an age of greater gravity and seriousness. It thus appears that in all that period of our life, when we have thrown off the habits of childhood, and have begun to think for ourselves, the important interests of eternity are too apt to be forgotten, and this important age seems to me not to be provided as it might be, with religious instruction peculiarly adapted to it. It is a period when the Christian parent or the guardian thinks he has done all he can. He has sown the good seed of instruction in the heart, and watered it, it may be with tears and earnest prayers; and he thinks that he may now rest from his labours, that he may now abate his watchfulness. And how frequently does it happen, that while he thus slumbers, the enemy comes and sows tares among the wheat, and the instructor looks in vain in the character of the man, for the fruits of those admonitions which he had so carefully instilled into the mind of the boy. It is the design of this meeting, my friends, to keep you in mind of early instruction, if you have enjoyed it, or to lead your attention to it now, if you have not had the privilege of a religious education.

The period of youth is, in many respects, the most important period of our life. It is the period when we are exposed to most danger, and it is the period when the character is generally formed. The opinions then received, are generally most pertinaciously adhered to through the rest of life.

It is not when the seed lies covered in the bosom of the soil that there is the most danger from an unpropitious season; though even then the parching heat may prevent its springing, or the too copious rain may sour it in its bed; neither is it when the plant has attained its full maturity, and has been hardened by its exposure to many a storm; but that is the period of the greatest danger, when the tender germ has just left the kindly protection of the earth, and is first exposed to the rude blast and the piercing cold.

And so it is with man, who has often been compared to the flower of the field. It is not when he enjoys the protection of a father's roof, and the advantage of parental instruction, though even then, a bad system of education may ruin his after-character. Neither is it after he has been long exposed to the temptations of the world. The character has in general, by that time, been formed, either in accordance with the practice of the world, or in opposition to these practices. The danger is then past, though it may not have been avoided. It is when the youth first goes out into the world that the danger is at its greatest: it is then that every impulse, especially if it be sinful, and therefore congenial to the mind, is apt to give a direction to the future character; and, consequently, that every temptation is too apt to bring destruction along with it.

Some of you may have received a religious education, and may be well acquainted with the doctrines of the gospel. But do not presume that, on this account, you are quite impregnable to the assaults of temptation, and may safely pass without a struggle, the most critical period of life.

In some respects, the very fact of having enjoyed a religious education, makes that time more critically dangerous, when you begin to enjoy it no longer. The plant that has been reared in a hot-house, and is guarded from all that could injure its infant growth, suffers more, when exposed to the inclemencies of the open sky, than that which has not been so carefully nurtured.

To one whose childhood has been protected by pious parents, sin is still by nature as agreeable as it is to others, and to him it has the additional charm of novelty. To another, the wickedness of the world has been gradually made known, as his mind gradually expands; but from such an individual, it is kept for a time almost secret, till at length it bursts all at once upon him. While under pious parents, the current of temptation has been kept from rushing upon him, but it has still been flowing on. It has not been diverted from its course, it has only been dammed up. The barrier that has been raised against it, cannot, however, stand for ever; it must, some time or other, give way; and the longer we have enjoyed its protection, the greater will be the torrent that shall burst upon us, when it is broken down. And if, my friends, it require an aid that is more than human, to enable us to stand against the natural stream, to preserve us against single, but successive temptations; surely when the enemy rushes in like a flood, it is the Spirit of the Lord alone that can raise up a standard against him.

Such are some of the dangers to which we are exposed from the world around us. There are others, which arise from the state of our own minds. We have begun to think for ourselves, and have thrown off that servile deference to authority which influences the minds of children. Formerly, for our parents to tell us anything was sufficient evidence for our believing it. We thought they could not be wrong; but we now perceive that we have a principle of reason within ourselves, by whose aid, we feel that we ought to inquire into the truth of all our opinions.

Among others, our religious opinions come to be re-tried, and there are many things that may lead us, on this most important subject, to false conclusions.

Our parents had told us of the purity and perfection of Christianity, and we fondly thought that they were living examples of that perfection which they taught us to aim at. But we have begun to discover that they are not the perfect creatures we took them to be. We thought them angels, and we find they are but men. We thought them infallible, and we find they have their errors and their weaknesses, and their sins, as well as ourselves. The character of a witness materially affects his testimony; and, as we have in general no ground for the religious opinions of childhood, but the testimony of parents, our altered views of their character are apt to occasion an alteration in our views, of the unchanging truths which they have taught us. We so associate together their characters, and the doctrines which they delivered to us, that when we begin to think of the former as weak and imperfect, we are too apt to conclude, that the latter are weak and imperfect also.

If, when we are thus beginning to mistrust our early opinions, we should hear of some who have bid fair in the Christian course, falling away, it will add strength to our suspicion, that the doctrines of the Bible may not be all that we thought them, and the natural aversion which we have to the truths under review, will prevent us from perceiving the fallacy of the reasoning by which we have arrived at this conclusion. When we have got thus far on the way to infidelity, the very circumstance of our having received these opinions in childhood, will seem another reason for despising them. We shall associate them with the other fables which we then listened to with pleasure, and received with confidence; and we shall think that we believed the one, for the same reason that we gave credit to the other; because of our inability to discover the gross deceits that had been palmed upon us by those who had full possession of our confidence. By a process of thinking, somewhat similar to this, we may come at last to think of the devil and of hell, as we now do of the stories of ghosts and witches, which once excited our alarm; and even to associate the inspired descriptions of heavenly glory, with gorgeous fables of streets of gold, and palaces of emerald, which we have read of in the volumes of eastern fiction.

Nor is this all the imaginary picture. God forbid that it should be the fate of any of us. But, my friends, it is too true a sketch of the feelings of not a few who have been brought up to acknowledge the gospel, but whose repeated violations of the law of God, have driven them to the fearful expedient of pacifying conscience, by the rejection of that book which the Almighty has been pleased to send us, as a revelation of his will; and sometimes, by the denial of the existence of the Eternal himself.

You see then, my friends, that at our time of life, we are exposed, from a variety of causes, to great danger; and even if we have received a religious education, it alone will not guard us from the evil that is in the world. The great question with each of us should be, "How shall a young man cleanse his way?" The same inspired writer who proposes the question, gives us also its answer; "By taking heed thereto according to the word." If we would take heed to our ways according to the word of God, we must know what that word is; and in order to this, we must not only read, but search the Scriptures. The study of the Sacred Scriptures then, will form the chief part of the business of our meetings. As to what plan we ought to adopt in attempting this, I acknowledge to you I feel considerable difficulty. The persons whose attention I wish chiefly to engage, are not children, or I should at once decide upon prescribing a passage to be committed to memory, and examining them on what had been thus prepared, with a view to interest the scholar in its meaning. But you are not children, and I wish to treat you as men. If any of yourselves have any plan to propose, I shall be glad to listen to it, and consider its merits.

In the mean time I shall humbly propose the plan which seems to me most eligible. I shall propose a certain subject, and ask such of you as choose to search the Scriptures, for passages connected with it. These you will mark, and be prepared to read. If any difficulty occurs to any of you in the passages you meet with, I shall be glad to explain it if I can; or, if not, to take it into consideration. Remarks on the different verses may occur to me as you read, which I shall make in as plain and familiar a manner as possible. I shall study at home the same subject which you are considering, and shall choose some passage connected with it, from which, after we have gone over your passages, I propose to deliver a *very short* address.

Let me remind you, however, that all we can do to obtain a correct knowledge of the Scriptures, and to attend to our way according to the dictates of inspired wisdom, will prove utterly vain, unless we are assisted with power from on high — unless we are enlightened by that Spirit, whose office it is to take of the things of Christ, and show them unto men. The most far-sighted and acute discerner of earthly things, is a blind man with regard to divine things. Let me entreat you then, seriously and fervently to offer up the petition we have read this evening: "Open thou mine eyes!" One word before I conclude, about the spirit we ought to manifest at these meetings. Let it be a spirit of deep humility. To know our own ignorance, and to be willing to learn from every one, are the first steps toward the acquisition of wisdom, whether earthly or heavenly. There is none of us so wise, but he may learn something from the rest; and none so ignorant but we may all learn something from him. And from this let me just remark, that if any of your friends, more advanced in life, shall condescend to honour us with their presence, and to listen to our exercises, they shall always receive a hearty welcome. If they know the truth, as it is in Jesus, they will rejoice to see their children seeking the way to Zion; and if they know it not, they may receive knowledge even at this little meeting, for which they may bless God through the ages of eternity.

May I allude, before concluding, to the distressing state of our native land from the stagnation of trade? "Shall there be evil in the city, and the Lord hath not done it?" We may depend upon it, that God does not afflict our country for nought. We may not be able to determine the cause for which these calamities have been sent, but that there is a cause, we may rest assured. And what, I ask, is more likely to bring the scourge of divine vengeance upon a nation, than its own iniquities? It were well if men would listen to the voice of Providence, which now speaks so loudly in every part of our land; and that, when the judgments of the Lord are abroad on the earth, men would learn righteousness.

The following is one of his short addresses to his class of young men, after it was formed: —

AN ADDRESS TO HIS CLASS.

"Happy is the man that findeth wisdom, and the man that getteth understanding," &c. — Prov. iii. 13 – 19.

It would be a very reasonable question for any of you to put to me to-night, "What has been your object in calling us together?" And I think I should speak the sincere language of my heart, in answering, "My object simply is to try to make you happy." Could I succeed in convincing you, that this is really my design, and that I have rational expectations of accomplishing it; I know that I should secure the willing attendance, and the earnest attention of all whose circumstances do not absolutely forbid them. Every one wishes to be happy. However different may be the pursuits in which men engage, and however diversified the objects on which they set their affections, this is the great sum of their desires, and this the point to which all their efforts tend. Every one of you feels the truth of this statement. You are all seeking after happiness; and yet, were I to question each one of you on this subject, I dare say I should receive the same answer from all, that this great object of your wishes has not yet been obtained. There is still another point in which I may venture to say, you all agree. And this is, "that though you have not yet found this object of your wishes, you have the expectation, that at some future period it will be obtained." The most miserable has this expectation. Take it away, and you leave a man in despair.

You feel then, that at present, you are not quite happy. Many of you may feel yourselves to be very miserable. You earnestly desire to be happy; and you have some vague hope, that at some time or other, you will be so.

This is a subject then, which is interesting to all of you. It is interesting to those who are most careless and indifferent about everything else. And yet, though a subject of such universal interest, there is perhaps no subject on which men have differed so widely. Why have we so many different characters in the world? It is just because men have such different notions of what will make them happy.

One man thinks, if he were rich, he would be happy, and he gives all his diligence to accomplish this object. He becomes rich, and in all probability, is more wretched than before. This is such a common idea, that we may be required to dwell on it a little longer. Especially in times like the present, it is most natural for him who labours hard for the pittance that barely furnishes the necessaries of life, to think that ease and plenty are all that is necessary to constitute true happiness. But you have only to come in contact with the rich, to know how different is the fact. I have said, that I wish to make you happy, and that I have rational expectations of accomplishing it. Some, I doubt not, would think it a good proof of the sincerity of my assertions, were I able and willing to lavish among you the good things of this life. This you know to be impossible; but, were my ability and my benevolence as unbounded as this supposition would require, I should feel that I had miserably failed to fulfil the expectations which I might have excited. No; wealth does not constitute happiness. Riches cannot give peace of mind; and, without this, what avails all bodily ease and luxury.

Some again, have affected to despise wealth, and have sought for encouragement in what have been deemed more dignified pursuits. But all have proved alike unsatisfactory. There is a want, a longing for something more, when the world has given all that it can. There is one who had tried all the means of happiness this world can afford, who gives it as the testimony of his experience, that "all is vanity and vexation of spirit." And I believe, in the moments of sober thought, this is the feeling of every individual in looking back upon the past. All has been unsatisfying. Expectations of happiness have been cruelly disappointed; and, if there have been a few hours of pleasure, they have been but few, and have often left the sting of remorse, or the bitterness of grief behind them. There may have been gleams of enjoyment which appeared but to vanish: but anything like lasting and satisfying happiness has not been experienced. And yet, with all that is unsatisfactory in the experience of the past, there is a strange delusion that still hangs over the future. In spite of experience, men will still hope to find that happiness which has hitherto deceived their expectations. We will not believe that earth cannot give it. The child looks forward to the frolics of boyhood, and the boy to the freedom and the pleasures of youth. The youth enters on speculations of gain or ambition, and the accomplishment of these will perfect his happiness. Manhood has not brought the longed-for satisfaction, but it has not ceased to expect it. Still we will look to the future for happiness, till we have no future to look to. And often, the nearer the end approaches, the stronger is the delusion. And it is thus that many of us slumber on from childhood to grey hairs, still dreaming of an imaginary bliss, which, in spite of all experience, we will not believe to be imaginary; ever deceived, and yet ever willing to be deceived again. And it is thus, alas, that too many slumber on, pleased with the deceitful vision, till the voice of death awakes them to the dread reality.

And is there, then, no such thing as happiness! Or, if there be, how are we to find it? If riches and honours, and fame, and learning and pleasure, have deceived the expectations of those who trusted to them for happiness, must we give up the search? There is such a thing as true enjoyment, and there is a way of finding it, which is patent to us all. The meanest, yea, the vilest have found it before us, and we need not despair. God has been pleased to "show us the path of life;" and if many have sunk to the grave without attaining the object of their wishes, it is because they would listen to the dictates of their own depraved propensities, rather than to the voice of their Creator. O let us not imitate so sad an example! Let us turn to the Bible, and be directed by it in this the most interesting of all inquiries.

He, to whom I have before alluded, as having tried all earthly things, and pronounced them "vanity;" while writing under the influence of the Divine Spirit, has the following words: "Happy is the man that findeth wisdom," &c. Prov. iii. 13 – 19. This points directly to the subject of our inquiries. It is ours, then, humbly to investigate what may be the meaning of the words, and to receive it as an intimation from Him who knoweth all things, who cannot be deceived, and who cannot lie.

It is evident, then, that the sense of the passage depends mainly upon the meaning we give to the words, "*wisdom*" and "*understanding*," (חכמה, תבונה.) If these are to be understood in the sense in which they generally pass current among us, the passage will seem at variance with the general remarks we have made about the unsatisfactory nature of all earthly things. It is true, the pursuits of learning and science are productive of a higher and a purer pleasure, than the gross and degrading gratification of avarice or sensuality. But still there are many called wise, whose wisdom has failed to make them happy. This, therefore, cannot be the meaning of the words. The Bible is never at variance with facts. Accordingly, we find the very author of our text bearing witness to the unsatisfactory nature of mere earthly wisdom. (Eccles. i. 16, to the end.) If ever the wisdom of any man could afford happiness, the wisdom of the wisest must have done so. But you have heard him rank it with the other unsatisfactory vanities of earth. We are told of the uncertainty of riches; and, therefore we are exhorted "not to labour to be rich." It is added in the same verse "Cease from thine own wisdom." Prov. xxiii. 4.

What then is the meaning of those interesting words, which form the chief ingredients of that happiness, after which all are seeking? They are not used in their ordinary sense: for, in that case, the passage would not be true, and would stand at variance with other parts of Scripture. It is always the safest way of interpreting Scripture language, and especially those phrases which are peculiar to Scripture, when we can make the divine word its own interpreter. If you turn to the twenty-eighth verse of the twenty-eighth chapter of Job, you will have a beautiful illustration of what I mean. There the very same words occur, which are found in our text, accompanied with a full and explicit explanation, "Behold the fear of the Lord, that is wisdom; and to depart from evil, is understanding." "*The fear of the Lord,*" you know, is a common expression in Scripture for *true religion.* It indicates a feeling of the profoundest reverence, mingled with adoring love, which is the right state of mind in which a creature should regard his Creator. To be truly happy, then, we must be truly religious. The *understanding* that is mentioned, is a *departure from evil.* This too, is an ingredient of happiness, and is the consequent of the former. True happiness is inseparably connected with holiness.

You will say, This is no new discovery. We have been often told so. Aye, but have you felt it to be a truth; and have you acted upon it as a truth? If so, whatever be your sorrows, you can tell that you have a joy which the world cannot give, and which it cannot take away. If you have not this joy, you have not yet laid hold on this true wisdom. Seek for her, for happy is the man that findeth her.

It appears then, that sin is the cause of all the misery that is in the world. There is a sense of guilt and a dread of punishment, which the most careless sometimes feel, and which must soon burst with overwhelming force upon them in that place where conscience will be ever awake. How blessed then is he " whose transgression is forgiven, whose sin is covered," &c. (Psalm xxxii.) This consciousness of guilt must form a great part of the unhappiness of every one, whose conscience is not seared as with a hot iron. In the gospel then there is a remedy for this. The blessedness mentioned in the Psalm may be ours, if we believe that Christ died for our sins. But the misery arising from a sense of guilt, is not the only misery connected with sin; nor is it this which constitutes the main part of the unhappiness of mankind. An awakened conscience has driven many to despair, and the thinking part of mankind are often oppressed by the unwelcome intrusions of its warning voice. But the gay, unthinking multitude, who never reflect, and who never think of futurity,—are they oppressed with a sense of guilt? They often are. And yet is it true, that many dance along from the cradle to the grave in whom the past has excited no remorse, and the future no anxiety. And yet these were not *happy*. They roved from pleasure to pleasure, seeking what they could not obtain. Their very love of novelty, showed that the last amusement could amuse no longer. They have sunk to the grave, and they are miserable now. There is a misery then connected with sin, independent of a sense of guilt, or rather, I should say, *Sin itself is misery*. It is sin which has stamped vanity on all the means of happiness which the world presents. It is sin which has mingled bitterness with every earthly pleasure. In this view of the matter, every sinner must be uuhappy, and that independent of the torments of conscience, or the foreboding of torments greater still. Misery must be mingled up with his very existence, and every enjoyment must be embittered by the principle of unhappiness which is in his own breast. One of the scripture names of the devil, means the *self tormentor;* and the appellation is applicable, in a certain degree, to every worker of iniquity. This is evidently the deadliest wound sin has given, but the religion of the Bible has a cure for this too.

In the gospel we are offered pardon, and this can disarm conscience and take the sting from death. But this is not all. We must be purified, as well as pardoned, ere our salvation be complete. The natural consequence of sin, is punishment proportioned to the enormity of the crime; a full pardon frees us from all the overwhelming consequences of our guilt. But sin itself is a punishment; and, so long as we are sinners, no pardon, however full or free, can save us from this punishment. While we remain depraved and unholy, we must be unhappy. A change of character then is the only hope of deliverance. And for this, most ample means are provided in the gospel of Christ. The very history of that atonement which procured our pardon, has a tendency while we meditate upon it, to promote our holiness. While we look to Christ, we are made like him. While we behold that glory with unveiled faces, we are changed into the same image from glory to glory. It is by believing in Christ then, and thinking much of his person and his history, that we shall find that wisdom, and get that understanding, which shall make us truly happy. For thus shall we fear the Lord, in the sense of that term; and thus too shall wè be led to depart from evil.

M.

ON FICTION, AS A MEDIUM OF RELIGIOUS INSTRUCTION.

Every age has its prevailing taste. And if we may judge of the mental appetite as we do of that of the body, from the food that is most relished by it, we should say, at present, novelty is the rage of the day. Whether we examine the tables of our drawing-rooms, or the shelves of our humblest circulating libraries, we find the greater proportion of the books, and perhaps nearly all those that bear the marks of frequent perusal, to be works of fiction. Nor is this to be wondered at. We have arrived almost at that state of intellectual luxury which characterized the Athenians when Paul visited their famous city. And it is just what might be expected, if the description given of them be applicable to our own countrymen in the present day. But we confess it does surprise, and in some degree alarm us, to find that this love of coloured fiction, in preference to sober fact, has infected the Christian part of our community too, and has exerted so wide an influence on the character of our religious publications.

We know that religious tales have been written by persons of eminent piety, and with the best of motives. We have even heard that real spiritual benefit has been obtained by the perusal of them. But allowing all this to be true, there is still room for the question, what is the tendency of such productions?

There is a general objection to common novels, that they give false views of the world; and the same thing may be said of all works of fiction. The sketches of Christian character contained in these religious tales, have no counterpart among living Christians.

It seems, indeed, essential to the nature of fiction, that everything should be overdone. Truth stamps a worth upon other productions, which must be made up here by something else. The volumes of Hume or Robertson are held in estimation as histories; but they would make but a sorry figure as novels.

Now, if this be true, here is the very serious evil in the works we are considering. Truth is wanting, and the judgment cannot be interested. To make up for this, the fancy must be entertained; and this is generally effected by over-wrought descriptions, and unlikely coincidences. What must be the effect of this on the mind of an unbeliever? He reads the lovely description, and he admires the picture. He turns to the world of reality around him, and sees nothing like it. And the too plausible conclusion is, "Well, if this be Christianity, these people, after all, are not what they pretend to be."

Equally pernicious must be the influence of this ideal perfection of Christian character, on the mind of a young disciple. He who has formed his notions of Christian society from the New Testament, will be prepared for the trials he may meet with, in his intercourse with Christian brethren, and in his fellowship with a Christian Church. He will lament that good men should differ in some of their opinions; and that sometimes there should spring from this, debates and strifes that are most unseemly. But he will not be stumbled by it: for he has read of a "contention so sharp" between two most eminent evangelists, that it caused their separation. He will be grieved that the love of many should wax cold; but he will be prepared to expect it. It will distress him much, if the faith of some be overthrown, who seemed to be the people of God. Still he will not be stumbled. He knows that there were similar declensions even among the first disciples, who professed the name of Jesus, at the peril of their lives. And in the midst of all these discouragments he will be sustained by the consideration, "Nevertheless, the foundation of God standeth sure."

Not so he who has overlooked the salutary lessons of these instructive facts, and has gathered his ideas of the religious world from the pages of some interesting fiction. When he comes in contact with realities, the beautiful vision that delighted him must vanish. Disappointments and discouragements will come thick upon him. His zeal must be damped, and his ardour quenched, and in all human probability his faith will be shaken.

It is a still stronger objection to works of fiction, that they place their reader in an ideal world, where he can enjoy the luxury of tender or sublime emotions, without undergoing the toil and the self-denial, which are inseparable from the conduct that usually produces such feelings. He forgets his own character, and identifies himself with the hero of the story. And if he but succeed in *supposing* the generous or benevolent deeds of this character to be his own; he succeeds to a certain degree in *actually appropriating* to himself the feelings which spring from such actions.

It is a strange paradox that men of the basest and most grovelling characters can sympathize with such feelings. It is strange, indeed, that a man who can be ravished with the beauties of nature should be capable of turning from the elevating contemplation of the work of God to the gratification of his grossest appetites. And yet such characters are to be found. The lives of some of our most illustrious poets furnish us with too conspicuous examples. The readers of fiction present us with a similar paradox; and the explanation in both cases is the same. The poet, in phrensy, forgets for a while the real world, and forgets his own real character, and so does the reader of fiction, though in a less degree. The only difference is, that the novelist does for his reader what the poet does for himself. The truth is, that the class of feelings to which we allude, are highly productive of pleasure; and no wonder that even the vicious love to indulge in them, when they can do so at a cheaper price than virtue. In a region of fancy such emotions can be cheaply purchased, and hence the universal charm of novels. Even the miser can dissolve in tenderness over a tale of suffering, when he knows that his gold is safe. And the narrowest spirit can dilate with generosity, if self-interest be not at stake. And finally, the most degraded profligate can admire and sympathize with virtue, if his vicious passions may still be gratified. Let any one who wishes for an exemplification of these remarks, read Rousseau's Eulogium on the character of Jesus Christ.

These general remarks, we think, are quite applicable to the religious novels of the day. We have not alluded to the pernicious principles contained in common novels: our observations have a regard to those qualities alone that are common to all works of fiction. Now it is indeed a serious evil, if by the process we have described, those delightful emotions which attend the deeds of philanthropy, can be *stolen* without paying their fair price in benevolent actions. But it is an evil more serious still, if, in this way, we can work ourselves into a state of sentimental excitement, and mistake this for that hallowed ecstasy which the faith of the gospel can alone afford. A mistake here is fatal, and we cannot help thinking that the class of publications we refer to make such a mistake easy. If an unknown author may be allowed to refer to his own experience, he can well remember perusing with intense delight, the fascinating pages of "No Fiction," and giving the sympathy of his tears to some of its affecting passages, when his whole soul was in direct opposition to the gospel of Jesus Christ.

There are many who look upon evangelical Christianity as a beautiful system, and who can delight to contemplate it, so long as it interferes not with *them*. They consider an eloquent sermon as a high intellectual treat. If ever they are offended with the preacher, or his doctrine, it is when conscience whispers that this may be all a reality, and may have an influence on their own destinies. The preacher is to them "as a very lovely song of one that hath a pleasant voice, and can play well upon an instrument." Give such persons religion dressed up in the form of a fiction, and it is just the thing they want. The song which charmed them remained in all its loveliness; and the truth which excited their alarm, is alarming no longer, when so closely wrapped with what is known to be fictitious.

If we may be allowed to add a single remark to a discussion already too lengthened, we would observe, that the style of the inspired writers seems to pronounce tacit condemnation on these high coloured and overstrained productions. They have surely adopted the best method of conveying instruction, who had all resources within their power, and almighty wisdom to direct their choice. Their method is a recital of *naked facts*. Here is no embellishment, no impassioned description, although the facts related are the most affecting which our earth has witnessed. They wished that the convictions of their readers should rest on *facts*, and that their feelings too should be excited by *facts*.*

The artist or the novelist may set before our imaginations the circumstances of the Redeemer's death, much more impressively than any of the evangelists have done. We may gaze upon the crucifix and weep; but our tears will not be the tears of repentance. And our indignation may burn against the persecutors of one so meek and so benevolent, while we continue more attached than ever to those sins that nailed the Lord of glory to the tree. It is the simple *fact* that the Son of God died for our sins, — as that fact illustrates the divine character, — which can make us abhor the sin we gloried in, and gladly suffer for the truth we once despised.

While we have so rich a store of facts, it is surely unwise to resort to fiction. We will venture to say, that one judicious volume of Christian biography, has been of more service to the cause of truth, than all the religious tales, or stories, "*founded on fact*," that have ever issued from the press.

The following fragment on a very important subject, appears to have been written about this time. I deeply regret that it is but a fragment, as from the very happy mode of illustrating the subject, which belongs to the first part of the paper, it would, I have no doubt, been a very admirable illustration of the doctrine had he lived to complete it: —

* We trust we shall not be misunderstood, as speaking against earnest appeals, founded on these facts.

ON THE OMNIPRESENCE AND OMNISCIENCE OF GOD

When we have offended a fellow man, and wish to escape his anger, the first thought that occurs, is to flee from his presence. We know that his observation is limited to one little spot; and that anywhere else we are safe.

Imagine, however, that such an individual possessed an active band of emissaries, scattered over a large extent of territory, with whom he can maintain an easy communication; or, that he himself is able to move with immense velocity in whatever direction he may please; and you can see how difficult it would be to escape from his presence. A well-regulated police will give some idea of this. Let an offender escape whither he will, a description of his person, and a warrant to apprehend him, is there before him. Suppose such a system perfect, and that all its operations are performed, not by numerous agents, but by one individual, possessed of the power of moving with the rapidity of lightning if you will, still this would afford but a poor conception of what is meant by omnipresence.

Flight would no longer be a means of escape; but concealment might. The eye of man cannot pierce the darkness, — nor can he guess the design that is formed in secret. And, however swift his motions, and minute his observations, some lurking place might still be found, which the most exquisite scrutiny could discover. The bare possibility of escape would be thus afforded, and that is all. But there is no such possibility of escape from God. "If we ascend up into heaven," &c. It is not by any change of place that God meets us wherever we turn. However difficult may be the conception, he is present everywhere. He fills heaven and earth with his presence. No wonder that David exclaimed, on contemplating the omnipresence of the Deity, — "Such knowledge is too wonderful for me." Psalm cxxxix. 15. If we wish to do anything in secret, it is the presence of a sentient being that we dislike; and the more acute and piercing his senses, the more would we avoid his presence. The mental and moral character of an individual is also a matter of importance. Thus darkness suspends the power of one of the human senses. Hence men can commit crime in the dark, which they would blush to perform in open day. And, in some instances, the presence of the inferior animals would be a matter of indifference, when the presence of human beings, especially of one esteemed for his virtues, would be felt as a most distressing intrusion. Now think of these remarks in their application to God?

"The darkness and the light are both alike to him." And, if we speak of a lurking place, behold, "hell is naked before him, and destruction hath no covering. All things are naked, and open," &c. And the Almighty Being, of whom these things are affirmed, is a being of uspotted purity.

Could a human being thus force himself on our bodily presence at all times, and in all circumstances, there would yet remain to us one retreat, whose secrets, without our consent, no human scrutiny might discover. Man may drive us from every other hiding-place, but he cannot come, unbidden, into the secret place of the soul. He may mark all our words and actions but our thoughts; his most keen-sighted penetration fails him there. The torture may be employed to force the will, and compel us to reveal what is passing within us. But in some cases of firm hardihood, the tyrant has found even his tortures ineffectual. There have been minds which refused to bend, though the body was broken on the torturing wheel. But there is no such repeal from the all-knowing Deity. It is his high prerogative to know the thoughts, and to try the views, of the children of men. Think then of that Almighty Presence, which is with us wherever we go. Think of that all-seeing eye, which not only can pierce the thickest darkness, and lay open the most secret hiding place; but which, without the medium of anything material, can gaze upon the naked soul, and tell the unuttered thoughts that are rising and passing within us.

There is still another way in which we may sometimes escape the anger of a fellow-man. If we can but avoid him for a season, we know that time will erase the remembrance of the offence, or at least, it will mitigate the fury of his passion. Thus Esau, who sought to kill his brother Jacob, received him, after the lapse of years, with cordial affection. But it is not so with God. "He is not a man, that he should repent."

God is present throughout space, in the world of mind, as well as the world of matter. He is present also throughout all duration, throughout time, throughout eternity.

The former was a difficult conception. This is still more so, and language fails to express it. It may be an easier way of conceiving the idea, to say, that all the past, and all the future, are to Him as the present, "Known unto him," &c. Hebrews iv. 6. It was some such conception that the philosophers had, who spoke of the *Eternal now*. Neither matter, nor spirit, nor duration itself, can remove us from this omnipresent God.

Hitherto we have been labouring to get some conception of the idea expressed by the term omnipresence.

Let us consider what effect it should produce on our minds, to know that God is omniscient and omnipresent.

In the illustration we set out with, we supposed the case of one endeavouring to escape the anger of the man whom he had offended. How terrible is the anger of an adversary, who is omnipresent! On the contrary, how delightful the thought of a Friend who never leaves us! Now, how do we regard Him who alone possesses this wondrous attribute? Is God our friend, or do we think of him only as our enemy? Alas, too many think of him merely as the destroyer of their pleasures, and the punisher of their sins. They would fain flee from his presence, but they cannot. The full impression of his omnipresence would be perfect misery. This they can, in some degree, avoid, if not by escaping from his presence, by banishing Him from their thoughts. The idea of God is an idea of pain. No wonder, then, if they can command the direction of their own minds, that we can say concerning them, "God is not in all their thoughts." But it will not be so always. There are cases in which conscience, roused by a deed of uncommon atrocity, and ever awake, has given some impression of an ever-present God. The murderer may flee from the scenes where he did the horrid deed, but they will not leave his thoughts; asleep or awake, the sword of justice will be seen hanging over him; and in many cases, he has been known to seek the hand of the avenger, to try if death would give relief from an existence of unmingled wretchedness. O what is the misery of those who have lifted up their eyes in hell! There conscience cannot slumber. There the unwelcome idea of a God of unrelenting justice, can be banished from the thoughts no longer.

THE END.

www.ingramcontent.com/pod-product-compliance
Lightning Source LLC
LaVergne TN
LVHW011151110826
845150LV00006B/1217

* 9 7 8 1 4 2 5 5 4 6 3 7 3 *